RESEARCH IN MARKETING

Volume 3 • 1980

RESEARCH IN
MARKETING

A Research Annual

Editor: JAGDISH N. SHETH
   *Department of Business
   Administration
   University of Illinois*

VOLUME 3 • 1980

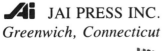 JAI PRESS INC.
Greenwich, Connecticut

CONTENTS

PREFACE   vii

PARADIGMS FOR MARKETING THEORY
    James M. Carman   1

A MODEL-BASED METHODOLOGY FOR ASSESSING
MARKET RESPONSE FOR NEW INDUSTRIAL PRODUCTS
    Jean-Marie Choffray and Gary L. Lilien   37

A TYPOLOGY OF CONSUMER NEEDS
    Janice G. Hanna   83

CONSUMPTION OF MASS COMMUNICATION:
CONSTRUCTION OF A MODEL ON INFORMATION
CONSUMPTION BEHAVIOR
    Preben Sepstrup   105

WHAT CAN BE DONE ABOUT INTERVIEWER BIAS?
    Donald S. Tull and Larry E. Richards   143

TEMPORAL DIMENSION OF CONSUMER BEHAVIOR: AN
EXPLORATION WITH TIME BUDGET
    M. Venkatesan and Johan Arndt   163

MARKETING MIX DECISION RULES FOR NON-PROFIT
ORGANIZATIONS
    Charles B. Weinberg   191

TESTING STOCHASTIC MODELS OF CONSUMER
CHOICE BEHAVIOR: A METHODOLOGY FOR
ATTACKING THE MANY-TO-ONE MAPPING PROBLEMS
    R. Dale Wilson   235

A MULTIVARIATE STOCHASTIC MODEL OF BRAND
CHOICE AND MARKET BEHAVIOR
    Fred S. Zufryden   273

PREFACE

The third volume of *Research in Marketing* is a significant departure from the first two volumes in several ways. First, the research papers deal with a more diverse set of topics than ever before. For example, there are research papers on marketing theory, industrial marketing, marketing mix for nonprofit organizations, and consumption of mass communication, in addition to papers on consumer behavior and market research. Second, there are fewer papers but many are significantly longer and truly represent minimonographs on a given topic of marketing science. Finally, the number of mathematical papers is more balanced than in previous volumes.

Given the diversity of content on the one hand, and the fewer number of papers on the other hand, I will not group them into subcategories, but instead briefly introduce each paper to the reader.

Based on the exchange system paradigm borrowed from the social exchange theory, Carman develops a definition of marketing as a process of voluntary exchange of some good between parties under a trust that both parties will complete the exchange and that it will provide utility. With this definition, Carman examines how the marketing exchange differs from social exchange by limiting itself from areas such as gift exchange, religion, marriage, and politics. At the same time, he aptly demonstrates that the exchange paradigm can be very useful in understanding vertical channels of distribution, regulation of monopoly and quasi-public goods, marketing by nonprofit organizations, and problems of restricted rights and information asymmetry. In my opinion, Carman's paper is likely to generate considerable interest and debate among marketing theorists.

Hanna's paper on a typology of consumer needs is equally innovative and thought provoking. Based on an extensive review of very diverse disciplines ranging from consumption economics, human values, and organization behavior to clinical and cultural psychology, she proposes that consumer needs can be classified into seven categories: physical safety, material security, material comfort, acceptance by others, recognition from others, influence over others, and personal growth. While there is a strong influence of Maslow and Alderfer in her thinking, she adds unique dimensions to their work on human consumption needs with respect to acceptance by, recognition from, and influence over others. This three-fold social need classification clearly goes beyond the conspicuous consumption and other-directed hypotheses provided by others. The typology of consumer needs, however, needs to be fully operationalized and tested before it can be accepted by marketing scholars.

Choffray and Lilien's research paper on a methodology for assessing market response for new industrial products is a refreshing change from the anecdotal and case history approach to researching industrial marketing management. Based on the organizational buying behavior literature, they propose a quantitative model of measuring market response to a new product. The model is hierarchical in nature and consists of the following four submodels: awareness model, feasibility model, individual evaluation model, and group decision model. The strength of the paper clearly lies in the quantitative formulation of behavioral principles inherent in most organizational buyer behavior models. In addition, the authors demonstrate the operationalization of their model with applications to the assessment of market potential for solar-powered industrial cooling systems.

The problem of interviewer bias is well known to all market and survey researchers. Tull and Richards review many procedures people have followed in order to minimize the interviewer bias. They range from avoiding interviewing itself to ignoring the bias. The latter can be very useful if it can be demonstrated that the interviewer bias is too small or insignificant to worry about or to spend considerable money and effort in eliminating it. Tull and Richards review the two popular methods of measuring the interviewer bias: comparison of recorded with true values, and experimental designs in which each interviewer is considered a treatment. They propose an alternative procedure of building a regression model for estimating the true values with a set of external predictor variables, and then comparing the actual values obtained through an interviewer with the estimated true values. Based on simulation of interviewer bias on data, they demonstrate that the regression approach is better and simpler than the experimental design approach presently used by large scale data collectors.

The fifth research paper by Preben Sepstrup is another example of a unique approach to understanding mass media information. It represents a first serious attempt to develop a theory of information consumption. The fundamental components of his theory of consumption of mass information are: size and type of information need, expected amount of information outside mass media, importance of topic, and expected costs of perceived information sources. The theory clearly treats the consumer as a highly rational individual who balances his costs versus benefits of information derived from mass media.

In recent years, time has replaced money as the scarce resource and an economic constraint for many human activities. It is, therefore, not surprising that marketing researchers have begun to take an active interest in studying how people budget their time for purchase and consumption activities. Venkatesan and Arndt report an exploratory study on a Norwegian panel of housewives with respect to allocation of time to different aspects of consumer decision process such as searching for information, shopping for products, and in postpurchase activities. While the substantive findings of their study are highly tentative and unique to Norwegian consumers, the authors aptly demonstrate that it is possible to gather time budget information from people with respect to their consumer behavior.

Weinberg's paper on marketing mix decision rules for nonprofit organizations is a significant contribution in several ways. First, it provides a mathematical framework for marketing mix decisions for nonprofit organizations. Second, it clearly demonstrates that much of the sophisticated model building approach generated for private enterprise marketing mix decisions can be extended to nonprofit organizations. Finally, it provides pricing implications for services offered by nonprofit organizations which are not only practical but socially highly desirable.

Weinberg is able to formulate an optimization decision rule in terms of maximization of usage of nonprofit service without any deficit budget and with respect to a given price, revenue derived from donors, and the marketing expenditures related to the donor and the user markets. He then demonstrates that the optimization rule for nonprofit organizations is comparable to the general Dorfman-Steiner power function popular in the marketing mix literature. He finally concludes that the best way to maximize usage given constant marketing expenditures is to lower the usage fees charged to patrons, which is generally more acceptable to the donors and the society at large. The concept of universal service which is prevalent in regulated monopolies such as utilities seems to clearly emerge from his mathematical formulation.

Dale Wilson's paper on a methodology for testing the many-to-one mapping problem in stochastic brand choice behavior earmarks the next phase in the maturity of brand choice literature. It goes beyond numerous empirical studies which have attempted to fit a given theoretical model to the brand choice panel data. It raises the concern that when many different model formulations all seemingly fit the same data, there is a real concern for the policy maker as to which model is a true representation of the brand choice reality. While the minimum chi-squared method has been the most popular method for selecting the best of all models that fit to a data bank, Wilson presents a more generalized procedure based on an F-test which evaluates the incremental differences in the fitness of the models. Furthermore, Wilson is able to link different stochastic models as elements of a generalized approach. The testing of his procedure (which ultimately uses the minimum Neyman chi-squared method), leads to the conclusion that the Linear Learning Model provides an effective model structure for predicting brand choice probabilities for the "Favorite Brand" Coffee data.

The last paper in this volume by Zufryden is a natural follow-up to the problem of many-to-one mapping raised in the previous paper. Rather than making a choice among several stochastic models, Zufryden develops a composite stochastic model by combining the properties of brand choice and purchase incidence phenomena at both the individual consumer and the aggregate market behavior levels. However, the uniqueness of Zufryden's model is the incorporation of any explanatory variables relevant to a market situation through the use of a Logit Model formulation within the structure of a first-order Markov process which underlies his composite stochastic model. The integration of prediction with explanation, purchase incidence with brand choice behavior, and individual customer with aggregate market behavior in a single model is a remarkable accomplishment. It is, therefore, very likely that the Zufryden model will become a benchmark in the history of stochastic models of brand choice behavior.

I hope this volume will demonstrate to the marketing scholars that the objective of *Research in Marketing* is to publish original research publications which are substantive enough to be treated as minimonographs. It offers an avenue for those scholars who feel that scholarly journals are too restrictive with respect to length and editorial expressions.

PARADIGMS FOR MARKETING THEORY*

James M. Carman, UNIVERSITY OF CALIFORNIA,

BERKELEY

When one reads much of the current marketing literature, and even the popular press, it sometimes appears that marketing is attempting to encompass all of social science and that most of the institutions in our society are looking to marketing for their survival (McGinniss, 1969; Simon, 1968; Farley and Leavitt, 1971; Kotler and Zaltman, 1971; Mindak and Bybee, 1971; Zaltman and Ver tinsky, 1971; Zikmund and Stanton, 1971; El Ansary and Kramer, 1974; White, 1973; Kotler, 1975; Gaedeke, 1977). Business institutions have long used marketing techniques, in addition to the marketing of their goods, in their public relations and financial relations activities. But use and misuse of marketing techniques have implications for business institutions and for society as a whole which need to be identified and evaluated. Thus, a discussion on the definition of marketing is more than a game for teachers of marketing to play with one

Research in Marketing, Volume 3, pages 1–36

Copyright © 1980 by JAI Press Inc.

All rights of reproduction in any form reserved.

ISBN: 0-89232-060-5

1

another. It is a discussion of concern to business executives who depend on conventional marketing systems for their continued good health.

In this paper, it is necessary to begin with a definition of marketing in order to focus on the development of frameworks for the discipline of marketing that we suggest are useful in the construction of marketing theory. This introduction is not intended as a comprehensive review of the development of marketing thought or typology of marketing theory.[1] Rather, it is intended only as an introduction to paradigms useful in marketing with special attention given to two of these: the general systems paradigm and the social exchange paradigm. The constructs of a new (or more accurately, newly structured) marketing paradigm—the Systems/Exchange Paradigm—are then defined. Finally, the specifications of the limits of the discipline of marketing are offered.

The paper then turns to a discussion of the social exchange paradigm and uses this paradigm to sharpen understanding of the ongoing debate over the universality of marketing. The third section of the paper uses four examples to show how the new Systems/Exchange Paradigm can limit the definition of the discipline of marketing. The fourth section then "exercises" the new paradigm by outlining its application to some problem areas for which marketers are almost uniquely equipped to provide solutions.

I. WHAT IS MARKETING?

The definition of marketing suggested here is similar to that which has been popular among a large number of scholars for over a decade (Ohio State University Marketing Staff, 1965; Sweeney, 1972). The italicized words are those discussed in more detail.

> Marketing is the *process* in a society by which individuals or public and private organizations identify the needs and wants of their respective clients, design and develop the *products, services, and ideas* to satisfy these needs and wants, communicate information about them, distribute them, and *exchange* them so as to create value for the parties involved.

The definition says marketing is a *process*. The study of that process is called the *discipline* of marketing. "Discipline" is preferable to science, because our study involves more than the use of the scientific method to explain and classify observable phenomena. It also involves problem-solving. The discipline is more appropriately classified as a *technical art* that has its foundation in the social sciences. For a discussion of the marketing as a science controversy, see Hunt (1976). The discipline contains a number of paradigms, and each paradigm draws on a number of theories. Thus, marketing is clearly not a single theory. The theories in the discipline are applied so as to become the operating *technologies* of practitioners engaged in the process.

Bagozzi (1976) defines a paradigm as stating what a discipline should study, what questions it should ask, and what rules should be followed in interpreting the answers obtained. As such, paradigms are the foundations of theory. They suggest units of analysis, constructs, and similar necessary elements of a calculus of theory in a discipline. However, they fall short of advancing propositions, axioms, lawlike generalizations, and testable hypotheses. Paradigms are not theories. The task is to determine which paradigms will lead to useful theories.

Our purpose here is: (1) to offer a suggestion as to what the discipline of marketing should study, (2) to do so by use of the social exchange paradigm, and (3) to suggest a new paradigm that is offered as being the central paradigm for the discipline of marketing. Six paradigms are frequently used by marketing scholars:

1. the microeconomics paradigm,
2. the persuasion/attitude change paradigm,
3. the conflict resolution paradigm,
4. the general systems paradigm,
5. the functionalist paradigm, and
6. the social exchange paradigm.

The microeconomic paradigm looks at an abstraction of a market, usually pure competition in a one-level structure. It tells us to study resource allocation by asking questions about supply, demand, transaction efficiency, and levels of information. The reason most often given by marketers for rejecting this paradigm is its excessive abstraction, not that it fails to ask the right questions. This may be an unwarranted criticism, for many operational theories do emanate from the abstract microeconomic model. Two quickly come to mind as theories that have been incorporated into what most of us would consider core marketing theory today. One of these is the group of theories dealing with small group competitive rivalry: monopolistic competition and oligopoly theory. The second is the group of models dealing with place theory and interregional marketing.

The persuasion/attitude change paradigm focuses on one aspect of the process of marketing—the information and persuasion required by one actor to achieve a desired behavior from another. It draws heavily on the theories of social psychology. Thus, the unit of analysis is the individual or small group. Stidsen and Schutte (1972) serve to represent this paradigm by suggesting that marketing focus on the communications which enable consumers and producers to significantly influence each other's goal attainment. This limited, though important, view of the process takes it out of consideration as the basic paradigm of the discipline of marketing.

The conflict resolution paradigm is a paradigm whose theories largely have been captured by other paradigms. As explained by Levy and Zaltman (1975), in sociology, political science, and social psychology, a large literature grew out of an effort in the 1950s to resolve conflicts in society without another world war. Much of this work is at the societal or macro level and focuses on the process of conflict emergence and resolution in a society. The constructs of this macro approach to conflict resolution remain somewhat disorderly. At least five approaches to social control of conflict have been identified: exchange, persuasion, authority, moral code, and tradition. Modern societies use all five, as we shall see, though the emphasis here is on exchange.[2]

On the other hand, applying constructs such as power, structure, and coalitions at the micro level has produced contributions to two other paradigms listed here: the social exchange paradigm and the microeconomic paradigm. Exchange transactions contain inherent conflict. The contributions of conflict constructs in exchange transactions are discussed here, and by virtually all marketers, as a part of the exchange paradigm. The second contribution is game theory. Microeconomics has been the major beneficiary of this theory. Oligopoly theory, for example, has developed not through extension of traditional economic theory but through constructs received from game theory (Telser, 1972; Friedman, 1977). Conflict resolution, its psychological theories, and its game theory have been identified here as a separate paradigm because there is evidence that it may yet have applications distinct from those now embodied in microeconomic theory and exchange theory (Rapoport, 1974).

The general systems paradigm focuses on the interrelationships between institutions in a system. We will argue that the systems paradigm is a necessary prerequisite to others used in marketing. The discipline must limit in some way the types of systems studied or the types of exchanges considered. Theory development using the systems paradigm (as with any paradigm) must begin by specifying the units of analysis, the constructs, the variables, and a set of generalizable and testable propositions. The unit of analysis is the item or group whose activities are studied. In marketing we often consider as the unit of analysis individuals, families, and organizations. Constructs are fundamental concepts that one uses in thinking about and analyzing an area. It is usually multidimensional and cannot be described by only a single measure. Brand loyalty, innovation, and riskiness are examples of constructs used in marketing. Variables are the unidimensional parts of a construct that we would like to (and often can) measure. Propositions specify the relationships between constructs. In marketing we attempt to specify the extent to which the risk aversion or innovativeness of an individual influences his or her loyalty for a particular brand.

Now, with regard to the general systems paradigm, one begins to build theory about a particular system with the following constructs. First, the definition of a system is a set of regularly interacting groups coordinated in such a way as to form a unified whole and organized so as to accomplish a set of goals. The goals of the system are stated in terms of optimum states of some objective functions, for example, Pratian optimum. Second, five constructs are required to specify the system:

1. the goals of the system,
2. the environment and constraints within which the system exists,
3. the resources of these units,
4. the functions these units perform,
5. the management and control mechanism for the system (Churchman, 1968).

Variables are required to measure performance, measure resources, measure functional flows, measure controls, and measure environmental influences. The units of analysis are the components that comprise the system.

The functionalist paradigm employs many theories, but all are concerned with decision-making regarding the functions performed by institutions within society. Our thesis is that a functional approach would require some systems specification before beginning analysis of the quality of decision-making within functions. Alderson has taken a parallel position with regard to the functionalist paradigm.

> Functionalism stresses the whole system and undertakes to interpret the parts in terms of how they serve the system. Some writers who are actually advocates of functionalism prefer to speak of the holistic approach because of emphasis on the system as a whole. . . (Alderson, 1957, p. 16).

> The writer has characterized his theoretical position as functionalist and has accepted the implied commitment to the total systems approach (Alderson, in Cox, Alderson, and Shapiro, 1964, p. 105).

Alderson saw himself as a functionalist because he wanted to sharpen the distinction between descriptive and normative theory. He attempted to build normative theory by focusing on the functions performed within the systems he studied. Nicosia's (1962) analysis of Alderson's functionalism will serve to review much of the history and interpretation of the systems approach to marketing. His analysis closes with a challenge that we face here with regard to the social exchange paradigm: "the challenge facing the student of marketing is that of operationalizing the conceptual schemata suggested by functionalism—that is, of translating them into empirical research instruments" (p. 413). We believe the descriptive-normative distinction does not need to be made here. The foundations for theory discussed here are useful in either kind of research.

The social exchange paradigm focuses on the phenomenon of exchange between social actors or institutions regardless of the functions being performed or the institutions involved. Special attention is given in the next section of this essay to this paradigm. The paradigm is flexible and has a smaller set of constructs than one might expect. One needs as elemental constructs:

- the goods being exchanged ('good' as used here is not restricted to a product);
- the value, utility, or reward associated with the goods (values can be estab-

lished by learning or reinforcement. Values can be personal as well as market established. They can change through time and are subject to diminishing marginal utility. Negative values are often called costs. Opportunity costs and sunk costs need to be considered.);

• a transaction;
• at least two actors.

However, it is our contention that before one can fruitfully employ the exchange theory paradigm to build marketing theory, the systems paradigm would dictate the necessity to specify what marketing system one was studying and what exchanges within that system are studied as marketing exchanges. In conventional products marketing, for example, buying and selling institutions are closely linked and somewhat interdependent. These institutions receive inputs from other institutions and generate outputs which are transmitted to other institutions. People within these institutions apply marketing technologies in the performance of this function. In economic systems, the inputs and outputs that flow through these institutions are goods which have measured economic value; the institutions transform them in order to alter their value; inputs are obtained in factor markets; and outputs are allocated in goods markets. This is too restrictive for our discipline. Marketing is concerned with the exchange of values between institutions beyond economic institutions—for example, churches—and also concerned with goods not counted as economic wealth—for example, prestige. However, the view advanced here is that with this broad view, the specification of the systems paradigm must precede employment of the social exchange theory paradigm. Before building theory with the social exchange framework, one needs to specify the units of analysis and all of the constructs of both the systems and social exchange paradigms.

Consistent with this thesis, a combined Systems/Exchange Paradigm is now introduced. This paradigm is a combination of the constructs of the two paradigms. The result appears in Table I. This new paradigm is offered as the basic paradigm of the discipline of marketing. This list of constructs will be used in later sections of this paper in order to show their usefulness in the analysis of marketing problems. Note that the list is equally useful in building both descriptive and normative theory.

The question is, how many elements in the definition of marketing above need to be present for the exchanges between institutions to be called "marketing"? One view is that it is marketing if any marketing technology is applied. For example, the state police department becomes a marketing institution when they promote safe driving, and hence, in this context, the state police and drivers constitute a marketing system. The more restrictive view is that a marketing system applies only to economic activity that contains all of the elements in the definition above and that must perform all of the functions listed there (Kotler, 1972). Thus, when the products and services are economic resources, the institu-

Table I.   Constructs of a Systems/Exchange Paradigm

1. The goals of the system under study.
2. The environment and constraints within which the system exists, including constraints on the entry of new actors.
3. The control mechanism for the system.
4. The actors (individuals, groups, establishments, or institutions) that comprise the system—their number, description, and internal structure.
5. The resources, relative size, and relative power of each actor.
6. The functions performed by the actors.
7. The linkage between actors.
8. The description, including heterogeneity, of the goods that are to be exchanged.
9. The ways in which values are assigned to the goods by each party.
10. Transaction cost functions, including the possibility for economies through routinization and the time interval between exchanges.
11. The level of information on goods, values, and alternatives available to actors in the exchange.
12. The rules governing exchanges, including time pressures to complete exchanges, the opportunity for collusion between buyers and sellers, and externally determined exchange rates.

tions are households and business organizations, and the institutions are linked by free markets, analyses of such systems are comfortable for a marketer. When these conditions are relaxed, either in terms of the institutions or the transfer process, the discipline is weakened in its ability to model the system accurately, to predict behavior and performance of the system, or to recommend control mechanisms.

The view advanced here and argued in the following sections is somewhere between these two poles. I believe that to be marketing, we must restrict the type of exchanges considered to those that:

1. include some degree of freedom for the traders to make a decision to trade or not to trade,
2. include the existence of some good that will provide utility,
3. include a trust that both parties will complete the exchange, and
4. consider systems in which resource allocation is the primary purpose.

This essay does not dispute the famous remark by Karl Popper that disciplines are distinguished by historical precedent and administrative convenience, while what man is about is the study of problems that "cut right across the borders of any subject matter or discipline" (Popper, 1963). If a *marketing technology* can be applied to solve a problem in driver safety, then it should be applied, and marketing theorists should be proud that it has been applied. It is not necessary for driver education to be a *marketing process*.

However, in the development of theory, the *marketing discipline* is well advised to stick to problem situations where all of the elements of the marketing process are present. (W. T. Tucker, 1974, p. 33, has made a similar point, as has the author (Carman, 1973)). This distinction is important because it is the application of some marketing concepts with an inaccurate systemic description that is at the heart of many of the problems raised here. Social exchange theory is a useful vehicle to use in explaining why I feel this distinction between technology, process, and discipline is so important. The next section considers this paradigm in more detail.

II. SOCIAL EXCHANGE THEORY

Social exchange theory, as a formal theory with that name, belongs to the discipline of sociology. However, it is much more multidisciplinary than that. Historic and present developments also can be found in psychology (Thibaut and Kelley, 1959) and anthropology (Levi-Strauss, 1969). Much in exchange theory appears to be economic theory, but economists (with a few exceptions, such as John R. Commons) have not been eager to claim it or attempt to fit general exchange theory into theories of market exchange. In contrast, the concept of an *exchange transaction* is a vital ingredient of marketing. Kotler says a transaction is *the* core concept of marketing—that "how transactions are created, stimulated, facilitated, and solved . . . is the generic concept of marketing" (Kotler, 1972, p. 49). Alderson (1965, p. 22) suggests that the transaction—the focus of the negotiation which leads to exchange—is one of two basic "units of action" of a marketing system. He goes on (pp. 83–86) to begin a formal analysis of transactions called the "Law of Exchange." Yet, the progress to date in building a general theory of social exchange has not been rapid or all that successful. If such a general theory is developed, it will contribute to all of social science, not marketing, psychology, sociology, or anthropology alone. For "exchange theory" is more of a frame of reference for the study of how "goods" (anything of value) move through a society (Emerson, 1976).

It may be useful to describe the differences in perspective between disciplines in a bit more detail. The anthropologist is interested in studying primitive societies with an eye toward understanding the evolution of these to complex societies. As far back as 1919 and 1922, anthropologists had defined one of the problems that concern us today. Sir James C. Frazer (1919) concluded, from the study of the exchange of women in the Old Testament and among Australian aboriginals, that (1) all exchanges derived from simple economic exchange, (2) institutions developed to support economic exchange, and (3) institutions permitted the development of more complex exchange. However, a few years later, another anthropologist (Malinowski, 1922) discovered a form of rather complex gift exchange, also in the Western Pacific, that appeared to have no economic significance at all. This debate on whether the initial, primitive motivation is the act of exchanging or the economic survival need to exchange goods rages today in anthropology, with intensity similar to the debate in marketing (Levi-Strauss, 1965). We will return to it in this essay.

The writings on exchange in sociology have been criticized as being so general as to be tautological (Emerson, 1976, pp. 341–343). On the other hand, the paradigm's simple structure permits one to use the framework from the perspective of dyadic social psychology (Thibaut and Kelley, 1959), operant psychology (Homans, 1961), or economic decision theory (Telser, 1972). Here we are concerned with how to use it to help build a unified theory of marketing. The work to date suggests that an understanding of complex exchange requires detailed analysis of social, economic, and legal institutions, as well as psychology and social mores. For us it is necessary to specify the types of exchanges, institutions, and functions with which marketing will be concerned. It may be necessary to limit the environments or rules governing the exchange or the functions being performed if we are: (1) to make contributions to a general theory of social exchange; (2) to gain insights that are not so general as to be trite; (3) to study necessary nonexchange topics, such as product management, production economies, and strategic planning; and (4) to be able to solve real problems.

This part of the paper will attempt to determine if any of the general system constructs listed earlier will restrict just which exchanges are marketing exchanges. We begin with consideration of four dimensions of the social exchange paradigm: (1) economic exchange vs. all social exchange, (2) free exchange vs. command exchange, (3) large group market exchange vs. bilateral negotiation, and (4) restricted exchange vs. indirect exchange. See Ekeh (1974) for another view on these points.

A. Economic Exchange vs. All Social Exchange

Under this dimension is considered the definition of "products, services, and ideas." Must they be economic goods or can they be economic neutrals? Actually, marketing has already made a considerable contribution to the resolution of this question. The writers in other social sciences worry more than marketers about restrictions to an economic man and goods with established market values. However, sociologists writing in social exchange are at least as explicit on the similarities and differences as are marketers (Chavannes, 1963, Homans, 1958, Knox, 1963, Belshaw, 1965, Blau, 1968). I hope it is not too optimistic of me to believe that most of us can agree that marketing applies to any exchange of goods (in the broad sense) that leads to an increase in the utility of at least one of the actors (with no loss in utility to the other). I suggest that things and activities that create utility are scarce social resources. Marketing is concerned with their allocation—not just the allocation of scarce resources with established economic value. Put more sharply, I believe marketing is concerned with resource allocation, but I define resources more broadly than would most economists.

Blau (1964, pp. 91–113) makes the distinction in another way, one that I find not very useful in making the difference before us. He believes that it is a clear obligation to reciprocate at a specific exchange rate that separates economic exchange from social exchange. Although this adds unnecessary legal, institutional trappings to our problem at this point, this issue is one that needs to be discussed. We shall return to it in later sections.

It is useful to consider some examples to see how far we can push these ideas. That is, on the basis of the good involved, can one meaningfully distinguish between economic and other social exchange transactions? The individual who gives anonymously to a charity gives up a classic economic asset and receives what? A good conscience? A feeling of fighting the welfare state? An excuse for not giving to other charities? Relief from the fund raiser? All are possible sources of utility. Although none has a market value that will increase national income, it is theoretically possible to measure their value through shadow prices. Note, also, that the output of this charity is not exchanged directly for the input. The charity is an institution that performs a particular type of resource redistribution function through generalized exchange. The institutional arrangements are important for a complete understanding of the process.

It is here that we reach one possible limit to the definition of marketing. If you do not agree with extending marketing to include this example, you have narrowed marketing. If you do agree, then you conclude that marketing cannot be narrowed by reference to the "things" that are exchanged. To narrow marketing, we must look to the other dimensions.

B. Free Exchange vs. Command Exchange

Exchanges create time, place, and possession utility and psychological or social utility that lead to the reallocation of scarce resources. Most writers in social exchange theory in all disciplines and all those cited here assume exchanges taken place as a result of free decisions by the actors. Ignorance, lack of information, deceit, or coercion may influence the rates of exchange, but at least bounded individual freedom is inherent in the definition of the exchange. Thus theft, robbery, and beggary are excluded. These are not exchange and not marketing.

Is there some necessary set of ingredients of freedom for marketing to take place? Certainly not the profit motive. Other utilities can be created. Enough freedom for marketing to take place can remain, even when some restrictions are placed on private ownership. COMSAT, AMTRAK, the U.S. Postal Service, and the Federal National Mortgage Association, among others, are all quasi-public corporations, some of which are expected to provide a return to their private investors. All are active participants in the economic marketing system. Neither private ownership nor the profit motive seem essential characteristics for an institution to employ marketing. The discipline can adequately deal with nonprofit and with public institutions as long as their goals and measures of performance are adequately defined and measured. Notice that these are constructs from the general systems paradigm. They help us define a marketing exchange. They teach us to focus on goals, measures of performance, and functions—not on whether payoffs are returns to entrepreneurs. Paul C. Roberts (1971) and others have attempted to build models of resource allocation through planning authorities that parallel market transactions. The differences always focus on distinctions in incentives (goals) and the signals concerning performance. However, the basic unit of analysis remains the exchange transaction.

However, some concept of freedom to exchange seems to be required for a marketing exchange transaction to take place. *We must assume two or more actors (traders), each possessing the use right to goods, including the potential to provide service, who may exchange among themselves in a mutually agreeable way.* Telser (1972) goes on, in his definition of economic exchange, to add, "Each has a preference describing the terms at which he is willing to change his holdings. No one is forced to trade and all are free to make contracts with anyone at mutually acceptable terms" (p. xiv). This definition is a simple statement of Kotler's first three axioms in his generic concept of marketing (Kotler, 1972). He takes a functionalist point of view with his fourth axiom which says that marketing is concerned with the study of how to alter the "mutually acceptable terms." In any case, these definitions do require freedom to exchange or not to exchange but do not require narrow definitions of private property, a price system, or a profit motive.

Now, marketers—for comparative purposes—may study resource allocation by command-based methods, where there is no freedom to set the terms of trade. We do this very naturally because our functionalist and systems paradigms come to the fore. Socialist and communist societies use political command systems to allocate scarce resources. Marketers are interested in these functions, and they therefore study the institutions and systems through which resource allocation takes place. They do comparative analyses on the relative efficiency of different systems. They attempt to design mixed systems.

But note, command-based systems do not usually completely do away with either private property, a price system, or the freedom to make some transaction decision in a market environment. The modern communist economy does not ignore the price system and free transactions. It merely attempts to regulate the allocation of scarce economic resources by controlling production (supply) and then controlling price (the rates of exchange) so as to attempt to bring market demand into equilibrium with that supply (Gogol, 1970, pp. 76–88). This latter case might be thought of as a "quasi-market" since buyers may have the freedom not to exchange.

Belshaw (1965, p. 117) points out that in all systems, from command to free market, the system depends on the establishment and recognition by the people of a legitimate source of authority to coordinate the system. It may be the family, the organization, the corporation, or the state. Once this authority is accepted, considerable individual freedom can be exercised in exchange transactions. It is only when it is not accepted that we have a police state and no freedom.

The marketing paradigms are concerned with the design of systems for exchange, given some source of authority that to some extent limits individual
freedom. Political mechanisms for resource allocation are mechanisms that can
take from the individual considerable freedom to make exchange transactions.
More will be said about political processes below. What I want to emphasize here
is that marketers cannot give up being functionalists. We cannot give up studying
the institutions that hold the legitimate authority to engage in exchange. We
cannot give up studying the system linkages that exist between these institutions.
We should not narrow marketing by giving up the functionalist, institutionalist,
and systemic paradigms. It is appropriate for marketing to study a system in
which some exchanges of resources are true market exchanges, some are free
exchanges but at exchange rates set by a government authority, and some resource transfers are by force.

C. Market Structure

The point is that something of the structure of the system and the functions
performed in that system need to be identified to meaningfully apply social
exchange concepts to marketing. Marketing and economics have developed
many schema for classifying the structure of exchanges. A basic construct in the
industrial organization field of economics is market structure, and most authorities in that field would begin all analyses with an analysis of competitive
structure. In this section, brief comment will be made about only two elements in
this list: the number of buyers and sellers and their relative power.

Marketing exchanges cover a continuum of structures with regard to the
number of buyers and sellers from competitive markets at one pole to bilateral
monopoly at the other. The nature of the exchange at these two poles is very
different. At the one end, buyers and sellers are completely powerless. The
power is in the invisible hand of the market. At the other end, an analysis of the
exchange depends completely on consideration of the relative power of the two
actors in the negotiation. Thus, the concept of relative power is a necessary part
of the marketing paradigms, but it would surely be incorrect to define marketing
as a discipline studying power relationships in society.

D. Restricted Exchange vs. Indirect Exchange

The structure of the exchange relationships and the importance of this structure
on social exchange theory is a topic that confuses anthropologists and sociologists, as well as marketers. There is not quite a standard terminology. I hope that
we can develop standard terminology in marketing. It is necessary to distinguish at least three types of exchange structure: restricted, generalized, and indirect. The first is straightforward, the second confusing, and the third controversial. Diagrams of these structures are shown in Figure 1.

Figure 1. A Classification of Exchange Structures

A.   Restricted Exchange

$$A \;\; {\overset{\leftarrow}{\rightarrow}} \;\; B$$

B.   Generalized Exchange

     1.   Chain Generalized

$$A \;\rightarrow\; B \;\rightarrow\; C \;\rightarrow\; A$$

     2.   Net Generalized

$$
\begin{array}{ccc}
A & & A \\
\downarrow & & \downarrow \\
C \;\rightarrow\; & B \;\rightarrow\; & A \\
\uparrow & & \uparrow \\
B & & C
\end{array}
$$

C.   Indirect Exchange

$$A \;\; {\overset{\leftarrow}{\rightarrow}} \;\; B \;\; {\overset{\leftarrow}{\rightarrow}} \;\; C \;\; {\overset{\leftarrow}{\rightarrow}} \;\; A$$

D.1. Restricted Exchange.   Restricted exchange is a two-party relationship in which A gives to B an exchange for B giving to A. We can expand the actors here to be organizations and not simply real people. There must be a *quid pro quo* in such relationships, and an attempt to maintain equality is evident. The parties expect that something of value is exchanged for something of similar value. It is well established in marketing that the exchange need not be face to face. Only an implicit meeting of minds is required. All dyadic market structure exchanges are of this type.

From here on, the going gets tougher. If ABC promotes a particular television program to be presented at 10:00 P.M. on Tuesday evenings, is there a transaction and is this marketing? It seems to fill all of the other requirements: there is an attempt to alter the demand structure through conception, promotion, distribution, and facilitation. What is the exchange? The viewer is giving up the opportunity to spend his time in some other way in order to watch the program. There is an exchange, but the values exchanged are not recorded in monetary terms. They are not easy to value, but the task is not impossible. The opportunity cost to the individual could be estimated. If his alternative was to watch another network, the cost is probably quite small. If it were to engage in his occupation at a rate of $10 per hour, the cost is relatively large. The value of the network is also estimable in terms of the effect on audience and hence advertising revenue. This value per individual is quite small. To sum up, the advertising of a television program may be marketing, but the value of the transaction is difficult to determine and may involve an opportunity cost.

D.2. Generalized Exchange. This is an exchange situation involving at least three actors and a one-way giving. That is, A gives to B who gives to C who gives to A. The distinction is that A and B do not *appear* to engage in even a simple restricted exchange transaction. A receives from C, not from B. Bagozzi (1975) provides a modern marketing example of this type of exchange. Ekeh (1974) divides generalized exchange into two types.

He would call what I have just described "chain generalized exchange." He would then define "net generalized exchange" as the situation of neighboring farmers in barn building or harvesting. All members of the group give collectively of their energy to build one neighbor's barn, knowing that at some time the receiver will reciprocate. Emerson (1976) points out that such exchanges are simply primitive examples of recognition of production theory. That is, there is more value added by working together than by the sum of all farmers working separately. He calls such a situation "productive exchange." This term is consistent with the notion that self-production may be an alternative to exchange. Robinson Crusoe constructed shelter because there was no innkeeper with whom he could exchange.

What makes the farmer example unique is that there is no employer. In formal production processes, the laborer exchanges his or her energy for a wage. In the farmer examples, one needs to appreciate the requirement for trust among the actors. There must be a *quid pro quo*. It is that an actor gives because he believes he will receive at some time from someone. The trust is the *quid pro quo. There is a meeting of the minds.* It is this that is central to my definition of an exchange. It is interesting and significant that generalized exchange does not require an elaborate institution structure. It has been found in primitive societies (Malinowski, 1922). Although the rates of exchange may not be well established, there is a *quid pro quo*. It does, however, require some social structure that has established norms or sanctions against deviation so that there is an expectation of reciprocation. I believe such exchanges are marketing.

A digression here to the early Middle Ages at this point should be useful to demonstrate that: (1) generalized exchanges are marketing, (2) productive exchanges are marketing, and (3) generalized productive marketing exchanges were important early in the development of the modern world. This digression also points out that while exchange theory is not necessary to analyze all transactions, how exchange "transactions are created, stimulated, facilitated and solved is the generic concept of marketing" (Kotler, 1972).

In the feudal period of Western Europe from 900 to 1200, what was the logic of lords, serfs, and knights? With regard to lords, why didn't unification take place? Why wasn't there a "lord of lords" who ran a federal government? The answer is simply that land was too plentiful, there was a shortage of people, there were no cities and no goods markets, and there were frequent attacks from outsiders. (For a longer description of this period, see North and Thomas (1973), chapters 2, 3, 4. The similarity of their account to Alderson's (1954) apocryphal story of the origin of marketing channels will be evident to marketing scholars.) A king could not govern so much undeveloped territory, so local lords were a convenience for all concerned.

If the lords had the land and the power, why serfdom? The serfdom system was one in which the serfs had considerable freedom to live and work on the lord's land. They exchanged their labor by working in the lord's fields and received in exchange the right to "strips" of land that they worked for their own use. The question is, why didn't the lord either take slaves or give the property to the serfs in exchange for goods instead of labor? (Note that the absence of a monetary system is not the answer.)

Slavery was not used because its costs would have been greater than the transaction costs of serfdom. Slaves could have easily escaped to another area so there would have been a need for expensive guards. Since the lord's manor was self-sufficient, there were many types of production chores to be done. More guards and supervisors would have been required than was true in situations where slavery was practiced. Obviously, the serfs preferred the system to slavery. Thus, slavery was not used because the exchange of labor for land was more efficient for both parties than was slavery.

Then why wasn't the system pushed to a more modern form of private farm with taxes paid to the lord? The answer is that there were no cities, poor transportation, few trading specialists, and no organized markets. The manor had to be self-sufficient. Self-sufficiency required coordination by the lord. He could not count on a market mechanism for coordination. Thus, he used a mixed command system of resource allocation that permitted him to coordinate the affairs of the manor by buying labor rather than by buying goods. The logic and survival of this system is understood through an analysis of marketing exchanges. This analysis could be pushed to an analysis of why and how the system changed after 1300, but here we will move on to the knights.

The knights were specialists in fighting rather than farming. They swore allegiance to the lord in return for a comfortable life. This private army was necessary because the king could not provide a mobile army to protect against attacking bands and there was no labor market in which to buy a mercenary army. Again transaction costs were lower and productivity higher with a grant of tenure to knights. This exchange was acceptable to all because defense is the classic example of a public good. An army big enough to protect the lord will also protect others in the castle. Therefore, lord and serf alike were satisfied with tenure to the knights. The knights are added to this digression because we must soon face the question of when exchanges for public goods are marketing and when they are not. Public goods require an institutional structure in which exchanges become indirect. In this case, serfs exchange with lords, lords exchange with knights, knights protect serfs.[3]

D.3. Indirect Exchange.   What is indirect exchange? It is a circular chain of restricted exchanges between three or more actors in a closed system. In other words, it will be circular and closed. As shown in Figure 1, A exchanges with B; B exchanges with C; C exchanges with A. Each exchange is a reciprocal, two-way transaction. Bagozzi uses an example involving a consumer exchanging with a bookseller, who exchanges with an advertising agency, who exchanges with a television station, who exchanges with the consumer. The *quid pro quo* exists in each exchange.

Indirect exchange results directly from the addition of social, economic, and legal institutions to the system. A key point to an understanding of why this structure is central to the controversy over the definition of marketing is that in indirect exchange we are dealing with a system of restricted exchanges. The system arises because of the institutional framework of the society. To understand the exchange system, one must understand the institutional framework. Levi-Strauss places great emphasis on this point. Sociologists, generally, emphasize the point that social theories should not be reducible to psychological theories of individual behavior (Turner, 1974, pp. 253–257). Similarly, in marketing our analysis must consider systemic functions and institutions and not simply dyadic exchanges. It is this kind of exchange system that we call "the process of marketing." It is a process of exchanges that has developed out of the specialization of labor supported by economic and legal institutions.

It is not indirect exchange that bothers me when we attempt to limit our definition of the discipline of marketing. Rather, what bothers me is the point at which we close the system of exchange and institutions. We consider this question next.

III. LIMITS ON THE DEFINITION OF MARKETING

This review of social exchange theory has helped to determine the necessary ingredients for an exchange to be a marketing exchange. We have said that the discipline of marketing should study the process of marketing as defined at the beginning of this essay and that the ingredients of the exchange must include: some degree of freedom for the traders to make a decision to trade or not to trade, the existence of some good that will provide utility, and a trust that both parties will complete the exchange.

Unfortunately, these elments do not quite do a complete job for us. Some limits on institutions and functions must also exist. Institutions and functions are a part of the general systems paradigm. Thus, the concept of the Systems/ Exchange Paradigm was introduced. Four examples will be offered in this section in order to demonstrate how the new paradigm limits the scope of marketing to considerably less than suggested by the social exchange paradigm. These four are *gift exchange, religion, marriage,* and *politics.* If these do not define the limits of marketing for you, they will at least define the grey areas.

Is gift exchange marketing? At the very least, it is necessary to distinguish between two types of gifts: true gifts and prestation gifts.

Prestations are gifts that create a clearly recognized obligation (Mauss, 1954). That is, the obligation to reciprocate is recognized and accepted. Many business gifts are of this type. Some primitive societies that had little concept of accumulating property seem to have used prestation systems as a means of accumulating wealth in the form of obligations. The *quid pro quo* clearly existed.

A true gift is a voluntary transfer without expectation or receipt of an equivalent. Blau (1964, p. 89) and many marketers would be concerned that, since only an intrinsic good feeling is received in return, there is no exchange. One could take that position. However, gifts could be considered like the charity example earlier. The giver of the gift gives up an economic asset and receives in return a good feeling from having given. "Do good and lend, not hoping for any return, and your reward shall be great" (Luke 6:35). It may not be necessary to receive a gift in return. There has been a reallocation of resources. The obligation in heaven causes it to approach prestation status. Is this marketing? Probably not if the resource allocations are minor. But that is not true at, say Christmas. Gifts are important to the economy and to marketers. Belk (1976) has studied gift selection using the social exchange paradigm.

Church marketing is only a bit different. The church is interested in your giving of your time, energy, support, and the internalizing of a particular set of religious beliefs that it hopes will alter your future behavior. Your utility is increased by the prospect of having your soul saved *and* by membership in a social organization. As a social organization, the church in societies with freedom not to worship would certainly be engaged in marketing. One could argue, I think, that the maintenance of moral standards and the saving of souls are not functions that are related in any way to resource allocation and should therefore be excluded from marketing. When the legitimate authority is God's, we are no longer studying marketing. Thus, the church ends up being marketing in some functions but not in others.

Marriage pushes us a bit farther in a similar direction. A great deal of marketing technology may go on in a marriage. Further, exchanges do take place. The exchange theory framework is useful in analysis of exchanges between lovers. What is missing is that the function of marriage in a society has very little to do with resource allocation. Its biological and sociological functions are basic, important, and unique. Now, anthropologists studying exchange have often used women for marriage as an example of a scarce resource being exchanged. Marketing may be involved at the stage of finding the woman. But after the marriage ceremony, the institution and its functions are not marketing.

Politics as marketing is, for me, the most elusive concept of all. To begin with, we may use political processes to elect those who have the power to command the allocation of resources. I suggest that the resource allocation is marketing but the election is not. Before I describe why, let us return to generalized exchange. Assume that C (citizen) gives to L (legislator), who gives to B (bureaucrat), who gives to C. Isn't this generalized exchange? My answer is no, because more than trust is involved. Political processes are different because an election vote is not a true giving and because the giver, C, gives up personal freedom to someone else with legitimate power. I would argue that political processes are not marketing processes because: (1) the giving is not a true exchange transaction, (2) individual freedom is given up, and (3) the functions and institutions are quite different from marketing paradigms. I would close the marketing system to exclude politics (as well as marriage and religion). It is appropriate that the discipline of political science studies these problems.

It may be useful to look at the democratic process a bit more closely. Here, as in marriage, the function of the institution is not principally resource allocation but governance of the group. Also, as in marriage, democracy involves giving up some amount of individual freedom for the good of the community.

When I give up a vote, what do I receive in exchange? A promise, perhaps. If elected, the candidate hopefully will spend my taxes in a way I prefer. Rathmell calls this a "nonvoluntary exchange" (Rathmell, 1974, pp. 31–32). However, if this is an exchange at all, it is an exchange with a far more complex set of functions than the exchanges defined above.

Consider now a public agency promoting some social idea—like not smoking. There is no exchange transaction with consumers. There may be generalized exchange from the congressional committee responsible for funding the agency, from constituencies and lobbying groups such as tobacco interests to the congressional committee, and a vote from the public in the districts of the congressmen on the committee. The agency, the lobbyists, and the congressmen may use marketing technologies. However, the functions here are not just concerned with resource allocation, and the political processes involved are far different from marketing processes.

The overlap between these two systems in our modern society is substantial. It is desirable to study the intersections between the two. A relatively new journal, *Public Choice,* was begun in 1966 largely because there exists sufficient general interest—political scientists with economic interest and economists with political science interests—to make a journal on the subject viable. However, scholars in these disciplines would not have defined the problem as one concerned with the definition of marketing. They see the distinction as one of alternative methods of resource allocation—by a market mechanism or by political mechanisms. They would say that "marketing" is concerned only with resource allocation through a system of free markets.

It is appropriate to study these alternative processes for resource allocation and to study systems which involve some mixture of both, just as we do in command-based exchange systems. Marketers can make a contribution to this process as long as we appreciate the differences in the systems involved. To be a productive discipline, we must not make marketing so general that it cannot produce useful knowledge. I have argued here that to be marketing, the exchanges must contain the ingredients of freedom, goods, and trust. I have also argued that the goals, functions, and institutions of the system must have resource allocation as their primary purpose. Politics fails to meet the freedom requirement. Marriage and religion fail to meet the resource allocation requirement.

IV. UNIQUE OPPORTUNITIES FOR STUDY WITHIN MARKETING

The limits just discussed should not suggest a narrow focus for marketing. Indeed, the purpose of this discussion of limits was to provide a background against which to develop some areas where marketing can use the Systems/Exchange Paradigm to increase our understanding of other areas of human endeavor. There is no shortage of work for us to do. Four areas are developed more fully. There are certainly many others.[4]

In this discussion, an attempt will be made to provide some examples of the usefulness of the list of fundamental constructs of the Systems/Exchange Paradigm provided in Table 1.

A. Vertically Integrated and Quasi-Integrated Systems

The merger wave of the past three decades has forced economists to analyze the social consequences of vertical mergers and integration in distribution systems. The commonly cited advantages of integration to the firm are market

foreclosure, cost savings resulting from coordination of production and marketing activities at two levels of the channel, the heightening of barriers to entry, the
potential for price discrimination, and the existence of excess profits at another
level in the channel. The public policy debate in recent years has brought these
arguments rather clearly into focus (Crandell, 1968; Bork, 1969; Needham, 1969;
Vernon and Graham, 1971; Posner, 1972). We will not review the analysis here.

Marketing scholars have made less of a contribution to this analysis than have
economists. Marketers have made more of a contribution in studying the efficiency of alternative structures of physical facilities (establishments) rather than
the vertical structure of institutions (Bucklin, 1966, 1970). The concern of this
work is design of efficient total vertical distribution systems without concern for
ownership of particular establishments or profit maximization of particular firms
in the system. This work employs static microeconomic theory and the total cost
approach of logistics to provide a basic analytic approach. The analysis concerns
itself with the number and location in space of establishments and with the
functions they perform and the flow of goods, title, and information through
them.

This line of development could fruitfully be extended by shifting the focus
from optimum establishment structure to optimum institutional structure. The
research question is, given a particular vertical distribution system and objective
function, what institutional and exchange structure is optimal? One finds hints on
how to answer this question in marketing, organization theory, and economic
theory. The proposition advanced here is that the Systems/Exchange Paradigm
presented in Table I is a rich and useful framework to answer such questions. To
support this proposition, we will refer to the work of Mayer Zald (1970) (an
organization theorist), Oliver Williamson (1971, 1975) (an economist), and
Louis Stern (a marketer). All implicitly are using at least a part of the Systems/
Exchange Paradigm.

Zald suggests a framework most like the one suggested here, but he is not
working on precisely the question defined above. He has suggested an integrating
framework for analyzing institutional performance that has eight dimensions:

goal structure (our No. 1 in Table I)
incentive systems (similar to our No. 3)
succession system (a part of our No. 4)
power structure (our No. 5)
demand structure (our No. 5 for buyers)
technology and production structure (similar to our No. 10)
information system (our No. 11)
allocation rules (our No. 12)

A marketer would feel very comfortable working within this framework.

Power has not historically been a major construct for marketers. Yet a research
tradition is emerging concerned with the analysis of the power structure among
institutions in the same vertical marketing channel. Louis W. Stern and his

students have been a major force behind this thrust (Rosenberg and Stern, 1971; El Ansary and Stern, 1972). While much more validation remains to be done, they have moved far down the road from definitions and conceptualizations of power to identification of the dimensions of power, to construction of measures of these dimensions, and to empirical testing of the measures (Bucklin, 1970, pp. 75–91). Working independently, Wilkinson (1974) has also contributed to this effort.

While not recognizing either the systems paradigm or the social exchange paradigm, Oliver Williamson comes closest to utilizing all of the Systems/Exchange Paradigm proposed here. He advances the idea that "it is transactions rather than technology that underlie the interesting issues of microeconomic organization" (1971, p. 253). His approach focuses on the transactional details of recurrent contracting under alternative modes of organization. In other words, he is interested in the effect the type of linkage between institutions (our No. 7) has on the social performance of a vertical channel system. In particular, he is interested in contrasting market coordination with coordination through other control techniques. In fact, the relationship of the work of Zald and Williamson to the Systems/Exchange Paradigm is much more fundamental than thus far indicated. Firms—all firms, not just vertically integrated ones—are the primary institutions for economic activity simply because of transactions costs (Posner, 1972, pp. 176–178). A producer could use fully negotiated transactions to buy the services of labor, the services of machines, materials, etc. The result would be very high transactions costs. Instead, routinized employment agreements and long-term contracts are used. The limit on this form of institutional organization is one of control. Thus, the systems design question is, when does an institution become so big that it is preferable to use market transactions to allocate resources rather than administrative directives within an institution? Williamson does not attempt to give a definitive answer to this question, but he does attempt to provide a way of looking at the question. To describe this work, we will use our framework rather than his.

No. 1. Goals of the system. Williamson has long been interested in identification of the appropriate objective function for a firm. He has concluded that most forms of profit maximization give very similar results. This led him to recognize that in all situations, the goals of different units within a vertically integrated system are going to be more in congruence than the goals of independent institutions within a channel. Thus, integrated organizations ought to work in harmony more easily than independent ones.

No. 2. Environmental constraints. Do the antitrust laws concerning vertical integration promote the most efficient vertical channel structures? Williamson's analysis certainly raises some doubts. These doubts are concerned not with the extreme examples of monopoly power through integration but with our faltering efforts to arrive at appropriate policies regarding exclusive dealing and forms of quasi-integration like franchising.

No. 4. Internal control systems. Williamson uses six concepts to define ways that integrated hierarchies increase efficiency. Two of these concern the institution's internal control system. One he calls *bounded rationality*, extended rational decision-making through "specialization of decision making and economizing on communication expense" (Williamson, 1975, p. 257). In other words, there is economy in administrative decisions as to what information not to process as well as economy in processing what is internalized. The second he calls *opportunism*, control techniques that curb small-numbers opportunistic suboptimization.

No. 5. Relative power. Williamson attempts to analyze the relative efficiency of integrated vs. market channels, where the intermediate channels are structured as bilateral oligopoly or monopoly and are consequently subject to market failure. He suggests that integrated channels may be preferable. In an intermediate market with a small number of buyers and sellers, price and quantity are determined through bargaining rather than large group competition. The results of such bargaining need not yield a socially desirable bargain, a complete contract which provides a procedure for handling every conteingency in an efficient manner, or a desirable distribution of risk within the channel. Marketers should certainly be able to contribute to an analysis of this problem.

No. 10. Transaction costs. Two other of Williamson's six ways that integrated hierarchies increase efficiency deal with transaction costs. First, integration "permits *small-numbers* bargaining indeterminacies to be resolved by fiat" (Williamson, 1975, p. 275). Second, "as compared with market modes of exchange, hierarchy provides for some purposes at least, a less calculative exchange *atmosphere*" (p. 258).

No. 11. The level of information available. Williamson suggests two ways that hierarchies can deal with information or its absence better than autonomous agents (1975, p. 257). One is by coordinating contingency plans so as to more efficiently absorb *uncertainty*. The other he calls *information impactedness*. Essentially, the concept is one that information is shared more efficiently within organizations than between organizations.

Williamson deals with all of the constructs in the Systems/Exchange Paradigm. Described here were only those where he feels his analysis has resulted in unique contributions. He has demonstrated, I believe, that those of us trained in marketing can carry this line of analysis much farther. Might it not be more appropriate for marketing scholars to work on problems involving true marketing exchanges than to apply our efforts to the marketing of political candidates?

B. Regulation of Monopoly, Externalities, and Quasi-Public Goods

One alternative method of resource allocation in situations where competition is doomed to failure is regulation. While regulation or public enterprise is not a popular choice if choice exists, often it does not. A free market for allocation of a public good, for example, fire protection, is doomed to failure because direct bargaining regarding an indivisible output among users must result in unanimous agreement among these users. Such exchange transactions, which involve multilateral bargains, require prohibitive transaction costs, high enforcement costs, and usually ''free riders,'' those that get the service and pay nothing (Samuelson, 1954). In fact, many goods have a degree of "publicness" in them. There may be a very large class of quasi-public goods (Evans, 1970). The analysis of efficiency in the allocation of such goods always focuses first on the efficiency of transactions and then on the wealth distribution effects.

The situation of regulated monopoly is slightly different. Here the good may be entirely private but economies of scale in production lead to a public choice to have a monopolistic producer selling in a market where price, quality, output, and terms of sale are regulated by government in an attempt to replace competition as the allocation mechanism. Modern governments also have the power to enforce their terms of trade. There are transaction costs of regulation too. They can on occasion be extremely costly. In smaller countries, monopoly profits may be preferred to regulation because the transaction costs are lower and the wealth redistributions that result are not all that different from those brought about by the taxes required to pay the regulators.

In regulated monopoly, there may be another cost. There is no reason to suppose that the regulator can replace a competitive market in allocation of the good. Thus in deciding whether to regulate, it is never sufficient to demonstrate that, without intervention, the market would operate imperfectly. One needs to compare the actual workings of the market with the prospective operation under regulation. This is clearly a very difficult task, but the Systems/Exchange Paradigm provides a guide to the analysis of regulated monopolies. Here the regulators and their political supervisors need to be treated as explicit institutions within the system. Transactions between regulators and regulated firm, between politicians and firm, and between regulators and politicians all need to be explicitly modeled. Such exchange transactions are marketing transactions and worthy of our attention. Medical care is an example of a delivery system in which some of the institutions are pleading for free enterprise and others are pleading for regulation. The medical care delivery system problem cries out for more detailed analysis using the Systems/Exchange Paradigm.

But we are getting a bit ahead of ourselves. It is worthwhile to return to a particular form of quasi-public good, those private goods that create external bads, and go into a bit more detail. Again our purpose is to emphasize that while these are problems of social policy or welfare economics, the analysis at least begins with a marketing analysis of transaction costs, for which the Systems/ Exchange Paradigm is a chief framework.

The usual welfare economics approach to externalities, say smoke pollution from a factory that provides jobs and useful products to the community, was to make the factory owners liable for the damage caused by the smoke or to tax the factory owner for an amount sufficient to let the government clean up the damage or to exclude the factory from the community. Ronald H. Coase (1960) did a careful economic analysis of the exchange transactions in this sytem and arrived at what has become known as the "Coase theorem." The theorem states that, with zero transaction costs *and* no wealth or income effects, the allocative results are invariant under changes in property rights. Regardless of the initial assignment of property rights, free exchange will result in efficient resource allocation under the restrictive assumptions of the theorem.[5] No penalty for external pollution is required. In other words, government regulation or restrictions on property rights may not be the best solution.

The problem is the two restrictive assumptions. Since the wealth effect is of less interest here, it will be disposed of first. Even with zero transaction costs, wealth will be redistributed. Just how depends on the initial distribution of property and whether the good being exchanged is a major proportion of the wealth of one actor. These redistributions are not developed here.

In order to determine outcomes and relax the zero transaction costs assumption, one must investigate construct No. 9 (assignment of values), construct No. 10 (transaction costs), and construct No. 12 (the rules of exchange) of our paradigm. The usual assumption is that if the externality affects a very large number of people, regulation will have lower costs than individual lawsuits or negotiated settlements between the polluter and the community. All solutions have costs. A lawsuit is a transaction cost designed to exchange the factory owner's money for the bad (smoke) received by a neighbor. The law profession and the courts are aware of the rising costs of regulation and settlement by suit. They also realize that the solutions they render are resource allocation decisions that could be made (save for wealth affects) in the marketplace. Marketers need to be carefully recording these transaction costs under various alternative arrangements if we are to contribute to the solution of what is, at its root, a marketing problem.

Certainly, some progress has been made, but generally not by marketers. Buchanan (1973), for example, has attempted to be more specific about the number of "bad-givers" and "bad-receivers" required for regulation to be preferable to private negotiations between the parties. Here we will stray from both his typology of situations and his analysis. Thus, any errors are those of the author and not Buchanan's. The typology, shown in Figure 2, is constructed by dividing the number of givers and receivers in a manner similar to a standard classification of market structures.

Buchanan also considers the case of whether bad-givers (polluters) have the right to pollute or whether the bad-givers have no rights to pollute and must exchange with the bad-receivers in order to gain these rights. This extension is necessary to consider that part of the Coase theorem dealing with whether differences in the initial assignments of property rights make any difference. It turns out that important differences can exist in cases IV, VII, and VIII. These dif-

Figure 2. Typology of Externality Structures

	One bad-receiver	Few bad-receivers	Many bad-receivers
One bad-giver	I	II	III
Few bad-givers	IV	V	VI
Many bad-givers	VII	VIII	IX

ferences are described in the discussion below, but the complexity of another dimension to the diagram in Figure 2 has been omitted.

The solutions of the nine situations shown are similar but not identical to those for finding the equilibrium price in market exchange. Situation I is like bilateral monopoly. An efficient allocation results through bargaining, transaction costs are low, and the Coase theorem holds even with transaction costs. Situations II and V are going to have solutions similar to situation I. Receivers will always form coalitions, for they have no reason not to do so. Transaction costs will differ very little from those in bilateral monopoly. An example would be an association of condominium unit owners who are negotiating with a single neighbor over some form of pollution.

Situation IV is one in which the outcome may depend on the initial assignment of rights. If the bad-givers do not have the right to pollute, they will be forced to negotiate with the one bad-receiver. They are very likely to do so through a coalition. The nuclear power industry dealing with a single state government is one example. Another would be residents of an island who dump raw sewage into a stream that flows downstream onto a single large ranch. The solution would be similar to that for situations II and V. On the other hand, if the bad-givers had the initial right to pollute, they are less likely to form a coalition. The one bad-receiver would have to bargain individually with each bad-giver for a price to cause the bad-givers not to pollute. Transaction costs will be greater and the solution more difficult to predict without knowing more about the situation and parties involved.

In situation III, the bad-giver clearly has the power, regardless of initial assignment of rights. This is a classic case for regulation. However, notice that today a class action suit would accomplish the same result without regulation. Transaction costs would be greater but, again, may not be prohibitive. The Sierra Club vs. the Disney Mineral King development is an interesting example here. Disney actually obtained the right to pollute from the U.S. Forest Service. The bad-receivers used an existing coalition to fight the development. Transaction costs were very high but perhaps less than under alternative arrangements.

Situation VI is a very interesting case. It is typical of oligopolistic heavy industry with pollution problems—steel, chemicals, wood pulp. The bad-givers will always want to deal as individuals and will attempt to divide buyers so as to demand high prices not to pollute if they hold the right and pay low prices if they do not hold the right. Regulation would appear to be a more efficient procedure than individual transactions.

Buchanan analyzes situation VII. The solution depends on the assignment of initial rights. If they lay with the bad-givers, the one receiver will have to negotiate separate agreements with each bad-giver or vacate his property. Since transaction costs are likely to be high, the latter course is likely. If the initial rights lay with the one bad-receiver, he can extract a monopoly price from bad-givers. Transaction costs may be low, but the result may not be the allocatively efficient one.

I can arrive at no general theoretical solution for situation VIII. The situation appears to be like that in bilateral oligopoly. Both givers and receivers realize the interdependencies of the situation. General solutions require knowing specific information about the characteristics and even personalities of the actors (No. 4), the initial assignment of rights, resources, and relative power (No. 5), the nature of the externality (No. 8), the value assignment process (No. 9), transaction costs (No. 10), the information available to actors (No. 11), and the rules governing exchanges (No. 12). Transaction costs in this structure are likely to be great and regulators very subjective to corruption.

Situation IX is also discussed by Buchanan. An equilibrium-like allocatively inefficient position is likely regardless of who holds the initial rights. For a single bad-receiver, there is little incentive to enter negotiations with a single bad-giver. Nothing will be gained. Small group coalitions are not likely to be productive for similar reasons. Bargaining coalitions of a size sufficient to insure gains to potential members are difficult and costly to form. An example of this situation is occupational health and safety. As long as workers are disorganized, employers do not even bother to collude in order to not provide safe work places. If employers are forced by the state to pay for workman's compensation, they will do some risk pooling and provide the safety devices required to minimize the cost of insurance premiums plus safety expenditures. The first viable bad-receiver coalition is the union which, with government enabling legislation, is able to bargain collectively for improved working conditions. The power of the union sanction may force the employers into coalitions. The transactions costs of such coalitions are not insignificant but are tolerable as long as unions perform other functions except negotiating over health and safety. Is more government intervention required? Recent legislation in the United States would indicate that many people believe it is. Will regulation be cost effective in this area? Will it create undesirable allocative inefficiencies? These are empirical questions that the Systems/ Exchange Paradigm will help to answer.

Jerome Rothenberg (1970) has suggested another approach to situation IX that he calls generic congestion. It arises from congestion through use of public goods such as a public beach. The users of the beach both create and receive the bad. Of course, others may receive the bad, for example, water pollution from the beach, and not all the public chooses to participate. The process is still allocatively inefficient, but now the whole user group loses by their self-imposed interaction. The study of exchanges between congesters may well prove fruitful in this case.

Regulation of monopoly and oligopoly, regulation of externalities, regulation of resources in short supply such as energy, and regulation of health and safety have all been areas of increasing government activity in recent years. Yet, economists, marketers, and activists like Ralph Nader and Louis Kohlmeier have all been very critical of the independent regulatory agencies (Kohlmeier, 1969). These events and others have spelled renewed popularity for the study of regulation by economists, political scientists, and sociologists (Kahn, 1970/71). The *Bell Journal of Economics,* which first appeared in 1970, continues to offer promise, and certainly reflects interest, of new breakthroughs in the theory of regulation. But what about marketers? The study of regulated monopoly as a technique of resource allocation is clearly within the province of the discipline, but few articles on the subject have appeared in our literature in recent years. Marketers have concentrated their attention more on the regulation of competition, for example, deception in advertising, than on the regulation of monopoly or quasi-public goods.

C. Marketing Exchanges by Not-for-Profit Institutions

A separate but similar topic of concern for marketers involves marketing in a number of rather diverse markets in which the seller is a quasi-public or eleemosynary institution. We include in this group the Postal Service, foundations, charities, hospitals, and educational institutions. Such institutions control large quantities of societal resources and it is not at all clear that either market or political processes work to cause such institutions to allocate their resources efficiently, relative to some societal welfare or preference function.

Many such institutions derive major proportions of their revenue in a fashion that does not meet a market test. For example, universities receive a substantial portion of their income from sources other than tuition. Medical care demanders frequently have their care paid for by "third parties." Pondy has suggested that the objective function of such institutions may be "maximizing discretionary resources" (Pondy, 1970), that is, maximizing their discretion to allocate resources independent of the desires of their sources of revenue.

Marketing scholars have studied the marketing problems of such organizations, but much more attention needs to be given to studying the relative effectiveness of alternative control mechanisms over resource allocation in quasi-public institutions (Tullock, 1966; F. K. Levy, 1968; Garrison, 1972).

An analysis of such exchange situations using the Systems/Exchange Paradigm (Table I) for a foundation or charity is presented now in order to demonstrate how the paradigm may be used. One would begin by defining the system within which the foundation or charity was operating. This task is not likely to be an easy one. A foundation or a charity is likely to be operating in a research system, a medical care system, a social service system, or an educational system. As such, it attempts, within the system, to conduct or support activities that others in the system are not supporting. Some such organizations may avoid being associated exclusively with a particular system. Assume here we are considering a medically-related organization like the Easter Seal Society for Crippled Children and Adults. Their system concerns a research system for physical and sensory disabilities and a medical care system for rehabilitation of crippled persons. In this system are special education public and private schools, physicians, proprietary hospitals, community hospitals, and social welfare agencies of local, state, and federal government. A listing of the institutions involved in such a system is not an easy undertaking.

1. It should be easier to specify the goals of the system—to make independent and near-normal living possible for those with physical and sensory handicaps.

2. The specification of relevant environmental factors again is not easy but also not impossible. The environmental factors would include: (a) health events such as rubella epidemics and trends in the incidence of stroke; (b) innovations in treatment of crippling disabilities; (c) changes in third party, including government, payment for rehabilitation services. An appreciation of these factors is necessary for an understanding of transaction behavior.

3. The control mechanism for the system largely is through the demand for such services and the availability of funds either from government, patients, or charitable giving. Again this is a complex system because most demand is not created by those who receive the services. Thus, an institution in the system seeks to remain healthy by identifying market segments who need its services and by increasing the flow of funds coming to it. This is precisely why Pondy's maximizing discretionary resource is a logical objective function for an institution. With a strong inflow of discretionary funds, an institution like Easter Seal has the ability to shift its services to those where there is the greatest demand.

4. As indicated above, the identification, description, and internal structure of the institutions in a system for providing rehabilitation services is difficult and very important in order to understand the exchange transactions taking place.

Government agencies have objective functions that are political; most medical providers in the system are profit maximizers; hospitals have survival goals; the eleemosynary institutions want to maximize discretionary resources. In conventional marketing systems we seldom have such disparity in institutional goals. Yet we know these disparities are very important in analyzing exchange transactions.

5. In systems with such diffuse institutions, the resources and relative power of these institutions is likely to be very different. In our example, government sources probably have the greatest financial resources and sometimes have the power of law to alter transactions in a particular way. The physician institutions have the power of their profession to refer their patients as they see fit. One would be lost in an analysis of exchange transactions in such a system if these vast differences in the nature and extent of power were not understood.

6. Similarly, while all institutions provide some rehabilitation functions, the functions performed by the various providers differ widely. Physicians uniquely provide drug therapies, general medical care, and referral services; special education institutions uniquely provide education services; other institutions provide unique social services. In analyzing transactions between client and provider and between providers, it is necessary to consider this different mix of functions performed. With regard to marketing functions, all institutions should be providing them, but the methods used are likely to be very different for the government agency, the for-profit physician, and the charitable institution such as Easter Seal.

7. Much less is known about the linkages between such institutions than is true for conventional commercial marketing channels. Our work in this field indicated that one must do primary data collection in order to specify all the linkages that exist between actors.

8. What is exchanged? At this step we can at last begin an analysis of exchange transactions. It is important here to emphasize the need to study transactions not only between Easter Seal and its clients but between client and other providers and between Easter Seal and other providers. Since all are interdependent in the system, analysis of exchanges between just two actors is not sufficient to understand the transaction from either a descriptive or normative point of view. An interesting aspect of the exchange between Easter Seal and its clients is that some clients receive services free of charge. That is, a client who is not covered by public or private insurance and has no funds can still receive services from the charitable institution. What then does the client exchange? Presumably a credit for Easter Seal as a charitable organization.

9. How does Easter Seal value such charity patients vis-à-vis those that have private insurance or those on Medicade or Medicare? How does the charity patient value services received for a zero money price vis-à-vis those received at a positive money price? Do patients value their time or delivery costs for charitable services differently than for services provided by government or private

providers? How does the existence of insurance influence these valuations? Little attention has been given to these questions and they are questions that lend themselves to analysis by marketers employing the exchange theory paradigm.

10. Transaction cost functions in health care delivery is a subject of great interest to the author. I believe this is another situation where the important problems concern transactions (marketing) rather than technology or manpower supply. Rehabilitation services provide an example of why I hold this hypothesis. Consider, for example, a stroke victim at the time of discharge from the hospital. He or she relies on the physician to advise on physical and speech therapy. The physician is not well equipped to answer this question. The social service department at the hostpial should have answers but may not have a clear idea of what services are available that are convenient for the patient. Also, the hospital may offer some of these services so the advice may not be unbiased. The patient and family have no way of shopping for rehabilitation services. To be paid by insurance, the services must be ordered by a physician. Thus, transaction costs tend to be high.

11. Concomitantly, the level of information is low. A normative marketing problem would be to develop ways to increase the level of information held by providers and available to clients.

12. The problems of the rules of exchange here have been discussed by others (Shortell, 1972; Harris, 1977). The patient is in strife, under a number of pressures, and cannot be expected to know about specialized health care services in advance. Providers collude and make side payments for referrals. Physicians fix prices through the use of relative value schedules. The government and the insurance companies attempt to alter delivery patterns and control costs by establishing rules or changing price schedules. We know that altering prices does change provider behavior. How does this behavior affect a charitable organization like Easter Seal? This analysis remains to be done.

In this example, we have not tried to answer questions but to raise them. Again, this example was intended to demonstrate that (1) the systems analysis paradigm is necessary for application of the general exchange paradigm, and (2) the Systems/Exchange Paradigm is useful in the analysis of a broad spectrum of marketing problems.

D. Some Problems of Freedom and the Right to be Informed

We have argued that at least limited rights of free, voluntary exchange are an essential part of the discipline of marketing. We have implied but not made explicit that this freedom to exchange is among the limited property use rights that are really *a necessary* rather than a sufficient *condition for the discipline too*. These rights need to be transferable if we are to have exchanges. Without private property, there would be no incentive to save and, like the Polynesians, we would live from what goods the gods made available for the cost of collection. It is this ability to hold, accumulate, and exchange property that leads us to efficiently husband resources. Thus, North and Thomas (1973) argue that it was the establishment of clear and unambiguous property rights that led to the rapid development of the Low Countries and England during 1500 to 1700 and led France and Spain to stagnate during that period. In a society where government places more and more restrictions on our use of property, do these incentives still exist? An answer to this question requires that we focus more on the systems elements of our paradigm (Nos. 2 and 3) than on the transaction elements.

However, the inability to obtain the information required to exchange effectively might also be viewed as a constraint on our freedom to exchange property. Information levels of traders is construct No. 11 in our paradigm. Whether one is negotiating in bilateral monopoly or dealing in a nearly competitive market, the actors must have information on goods and prices. By definition, competitive markets provide clear information on the exchange rates that are available to prospective buyers and sellers. These traders are free to trade or not trade at prevailing prices as they see fit. Price and the availability of price and quality information are central not only for efficiency but for protecting the freedom of the traders. However, the asymmetry of information problem is well-known in most markets today. Much of the current consumer movement is concerned with protecting the rights of consumers to have adequate and accurate price and quality information about the increasing number and complexity of alternatives available to the marketplace.

But in political resource allocation, where revenues are taxes, and in public goods, where revenues are purposely separated from outputs, buyers are not clear as to what alternative uses of resources are possible, have little control (or only after a considerable lag) over the quality of these outputs, and have very little control over their cost. The payoff of an output from one of these organizations is often diffused so broadly through the society that the individual is likely to have trouble evaluating the payoff for himself. In short, the "buyer" may not know what alternatives exist, have little information on the impact of these alternatives, and is not free to veto the alternative chosen anyway.

Put more sharply, we have very little definitive theory on the effectiveness of information flows and social control in nonmarket resource allocation. The politician would counter that the social cruelty of the free market systems has also not been studied carefully enough. For example, after spending seventy years building a society that is completely dependent on cheap energy, doesn't the market violate personal freedoms by raising the price of gasoline by a factor of three? Thus, many politicians actively resist letting the price system do its job. They might argue that the long use of cheap energy creates a kind of property or use right much the way that continued use of a path over private property can create a use right. An analysis of this issue would involve a comparison of control mechanisms and of limitations on freedom between free exchange and command exchange and on the wealth redistribution effects of unregulated energy prices. Such a comparison is partially within the discipline of marketing as it was defined earlier in this essay. Levy and Zaltman (1975) provide an excellent beginning for this work by focusing on the relative efficiency of conflict resolution under differing channel structures, competitive structures, and political allocation systems.

V. SUMMARY

This paper has suggested that the question of a narrow or broad definition of marketing is probably not as important as is the impact that the definition has on the research which marketers undertake. As a framework for the development of theory in the discipline of marketing, a Systems/Exchange Paradigm was introduced. This paradigm is viewed as a companion to the systems/functionalist paradigm (that Alderson would have simply called "functionalist") of marketing. These two, which are closely related, appear to be sufficient for organizing all normative and descriptive theory in the discipline.

With regard to closing the systems defined as the discipline of marketing, an analysis of gifts, marriage, religion, and politics led to the generalization that marketing exchanges: (1) should be conducted for the primary purpose of resource allocation; (2) require ingredients of freedom and trust for the parties; (3) exist in an environment with sufficient property rights for the parties to exchange use rights. 'Resources' here include a very broad category of 'goods.' By these criteria, politics, marriage, and religion were excluded from our discipline.

As a way of suggesting the usefulness of the Systems/Exchange Paradigm, it was used to outline analyses of four neglected areas of research in marketing. The first of these concerns the optimal design of vertical channels of distribution. The point is made that the choice between market allocation of resources and administrative allocation of resources is one of the fundamental questions of economic organization. The Systems/Exchange Paradigm helps us to see that what marketers view as one important question of their discipline is in reality a central question of societal organization.

The second area for research discussed concerns the question of when government regulation is superior to market exchange in situations of public goods, legalized monopolies, externalities, very scarce resources, and health and safety. The Coase theorem on the social costs of dealing with externalities is extended in this section.

The third area for research concerned marketing exchanges by not-for-profit institutions. In this section, an analysis of exchanges by a charity was outlined using the Systems/Exchange Paradigm. The last problem area suggested concerned the impact that restraints on property rights and information asymmetry have on the ability and willingness of actors to engage in exchanges and the impact of these problems on allocative efficiency. This problem area is concerned with a unit of analysis that is more likely to be the individual than was true of the other examples.

The range of these problems is broad. The definitions of the process of marketing and the discipline of marketing as defined here are broad. While government social intervention programs were largely excluded from marketing, the many interesting problems of mixed economies using market and political processes for resource allocation were certainly not excluded. However, our testing of the limits of the discipline does suggest that marketing is concerned with the resource allocation functions of the society. When the primary function of a societal process is other than resource allocation, we have stepped beyond marketing.

FOOTNOTES

*This essay represents an evolving of my conscious thinking on this subject that began in 1970 or 1971. A conference on social marketing in Urbana in December 1972 catalyzed this thought process. Some of these ideas appeared in 1973 (Carman, 1973). Many people have contributed to the ideas contained here. Most of them appear in the references. Among those not listed there are David A. Revzan and Robert M. March.

1. In this spirit, *all* of the standard comprehensive books on marketing theory are excluded from the references and are not reviewed.

2. Charles E. Lindblom's (1977) important new book on political-economic systems provides an excellent example of how the paradigms developed here can be used either for analysis of marketing or of political economy.

3. Jagdish Sheth has pointed out that the Hindu traditional story of the origin of the caste system describes four similar functions: the teachers who were divine and received gifts; the fighters who protected treasure and assured good government; the agricultural workers with the power of work; the laborers who served the other three. Although the true historic roots of the system include racial, social, religious, and political functions as well, it is important to note the existence of complex generalized exchanges in this system that date from ancient times.

4. Bagozzi (1978) is attempting to extend the work of Thibaut and Kelley to harmonize more directly with utility theory. Thibaut and Kelley start with psychological concepts, build upward to the dyad, and then, using exchange theory, build upward to the small group. Bagozzi is attempting to work with exchanges between dyads or small groups in understanding marketplace behavior. Economic theory does not deal well with small group exchanges. These are problems that fall naturally into the realm of marketing and problems where the exchange theory framework can be of value.

5. It may be useful here to distinguish between allocative (or social) efficiency and transaction (or technical) efficiency. Allocative efficiency is perfect when the value of the marginal product of a resource is equal in all of its uses. That is, the marginal revenue product of the resource in all its uses is equal to its price. Transaction efficiency refers to the cost of accomplishing the transaction. It is maximum when the cost of the transaction is minimum. In the whole economy, a technically efficient system would result in using administrative allocations within organizations and market allocations in such combination that the costs of making all allocations would be a minimum.

REFERENCES

Alderson, W., "Factors Governing the Development of Marketing Channels," in *Marketing Channels for Manufactured Products,* Richard M. Clewett (ed.). Homewood, Ill.: Richard D. Irwin, Inc., 1954.

Alderson, W., *Marketing Behavior and Executive Action.* Homewood, Ill.: Richard D. Irwin, Inc., 1957.

Alderson, W., *Dynamic Marketing Behavior.* Homewood, Ill.: Richard D. Irwin, Inc., 1965.

Bagozzi, R. P., "Marketing as Exchange." *Journal of Marketing* 39 (October 1975): 32–39.

Bagozzi, R. P., "Science, Politics, and the Social Construction of Marketing." *Proceedings of the American Marketing Association,* Memphis, August 1976.

Bagozzi, R. P., "Marketing as Exchange: A Theory of Transactions in the Marketplace." *American Behavioral Scientist,* March/April 1978.

Belk, R. W., "It's the Thought that Counts: A Signed Digraph Analysis of Gift-Giving." *Journal of Consumer Research* 3 (December 1976): 155–162.

Belshaw, C. S., *Traditional Exchange and Modern Markets.* Englewood Cliffs, N.J.: Prentice-Hall, Inc., 1965.

Blau, P. M., *Exchange and Power in Social Life.* New York: John Wiley & Sons, 1964.

————, "Interaction: Social Exchange," in *International Encyclopedia of the Social Sciences,* Vol. 7, David L. Sills (ed.), pp. 452–458. New York: Macmillan Co., 1968.

Bork, R. H., "Vertical Integration and Competition Processes," in *Public Policy Toward Mergers,* J. F. Weston and S. Peltzman (eds.), pp. 139–149. Pacific Palisades, CA.: Goodyear Publishing Company, Inc., 1969.

Buchanan, J. M., "The Institutional Structure of Externality." *Public Choice* 14 (Spring 1973): 69–82.

Bucklin, L. P., *A Theory of Distribution Channel Structure.* Berkeley: Institute of Business and Economic Research, University of California, 1966.

————, ed., *Vertical Market Systems,* pp. 158–174. Glenview, Ill.: Scott, Foresman and Company, 1970.

Carman, J. M., "On the Universality of Marketing." *Journal of Contemporary Business* 2 (Autumn 1973): 1–16.

Chavannes, A., cited in John B. Knox, "The Concept of Exchange in Sociological Theory: 1884 and 1961." *Social Forces* 41 (1963): pp. 341–346.

Churchman, C. W., *The Systems Approach.* New York: Delacorte Press, 1968.

Coase, R. H., "The Problem of Social Cost." *Journal of Law and Economics* 3 (October 1960): 1–44.

Cox, R., Alderson, W., and Shapiro, S. J. (eds.), *Theory in Marketing: Second Series.* Homewood, Ill.: Richard D. Irwin, Inc., 1964.

Crandall, R. W., "Vertical Integration and the Market for Repair Parts in the United States Automobile Industry." *Journal of Industrial Economics* 16 (July 1968): 212–234.

Ekeh, P. P., *Social Exchange Theory: The Two Traditions.* London: Heinemann Ltd., 1974.

El Ansary, A. I., and Kramer, O. E., "Social Marketing: The Family Planning Experience." *Journal of Marketing* 37 (July 1974): 1–7.

El Ansary, A. I., and Stern, L. W., "Power Measurement in the Distribution Channel." *Journal of Marketing Research* 9 (February 1972): 47–52.

Emerson, R. M., "Social Exchange Theory," in *Annual Review of Sociology,* Vol. 2, A. Inkeles, J. Coleman, and N. Smelser (eds.), pp. 335–362. Palo Alto, CA.: Annual Reviews, Inc., 1976.

Evans, D. K., "Private Good, Externality, Public Good." *Scottish Journal of Political Economy* (February 1970): 79–89.

Farley, J. U., and Leavitt, H. J., "Marketing and Population Problems." *Journal of Marketing* 35 (July 1971): 3–12.

Frazer, J. G., *Folklore in the Old Testament,* Vol. 2. London: Macmillan & Co., 1919.

Friedman, J. M., *Oligopoly and the Theory of Games.* New York: North Holland Publishing Co., 1977.

Gaedeke, R. M., *Marketing in Private and Public Nonprofit Organizations: Perspectives and Illustrations.* Santa Monica: Goodyear Publishing Co., Inc., 1977.

Garrison, L. C., "The Needs of Motion Picture Audiences." *California Management Review* 15 (Winter 1972): 144–152.

Gogol, B., *Organization of Domestic Trade in the USSR.* Moscow: Progress Publishers, 1970.

Harris, J. E., "The Internal Organization of Hospitals: Some Economic Implications." *Bell Journal of Economics* 8 (Autumn 1977): 467–482.

Homans, G. C., "Social Behavior as Exchange." *American Journal of Sociology* 63 (May 1958): 597–606.

Homans, G. C., *Social Behavior: Its Elementary Forms*. New York: Harcourt Brace & World, 1961.

Hunt, S. D., "The Nature and Scope of Marketing." *Journal of Marketing* 40 (July 1976): 17–28.

Kahn, A. E., *The Economics of Regulation*. New York: John Wiley & Sons, Vol. 1, 1970; Vol. 2, 1971.

Knox, J. B., "The Concept of Exchange in Sociological Theory: 1884 and 1961." *Social Forces* 41 (1963): 341–346.

Kohlmeier, L. M., *The Regulators*. New York: Harper and Row, 1969.

Kotler, P., "A Generic Concept of Marketing." *Journal of Marketing* 36 (April 1972): 46–54.

Kotler, P., *Marketing for Nonprofit Organizations*. Englewood Cliffs, N.J.: Prentice-Hall, Inc., 1975.

Kotler, P., and Zaltman, G., "Social Marketing: An Approach to Planned Social Change." *Journal of Marketing* 35 (July 1971): 3–12.

Levi-Strauss, C., *The Elementary Structure of Kinship*. Boston: Beacon Press, 1969.

Levy, F. K., "Economic Analysis of the Non-Profit Institution—The Case of the Private University." *Public Choice* 4 (Spring 1968): 3–18.

Levy, S., and Zaltman, G., *Marketing, Society, and Conflict*. Englewood Cliffs, N.J.: Prentice-Hall, 1975.

Lindblom, C. E., *Politics and Markets*. New York: Basic Books, Inc., 1977.

Malinowski, B., *Argonauts of the Western Pacific*. London: Routledge and Kegan Paul, 1922.

Mauss, M., *The Gift*. In English, London: Cohen and West; and New York: The Free Press, 1954.

McGinniss, J., *The Selling of the President: 1968*. New York: Trident Press, 1969.

Mindak, W. A., and Bybee, H. M., "Marketing's Application to Fund Raising." *Journal of Marketing* 35 (July 1971); 13–18.

Needham, D., *Economic Analysis on Industrial Structure*. New York: Holt, Rinehart and Winston, 1969.

Nicosia, F. N., "Marketing and Alderson's Functionalism." *Journal of Business* 35 (October 1962): 403–413.

North, D. C., and Thomas, R. P., *The Rise of the Western World*. Cambridge: University Press, 1973.

Ohio State University Marketing Staff, "A Statement of Marketing Philosophy." *Journal of Marketing* 29 (January 1965): 43–44.

Pondy, L. R., "Toward a Theory of Internal Resource-Allocation," in *Power in Organizations*, M. N. Zald (ed.), pp. 270–311. Nashville: Vanderbilt University Press, 1970.

Popper, K., *Conjectures and Refutations*. New York: Harper and Row, 1963.

Posner, R. A., *Economic Analysis of Law*. Boston: Little, Brown and Co., 1972.

Rapoport, A., *Game Theory as a Theory of Conflict Resolution*. Boston: D. Reidel Publishing Co., 1974.

Rathmell, J. M., *Marketing in the Service Sector*. Cambridge: Winthrop Publishers, Inc., 1974.

Roberts, P. C., "An Organizational Model of the Market." *Public Choice* 10 (Spring 1971): 81–92.

Rosenberg, L. J., and Stern, L. W., "Conflict Measurement in the Distribution Channel." *Journal of Marketing Research* 8 (November 1971): 437–442.

Rothenberg, J., "The Economics of Congestion and Pollution: An Integrated View." *American Economic Review* (May 1970): 114–116.

Samuelson, P. A., "The Pure Theory of Public Enterprise." *Review of Economics and Statistics* 36 (November 1954): 387–389.

Shortell, S. M., *A Model of Physician Referral Behavior: A Test of Exchange Theory in Medical Practice*. Chicago: University of Chicago, Center for Health Administration Studies, 1972.

Simon, J. L., "A Huge Marketing Research Task—Birth Control." *Journal of Marketing Research* 5 (February 1968): 21-27.

Stidsen, B., and Schutte, T. F., "Marketing as a Communication System: The Marketing Concept Revisited." *Journal of Marketing* 36 (October 1972): 22-27.

Sweeney, D. J., "Management Technology or Social Process." *Journal of Marketing* 36 (October 1972): 3-10.

Telser, L. G., *Competition, Collusion and Game Theory*. Chicago: Aldine-Atherton, 1972.

Thibaut, J., and Kelley, H. H., *The Social Psychology of Groups*. New York: John Wiley & Sons, 1959.

Tucker, W. J., "Future Directions in Marketing Theory." *Journal of Marketing* 38 (April 1974): 30-35.

Tullock, G., "Information without Profit." *Public Choice* 1 (1966): 141-160.

Turner, J. H., *The Structure of Sociological Theory*. Homewood, Ill.: The Dorsey Press, 1974.

Vernon, J. M., and Graham, D. A., "Profitability of Monopolization by Vertical Integration." *Journal of Political Economy* 79 (July-August 1971): 924-925.

White, T. H., *The Making of the President: 1972*. New York: Atheneum Publishers, 1973.

Wilkinson, I. F., "Researching the Distribution Channel for Consumer and Industrial Goods: The Power Dimension." *Journal of the Market Research Society* 16 (January 1974): 12-32.

Williamson, O. W., "The Vertical Integration of Production: Market Failure Considerations." *American Economic Review* 61 (May 1971): 112-123.

————, *Markets and Hierarchies: Analysis and Antitrust Complications*. New York: The Free Press, 1975.

Zald, M. N., ed., *Power in Organizations*. Nashville: Vanderbilt University Press, 1970.

Zaltman, G., and Vertinsky, I., "Health Service Marketing: A Suggested Model." *Journal of Marketing* 35 (July 1971): 19-27.

Zikmund, W. G., and Stanton, W. J., "Recycling Solid Wastes: A Channel-of-Distribution Problem." *Journal of Marketing* 35 (July 1971): 34-39.

A MODEL-BASED METHODOLOGY FOR ASSESSING MARKET RESPONSE FOR NEW INDUSTRIAL PRODUCTS

Jean-Marie Choffray, ESSEC
Gary L. Lilien, M.I.T.

ABSTRACT

Industrial marketers face the difficult problem of developing product designs and associated communication strategies for new products aimed at heterogeneous audiences. This paper details the structure of an operational model of industrial response to marketing strategy. Four submodels make up this structure—an awareness model, a feasibility model, an individual evaluation model, and a group interaction model. Methods of structuring and calibrating these submodels are discussed, as are the associated measurements. The use of the new methodology to develop industrial marketing strategy—including product design and positioning trade-offs as well as communication program development—are reviewed. The

Research in Marketing, Volume 3, pages 37–81
Copyright © 1980 by JAI Press Inc.
ISBN: 0–89232–060–5

paper uses illustrations from applications of the methodology and concludes with a detailed example reviewing the assessment of the market potential for solar-powered industrial cooling systems.

1. INTRODUCTION: THE NEW INDUSTRIAL PRODUCT DEVELOPMENT PROBLEM

New products account for a significant portion of the sales volume of industrial companies. McGuire and Bailey (1970) indicate that for the majority of industrial companies, over 25 percent of sales volume is attributable to products introduced within the last five years. Several studies (de Simone, 1967; Booz, Allen and Hamilton, 1965, for example) also show the importance of new products in determining company growth.

However, new products are risky. The Booz, Allen and Hamilton study shows that over 70 percent of the money spent on new product activities is associated with products that are not commercial successes. A recent analysis of the success probabilities of new industrial products at different stages in their development by Mansfield and Wagner (1975) suggests that less than one-third of new industrial product projects become economic successes.

Mansfield and Rapoport (1975) report on the cost of new product development. The major components of this cost, across many industries, are associated with the development of a prototype plant, new tools, and manufacturing facilities. This suggests the importance of market analysis prior to that stage of development.

A number of attempts have been made to identify the causes of new industrial product failures (Briscoe, 1973; Rothwell et al., 1974; Cooper, 1975; Mansfield and Wagner, 1975). The results of these studies are quite consistent: more emphasis is needed on analysis of organizational purchasing behavior and on fostering a closer integration of market research with product development. As Levitt (1960) points out, and as is confirmed by careful empirical work by von Hippel (1977), the high rate of failure of many new industrial products is linked to the policy of selling what R&D can produce rather than of satisfying customer needs.

This paper presents a model-based methodology to assess short-run market response to a new industrial product. The methodology comprises a set of models that addresses the issues of new product awareness, organizational feasibility, decision participants' perceptions, and group choice. Although the structure has been developed to treat medium-priced capital equipment, the modularity of its submodels offers considerable flexibility. In a particular application of the methodology, any of its submodels can be adapted to account for the unique situation encountered by the new industrial product investigated.

Once the model components have been calibrated, the methodology provides a flexible decision aid for developing new industrial products. It provides key diagnostic information about areas of high potential for product redesign; areas of resistance to the new product concept among decision participants; and opportunities for developing differentiated communication strategies.

The methodology can therefore be used to assess design trade-offs, in terms of expected market response, and product profitability. The analysis of the buying behavior of organizations in the target market, on which the methodology rests, also allows a quantitative treatment of new industrial product positioning issues and communications programs development (including target audience definition and copy design).

The paper proceeds as follows: the next section briefly reviews the literature about organizational buying and identifies those variables and relationships that are essential to the new product adoption process. We then develop an operational model of market response and review the issues associated with designing the model components. A measurement methodology is then described which provides the necessary input to each of the model's components. The use of the procedure to aid the new industrial product development process is then reviewed, using a solar-powered cooling system for industrial use as a case example. That extended example shows: which design improvements in solar cooling will have most effect on potential demand; who (what job responsibilities) are the key decision influences in the market; how the market can be segmented according to the structure of the decision-making unit; and what types of communications programs (issues, media) are most likely to be cost effective in boosting the potential sales of the new product.

The time/cost and other implementation issues associated with the methodology are reviewed, along with a discussion of the situations which justify its use.

2. ORGANIZATIONAL BUYING: BACKGROUND

As Webster (1978) points out, the amount of rigorous analysis given to industrial marketing problems is quite small relative to that given consumer marketing problems. There are several reasons for this: industrial products, from sulfuric acid to computer software and nuclear power plants, are more diverse than consumer products. Industrial companies tend to be production-oriented, and direct a smaller portion of their financial resources to marketing research activities than do consumer goods manufacturers. Most importantly, organizational buying behavior is far more complex and requires new and different modeling solutions.

For many industrial products—especially for capital equipment—a multi-person decision process is the normal mode of behavior. This decision process is characterized by the involvement of several individuals, with different organizational responsibilities, who interact with one another in a decision-making structure specific to each organization, and whose choice alternatives are limited by environmental constraints and organizational requirements.

Previous work on industrial buying behavior has been essentially concerned with (1) the development of integrated conceptual models and (2) the empirical verification of hypotheses pertaining to specific aspects of this behavior.

Robinson and Faris (1967) develop a descriptive model of industrial buying behavior that categorizes this process according to purchase situations. Webster and Wind (1972) propose a descriptive model of organizational buying. They introduce the concept of a "buying center" which includes those individuals involved in a purchase decision. Response of the buying center is analyzed as a function of four classes of variables: individual, interpersonal, organizational, and environmental. Sheth (1973) develops a model that tries to encompass all industrial buying decisions. The model distinguishes three main elements of industrial buying: (1) the psychological characteristics of the individual involved, (2) the conditions which precipitate joint decision-making, and (3) the conflict resolution procedures affecting joint decision-making.

In addition, a number of empirical studies have dealt with certain aspects of industrial buying behavior. These studies are mainly (1) observations of actual purchase decisions (Cyert et al., 1956; Brand, 1972), (2) analyses of the involvement of various organizational functions in industrial purchasing (Harding, 1966; Scientific American, 1969; Buckner, 1967), and (3) studies of the behavior and decision styles of individual decision participants (Lehman and O'Shaughnessy, 1974; Cardozo and Cagley, 1971; Hakanssan and Wootz, 1975; Wilson, 1971; Sweeney et al., 1973; Scott and Bennett, 1971; Wildt and Bruno, 1974; Scott and Wright, 1976).

A limitation of current models of organizational buying behavior is their lack of parsimony. Typically, available models provide a detailed conceptual structure for the study of industrial buying that is too complex to be operationalized. Moreover, from a managerial standpoint, the influence of many of the intervening variables singled out in these models have only been empirically validated in a limited way.

Recognizing these limitations, we develop an operational model of organizational buying that is more concise than currently available models. It focuses on the links between the characteristics of an organization's buying center and three major stages in the industrial purchasing decision process: (1) the elimination of alternatives that do not meet organizational requirements, (2) the formation of decision participants' preferences, and (3) the formation of organizational preferences.

Although simple, this model is consistent with the current state of knowledge in the field. It operationalizes the concept of the buying center and deals with issues of product feasibility, individual preferences, and organizational choice. And it specifically addresses the sequential process involved in considering purchase of a new industrial product. The next section develops that model in detail.

3. A MODEL OF ORGANIZATIONAL RESPONSE

A complete, operational model of industrial response to a new product requires that organizational heterogeneity be explicitly handled. The model proposed here considers the following sources of heterogeneity:

1. Potential customer organizations differ in their "need specification dimensions," that is, in the dimensions they use to define their requirements. They also differ in their requirements along these dimensions.

2. Potential customer organizations differ in the composition of their buying centers: in the number of individuals involved, in their responsibilities, and in the way they interact.

3. Decision participants, or individual members of the buying center, differ in their sources of information as well as in the number and nature of the evaluation criteria they use to assess product alternatives.

The consideration of these sources of organizational heterogeneity in an aggregate model of industrial response requires that members of the buying center be grouped into "meaningful" populations. Here, we use "decision participant category" to refer to a group of individuals whose responsibilities in their respective organization are essentially similar. Examples of such participant categories are "production and maintenance engineers," "purchasing officers," "plant managers," etc.

Our objective is to gain leverage by focusing on areas where individual or organizational homogeneity allows meaningful aggregation. To this end, we assume:

A1. Within potential customer organizations, the composition of the buying center can be characterized by the categories of participants involved in the purchasing process.

A2. Decision participants who belong to the same category share the same set of product evaluation criteria as well as information sources.

Assumption 1 is operationalized in Section 4.2; Assumption 2 is consistent with current knowledge. Sheth (1973) contends that individuals whose task orientation and educational backgrounds are similar tend to have common expectations about industrial products and suppliers. Recent work (Choffray and Lilien, 1976) indicates that meaningful differences exist in both the number and nature of the evaluation criteria used by various decision participant categories.

Figure 1 presents the general structure of our industrial market response model. The structure of this response model states that for an organization to select product a_0 for purchase, at least one decision participant in that organization must be aware of a_0 as an alternative; product a_0 must meet the organization's technical and financial requirements as well as the constraints imposed on that organization by its environment; and product a_0 must be the choice of the buying center in that organization (resulting from the interaction among its various members).

Figure 1. General Structure of an Industrial Market Response Model

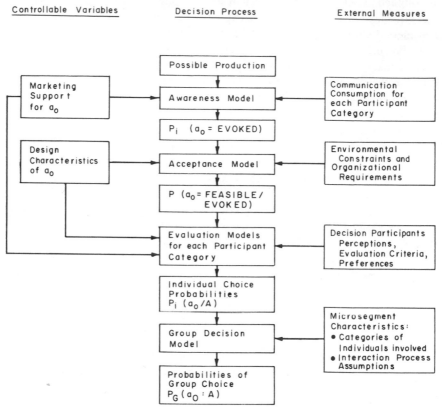

Our model and associated measurement methodology focuses on the following issues: (1) identification of ''microsegments'' or organization, homogeneous in the structure of their buying centers or decision-making units (DMU's); (2) within each microsegment, determination of the fraction of customers who are aware of the product; (3) within that microsegment, and assuming awareness, determination of the fraction of organization for whom the product is feasible, and (4) determination of the fraction of customer-organizations in the microsegment that prefer the product to other alternatives.

Multiplication of the fractions in (2), (3), and (4) gives an estimate of segment market share. The next step is (5) determination of product sales, predicted as the product of segment market share times total segment forecast sales (market potential). Summing this quantity over segments gives the product-sales estimate.

This modeling and measurement sequence makes certain key assumptions. The process of choice—essentially one of sequential screening—is consistent with current choice theory (Tversky, 1972). It will assume that organizations in a "microsegment" (having similar DMU's), use the same dimensions for screening product alternatives. Similarly, as noted above, the methodology assumes that individuals with similar backgrounds and job responsibilities structure preferences similarly. Both these assumptions can be challenged, but both are reasonable a priori and make the procedure operational.

Stated analytically, then, the probability that product a_0 in evoked set A is the organization's choice (given that the organization is in the market to purchase a product in the class) can be written as:

$Pr(a_0 = \text{ORGANIZATIONAL CHOICE}) =$
  $Pr (a_0 = \text{GROUP CHOICE/INTERACTION, FEASIBLE, EVOKED})$
  $\times Pr (a_0 = \text{FEASIBLE/EVOKED})$
  $\times Pr (a_0 = \text{EVOKED})$

Each element of this structure is reviewed next.

3.1. The Awareness Model

3.1.1. Purpose. The awareness model links the level of marketing support for product a_0—measured in terms of spending rates for such activities as *P*ersonal *S*elling (PS), *T*echnical *S*ervice (TS), and *AD*vertising (AD)—to the probability that a decision participant belonging to category i (say production and maintenance engineers), will evoke a_0 as a potential solution to the organizational purchasing problem. Let

$$P_i (a_0 = \text{EVOKED})$$

denote this probability. Hence, we postulate that

$$P_i (a_0 = \text{EVOKED}) = f_i(\text{PS, TS, AD})$$

The evoking function will be calibrated separately within each microsegment, leading (perhaps) to different structures. Only controllable variables have been included here in line with our objective of making the structure operational.

This formulation also assumes that individuals who belong to the same participant category share essentially the same sources of information. It is reasonable to expect, however, that the awareness functions $f_i(\cdot)$'s will exhibit substantial differences across categories of decision participants as a result of their different levels and sources of information.

When several decision participant categories are involved in the purchasing process, the probability that product a_0 will be evoked as an alternative is the probability that at least one member of the buying center will evoke it. Thus:

$$P_G(a_0 = \text{EVOKED}) = 1 - \text{II}_i (1 - P_i(a_0 = \text{EVOKED}))$$

where index i covers all decision participant categories characterizing the purchasing process of the particular microsegment to which the organization belongs. This assumes that these probabilities are independent. Our experience
with organizational communication between job functions leads us to believe this
assumption is not unrealistic.

3.1.2. Analytical Structure.   The functional form of each of the awareness
functions $f_i(\cdot)$'s can either be derived empirically through a field study or can be
provided by the product manager judgmentally. In the first case, a survey is
performed for a sample of individuals from each participant category, exposed to
various levels of the control variables PS, TS, and AD. Individuals are asked
what brand(s) of product in the class they are aware of, their media consumption
patterns, the last time they saw a salesman, etc. (See Morrill, 1970, for a
description of a large-scale study of this nature.) These measurements can then
be used as input to a set of multiple discriminant analyses or probit analyses
which allow the development and calibration of analytical forms for each of the
$f_i(\cdot)$'s. In some recent work by Lilien and Rao (1979), a generalized logistic
function has been used to calibrate an awareness model. In that study, advertising
weight was found to affect the level of product awareness.

   In many cases, however, the second approach will be used due to time and cost
constraints. It is based on a "decision calculus" approach (see Little, 1970),
that relies on the manager's experience with the product and its market to infer
what the $f_i(\cdot)$'s are for each decision participant category.

   In this case, a base point (c) is provided by current marketing effort level and
current awareness. Allowing for forgetting, a manager might be asked what
would happen to awareness

Figure 2. Decision Calculus Calibration

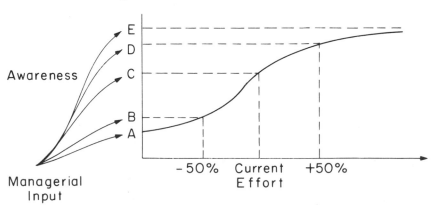

- with a 50 percent increase in marketing effort (D)
- with a 50 percent decrease in effort (B)
- with a level of marketing effort which is essentially unlimited (E)
- with marketing effort set to zero (A)

Figure 2 displays the results of a decision calculus-type calibration.

3.2. The Acceptance Model

3.2.1. Purpose. The second element of the market response model is the acceptance model which accounts for the process by which organizations screen out infeasible products. Typically, the methodology assumes that potential customer organizations specify their purchasing needs along a set of ''need specification dimensions.'' Examples of such dimensions are: initial product cost; operating cost; technical features, etc. Companies have specific requirements along these dimensions which limit the range of products that they can consider for final purchase.

Alternatively, need specification dimensions can be viewed as product design dimensions along which the new product characteristics can be defined. Let the new product a_0 be characterized by a vector of features $x_0 = \{x_{01} .. x_{0l}\}$ defined along organizational need specification dimensions $\{X_i\}$, $i=1 \ldots l$.

The acceptance model relates the design characteristics X_0 of product a_0 to the probability that it will fall in a potential customer's feasible set of alternatives. Let this probability be denoted by

$$P_G (a_0 = \text{FEASIBLE/EVOKED}) = g(X_0)$$

Although organizations in the potential market may differ in their need specification dimensions, as well as in their requirements along these dimensions, the acceptance model $g(\cdot)$ assumes that the process by which organizations eliminate infeasible alternatives is essentially similar across potential customer organizations.

3.2.2. Analytical Structure. The notions of feasible sets of alternatives and of organizational need specification dimensions suggest that the models most suitable at this level are of the conjunctive type. Conjunctive models are multiple cutting-point models in which a set of acceptable levels is defined by each potential customer organization along its relevant set of need specification dimensions. To be feasible to a given organization, a product alternative has to fall in the acceptance region along each of these dimensions.

Several models can be used to approximate the process of organizational elimination of unfeasible alternatives. We propose two convergent approaches to specify $g(\cdot)$. Both approaches require information about the maximum (or minimum) requirement along each relevant need specification dimension from a sample of organizations in the potential market for the new product.

The first approach is probabilistic and requires fitting individual Beta probability density functions to the empirical distribution of normalized company requirements along each specification dimensions. The joint probability that X_0 falls in the feasible region for a given organization chosen at random in the potential market for the new product is then assessed as:

$$p(a_0 = \text{FEASIBLE/EVOKED})$$

$$= \prod_{i=1}^{l} p(X_{oi} = \text{FEASIBLE/EVOKED})$$

assuming that company requirements along the l specification dimensions are mutually independent. If such is not the case, principal component analysis can be used to identify a smaller set of independent composite specification dimensions.

The specification of each function $p(X_{oi} = \text{FEASIBLE})$ from the empirical distribution of company requirements can be made using a Beta density function of the form

$$f(x) = \begin{cases} \dfrac{1}{B(\alpha,\beta)} \, x^{\alpha-1} \, (1-x)^{\beta-1}; & 0 < x < 1 \\ 0 & \text{otherwise} \end{cases}$$

where $\quad B(\alpha,\beta) = \displaystyle\int_{0}^{1} x^{\alpha-1}(1-x)^{\beta-1}dx \qquad \alpha, \beta > 0$

The Beta distribution is very inflexible and can approximate a variety of empirical shapes. Its two parameters (α,β) can be estimated by the method of moments.

In order to use the Beta function, company requirements along each specification dimension must first be normalized to lie within the range [0,1]). A simple transformation used to accomplish this is

$$y_{iJ} = \frac{Y_{iJ} - \min(Y_J)}{\max(Y_J) - \min(Y_J)}$$

where y_{iJ} stands for the normalized requirement of company i on specification dimension J; Y_{iJ} stands for the observed requirement of company i on specification dimension J (say Y_{iJ} = \$900 per ton of cooling, for company i, where J = maximum acceptable cost per ton of cooling; max (Y_J), min (Y_J) stand for the maximum and minimum values observed for specification dimension J.

Once the parameters of the Beta function have been estimated for each specification dimension, the integral form:

$$\frac{1}{B(\alpha_j\beta_j)} \int_0^{y_{ij}} x^{\alpha j-1} (1-x)^{\beta j-1}\, dx$$

can be used to estimate the probability that a system with characteristic Y_{ij} (normalized value y_{ij}) is feasible for a randomly selected organization.

As a simplified example, (with a normal rather than a beta density) suppose there are only two need-specification dimensions, cost/unit and annual maintenance cost, and suppose, for simplicity, we calculated the marginal distributions across organizations, as follows:

Cost/Unit: Normal~mean = $1,000, sd = $100
Annual maintenance cost: Normal~mean = $ 100, sd = $10

If these distributions are independent, then we would find the fraction of organization who find a product with cost = $1100 *and* maintenance cost = $100 *feasible* as

$$(1 - \Phi\left(\frac{(1100-1000)}{100}\right)) \times (1 - \Phi\left(\frac{(100-100)}{10}\right)) =$$

$$(1 - \Phi(-1)) \times (1 - \Phi(0)) = (.159)(.5) = .079.$$

(where Φ is the cumulative standard normal distribution function). Thus, we would estimate that 7.9 percent of the organizations in that sector would find that "design" (i.e., cost = $1100, maintenance = $100) feasible.

The second approach uses regression on a logit-transferred dependent variable to relate the fraction of organizations in the potential market that would find product design X_o feasible to the individual characteristics $[x_{o1}, \ldots x_{ol}]$ of this product. The logit approach therefore assesses the relative importance of the various features of the new product in the determination of its market acceptance rate.

Calibration of the logit model first requires that a sample of "artificial" designs for the new product be randomly generated through simulation. Let this set of designs be denoted $[X_i, i=1 \ldots l]$. For each such design, the fraction of organizations in the sample that would find it feasible is computed. Let P_j, $j=1 \ldots M$ denote these numbers. The model

$$l_n \frac{\hat{p}_j}{1-\hat{p}_j} = \beta_0 + \sum_{i=1}^{l} \beta_i x_{ji} + \epsilon_j$$

is then assessed by weighted least squares.

Both approaches have their respective advantages. The logit approach gives a confidence interval around the estimate of the market acceptance rate corresponding to the specific features of a new product. It also provides an estimate of the relative importance of organizational requirements in the determination of the rate of market acceptance within a small region around the likely value. The probabilistic approach, on the other hand, explicitly models interaction between organizational requirements. As a result, it is particularly suitable to investigate new product design trade-offs, and is accurate at extremes of the feasibility requirements (when initial cost is very large, say).

Independent of the approach followed, the feasibility model $g(\cdot)$, once specified, can be input to a simulation that (1) quantifies product design trade-offs, and (2) allows accurate prediction of the rate of market acceptance corresponding to specific designs of the new product.

3.3. The Organizational Decision Models

Feasibility of a product for a given organization is only one step toward adoption. Usually, several alternatives are feasible in any purchase situation. The one that is retained for final adoption is related to the individual preferences of decision participants and of their mode of interaction.

The methodology proposed here explicitly addresses these two issues. First, it investigates the formation of individual preferences for feasible product alternatives for each category of decision participants. Second, it proposes ways to formalize the interaction process among decision participant categories within each microsegment.

3.3.1. Models of Individual Preference Formation

3.3.1.1. Purpose. Individual evaluation models relate evaluations of product characteristics to preferences for each category of decision participant. The models permit the analysis of preference response to changes in product positioning. They therefore feed back important information for the development of industrial communication programs that address the issues most relevant to each category of participant. Let

$$P_i(a_o;A/FEASIBLE, EVOKED)$$

denote the probability that an individual belonging to category i will choose a_o from the set of feasible alternatives A. It is developed as:

$$P_i(a_o;A/FEASIBLE, EVOKED) = h_i(E_{oj})$$

where E_{oj} refers to individual j's evaluation of alternative a_o along those performance evaluation criteria $C_i = [c_i, \ldots , c_{in}]$ common to all individuals belonging to category i. These criteria will typically be calculated by factor-analyzing product attribute perceptions data.

3.3.1.2. Analytical structure. Most empirical studies of how individuals perceive and evaluate product alternatives have been done in the consumer goods area (see Allaire, 1973; Hauser and Urban, 1977; and Urban, 1975, for example). These methodologies share the same theoretical foundations. They all assume the existence of an n-dimensional perceptual space common to all consumers. An individual's perception of a product may then be thought of in terms of the coordinates of this product on the set of relevant perceptual dimensions. Operationally, an individual's perception of a product is provided by his ratings of the product on a set of perceptual items representing the salient attributes in the product class.

In order to relate individual preferences to product perceptions, the methodologies developed in the consumer area suggest the reduction of the perceptual space to a subspace of lower dimensionality whose coordinate axes express how these individuals structure basic product attributes into higher-order performance evaluation dimensions (Hauser and Urban, 1977) or choice criteria (Howard and Sheth, 1969). An individual's evaluation of a product may then be viewed as the projection of this product on his relevant evaluation criteria.

Straightforward application of these methodologies in the case of industrial adoption decisions raises substantial problems due to the multi-person nature of these decisions. The methodology proposed here therefore attempts to answer the following questions:

1. How do different categories of decision participants differ in the way they *perceive* available alternatives, including the new product?

2. How do these groups of decision participants differ in the way they *structure* basic product attributes into higher-order evaluation criteria?

3. How do these evaluation criteria affect product *preferences* for each of these different groups of individuals?

An answer to the first question is essential for developing sensible communication programs aimed at reducing resistance to the new product within specific participant categories. In the same way, answers to the other two questions aid in the study of positioning trade-offs for the new product.

Perceptual Analysis.   As stated earlier, implementation of our methodology requires that decision participants be grouped into homogeneous categories with respect to their task orientation or job responsibility. The perceptual analysis part of the methodology aims at answering the two following questions: For each category of decision participant, are feasible products perceived differently? This step of the analysis is called product discrimination analysis. Alternately, for each feasible product, do the categories of decision participants exhibit substantial perceptual differences? This step of the analysis is called differential perception analysis.

The formal analysis of product discrimination is tested via one-way multivariate analysis of variance. Then, for each feasible product alternative, differential perceptions across participant categories are tested via multivariate profile analysis. If the groups differ in their perception of an alternative, univariate analyses of variance are performed to isolate those items that are the major sources of these differences.

Product Evaluation Analysis.　　Figure 3 outlines the steps that are used to assess differences in the evaluation criteria used by each category of decision participants. First, variance-covariance matrices between all perceptual items are

Figure 3. Outline of Evaluation Space Methodology

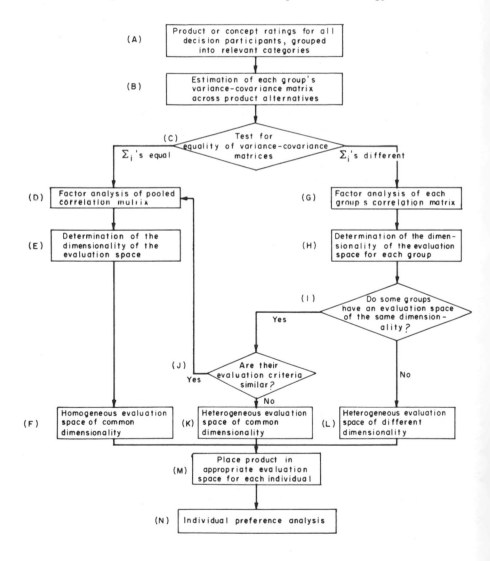

computed using the ratings obtained for all feasible product alternatives from each individual in every participant category (B). Then, a test for equality of all participant categories' covariance matrices is performed and allows for an early detection of possible differences in the way individuals in each of these groups structure the relevant product attributes into higher-order evaluation criteria (C). The Box test is used for this purpose.

If the hypothesis of equal covariance matrices is accepted, the correlation matrix between perceptual ratings is computed across all individuals and factor analyzed (D). The dimensionality of the common evaluation space is determined (E) by the parallel analysis method (Humphreys and Ilgen, 1969). The exact composition of the evaluation criteria common to all categories of decision participants is then appraised (F).

Rejection of the hypothesis of equal covariance matrices across decision categories requires separate factor analysis for each group (G). The dimensionality of the evaluation space is then determined for each group (H). If the number of evaluation criteria is different for each participant category, the analysis concludes at the existence of differences in the evaluation space harbored by different categories of participants. On the other hand, when some groups have an evaluation space of the same dimensionality, additional tests (J) for the equality of evaluation criteria are necessary (Choffray and Lilien, 1976). These tests investigate all subsets of participant groups with the same dimensionality for equality of evaluation criteria. If all evaluation criteria are found to be identical, these participant categories have a common evaluation space, so that a factor analysis of their pooled correlation matrix is not required (D). If at least one of their evaluation criteria is different, the analysis concludes at the existence of heterogeneous evaluation spaces across those decision groups with the given dimensionality.

The final step of the analysis is concerned with the behavioral relevance of the differences in the evaluation criteria used by the different categories of participants. This step is called preference estimation (N) and is concerned with linking individual preferences to product coordinates in the appropriate evaluation space.

Following Allaire (1973), for each participant category, several functional forms are tested by regression analysis and the best one retained. Here the dependent variable is stated product preference (rank-ordered or ratio-scaled from paired-comparison data), while the independent variables are the evaluation criteria. These models of individual preference formation may lead to the identification of decision style differences among participant categories. Once calibrated, these models are used to predict preference for feasible product alternatives. They can also be used in a "sensitivity-analysis" mode to assess likely changes in individual preferences caused by a change in the positioning of the new product on the respective evaluation criteria of each participant category.

Once calibrated, individual preferences can be transformed into probability of choice in one of several ways. First, we can assume that an individual will choose his first preference product. Secondly, a transformation, relating ratio-scaled preference to probability of purchase such as

$$\text{Prob (purchase of } a_0) = \frac{(\text{Pref } (a_0))^\beta}{\sum_i (\text{Pref } (a_i \epsilon A))^\beta}$$

can be used. (See Silk and Urban, 1977 for the use of a model of this type in predicting purchase from preference data.)

3.3.2. Models of Group Interaction

3.3.2.1. Purpose.   Prior to calibrating group interaction models, our methodology calls for identification of those participant categories involved in the new product adoption process within potential customer organizations. Part of our methodology, called microsegmentation analysis, is concerned with measuring the composition of the buying center within potential customer organization and with identifying groups of firms which exhibit similar patterns of adoption process involvement. This part of our methodology is described later.

Models of group interaction map individual probabilities of choice for feasible alternatives into group probabilities of choice. In our methodology, this aggregation is made for each microsegment of organization identified in the potential market for the new product.

3.3.2.2. Analytical structure.   We propose four models of group choice. Each one corresponds to different assumptions about the nature of the interaction process. We distinguish a Weighted Probability Model, a Voting Model, a Unanimity Model, and an Acceptability Model. All of them are proposed for a typical organization of an unspecified microsegment of the potential market.

Weighted Probability Model. The Weighted Probability model assumes that the group, as a whole, is likely to adopt a given alternative, say $a_0 \ \epsilon A$, proportionally to the relative importance of those members who choose it.

Let

$$P_G(a_j; A) = \text{probability that the group chooses } a_j$$

w_i = relative importance, on the average, of decision participant d_i, $i=1, \ldots r$ in the choice process. So,

$$\sum_{i=1}^{r} w_i = 1$$

Then the weighted probability model postulates that

$$P_G(a_0; A) = \sum_{i=1}^{r} w_i P_i(a_0; A)$$

We can interpret this as a two-step sampling process where in step one, the organization samples a decision-maker from the set of decision participants proportionally to each participant's relative importance in the choice process. In step two, the sampled decision-maker selects an alternative according to his own choice probabilities.

There are two interesting special cases of the weighted probability model: (1) *Autocracy:* If $w_e = 1$, then all other $w_{i \neq e} = 0$; then a single decision participant, d_e is responsible for the group choice. (2) *Equiprobability:* If $w_i = 1/r$, for all i, then every decision participant has equal weight in the process. This is an appealing model, as it is a sort of zero-information or naive model. The industrial marketing manager need only identify the decision participants and does not have to measure or provide subjective estimates of the importance coefficients.

The equiprobability form of the weighted probability model has received some empirical support, both in dyadic decision making (Davis et al., 1973) and in group decisions involving more than two participants (Davis, 1973). Moreover, the model was found to accurately describe group risk shifts (Davis, 1973).

One must be careful, however, in interpreting these results. Indeed, although the cumulative frequencies of actual group decisions were reproduced accurately by the equiprobability model, these experiments mainly involved ad hoc groups whose members had little experience in working together. The equiprobability model might then be a reasonable approximation to organizational choice behavior in situations that involve decision participants from different departments who are not accustomed to working together.

As an example, consider an organization with three decision participants d_1, d_2, d_3 and three alternatives $A = [a_0, a_1, a_2]$.

Individual Choice Probabilities $P_i(a_j;A)$

a_j	$P_1(a_j;A)$	$P_2(a_j;A)$	$P_3(a_j;A)$
a_0	.2	.3	.7
a_1	.5	.2	.2
a_2	.3	.5	.1

Then $P_G(a_0;A) = .2w_1 + .3w_2 + .7w_3$. An equiprobability model with $w_i = 1/3$, i=1,2,3 will yield $P_G(a_0;A) = .4$. An autocratic model with $w_1 = 1$ will yield $P_G(a_0;A) = .2$; with $w_3 = 1$ will yield $P_G(a_0;A) = 7$. These are upper and lower bounds on $P_G(a_0;A)$ for the weighted probability model. In terms of our example: $.7 \geq P_G(a_0;A) \geq 2$.

The Voting Model.   The voting model attributes the same weight to all individuals involved in the decision process. It states that the probability that the group will choose alternative a_0 is equal to the probability that a_0 is selected by the *largest number* of decision participants. Let

$$X_{ij} = \begin{cases} 1 & \text{if } d_i \text{ chooses } a_j \\ 0 & \text{otherwise} \end{cases}$$

Then

$$\Pr(X_{ij} = 1) = P_i(a_j; A)$$

Let

$$Z_j = \sum_{i=1}^{r} X_{ij} \quad \text{then}$$

$$P_G(a_0; A) = \text{Prob}\,[Z_0 = \max_j (Z_j)]$$

In terms of the previous example, we get $P_G(a_0; A) = .417$. This compares with .4 for the equiprobability model.

The Unanimity Model.   This model assumes that, in order to be accepted by the group, an alternative, say a_0, has to be the actual choice of all decision participants involved in the choice process. Thus a group might, in theory, "vote" over and over again until unanimity is reached. Empirical studies of the industrial adoption process indicate that this model does capture some of the essence of the multi-person choice involved in this process (Buckner, 1967). This model reflects the so-called management by consensus, reportedly practiced by Japanese businessmen.

Formally, the unanimity model implies that

$$P_G(a_0; A) = \frac{\prod\limits_{i=1}^{r} P_i(a_0; A)}{\sum\limits_{j=0}^{n} \prod\limits_{i=1}^{r} P_i(a_j; A)}$$

assuming that individual preference distributions are mutually independent. This is the conditional probability that the product a_0 is selected, given that the group reaches unanimity.

Acceptability Model.   This model assumes that if a group does not reach unanimous agreement, it is most likely to choose the alternative that "perturbs" individual preference structures least. This may be referred to as "management by exception." Suppose the following pattern of individual preferences holds in a group of two.

Decision Participant	Preference Pattern	Probability of Getting Pattern θ_k
d_1	$\theta_{1e}: a_0 \geqslant a_1 \geqslant a_2$	$P_1(\theta_{1e}/A)$
d_2	$\theta_{2h}: a_2 \geqslant a_0 \geqslant a_1$	$P_2(\theta_{2h}/A)$

where θ_{ik} means that individual i exhibits a preference structure θ_k. Given the pattern of preference structures $\gamma_{eh} = [\ \theta_{ie}, \quad \theta_{2h}]$, we define the perturbation $Q(A_j \mid \gamma_{eh})$ associated with the choice of alternative a_j as the total number of preference shifts necessary for a_j to be everyone's first choice. In the above example, we get:

$$Q(a_0 \mid \gamma_{eh}) = 1$$

$$Q(a_1 \mid \gamma_{eh}) = 3$$

$$Q(a_2 \mid \gamma_{eh}) = 2$$

Assuming that all preference shifts are strictly comparable, we have:

$$P_G(a_0 \mid \gamma_{eh}) = 3\, P_G(a_1 \mid \gamma_{eh})$$

$$P_G(a_0 \mid \gamma_{eh}) = 2\, P_G(a_2 \mid \gamma_{eh})$$

As $\quad \sum_{j=0}^{n} P_G(a_j \mid \gamma_{eh}) = 1$, we get

$$P_G(a_0 \mid \gamma_{eh}) = 6/11$$

$$P_G(a_1 \mid \gamma_{eh}) = 2/11$$

$$P_G(a_2 \mid \gamma_{eh}) = 3/11$$

Formally, given the distribution of preferences $P_i(\theta|A)$ for each decision participant, we can compute the probability that a specific pattern of preference structures γ_w will occur across individuals.

Thus, we get

$$Pr[\gamma_w] = Pr\ [\theta_{1k}, \theta_{2k}, \ldots \theta_{rk}]$$

$$= \prod_{i=1}^{r} P_i(\theta_{ik}|A) \qquad \text{where } w = 1, \ldots k^r$$
$$\text{and} \quad k = 1, \ldots (n+1)!$$

assuming that individual preference distributions are mutually independent.

Letting $Q(a_j \mid \gamma_w)$ be the perturbation associated with alternative a_j in the pattern γ_w, we postulate that the ratio of probability of group choice equals the ratio of needed preference perturbation to achieve first preference within the group:

$$\frac{P_G(a_j|\gamma_w)}{P_G(a_e|\gamma_w)} = \frac{Q(a_e|\gamma_w)}{Q(a_j|\gamma_w)}$$

Moreover, if $Q(a_e|\gamma_w) = 0$, then

$$P_G(a_e|\gamma_w) = 1 \text{ and}$$

$$P_G(a_j|\gamma_w) = 0 \text{ for } j \neq e \text{ (This is a case of unanimous}$$
$$\text{first preference.)}$$

As the total number of possible preference shifts is fixed, these conditional probabilities are uniquely determined. Hence, the unconditional probabilities of group choice are given by:

$$P_G(a_j;A) = \sum_w P_G(a_j|\gamma_w) \cdot Pr[\gamma_w]$$

Although conceptually simple, the acceptability model entails combinatorial difficulties. Its justification follows from the observation that many groups seem to choose "everybody's second choice," or more precisely, the alternative that perturbs individual preferences least.

The models above are intuitively appealing but by no means exhaustive. An alternative to explicit modeling is to simulate the impact of different interaction assumptions on the estimate of group response. This approach is particularly suitable when neither the manager in charge of the new product nor sales people have an accurate understanding of the interaction process that characterizes decision-making within each microsegment. This approach allows them to consider various types of assumptions and assess the sensitivity of group response to these assumptions.

4. IMPLEMENTATION OF THE INDUSTRIAL MARKET RESPONSE METHODOLOGY

Implementation of the structure described above requires a set of measurements that provides input to the various submodels. This section reviews the measurement steps involved in a typical implementation of the response model. These measurements are summarized in Figure 4.

4.1. Measurements at the Market Level

The first measurement step, called macrosegmentation following Wind and Cardozo (1974), specifies the target market for the new product. The purpose of macrosegmentation is to narrow the scope of the analyses to those organizations most likely to purchase the product. Bases for macrosegmentation might be as

Figure 4. Major Measurements Needed for Calibrating the Industrial Market Response Model

Data Type	Source	Target
1. Hard	1.1. Market	1.1.1 Macrosegmentation: Target Market Definition
	1.2. Organizations	1.2.1 Identification of Need Specification Dimensions; Measurement of Organizational Requirements.
		1.2.2 Microsegmentation: Grouping of Organizations on the Basis of Buying Center Composition
	1.3. Decision Participants	1.3.1 Production Awareness and Communication Consumption Patterns
		1.3.2 Production Evaluations and Preferences
2. Soft	2.1. Industrial Marketing Manager	2.1.1 Judgmental Estimates of Interaction Process

general as S.I.C. code classification, geographic location, etc. The output of this measurement step is an estimate of the maximum potential market for the product. Let Q denote that maximum potential.

4.2. Measurements at the Customer-Organization Level

Two major types of measurements have to be obtained at this level. If the potential market for the product contains a large number of customers, a representative sample can be drawn. In other cases, gathering data from all potential customers might be considered.

Organizations' need specification dimensions have to be identified first, and then the requirements of each firm in the sample along these dimensions must be assessed. Identification of these dimensions follows discussions with potential decision participants. Group interview methods (see Wells, 1974) are particularly suitable for this purpose. It is the authors' experience that such interviews with members of the buying center of a few (3–5) potential customers are generally sufficient to identify the set of relevant specification dimensions.

Survey questions are developed next. These questions request the maximum (or minimum) value along each specification dimension beyond which the organization would reject a product out of hand. In order to reduce individual response bias, respondents are allowed to use any information sources in their organization (including colleagues) to provide their answers. These answers are the main input to the acceptance model. Figure 5 gives an example of these questions for an industrial air conditioning system.

Next, information is collected on the composition of the buying center and the respective organizational responsibilities of its members. This information allows the development of a decision matrix (see Figure 6 for an example) that requests the percentage of the task responsibilities for each stage in the purchasing process associated with each category of decision participants. This instru-

Figure 5. Sample Question for Evaluation of Need Specification Dimension

2.1 Suppose your company had decided to install an a/c system in a *new* plant and has identified
several different systems for consideration. In screening these alternatives, your company *will
eliminate* any system,
   a. If its expected life is *less than* _____ years.
   b. If its initial investment cost is *more than* _____ $/ton of cooling.
   c. If it is covered by a complete warranty of *less than* _____ months.
   d. If it is successfully operating in *less than* _____ other industrial installations.
   e. If its annual operating cost (maintenance included) is *more than* _____% of its initial
       investment cost.

ment has been shown to give consistent estimates of involvement in the decision
process when completed by different members of the same organization (Choffray, 1977). This corroborates earlier observations by Wind and Kelly (1974).

We next develop a microsegmentation scheme that uses cluster analytic
procedures to identify microsegments of potential customers that are homogeneous in the composition of their buying centers. Figure 7 outlines the main
steps in this analysis.

First, the decision matrix is used to measure involvement in the adoption
process for a sample of organizations in the potential market. Let x_{ijh} denote the
entry in row j and column h of the decision matrix for company i. This value
represents the "percentage" of the task responsibilities associated with decision
phase h that are part of the role of participant category j in the adoption process
for company i. We then have

$$x_{ijh} \geq 0 \qquad \text{for all i, j, h}$$

$$\sum_{j} x_{ijh} = 1.0 \qquad \text{for all i and h}$$

Second, an index of inter-organizational similarity or dissimilarity must be
selected. One measure of the degree of dissimilarity between two organizations
(r,s) in the structure of their adoption process is the distance function

$$D_{rs}^2 = \sum_{J, h} (\sigma_{rjh} - \sigma_{sjh})^2$$

where
$$\sigma^{ijh} \begin{cases} = 1 \text{ if } x_{ijh} > 0 \\ = 0 \text{ if } x_{ijh} = 0 \end{cases}$$

Third, cluster analytic procedures are used to identify groups of organizations
which exhibit similar patterns of involvement in their adoption process. Choffray
(1977) presents criteria to determine the number of such microsegments which
should be retained for final analysis.

The final step of the microsegmentation analysis concerns the identification of

Figure 6. Sample Decision Matrix: Industrial Air Conditioning Study

Decision phases / Decision Participants	1 Evaluation of a/c needs, specification of system requirements	2 Preliminary a/c budget approval	3 Search for alternatives, preparation of a bid list	4 Equipment and manufacturer evaluation*	5 Equipment and manufacturer selection
COMPANY PERSONNEL					
Production and Main-tenance Engineer	%	%	%	%	%
Plant or Factory Manager	%	%	%	%	%
Financial controller or accountant	%	%	%	%	%
Procurement or pur-chasing department	%	%	%	%	%
Top Management	%	%	%	%	%
EXTERNAL PERSONNEL					
HVAC/Engineering firm	%	%	%	%	%
Architects and Build-ing Contractor	%	%	%	%	%
a/c equipment manu-facturers	%	%	%	%	%
COLUMN TOTAL	100 %	100 %	100 %	100 %	100 %

* *Decision phase 4 generally involves evaluation of all alternative a/c systems that meet company needs while Decision phase 5 involves only the alternatives (generally 2-3) retained for final selection.*

Figure 7. Outline of the Microsegmentation Methodology

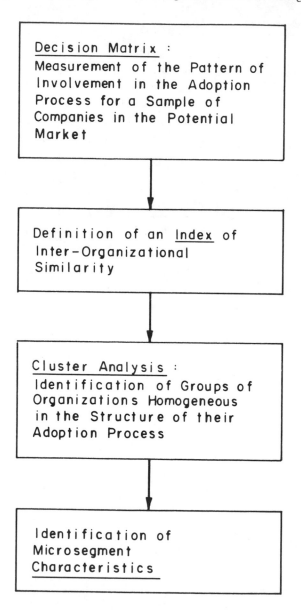

microsegment characteristics in terms of: general pattern of decision process involvement; and external company measures such as size, growth rate, etc. Analysis of variance or other statistical methods can be used for this purpose.

Let S, . . S_n denote the microsegments identified in the potential market for the new product and V_1, . . V_n their relative size in terms of market potential. Each microsegment S_q is further characterized by a set of participant categories DEC_q that are usually involved in the adoption process for the companies it comprises. For instance, in segment S_1, corporate managers along with design engineers might be the major categories of participants involved. In S_2, production engineers are involved, too, etc.

4.3. Measurements at the Decision Participant Level

For each decision participant category, product awareness, perceptions, and preferences are measured at the individual level.

Product awareness can be obtained through survey questions asking each potential decision participant what product(s) or brand(s) of product they think of in a specified product class. Several other methods commonly used in consumer goods marketing to measure brand awareness (see Johnson, 1974) can also be used. Both measurements are used to calibrate the awareness submodel.

The measurement of individual perceptions, evaluations, and preferences for product alternatives requires more complex methods. In industrial markets it is often difficult to expose potential buyers to a physical product due to transportation and time constraints. For this reason, the use of concept statements, accurately describing each product in the class considered, is a reasonable alternative. Due to the technical orientation of potential buyers, the use of concept statements to measure individual perceptions and preferences seems as suitable for industrial markets as in consumer markets, where the method has been used with considerable success (Hauser and Urban, 1977). Figure 8 gives a sample concept statement for solar-powered air conditioning.

Individual product perceptions can then be recorded along each of a set of perceptual scales that include the relevant attributes used by individuals to assess products in this class. Figure 9 develops the measurement procedure used for solar air conditioning.

Preference data can be collected in several ways. Two convergent methods, rank-ordered preferences and constant sum-paired comparisons, were used in the solar cooling study (see Figure 10). The latter method allows the evaluation of a ratio-scaled preference score via Torgerson's least squares procedure (1958). Preference rankings obtained by the two methods can then be used to assess respondents' inconsistency in preference judgment.

An important assumption inherent in the measurements of individual percep-

Figure 8. Sample Concept Statement: Solar Air Conditioning Study

Solar Absorption a/c System: SOLABS

SOLABS consists of a standard absorption chiller as used in ABSAIR and a hot water solar collector which replaces the boiler in a standard absorption a/c system. As it uses solar energy as a power source, SOLABS is less sensitive to fuel shortages and power fluctuations than other industrial a/c systems.

The solar collector used by SOLABS is a flat type that is located on the roof of the building. In some cases, collectors can even replace the roof. Collectors come in panels of various standard sizes that are attached to one another by normal plumbing connections. Two water storage tanks are also part of SOLABS and are generally buried in the ground. One of these tanks is for chilled water, to meet the immediate demands of the absorption system. The other one is for hot water, to meet a/c needs during periods of little sunshine or alternatively to provide heating during these same periods. When the system is used exclusively for a/c, water storage capacity need not be large as more solar energy is available when cooling is most needed. A small backup heating and cooling system can be used to make up for prolonged periods of low sunshine.

Solar energy alone can provide 40%–60% of all building a/c requirements, significantly reducing energy costs. In addition, warm water produced by the solar collector can be used for manufacturing or domestic water needs. In colder climates, this system can provide 30%–40% of heating requirements.

The initial cost of SOLABS is at least 50% higher than for non-solar systems, depending on the size of the installation. The operating cost of SOLABS, however, is considerably lower than for other systems due to a reduction of at least 40% in a/c energy consumption (depending on the geographical location). Maintenance costs for SOLABS are similar to those for ABSAIR.

SOLABS produces no pollution. As it requires a minimum of moving parts, SOLABS is very quiet and vibration free.

The solar a/c concept is not new. Several well-known manufacturers produce components and one such system was in operation at the University of Florida as early as 1960. Currently, there is a new school in Atlanta, Georgia that is air-conditioned by SOLABS and there are several projects to install similar a/c systems in different parts of the U.S.

tions and preferences is that these measurements are obtained from actual decision participants. To minimize this potentially important source of bias, the authors suggest a two-stage sampling procedure. First, a member of top management in each company in the sample is identified, using published sources of information. He is asked to specify those members of his organization that, in his judgment, would be most likely to participate in the purchase of a product in the class. Only individuals identified at this second stage are interviewed or mailed a copy of the survey instrument.

Figure 9. Sample Evaluation Scheme: Solar Air Conditioning

Ratings for SOLABS (Circle one number for each item)

	Strongly Disagree						Strongly Agree
1. The system provides reliable air conditioning.	1	2	3	4	5	6	7
2. Adoption of the system protects against power failures.	1	2	3	4	5	6	7
3. The effective life of the system is sensitive to climate conditions.	1	2	3	4	5	6	7
4. The system is made up of field-proven components.	1	2	3	4	5	6	7
5. The system conveys the image of a modern, innovative company.	1	2	3	4	5	6	7
6. The system cost is acceptably low.	1	2	3	4	5	6	7
7. The system protects against fuel rationing.	1	2	3	4	5	6	7
8. The system allows us to do our part in reducing pollution.	1	2	3	4	5	6	7
9. System components produced by several manufacturers can be substituted for one another.	1	2	3	4	5	6	7
10. The system is vulnerable to weather damage.	1	2	3	4	5	6	7
11. The system uses too many concepts that have not been fully tested.	1	2	3	4	5	6	7
12. The system leads to considerable energy savings.	1	2	3	4	5	6	7
13. The system makes use of currently unproductive areas of industrial buildings.	1	2	3	4	5	6	7
14. The system is too complex.	1	2	3	4	5	6	7
15. The system provides low cost a/c.	1	2	3	4	5	6	7
16. The system offers a state of the art solution to a/c needs.	1	2	3	4	5	6	7
17. The system increases the noise level in the plant.	1	2	3	4	5	6	7

4.4. Measurement at the Managerial Level

The measurements described above are used to calibrate the three first components of the industrial market response model. Development of group choice models, however, requires assumptions about the type of interaction that takes place between decision participant categories.

As suggested earlier, the measurement methodology relies on the marketing manager's experience with the product class. The final input to the industrial

Figure 10. Sample Preference Measurement Scheme: Solar Cooling Study

You have just rated three alternative industrial air conditioning systems. Now we would like to know your overall preferences for these systems, listed below. *Assume that all three systems satisfy the requirements you stated in question 2.1.* Write a "1" next to the one which would be your first choice, a "2" next to your second choice and a "3" next to your third choice.

Conventional Absorption a/c system	ABSAIR	_____
Conventional Compression a/c system	COMAIR	_____
Solar Absorption a/c system	SOLABS	_____

Assume your company has reduced the choice of system alternatives to two, *both meeting the requirements you stated in question 2.1.* For each of the pairs listed below, allocate 11 points between the alternatives in a way which reflects your relative preference for the two systems.

a. COMAIR vs. SOLABS

Conventional Compression a/c system	COMAIR	_____
Solar Absorption a/c system	SOLABS	_____
Total	=	11

b. ABSAIR vs. COMAIR

Conventional Absorption a/c system	ABSAIR	_____
Conventional Compression a/c system	COMAIR	_____
Total	=	11

c. SOLABS vs. ABSAIR

Solar Absorption a/c system	SOLABS	_____
Conventional Absorption a/c system	ABSAIR	_____
Total	=	11

response model consists of the manager's specification of those models of interaction which best reproduce his understanding of the purchasing decision process for the companies which fall in each microsegment.

In terms of the models proposed earlier, the manager's estimates for microsegment S_q might be:

Model	Fraction of Segment S_q Using this Model
Weighted Probability Model	α_{1q}
Voting Model	α_{2q}
Unanimity Model	α_{3q}
Acceptability Model	α_{4q}

with $\sum_e \alpha_{eq} = 1$ for each microsegment q. If the manager considers that the companies within a particular microsegment exhibit homogeneity in the nature of their conflict-resolution process, only one $\alpha_{eq} = 1$, and the others $= 0$.

Note that we segment organizations according to *who* is involved; the group decision models determine *how* they interact. It is usually most convenient, in practice, to assume one interaction model per microsegment, however.

5. ASSESSING RESPONSE TO INDUSTRIAL MARKETING STRATEGY: INTEGRATING MEASUREMENTS AND MODELS

The information provided by the measurement methodology and fed into the various models components leads to an estimate of market response. $M_q(a_0)$ denotes the estimated share of microsegment S_q that finally purchase product a_0. Hence

$$M_q(a_0) = \sum_e \alpha_{eq} P_r[a_0; A/MOD_e, DEC_q]$$

where $P_r[a_0; A/MOD_e, DEC_q]$ denotes the probability that a_0 is the organizational choice, given the involvement of decision categories DEC_q and an interaction model MOD_e.

Given a maximum potential sales of Q for product a_0, we can estimate expected sales of a_0 by computing

$$Sales (a_0) = Q\left[\sum_{q=1}^{S} V_q M_q(a_0)\right]$$

The model based methodology presented here provides a sensible framework to assess response to industrial marketing strategy for new industrial products. The model is quite general and its components can easily be adapted to account for the different problems of specific new industrial products. In particular, the model clearly encompasses single-person decision-making as a special case. In fact, any part of the submodel can be deleted if it is irrelevant, resulting in model simplifications as well as in fewer measurements. So, the group decision model would be ignored in case of single-person decision-making, as would the microsegmentation methodology. The acceptance model and associated measurements, on the other hand, become irrelevant for industrial products that lead mainly to straight-rebuy situations, and can therefore be omitted from the model.

6. APPLYING THE METHODOLOGY: SOLAR AIR CONDITIONING CASE STUDY

This section reviews a case example using the methodology developed here. It incorporates the measurement procedures outlined in Section 4 and the analysis presented here parallels the theoretical developments discussed in Section 3.

6.1. Background

Currently, over 25 percent of the energy used in the United States is consumed by heating and cooling of buildings and by providing hot water (Westinghouse

Phase 0 report, 1974). At a conversion efficiency of 10 percent, 11,000 square miles of solar collectors (or 0.3 percent of United States land area) could have satisfied the 1970 water and space heating and cooling needs of the United States (Williams, 1974).

Space cooling is the fastest growing area of United States energy use, projected to account for over 5 percent of United States energy demand by 1980 (Westinghouse Phase 0 report, 1974). A substantial portion of this demand is for use in industrial buildings. Thus, a considerable amount of fossil fuel could be saved by wide-scale adoption of solar-powered cooling systems.

Recognizing the potential for this saving, the United States Energy Research and Development Administration, together with the United States Economic Development Administration, is sponsoring a multi-year study to (1) demonstrate the technical feasibility of solar-powered cooling in a commercial–industrial setting, and (2) to evaluate the potential market for such a system. (Lilien et al., 1977, gives complete details.)

There are two major classes of cooling systems in wide use today— compression systems and absorption systems, comprising about 90–95 percent and 5–10 percent of the market respectively.

Compression cooling, the most familiar system used in cars, room air conditioners, most refrigerators, etc., uses a single refrigerant in conjunction with an evaporator, a compressor, and a condensor. In the evaporator, the refrigerant, under pressure, passes through an expansion valve and vaporizes. As it evaporates, the refrigerant absorbs heat from the vehicle (water or air) that it is cooling. The refrigerant vapor is then compressed and sent to the condensor where it rejects heat to the environment. Finally, the refrigerant returns to the evaporator to start the cycle again. The initial cost of compression cooling systems is the lowest available and it is also the most efficient convertor of thermal or electric energy into cooling.

An absorption chiller uses a refrigerant (e.g., water) and an absorbent (e.g., lithium bromide) in conjunction with an evaporator, absorber, generator, and condenser. In the evaporator, the refrigerant, in a vacuum, is vaporized by a sprayer. As it evaporates, the refrigerant absorbs heat from the water that is used to cool the building. The refrigerant vapor is then absorbed by the solution in the absorber. The resulting solution is heated in the generator to drive off the refrigerant. At the condensor, the refrigerant vapor condenses and rejects heat to the environment. The refrigerant then returns to the evaporator to start the cycle again.

Initial costs for absorption systems tend to be significantly higher than for compression systems. They are particularly inefficient at sizes under 100 tons, making single family residential applications (around 5 tons) inappropriate. These systems are generally used by firms (such as pharmaceutical companies) that use steam for other industrial processes and who wish to make additional use of that steam.

The solar cooling system investigated in this study uses an absorption cycle in which the necessary heat to drive off the refrigerant is captured by solar collectors.

6.2. The Industrial Cooling Adoption Process: Background and Measurement

An objective of the market analysis was to obtain an understanding of the technical, economic, and organizational issues associated with the adoption of industrial cooling systems in general and solar cooling in particular. Specifically, we wish to determine (1) what kinds of decision variables are important in the adoption process for solar cooling, and (2) who takes part in, or influences, that decision process.

To this end, a series of in-depth personal and group interviews were conducted with personnel from industry and heating, ventilating, and air conditioning (HVAC) consulting firms. As these interviews progressed, a questionnaire was gradually developed, refined, and pilot-tested. Two versions of the questionnaire were finally developed—one for internal, company people and a second for outside consultants. Both these questionnaires requested data of the sort indicated in Section 4.

The questionnaire was administered as follows: a sample of firms was selected by size, S.I.C. code, and geographic area, and a senior management member was identified. He was sent a personal letter asking for names of two or three members of his organization most likely to be involved in the adoption decision process for industrial cooling equipment. A detailed questionnaire was then sent to the individuals mentioned. This two-step sampling procedure increased the likelihood of reaching key people in the adoption decision for this class of product. The return rates were 27 percent and 46 percent respectively.

6.3. Feasibility Analysis

Figure 11 gives some descriptive statistics about company requirements for industrial air conditioning systems. Figure 12 gives the regression results using the logit model described in Section 3.2 to assess system feasibility.

These results point to the overall importance of a system's cost in the determination of acceptance, evidenced by the high value of the corresponding standardized regression coefficient.

In order to assess market potential, probability estimates of likely characteristics of the new solar air conditioning system along each specification dimension were obtained from experts. These levels and their associated likelihood of occurrence are shown in Figure 13. Using these values as input, market acceptability was calculated as 2.00 percent, as noted in Figure 14.

By linking system characteristics to market acceptance, the feasibility analysis

Figure 11. Range of Company Requirements

	Minimum	Mean	Median	Maximum
1) Expected life of the system should be greater than:	5 years	11.6 years	10 years	20 years
2) Initial investment cost of the system per ton of air conditioning should be less than:	$100	$983	$1000	$3000
3) Warranty period should be greater than:	1 month	15.4 months	12 months	60 months
4) The number of successful installations in the field should be at least:	0	17.6	5	100
5) The annual operating cost as a percent of initial cost should be less than:	5%	14.0%	10%	50%

Figure 12. Results of the Logit Regression Analysis: Solar Cooling Study

Variable	Estimated Coefficient	Standardized Coefficient
Expected system's life	.071	.236*
Initial Investment Costs	− .001	−.676*
Warranty Period	.011	.119*
Number of successful Installations	.001	.022
Annual Operating Cost	− .084	−.733*
CONSTANT	−2.857	
$F(5,137) = 58.42$		
$R^2 = .69$		

*Significant at the level $< .01$.

Figure 13. Expert Estimates of Solar Absorption System Characteristics

	Low	Most Likely	High
Likelihood	1/6	2/3	1/6
Expected life (years)	10	15	20
Initial Investment (per ton)	1500	2000	2500
Warranty Period (months)	12	24	60
Number of Successes	5	25	100

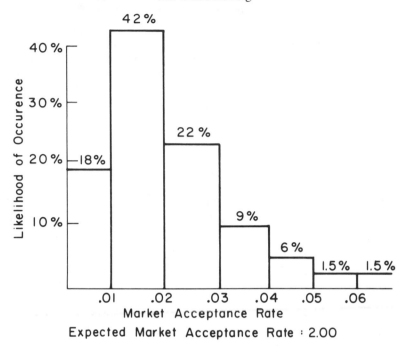

Figure 14. Simulated Distribution of Market Acceptance for Solar Absorption
Air Conditioning

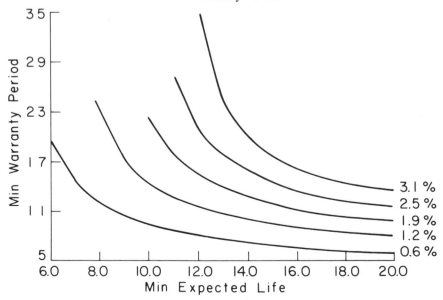

Figure 15. Solar Absorption Iso-Acceptance Trade-off Curves—Expected Life
vs. Warranty Period

provides a tool to investigate design trade-offs. As an example, holding all other dimensions at their median value, Figure 15 displays trade-offs between warranty period and expected life. From these curves, we see that potential customers become increasingly concerned about warranty issues the shorter the expected life of the system. Moreover, these curves suggest the existence of a saturation level for the warranty period. After the warranty exceeds 23 months, it becomes hard to further increase system acceptance by increasing the warranty period.

6.4. Perceptual Analysis

Analysis of the responses by the different groups of decision participants to the different concepts, using the methods developed in Section 3.3, indicated that each group of decision participants perceived the three alternatives differently. Perceptual differences for each concept were also found between each group. For example, analysis of the perceptual differences via one-way univariate analysis of variance suggests that plant managers view solar cooling as a more substantial means of protection against power failures than do HVAC consultants. They also consider it more cost effective than HVAC consultants. Finally, plant managers view the solar system as a complex system whose components have not been fully tested, but that provides a state-of-the-art solution to industrial cooling needs. HVAC consultants' perception of the solar systems differ considerably in this last respect.

6.5. Evaluation Space Analysis

Careful analysis of the evaluation spaces of each category of decision participants showed significant structural differences. Corporate Engineers and Plant Managers had 2 dimensional evaluation spaces, interpreted in Figure 16.

The issue of industrial cooling systems' initial costs does not appear as clearly for Plant Managers. Modernness, energy savings, and protection against fuel rationing and power failure, on the other hand, account for a substantial portion

Figure 16. Comparison of Factor Solutions for CE, PM

	Factor A	Factor B
Corporate Engineer (CE)	Field Tested First Cost Reliability Noise Level	Reduced Pollution Energy Savings/Protection Modernness
Plant Manager (PM)	Energy Savings/Protection Low Operation Cost Reduced Pollution Modernness	Reliability/Field Tested Modularity Noise Level

Figure 17. Comparison of Factor Structures for PE, TM, and HC

	Factor A	Factor B	Factor C
Production Engineer (PE)	Energy Savings/ Protection Low Operating Cost Modernness Reduced Pollution	Modularity Noise Level	Complexity Field Tested/ Reliability
Top Manager (TM)	Energy Savings/ Protection Low Operating Cost Modernness Protection against power failure Reduced Pollution	Reliability/ Field Tested Initial Cost Complexity	Noise Level
HVAC Consultant (HC)	Modernness Reduced Pollution Energy Savings/ Protection	Field Tested/ Reliability	Noise Level Initial Cost

of the variance in Plant Managers' perceptions. Corporate Engineers see the system's reliability and first costs as primary issues.

Similarly, Figure 17 presents an interpretation of the factor solutions for the other three groups, TM, PE, and HC. The composition of the first factor indicates minor differences between these groups in terms of their first evaluation criteria (TM include protection against power failures, and HC do not place the same emphasis on low operating cost). Major differences, however, arise in the second and third factors. Production Engineers (PE), emphasize system complexity and modularity more than other groups. First cost comes out clearly as an essential element in top managers' (TM) evaluation of industrial cooling equipment.

6.5. Preference Analysis

The relevance of these differences for marketing strategy formulation can be formally assessed by linking individuals' preferences for the three alternative industrial cooling systems to their evaluation of these alternatives. For this purpose, a linear regression model was fitted with rank order preference used as the response variable and individual product evaluations (estimated individual factor scores) used as independent variables. (Hauser and Urban, 1977, suggest that least squares regression closely approximates monotonic regression for integer rank-ordered preference variables.)

The results of this analysis are summarized in Figure 18. Separate evaluation spaces were used for each group of participants. Note the following: first, rank order preference (1st, 2nd, 3rd, etc.) was the dependent variable. Thus, "the lower the better" in terms of product evaluation (i.e., a negative regression coefficient is good.) Second, the factors are *not* named because they mean different things to different groups. See Figures 16 and 17 for interpretation. Finally, since a principle axes solution was used, with a varimax rotation, the factors are orthogonal and, thus, more readily interpretable.

The results suggest important differences in the way product evaluations are related to individual preferences within each group. First, consider Corporate Engineers and Plant Managers. Corporate Engineers find reliability and first cost important, while Plant Managers find modernness, fuel savings, and low operating costs to be most significant.

The comparison of the other three groups is most interesting. Production Engineers find modernness, low operating cost, and protection against fuel rationing most important. But they seem to favor less field proven, less noisy, and less easily substitutable equipment. Production Engineers are perhaps the only individuals in the decision process who will work with this equipment directly, and seem to favor that equipment which makes their job more challenging. Top Managers also find modernness, protection and low operating cost most important, but weight reliability and initial cost heavily as well, in the expected direction. Finally, HVAC consultants do not seem concerned about modern image, low operating cost, and fuel rationing protection. Their concerns are immediate—they weigh initial cost and noise level most heavily and, secondarily, reliability and the presence of field proven components.

Hence, each of these groups not only evaluates the various alternatives differently, but links product evaluations and individual preferences differently as well. It is important to note that preference regressions were also run assuming a common evaluation space and heterogeneous preference parameters, and suggested neither the positive association with less substitutable, less proven equipment noted above for Production Engineers (PE), nor the absence of association with modernness, low operating cost, and fuel rationing protection for

Figure 18. Preference Regression Estimates

Group	Constant	Factor A Regression Coefficients	Factor B Regression Coefficients	Factor C Regression Coefficients	No. of Observations
CE	2.02	−.46	−.10	×	115
PM	2.00	−.25	−.19	×	84
PE	1.99	−.39	.27	(.09)*	66
TM	1.99	−.37	−.18	−.13	123
HC	1.99	(−.02)*	−.31	−.45	273

*not significantly different from 0 at the .10 level

HVAC consultants (HC). The derivation of the evaluation space for each category of decision participant is, then, an important step in the development of accurate and behaviorally relevant models of industrial product evaluation.

6.6. Microsegmentation

Analysis of the decision matrices from the responding companies led to the identification of four microsegments. Figure 19 gives the sizes of these microsegments as well as the key decision participants in the equipment selection phase of the decision process. Figure 20 gives a qualitative interpretation of the results of the analysis of variance run on company characteristic. Companies in Segment 4 are smaller, more satisfied with their current cooling system, and more concerned with the economical aspects of cooling. They are characterized

Figure 19. Major Microsegments of Organizations in Potential Market for Solar A/C

	Segment 1	Segment 2	Segment 3	Segment 4
Microsegment size in Potential Market	12%	31%	32%	25%
Major Decision Participants in A/C Equipment Selection Decision	Plant Managers (1.00)	Production Engineers (.94)	Production Engineers (.97)	Top Management (.85)
(Frequencies of Involvement)	HVAC Consultants (.38)	Plant Managers (.70)	HVAC Consultants (.60)	HVAC Consultants (.67)

Figure 20. Relative Characteristics of Organizations in Each Segment

	Segment 1	Segment 2	Segment 3	Segment 4
Satisfaction with current a/c system	medium high	low	medium low	high
Consequence if new a/c less economical than projected	medium high	low	medium low	high
Consequence if new a/c less reliable than projected	medium high	low	high	medium low
Company size	medium	large	large	small
Percentage of plant area requiring a/c	medium large	small	large	medium
Number of separate plants	medium large	small	large	medium small

by a more frequent involvement of managerial function, and they rely on external sources of expertise (HVAC consultants) to assist them.

Segments 1 and 3 do not differ much by size of firm, but segment 3 companies have more plants, larger cooling needs, and are more concerned with reliability of cooling than segment 1. Thus companies in Segment 3 rely on engineering functions for air conditioning assessment while Segment 1 relies on management functions.

Segment 2 groups large companies with a small number of plants. Such companies tend to have decisions made at the plant level, as indicated by the high frequency of involvement of Plant Managers and Plant Engineers.

6.7. Market Potential Assessment

Discussions with decision-makers in the industry suggested that the use of a weighted probability model to evaluate the interaction process between participant categories would be generally "acceptable." Thus, to get conditional probability of choice given feasibility, we use the equation:

$$P_G(a) = \sum_i w_i\, P_i(a)$$

where i = decision participant category and $P_i(a)$ = first preference for solar.

Figure 21 gives the conditional probability of group choice for each segment.

Figure 21. Microsegment Response

Segment	Size	Conditional Probability of Group Choice Given Feasibility $(P_1w_1 + P_2w_2)$
1	.12	.44 × .72 + .15 × .28 = .359
2	.31	.50 × .57 + .44 × .43 = .474
3	.32	.50 × .62 + .15 × .38 = .367
4	.25	.45 × .56 + .15 × .44 = .318

Our model suggests putting these pieces together as

Penetration = Choice level, given feasibility
           × feasibility, given awareness
           × awareness

For awareness, it was found that 15 percent of company people and 41 percent of HVAC consultants were aware of solar a/c.

Thus, the probability that the group will be aware is 1 − probability that no one is aware or $1 - \Pi (1 - P(\text{aware}))$. Thus we get awareness by segment as

$$
\begin{array}{lll}
\text{Segment 1:} & 1 - .85 \times .59 & = .50 \\
\text{Segment 2:} & 1 - (.85)^2 & = .28 \\
\text{Segment 3:} & 1 - .85 \times .59 & = .50 \\
\text{Segment 4:} & 1 - .85 \times .59 & = .50
\end{array}
$$

considering only the major decision-participants from Figure 19.

To develop total market response, we take feasibility $= .02$ and calculate likely response as .32 percent as in Figure 22. A similar calculation assuming 100 percent awareness (perhaps on the basis of a heavy media campaign) would yield an expected share of 0.77 percent.

Figure 22. Calculation of Expected Response

Segment	Size	×	Awareness	×	Feasibility	×	Group Choice	=	Response
1	.12	×	.50	×	.02	×	.359	=	.00043
2	.31	×	.28	×	.02	×	.474	=	.00082
3	.32	×	.50	×	.02	×	.367	=	.00117
4	.25	×	.50	×	.02	×	.318	=	.00080
							Response	=	.0032

Applying these numbers against projected total a/c sales gave an estimate of total solar a/c potential: $15 million in 1980 and $17.9 million in 1985.

7. USE OF THE METHODOLOGY

The methodology has important implications for the design of industrial products as well as for the development of associated communications programs.

7.1. Improving Product Design

An important problem in the development of a new industrial product is the determination of those specific features that the product should incorporate. The product acceptance portion of the methodology provides actionable information for making such decisions.

First, the analysis forces management to identify and evaluate organizational need specification dimensions. Second, the acceptance model assesses design trade-offs in terms of market potential.

The acceptance model forces industrial marketing managers to explicitly analyze product design and pricing decisions. Moreover, given data about R&D, production and distribution costs, a complementary model can optimize industrial product features within the firm's constraints.

Figure 23. Sensitivity of Market Feasibility to Changes in Design Characteristics

Base Case	Expected Life	Investment	Warranty Period	# Successes	Operating Cost	Expected Feasibility
	15	2000	24	25	7	2.00%
1	20	nc	nc	nc	nc	2.90%
2	10	nc	nc	nc	nc	1.40%
3	15	2500	nc	nc	nc	1.25%
4	15	3000	nc	nc	nc	0.76%
5	15	1500	nc	nc	nc	3.3%
6	15	2000	36	nc	nc	2.3%
7	15	2000	12	nc	nc	1.8%
8	15	2000	24	5	nc	1.9%
9	15	2000	24	100	nc	2.2%
10	15	2000	24	25	10	1.64
11	15	2000	24	25	5	2.4%

nc indicates no changes from the Base Case.

As an example, Figure 23 shows the effect of design changes on market feasibility for solar a/c. It shows the relative sensitivity of market feasibility to design feature changes one at a time. Similar analyses can be run for joint effects.

7.2. Developing and Testing Communication Programs

Industrial communication programs, including advertising and sales presentations, affect response through the awareness model and the individual evaluation models.

The analysis of individual preferences for each category of decision participant allows analysis of product positioning. For example, our analysis showed that Plant Managers were more concerned about low operating cost, additional protection offered by the system, and substitutability of its components than were Corporate Engineers. The latter category of participant on the other hand, placed considerable emphasis on the system's first cost and reliability.

Following identification of the relevant evaluation criteria for each category of participant, average product evaluations can be assessed for each product in the class investigated. Results of this analysis can be used in three different ways: to identify those attributes of the new product that are not perceived by certain categories of decision participants as management wants, so that corrective action can be taken in a product communication strategy; to develop a communication program that addresses the specific needs of each group of decision participant; and to simulate the impact of changes in communication content on the preferences of each category of individuals.

7.3. Targeting Industrial Communication Programs

The microsegmentation methodology tells what categories of decision participants are most likely to become involved in the purchase decision. By isolating microsegments of organizations, the methodology provides an accurate description of the structure of the purchasing decision process. For example, in the industrial cooling study, the four microsegments identified showed substantial differences in terms of the number of decision phases in which each category of participant is involved; the number of participant categories involved in each stage of the process; and the frequency of involvement of each category of participant in each decision phase.

This information allows development of differentiated communication strategies, targeted at those categories of individuals most influential in the various microsegments. Typically, the microsegmentation results can be used to eliminate from a communication program categories of individuals that are involved in the decision process less often than management expected; concentrate communication efforts on those categories of individuals that are involved in the purchasing process in the largest microsegments; and predict the structure of the decision process for a specific firm on the basis of its external characteristics.

In addition, as categories of decision participants differ in their level and sources of information, the microsegmentation analysis provides additional help in the selection of communication vehicles.

For example, suppose we had our choice of improving preference among only one of the four key groups of solar a/c influences. Figure 24 suggests that we get

Figure 24. Preference Sensitivity Analysis

	Change in Share with 10% Preference Improvement in Group
Plant Manager	+4.7%
HVAC Consultant	+8.1%
Production Engineer	+5.3%
Top Manager	+4.0%

the most leverage by addressing HVAC consultants, as a 10 percent preference improvement among that group leads to a relative projected share increase of 8.1 percent vs. 5.3 percent for production engineers, the next highest group.

7.4. Cost/Value of Implementation

By now, the managerial reader (if not thoroughly exhausted) is certainly convinced that the procedure is too complicated and expensive for him. The same argument was made at the introduction of pre-test-market simulators in the packaged goods area a few years ago. Use of these procedures is now a well-established, standard practice.

The procedure is complex. But organizational purchasing is complex—simple procedures bypass the very richness of that process that makes industrial marketing challenging! But the procedure is conceptually simple (see Figure 1). It is based on breaking down the purchasing process into steps that are readily model-able and measurable, constructing the appropriate measurements and consistently and accurately analyzing the results.

The time and cost considerations for implementation vary, depending primarily on the number and distribution of potential customers. Personal administration of the survey instrument will cut down non-response bias and develop data with generally more integrity. However, if a manufacturer has 50 customers, one in each state, travel costs are going to be enormous.

If we assume that customers can be found in two or three relatively concentrated areas, the total cost to perform this analysis (at this writing), would be in the $30–$60 K range. It would also take 10 to 15 weeks from conception to reporting (assuming the software was already operational).

A lot of money to study the market potential for a new industrial product? Maybe and maybe not. A company we know had no other way to study the market potential for a new industrial product than to build a prototype. It cost $800,000. It was a dud. It was also a preventable loss, given prior application of the procedure proposed here.

8. CONCLUSIONS

The methodology described here provides some powerful new procedures to support the marketing of new industrial products. It explicitly addresses issues of product feasibility, individual preference formation, and organizational decision-making. It provides a new framework to operationalize the concept of the buying center.

A set of measurements provide input to each model component. The methodology provides tools to measure involvement in the purchasing decision process and uses this information to abstract microsegments of organizations homogeneous in decision-making structure.

To date, the procedure has been used to: develop a market introduction plan for an industrial air conditioning system powered by solar energy; design an "intelligent" computer terminal and develop a supporting communication program; and evaluate the market for or support the introduction of thermic diode solar panels, photovoltaic systems, and copier systems.

Some of the submodels are still being improved, as are some of the measurement tools. We are currently working on extensions and generalizations of the feasibility models that will combine the benefits of the probability and logit models. We are also incorporating a time dimension with a manufacturing experience curve component, to allow evaluation of product potential sales over time.

The general structure, however, is currently operational and can produce much-needed information for better industrial marketing decisions for new products. As such, the model and associated measurements should be viewed as a first, but important, step in the development of better tools for industrial marketing.

REFERENCES

Allaire, Yvan, "The Measurement of Heterogeneous Semantic, Perceptual and Preference Structure." Unpublished Ph.D. Thesis, Massachusetts Institute of Technology, 1973.

Booz, Allen and Hamilton, *Management of New Products.* 1965.

Brand, Gordon T., *The Industrial Buying Decision.* New York: Wiley, 1972.

Briscoe, Geoffrey, "Some Observations on New Industrial Product Failures." *Industrial Marketing Management* 2 (February 1973): 151–162.

Buckner, Hugh, *How British Industry Buys.* London: Hutchinson and Co., 1967.

Cardozo, Richard N., and Cagley, James W. "An Experimental Study of Industrial Buyer Behavior." *Journal of Marketing Research* 8 (August 1971): 329–334.

Choffray, Jean-Marie, "A Methodology for Investigating the Structure of the Industrial Adoption Process and the Differences in Perceptions and Evaluation Criteria among Potential Decision Participants." Unpublished Ph.D. thesis, Massachusetts Institute of Technology, Sloan Scool of Management, April 1977.

Choffray, Jean-Marie, and Lilien, Gary L., "Models of the Multiperson Choice Process with Application to the Adoption of Industrial Products." M.I.T., Sloan School Working Paper No. 861–76, June 1976.

Choffray, Jean-Marie, and Lilien, Gary L., "Industrial Adoption of Solar Air Conditioning: Measurement Problems, Solutions and Marketing Implications." M.I.T., Sloan School Working Paper No. 894–76, December 1976.

Choffray, Jean-Marie, and Lilien, Gary L., "An Operational Model of Market Response to New Industrial Products." *Journal of Marketing,* Vol. 42, No. 2 (April, 1978).

Choffray, Jean-Marie, and Lilien, Gary L. "Organizational Acceptance of Product Alternatives: Models, Measurements and Applications." M.I.T., Sloan School Working Paper (forthcoming).

Cooper, Robert G., "Why New Industrial Products Fail." *Industrial Marketing Management* 4 (December 1975): 315–326.

Cyert, Richard M., et al., "Observation of a Business Decision." *Journal of Business* 29 (October 1956): 237–248.

Davis, James H., "Group Decision and Social Interaction: A Theory of Social Decision Schemes." *Psychological Review,* Vol. 80, No. 2 (March 1973): 97–125.

Davis, J. H., Cohen, J. L., Hornik, J., and Rissman, K., "Dyadic Decision as a Function of the Frequency Distributions Describing the Preferences of Members Constituencies." *Journal of Personality and Social Psychology,* Vol. 26, No. 2 (1973): 178–195.

de Simone, Daniel V., *Technological Innovation: Its Environment and Management.* Washington, D.C.: U.S. Department of Commerce, 1967.

Hakansson, Hakan, and Wootz, Bjorn, "Supplier Selection in an Industrial Environment—An Experimental Study." *Journal of Market Research* 12 (February 1975): 46–51.

Harding, Murray, "Who Really Makes the Purchasing Decision." *Industrial Marketing* 51 (September 1966): 76–81.

Hauser, John R., and Urban, Glen L., "A Normative Methodology for Modeling Consumer Response to Innovation." *Operations Research*, Vol. 25, No. 4 (July–August 1977): 579–619.

Howard, John A., and Sheth, J. N. *The Theory of Buyer Behavior*. New York: Wiley, 1969.

Humphreys, L. G., and Ilgen, D. R., "Note on a Criterion for the Number of Common Factors." *Educational and Psychological Measurement* 29 (1969): 571–578.

Johnson, Roger M., "Measuring Advertising Effectiveness," in Robert Ferber (ed.), *Handbook of Marketing Research*, pp. 4:151–164. New York: McGraw-Hill, 1974.

Kelly, Patrick J., "Functions Performed in Industrial Purchasing Decisions with Implications for Marketing Strategy." *Journal of Business Research* 2 (October 1974): 421–434.

Lehmann, Donald R., and O'Shaughnessy, John, "Differences in Attribute Importance for Different Industrial Products." *Journal of Marketing* 38 (April 1974): 36–42.

Levitt, Theodore, "Marketing Myopia." *Harvard Business Review* 38 (July–August 1960): 45–56.

Lilien, Gary L., et al., "A Socio-Economic and Marketing Study for a Standard Fomento Factory in Puerto Rico." OR/MS Dialogue Inc. Report, September 1977.

Lilien, Gary L., and Rao, Ambar G., "A Model Linking Sales Response to Advertising with Immediate, Behavioral Variables." Presented at ORSA/TIMS meeting, May 1977, San Francisco, California.

Little, John D. C., "Models and Managers: The Concept of a Decision Calculus." *Management Science*, Vol. 16, No. 8 (April 1970): 466–485.

McGuire, Patrick E., and Bailey, Earl L., *Sources of Corporate Growth*. New York: The Conference Board, No. 24. 1970.

Mansfield, Edwin, and Rapoport, John, "Costs of Industrial Product Innovations," *Management Science*, 21 (August 1975): 1380–1386.

Mansfield, Edwin, and Wagner, Samuel, "Organizational and Strategic Factors Associated with Probabilities of Success in Industrial R&D." *The Journal of Business* 48 (April 1975): 179–198.

Morrill, John E., "Industrial Advertising Pays Off." *Harvard Business Review* 48 (March–April 1970): 4–14.

Robinson, Patrick J., and Faris, Charles W., *Industrial Buying and Creative Marketing*. Allyn and Bacon, Inc., 1967.

Rothwell, R., et al., "SAPPHO updated—Project SAPPHO Phase II." *Research Policy* 3 (1974): 258–291.

Ryser, Herbert J., *Combinatorial Mathematics*. The Mathematical Association of America, Inc., 1963.

Scientific American, *How Industry Buys/1970*. New York: 1969.

Scott, Jerome E., and Bennett, Peter D., "Cognitive Models of Attitude Structure: 'Value Importance' is Important," in Fred C. Allvine (ed.), *Relevance in Marketing: Problems, Research, Action*, 33. Chicago: American Marketing Association, 1971.

Scott, Jerome E., and Wright, Peter, "Modeling an Organizational Buyer's Product Evaluation Strategy: Validity and Procedural Considerations." *Journal of Marketing Research* 13 (August 1976): 211–224.

Sheth, Jagdish N., "A Model of Industrial Buyer Behavior." *Journal of Marketing* 37 (October 1973): 50–56.

Silk, Alvin J., and Urban, Glen L., "Pre-Test Market Evaluation of New Packaged Goods: A Model and Measurement Methodology." *Journal of Marketing Research* 15 (May 1978): 171–191.

Sweeney, Timothy W., et al., "An Analysis of Industrial Buyers' Risk Reducing Behavior: Some

Personality Correlates,'' in Thomas V. Greer (ed.), *Increasing Marketing Productivity,* 35. Chicago: American Marketing Association, 1973.

Torgerson, Warren N., *Theory and Methods of Scaling.* New York: Wiley, 1958.

Tversky, Amos, "Elimination By Aspects: A Theory of Choice." *Psychological Review,* Vol. 79, No. 4 (July 1972): 281–299.

Urban, Glen L., "Perceptor: A Model for Product Positioning." *Management Science.* 21 (April 1975): 858–871.

von Hippel, Eric A., "Has a Customer Already Developed Your Next Product?" *Sloan Management Review* 18 (Winter 1977): 63–74.

Webster, Frederick E., Jr., and Wind, Yoram, *Organizational Buying Behavior.* New York: Prentice Hall, 1972.

Webster, Frederick E., Jr., "Management Science in Industrial Marketing." *Journal of Marketing,* Vol. 42, No. 1 (January 1978).

Wells, William D., "Group Interviewing," in Robert Ferber (ed.), *Handbook of Marketing Research,* pp. 2: 133–146. New York: McGraw-Hill, 1974.

Westinghouse Electric Corporation, *Solar Heating and Cooling of Buildings: Phase 0.* May 1974.

Wildt, Albert R., and Bruno, Albert V., "The Prediction of Preference for Capital Equipment Using Linear Attitude Models," *Journal of Marketing Research* 11 (May 1974): 203–205.

Williams, Richard J., *Solar Energy: Technology and Applications.* Ann Arbor: Ann Arbor Science Publishers, 1974.

Wilson, David T., "Industrial Buyers' Decision-Making Styles." *Journal of Marketing Research* 8 (November 1971): 433–436.

Wind, Yoram, "Organizational Buying Center: A Research Agenda." The Wharton School, University of Pennsylvania.

Wind, Yoram, and Cardozo, Richard, "Industrial Market Segmentation." *Industrial Marketing Management.* 3 (1974): 153–166.

A TYPOLOGY OF CONSUMER NEEDS*

Janice G. Hanna, GEORGIA STATE UNIVERSITY

ABSTRACT

In this paper the author has attempted to expand our knowledge of fundamental-level consumer needs by identifying and classifying those basic human needs which may be satisfied through consumption activities. The approach was to examine human need classifications developed to explain human behavior in other behavioral science disciplines; the outcome of this analysis was a proposed consumer needs typology.

I. INTRODUCTION

Consumer needs, or motives,[1] is a central construct in each of the comprehensive theories of consumer behavior (Andreason, 1965; Engel, Kollat, and Blackwell, 1968; Howard and Sheth, 1969; Nicosia, 1966). Given the centrality of consumer needs to the understanding of consumer behavior, it is surprising that there

Research in Marketing, Volume 3, pages 83–104
ISBN: 0-89232-060-5

is no discernible systematic body of knowledge on the nature of consumers' basic needs or motives. The history of the study of consumer motivation serves to illustrate this conclusion.

In the 1950s, the study of consumer motivation focused primarily on methodology, that is, the use of the projective technique to elicit underlying personality characteristics which would explain individual differences in product choice (Dichter, 1960; Haire, 1950). In the 1960s, the emphasis shifted to a study of the nature of the personality traits themselves. Consumers were classified as high or low on personality scales of achievement, affiliation, dominance, exhibition, or the like, for the purposes of explaining individual differences in brand choice or product use (Cohen, 1967; Evans, 1959; Koponen, 1960; Sparks and Tucker, 1971; Tucker and Painter, 1961; Westfall, 1962). Finally, the study of consumer motivation in the 1970s has focused on secondary-level needs, equivalent to relevant product attributes, for determining brand choice. For example, the relevant product attributes for choosing a brand of toothpaste may be breath-freshening, decay-preventive, and good-tasting. The study of the role of relevant product attributes in the formation of attitudes towards brands has very nearly dominated the marketing and consumer behavior literature for the entire decade of the 1970s (Cohen, Fishbein, and Ahtola, 1972; Hansen, 1976; Jacoby, 1976; Lutz, 1975; Sheth, 1974; Sheth and Talarzyk, 1972; Wilkie and Pessemier, 1973). In summary, the study of consumer motivation has at one time or another focused on the projective methodology, personality traits, or relevant product attributes. The systematic study of the basic needs themselves is absent from the literature.

What are the basic human needs which the consumer attempts to satisfy through his/her purchase, use, and disposition of products and brands? It is the purpose of this paper to (1) review human need classifications from the behavioral science disciplines, (2) propose a typology of *consumers' basic needs,* and (3) consider the typology's theoretical and research implications for the study of consumer behavior.

II. REVIEW OF CONSUMER NEED CLASSIFICATIONS

It is generally agreed in the psychological and consumer behavior literatures on motivation that motives function to arouse and to direct one's behavior (Cofer and Appley, 1964; Howard and Sheth, 1969). Here, a consumer need, or motive, will be defined as a state of the individual which arouses and directs his/her consuming activities toward attaining a specific goal. The nature of the goal infers the nature of the need. For example, if a consumer's goal is to attain acceptance by others through the purchase and use of products and brands, then he/she must have had a need to be accepted by others.[2]

From the economics literature, there are at least a few sources which would imply a classificatory scheme of consumers' basic needs. Katona's (1971) description of the affluent consumer suggested three consumer needs. He stated that the affluent consumer takes for granted the "necessities" of life, and after satisfying his/her "fun and comfort" needs, will aspire to fulfill "cultural, artistic, and spiritual" needs. On the other hand, the descriptions of the affluent consumer offered by Galbraith (1958) and Rostow (1961) suggested only two consumer needs, that is, for the "basics of food, shelter and clothing" and a "vast wealth of material possessions." According to Galbraith, the consumer will continue to endlessly accumulate a greater and greater wealth of material possessions, whereas Rostow sees the consumer finally becoming satiated with material goods, hopelessly bored, and spiritually stagnant.

In the marketing and consumer behavior literature, too, there are only a few studies which focus on the content of the various kinds of consumers' fundamental needs. They are reviewed here.

Fennel (1975) recognized the need for a generalized typology of motives specific to the consumer, and proposed that consumer motivation be described in terms of the consumer's perception of the product-use situation. She outlined five motivating product-use situations which should differentially influence brand choice. They were the aversive, anticipated aversive, normal depletion, product-related aversive and the positive product-use situations. According to Fennel, the aversive product-use situation will motivate consumers to buy that brand which will deal with, in order to escape from, the aversive situation. Examples of aversive product-use situations may be an extra dirty laundry or a severe headache. Second, the anticipated aversive product-use situation will motivate the consumer to buy that brand which will prevent an undesirable situation. Examples may be fear of censure if laundry is not up to socially acceptable standards, or concern over social inadequacy if the headache is not overcome. Third, Fennel proposed that the normal depletion product-use situation will motivate buying of a product to maintain a normal supply of the product. A constant normal supply of the product will allow, for example, the consumer to do the laundry when the clothes are soiled, or to take a headache remedy when one has a headache. Fourth, the product-related aversive product-use situation motivates the consumer to resolve the conflict of using a given product which may have negative outcomes originating in the product itself by seeking brands offering product-in-use assurances. Examples may be concern that a laundry detergent may damage the fabric, or that a headache remedy may have bad side effects. Fifth, according to Fennel, there is a positive product-use situation which the consumer perceives as an opportunity for fun, novelty, complexity, aesthetic or sensory pleasure, and which motivates the consumer to seek brands which promise diversion or enjoyment. Examples of positive product-use situations may be a dishwashing detergent with a fresh scent, or alphabet breakfast cereal. Fennell's classification is, however, a classification of product-use situations which act as a *stimulus* to consumer motives, rather than being the motives themselves.

Sheth has also proposed a generalized classification of needs. Although not conceptualized to be specific only to the domain of consumer behavior, Sheth has discussed its applicability to consumer choice behavior especially in choice of a mode of travel (1976) and choice of a scientific and technical information system (1977). He stated that individual choice behavior is influenced by five needs—functional, social, situational, emotional, and epistemic. And choice of an alternative depends on how closely evaluations of an alternative match with the expectations of the user in terms of the five needs. According to Sheth, an alternative satisfies the functional need through its physical or functional purpose for existence. An alternative satisfies the social need through its association with selected demographic, socio-economic, or cultural-ethnic segments of society. When a set of contingencies arise, which either facilitate or inhibit the satisfaction of functional or social needs, an alternative must satisfy the situational need. An alternative satisfies the emotional need by the affective feelings it arouses, feelings such as guilt, love, respect, anger, fear, beauty, or serenity. And an alternative satisfies the epistemic need by offering something different or new.

A. Consumer Values

Finally, a recent literature on consumer values has emerged based on Rokeach's (1973) personal value survey (Boote, 1975; Howard, 1977; Munson, 1978; Scott and Lamont, 1974; Vinson and Munson, 1976; Vinson, Munson, and Nakanishi, 1977; Vinson, Scott, and Lamont, 1977). A value, according to Rokeach (1968), is "a centrally held enduring belief which guides actions and judgements across specific situations and beyond immediate goals to more ultimate end-states of existence." The personal value survey contains eighteen terminal and eighteen instrumental values, where terminal values have to do with preferred end-states of existence, for example, family security, a comfortable life, social recognition, a sense of accomplishment, or a world of beauty; and where instrumental values relate to modes of conduct, for example, clean, polite, independent, imaginative, or intellectual. Some of these personal values, particularly the preferred end-states, would seem to describe basic human needs that could be satisfied through consumption activities.

Vinson, Scott, and Lamont (1977) described the consumer's value system as arranged along three mutually dependent levels. Most basic are the global or generalized personal values of which there are only a few dozen. These are the values to which Rokeach refers; they are the centrally held and enduring beliefs which guide actions and judgements across specific situations. The least centrally held values include the evaluative beliefs about the attributes of products and brands, of which there may be thousands. In between the most and least centrally held values, Vinson, Scott, and Lamont propose the domain-specific values, of which there may be hundreds. They assume that people acquire values through experience in specific situations or domains of activity. For example, consumption-related domain-specific values may be, according to Vinson, Scott, and Lamont, that products should be safe, non-polluting, durable, comfortable, exciting, or beautiful.

Scott and Lamont (1974) simultaneously factor-analyzed importance ratings by 204 Colorado consumers of Rokeach's 32 global values, 32 consumption domain-specific values, and 5 product attributes of the automobile. The consumption domain-specific values reduced to five factors defining the consumer value dimensions of ethics in business conduct, social-responsibility of business, ease of use and repair of products, aesthetic aspects of products, and shopping convenience.

Unfortunately, these studies seemed to have mistakenly equated relevant product attributes with the more general consumption domain-specific values. However, in one study by Boote (1975), which investigated the relationships between terminal values, instrumental values, choice criteria, beliefs, attitudes, and purchase, he appeared to have more accurately operationalized terminal values at the more general level of consumption domain-specific values, as follows:

To have plenty of food on hand at all times to meet my kind of requirements,

To enjoy a high level of physical comfort at home,

To have something to do to entertain myself when I have leisure time at home,

To have a beautiful home,

To have a feeling of accomplishment with everything I do,

To have household possessions which are different from those of other people I know, and

To make or do things which express my distinctive personality or talents.

The measurements taken were of the importance ratings by 124 women homemakers in Norwalk, Connecticut, on each of the consumption domain-specific values.

In this paper, the author attempts to expand knowledge of fundamental-level consumer needs by identifying and classifying those basic human needs which may be satisfied through consumption activities. The approach was to examine human need classifications developed to explain human behavior in other behavioral science disciplines; the outcome of this analysis is a proposed consumer needs typology.

III. INTERDISCIPLINARY REVIEW OF HUMAN NEED CLASSIFICATIONS

Every behavioral science discipline has recognized the importance of the need, or value, construct for understanding human behavior. And at one time or another in the development of a discipline, efforts at ordering and describing different types of needs relevant within the discipline's domain of human activities have been recorded.

Examples of human need classifications are, in the field of organizational behavior, Maslow's (1943, 1970) theory of human needs and Aldefer's (1969) theory of workers' needs. Spranger's (in Vernon and Allport, 1931) personal values and Murray's (1938) viscerogenic and psychogenic needs are human need classifications in personality psychology. And Rokeach's (1968, 1973) personal values and Katz's (1960) motivational bases of attitude are human need classifications in social-psychology. Finally, Riesman's (1950) social character in sociology and F. Kluckhohn's (1961) value orientations in cultural anthropology represent efforts at classifying human needs, or values, in these disciplines.

It is not the purpose here to review the application of these human need classifications to the study of consumer behavior. Rather we discuss the need classifications as they were conceptualized to explain human behavior in their respective disciplines.

A. Organizational Behavior

Of the theories of human needs, Maslow's (1943, 1954, 1970) has by far had the most notable impact on the study of workers' motivations (Schneider and Alderfer, 1973). According to Maslow, most individuals will pursue satisfaction of certain specific types of human needs: physiological, safety, belongingness, esteem, and self-actualization. Physiological needs include the need for food, water, air, and the like. Safety needs include the need for security, stability, and the absence from pain, threat, or illness. Belongingness needs involve the need for love and affection, for friends, and for one's place in a group. Esteem needs include both a need for personal feelings of achievement, or self-esteem, and also a need for recognition or respect from others. Finally, self-actualization needs involve the need for a feeling of self-fulfillment, or the realization of one's potential. Maslow also proposed that the needs are arranged in a hierarchy of pre-potency so that once a lower level need—for example, physiological—is satisfied, the individual becomes motivated by the next higher level need—for example, safety—and so on through the hierarchy.

Alderfer (1969, 1972) too, proposed a human needs theory to explain workers' behavior. His ERG theory classifies workers' needs into three broad categories: existence, relatedness, and growth. Existence needs include all of the various physiological and material desires, for example, the classic drives of hunger and thirst as well as other material needs like work-related pay, fringe benefits, and physical safety. Existence needs are characterized first by the goal of obtaining a material substance, and second, by a person's satisfaction tending to be correlated with another person's frustrations when resources are limited. Relatedness needs concern the desires people have for relationships with significant others that can be characterized by a mutual sharing of thoughts and feelings. The basic quality of relatedness needs is different from existence needs because relatedness needs cannot be satisfied without mutuality. For all the parties in a relationship, their satisfaction (and frustration) tends to be correlated. Growth needs include desires of a person to have creative and productive effects upon one's self and upon the environment. Satisfaction of growth needs occurs when a person engages problems which call upon him/her to utilize his/her capacities fully and to develop new capabilities. The psychological sense a person has from fulfilling his/her growth needs is that of a greater wholeness or fullness as a human being.

B. Personality Psychology

Spranger (in Vernon and Allport, 1931) posited a six-fold classification of personal values. Each value represents a separate ideal, or pure (as opposed to mixed) characterization of man. The values are: theoretical, economic, aesthetic, social, political, and religious. According to Spranger, the dominant interest of the theoretical man is the discovery of truth. His/her chief aim in life is to order and to systematize his/her knowledge. The economic man is characteristically interested in what is useful. His/her interest in utility embraces the practical affairs of the business world—the production, marketing and consumption of goods, the elaboration of credit, and the accumulation of wealth. The aesthetic man sees his/her highest value in form and harmony. Each single experience is judged from the standpoint of grace, symmetry, or fitness. He/she finds his/her chief interest in the artistic eposides of life. The highest value for the social type of man is love of people, whether one or many. The social man prizes other persons as ends, and is therefore kind, sympathetic, and unselfish. The political man is interested primarily in power. He/she wishes above all else for personal power, influence, and renown. Finally, the religious man considers the highest value to be unity. He/she seeks to comprehend the cosmos as a whole, and to relate one's self to its embracing totality.

Murray (1938) proposed a list of twenty-eight secondary, or psychogenic, human needs and twelve primary, or viscerogenic, human needs. We focus our discussion on the secondary, or psychogenic, needs. The first five psychogenic needs pertain chiefly to needs associated with inanimate objects:

Acquisition—The need to gain possessions and property, to grasp, snatch or steal things, to bargain or gamble, to work for money or goods.

Conservance—The need to collect, repair, clean and preserve things, to protect against damage.

Order—The need to arrange, organize, put away objects, to be tidy and clean, to be scrupulously precise.

Retention—The need to retain possession of things, to refuse to give or lend, to hoard, to be frugal, economical and miserly.

Construction—The need to organize and build.

Needs which are commonly manifested in ambition, will to power, desire for accomplishment and prestige are:

Superiority—This need includes both the needs for Achievement (will to power over things, people and ideas) and for Recognition (efforts to gain approval and high social status).

Achievement—The need to overcome obstacles, to exercise power, to strive to do something difficult as well and as quickly as possible.

Recognition—The need to excite praise and commendation, to demand respect, to boast and exhibit one's accomplishments, to seek distinction, social prestige, honours or high office.

Exhibition—The need to attract attention to one's person, to excite, amuse, stir, shock, thrill others, self-dramatization.

Needs which involve the defense of status or the avoidance of humiliation include:

Inviolacy—This need includes desires and attempts to prevent a depreciation of self-respect, to preserve one's "good name," to be immune from criticism, to maintain psychological "distance." It is based on pride and personal sensitiveness. The Inviolacy need includes the needs for Infavoidance, Defendance, and Counteraction.

Infavoidance—The need to avoid failure, shame, humiliation, ridicule, to refrain from attempting to do something that is beyond one's powers, to conceal a disfigurement.

Defendance—The need to defend oneself against blame or belittlement, to justify one's actions, to offer extenuations, explanations and excuses, to resist "probing."

Counteraction—The need to overcome defeat by restriving and retaliation, to select the hardest tasks, to defend one's honour in action.

The next five needs, according to Murray, have to do with human power exerted, resisted, or yielded to. It is a question of whether an individual initiates independently his/her own behavior and avoids influence, whether he/she copies and obeys, or whether he/she commands, leads, and acts as an exemplar for others.

Dominance—The need to influence or control others, to persuade, prohibit, dictate, to lead and direct, to restrain, to organize the behavior of a group.

Deference—The need to admire and willingly follow a superior allied other, to cooperate with a leader, to serve gladly.

Similance—The need to emphathize, to imitate or emulate, to identify onself with others, to agree and believe.

Autonomy—The need to resist influence or coercion, to defy authority or seek freedom in a new place, to strive for independence.

Contrarience—The need to act differently from others, to be unique, to take the opposite side, to hold unconventional views.

The next two needs are for aggression and for abasement.

Aggression—The need to assault or injure another, to murder, to belittle, harm, blame, accuse or maliciously ridicule a person, to punish severely, sadism.

Abasement—The need to surrender, to comply and accept punishment, to apologize, confess, atone, self depreciation, masochism.

The next need rests on the supposition that there are in everybody primitive, asocial impulses, which must be restrained if the individual is to remain an accepted member of his/her culture.

Blamavoidance—The need to avoid blame, ostracism or punishment by inhibiting asocial or unconventional impulses, to be well-behaved and obey the law.

The next five needs have to do with affection between people: seeking it, exchanging it, giving it, or withholding it.

Affiliation—The need to form friendships and associations, to greet, join, and live with others, to cooperate and converse sociably with others, to love, to join groups.

Rejection—The need to snub, ignore or exclude another, to remain aloof and indifferent, to be discriminating.

Nurturance—The need to nourish, aid or protect a helpless other, to express sympathy, to "mother" a child.

Succorance—The need to seek aid, protection or sympathy, to cry for help, to plead for mercy, to adhere to an affectionate, nurturant parent, to be dependent.

Play—The need to relax, amuse oneself, seek diversion and entertainment, to "have fun," to play games, to laugh, joke and be merry, to avoid serious tension.

Finally, there are two complementary needs which, according to Murray, occur with great frequency in social life, the need to ask and the need to tell.

Cognizance—The need to explore (moving and touching), to ask questions, to satisfy curiosity, to look, listen, inspect, to seek knowledge.

Exposition—The need to point and demonstrate, to relate facts, to give information, explain, interpret, lecture.

C. Social-Psychology

Rokeach (1968, 1973) proposed a list of personal values in order to study the relationship between people's values and attitudes. He believed that values and attitudes were cognitively connected and internally consistent. And further, that a change in one part of the value-attitude system would affect the other part. Because values are more centrally held enduring beliefs than attitudes, he assumed them to be more resistant to change and to have the greater influence in the value-attitude relationship. His personal value survey contained eighteen terminal values and eighteen instrumental values, where terminal values have to do with preferred end-states of existence and instrumental values related to modes of conduct. The eighteen terminal values include:

A comfortable life (a prosperous life)
An exciting life (a stimulating, active life)
A sense of accomplishment (lasting contribution)
A world at peace (free of war and conflict)
A world of beauty (beauty of nature and the arts)
Equality (brotherhood, equal opportunity for all)
Family security (taking care of loved ones)
Freedom (independence, free choice)
Happiness (contentedness)
Inner Harmony (freedom from inner conflict)
Mature love (sexual and spiritual intimacy)
National security (protection from attack)
Pleasure (an enjoyable, leisurely life)
Salvation (saved, eternal life)
Self-respect (self-esteem)
Social recognition (respect, admiration)
True friendship (close companionship)
Wisdom (a mature understanding of life)

And the eighteen instrumental values are:

Ambitious (hard-working, aspiring)
Broadminded (open-minded)
Capable (competent, effective)
Cheerful (lighthearted, joyful)
Clean (neat, tidy)
Courageous (standing up for your beliefs)
Forgiving (willing to pardon others)
Helpful (working for the welfare of others)
Honest (sincere, truthful)
Imaginative (daring, creative)
Independent (self-reliant, self-sufficient)
Intellectual (intelligent, reflective)
Logical (consistent, rational)
Loving (affectionate, tender)
Obedient (dutiful, respectful)
Polite (courteous, well-mannered)
Responsible (dependable, reliable)
Self-controlled (restrained, self-disciplined)

Katz (1960), too, was interested in the underlying cognitive structure of attitudes, and proposed that attitudes function to serve the individual according to their motivational basis. The four motivational bases of attitude were for adjustment, ego-defense, value expression, and knowledge. The adjustment motive involves the need of people to make the most of their external world and what it has to offer. Specifically, people have a need to maximize reward or to minimize punishment in their external environment. The ego-defense motive involves the need of people to live with themselves, and thereby a need to protect one's ego from one's own unacceptable impulses and from knowledge of threatening forces from without. The value-expression motive focuses on the need for self-expression, self-development, and self-realization. Finally, the knowledge motive involves the individual's need to give adequate meaning, understanding, clarity, and consistency to one's external environment.

D. Sociology

In order to analyze the social character of the American "new middle class," Riesman (1950) posited a typology of social character for describing societies. He proposed that a society's social character can generally be categorized as predominantly one or two of the following types: traditional-directed, inner-directed, or other-directed. Tradition-directed people in a society are guided by a rigid set of rules, usually backed by powerful religious beliefs which prescribe what should be done, under what circumstances, and why. In contrast, inner-directed people turn to their own inner values and standards for guidance to decide for themselves in view of their own long-term self-interest what would be the proper course to take. Other-directed people direct their behavior so as to secure the esteem and approval of their immediate peers.

Riesman asserts that the tradition-directed person is almost gone from the United States society today, and that the social character of U.S. society is predominantly both inner- and other-directed. He also observed a slow shift in the American "new middle class" social character from inner-directedness to other-directedness.

E. Cultural Anthropology

F. Kluckhohn (1961) proposed a classification of value orientations in order to study differences in values among cultures. She assumed that there were a limited number of common human problems for which all peoples at all times must find some solutions, that solutions of all problems are variable but within a range of possible solutions, and that while all solutions are present in all societies at all times, solutions are differentially preferred by societies. The answers to each of five common human problems comprised Kluckhohn's classification of value orientations.

To the question "What is the character of innate human nature?" a society's human nature value orientation may be either evil, good-and-evil, or good. To the question "What is the relation of man to nature?" a society's man-nature value orientation may be one of the following: subjugation to nature, harmony with nature, or mastery over nature. And to the question "What is the temporal focus of human life?" the time value orientation of a society may be either past, present, or future. To the question "What is the modality of human activity?" a society's activity value orientation may be either being, being-in-becoming, or doing. And finally to the question "What is the modality of man's relationship to other men?" the relational value orientation of a society may be either lineal (recognized leaders of important families make decisions), collateral (almost everyone comes to agree on a decision), or individualistic (everyone holds own opinion and votes on a decision).

According to the theory, in each culture most individuals are characterized by a dominant profile of value orientations. For example, the dominant value orientations in the United States culture were predicted to be: a conception of human nature as evil but perfectable, a mastery over nature, future time, doing, and individualistic (Kluckhohn, 1961).

IV. PROPOSED TYPOLOGY OF CONSUMER NEEDS

What are the basic human needs which the consumer attempts to satisfy through his/her purchase, use, and disposition of products and brands? To answer this question, the author proposed a typology of fundamental consumer needs. The consumer needs were defined specific to the domain of consuming activities, and conceptualized at a level more fundamental than relevant product attributes. Seven consumer needs and their definitions are presented in Table I. A brief discussion of each consumer need and its related consumer behavior follows.

The first consumer need is Physical Safety—the need to consume products so as to avoid harm or danger in their use, and to preserve clean air and water in the environment. There are several concepts in the consumer behavior and marketing literature which may infer this underlying consumer need. Specifically, perceived physical risk that a brand may be unsafe, harmful, or injurious to the

Table I.   A Typology of Consumer Needs

Physical Safety	The need to consume products so as to avoid harm or danger in their use, and to preserve clean air and water in the environment
Material Security	The need to consume an adequate supply of material possessions
Material Comfort	The need to consume a large and/or luxurious supply of material possessions
Acceptance by Others	The need to consume products so as to be associated with a significant other or a special reference group
Recognition from Others	The need to consume products so as to be acknowledged by others as having gained a high status in one's community
Influence over Others	The need to feel one's impact on others' consumption decisions
Personal Growth	The need to consume products so as to be or become one's own unique self

health would surely infer an underlying need on the part of the consumer for Physical Safety. The socio-ecologically conscious consumer who purchases returnable bottles, phosphate-free detergent, and lead-free gasoline because he/she makes product and brand choices on the basis that its attributes do not harm the environment may also be expressing a need for Physical Safety, in this case from the environment. Fear appeals in advertising to promote the use of seat belts or to demarket cigarettes suggest that advertisers believe consumers have a need for Physical Safety. And the Consumerism issues of health and safety of products, nutrient labeling, and open dating would suggest that consumerists and government policy makers, too, assume consumers have a need for Physical Safety.

The second consumer need, for Material Security—the need to consume an adequate supply of material possessions—may be inferred from the consumer behavior concepts, perceived financial risk, and perceived performance risk. Consumers who perceive financial risk in the choice of a brand because he/she may lose money, either because the brand may not work at all or because it may cost more than it should to keep it working, may be expressing an underlying need for material security. Similarly, consumers who perceive performance risk in the choice of a brand because the brand may have something wrong with it or it may not work properly also may have a need for Material Security.

The third consumer need is Material Comfort—the need to consume a large and/or luxurious supply of material possessions. The materialism value, the self-indulgent consumer who is marked by a great urgency of wants, the credit card lifestyle, and the inability to delay gratification, would all seem to infer an underlying consumer need for Material Comfort. Further, from the multi-attribute attitude studies, we observe that the relevant product attributes which determine brand attitude are very often of the nature—comfort, luxury, spaciousness, style, and convenience. Here too, we may infer an underlying need on the part of the consumer for Material Comfort.

The fourth consumer need, Acceptance by Others—the need to consume products so as to be associated with a significant other or a special reference group—may be inferred from several consumer behavior concepts. Consumers who perceive social risk in the choice of a brand because it may affect the way others think about him/her may be experiencing an underlying need for Acceptance by Others. And where the expectations that relevant others have of the consumer actually influence his/her product or brand choice (subjective norm or social compliance), certainly the consumer must have had an underlying need to be Accepted by Others. Early and late majority adopters of an innovation also may be satisfying a need to be Accepted by Others.

The fifth consumer need is Recognition from Others—the need to consume products so as to be acknowledged by others as having gained a high status in one's community. Conspicuous consumption, where a consumer chooses products and brands that will be seen and admired by relevant others, and status consciousness, where a consumer chooses products and brands to achieve status or gain prestige for him/herself in the eyes of relevant others, may infer the underlying need for Recognition from Others.

The sixth consumer need, Influence over Others—the need to feel one's impact on others' consumption decisions—may underlie the behavior of opinion leaders and consumerists. Opinion leaders who influence their friends' and relatives' choice of a whole variety of products and brands, from fashions to instant coffee or microwave appliances, may be exhibiting an underlying need to Influence Others. And consumerists, politically involved in and actively leading the Consumerism Movement, surely express a need to Influence Others as they try to influence not only what consumers purchase, but also what information consumers use in making purchase decisions, and how consumers will go about complaining when they are dissatisfied with a product or brand.

Finally, the seventh consumer need is the need for Personal Growth—the need to consume products so as to be or become one's own unique self. Of course, the self-actualizing consumer who attempts to fulfill him/herself through his/her purchases and to do the best he/she is capable of doing in his/her purchase decisions must certainly be satisfying the need for Personal Growth. The great diversity of goods and services, and the variety of specialty shops available in an affluent society, and in particular the recent emergence of personal growth services such as Transcendental Meditation groups, Yoga, or dance classes, all may infer an underlying consumer need for Personal Growth. Furthermore, innovators who are the first to try a new product or brand, and certain impulse buying behavior of a curiosity nature, may also infer the Personal Growth consumer need. And too, consumers who perceive psychological risk that a brand may not fit in well with one's self-image or self-concept or the way one thinks of him/herself may be experiencing the need for Personal Growth.

The consumer needs typology is proposed to be a general typology of fundamental consumer needs across all individual consumers, products, and product purchase, use, and disposition situations. All of the needs exist for a consumer, although at any one point in time one need or a subset of these needs may be more dominant and influence choice within a product class. Thus, it is only the relative dominance of the consumer needs that may be expected to vary according to different individuals, different products, or different product purchase, use, or disposition situations.

V. COMPARISON OF CONSUMER NEEDS TYPOLOGY WITH OTHER HUMAN NEED CLASSIFICATIONS

In Table II, each of the proposed consumer need types is compared with selected levels of the need classifications from the other behavioral science disciplines. Beginning with the consumer need for Physical Safety, we examine the content of each of the proposed consumer need types for corresponding content from the other human need classifications.

Table II. Comparison of Content of Consumer Needs with Content of Selected Levels of Other Human Need Classifications

Discipline	Classification	Author	Consumer Needs						
			Physical Safety	Material Security	Material Comfort	Acceptance by Others	Recognition from Others	Influence over Others	Personal Growth
Organizational Behavior	Human Needs	Maslow	Safety	Safety		Belongingness	Esteem		Self-actualization
	Workers' Needs	Alderfer	Existence	Existence		Relatedness	Relatedness		Growth
Personality Psychology	Personal Values	Spranger (Vernon and Allport)		Economic	Economic	Social		Political	Theoretical Aesthetic Religious
	Psychogenic Needs	Murray (Edwards)		Conservance Retention	Acquisition	Deference Similance Blamavoidance Affiliation	Recognition Exhibition	Achievement Dominance	Autonomy Contrarience Cognizance
Social Psychology	Personal (Terminal) Values	Rokeach		Family security	A comfortable life	Mature love True friendship	Sense of accomplishment Social recognition		A world of beauty Freedom Wisdom
	Motivational Bases of Attitude	Katz		Adjustment		Ego-Defense			Value-expression
Sociology	Social Character	Riesman		Inner-directed		Other-directed	Other-directed		
Cultural Anthropology	Value Orientations	F. Kluckhohn	Mastery of Nature						Individualistic

We observe that Maslow's safety need (the need for . . . absence from pain, threat or illness), Alderfer's existence need (need for . . . physical safety), and F. Kluckhohn's mastery of nature value orientation correspond with the content of the consumer need for Physical Safety (the need to consume products so as to avoid harm or danger in their use, and to preserve clean air and water in the environment).

Second, there are need levels from almost all of the other need classifications which correspond with the content of the consumer need for Material Security (the need to consume an adequate supply of material possessions). They are Maslow's safety need (the need for security, stability, . . .) and Alderfer's existence need (. . . material needs like work-related pay, fringe benefits . . .). The Material Security consumer need also corresponds with the content of Spranger's economic value (interest in . . . consumption of goods), Murray's needs for conservance (to collect, repair, clean and preserve things, to refuse to give or lend, to hoard, to be frugal, economical and miserly), Rokeach's family security value (taking care of loved ones), and Katz's adjustment motive (need of people to make the most of their external world and what it has to offer, to maximize reward or to minimize punishment). Also Riesman's inner-directed social character (emphasis on long-term benefit of the individual) corresponds to the consumer need for Material Security.

Third, the content of the consumer need for Material Comfort (the need to consume a large and/or luxurious supply of material possessions) is supported by the content of Spranger's economic value (interest in . . . consumption of goods, . . . and the accumulation of wealth), by Murray's psychogenic need for acquisition (to gain possessions and property, . . . to work for money for goods), and by Rokeach's personal value of a comfortable life (a prosperous life).

Fourth, Maslow's human need for belongingness (the need for love and affection, for friends, and for one's place in a group) and Alderfer's relatedness need (the desire people have for relationships with significant others that can be characterized by a mutual sharing of thoughts and feelings) qualitatively correspond with the consumer need for Acceptance by Others (the need to consume products so as to be associated with a significant other or a special reference group). So too, do Spranger's social value (love of people) and Murray's psychogenic needs for deference (to admire and willingly follow a superior . . .), similance (. . . to imitate or emulate, to identify oneself with others . . .), blamavoidance (to avoid blame, ostracism or punishment by inhibiting asocial or unconventional impulses . . .), and for affiliation (to form friendships and associations, . . . to join others . . . , to cooperate and converse sociably with others, to love, to join groups). Rokeach's personal values of mature love (sexual and spiritual intimacy) and true friendship (close companionship), Katz's motive of ego-defense (need of people to live with themselves, to protect one's ego from one's own uncontrollable impulses and from threatening forces from without), and Riesman's other-directed social character (emphasis on . . . approval of immediate peers) also correspond with the content of the Acceptance by Others consumer need.

Fifth, the content of the consumer need for Recognition from Others (the need to consume products so as to be acknowledged by others as having gained a high status in one's community) corresponds with Maslow's human need for esteem (need for recognition or respect from others), and Alderfer's relatedness need (the desire people have for relationships with significant others . . . including esteem of others). It also corresponds with Murray's psychogenic needs of recognition (to excite praise of commendation, to demand respect, to . . . exhibit one's accomplishments, to seek distinction, social prestige, . . .) and exhibition (to attract attention to one's person . . .), with Rokeach's personal values of sense of accomplishment (lasting contribution) and social recognition (respect, admiration), and with Riesman's other-directed social character (emphasis on esteem . . . of immediate peers).

Sixth, Spranger's political value (wishes for personal power, influence, and renown) and Murray's psychogenic needs of achievement (will to power over things, people and ideas) and dominance (to influence or control others, . . . to lead and direct, to organize the behavior of a group) correspond with the content of the consumer need to Influence Others (the need to feel one's impact on others' consumption decisions).

Finally, the consumer need for Personal Growth (the need to consume products so as to be or become one's own unique self) corresponds qualitatively with Maslow's self-actualizing human need (need for a feeling of self-fulfillment, or realization of one's potential) and Alderfer's growth need (desire to have creative and productive effects upon him/herself and upon his/her environment . . .). It also corresponds with Spranger's theoretical value (interest in ordering and systematizing one's knowledge), aesthetic value (interest in artistic episodes of life), and religious value (interest in unity of oneself with the totality of the universe), and with Murray's psychogenic needs for autonomy (to resist influence or coercion, to defy an authority or to seek freedom in a new place, to strive for independence), contrarience (to act differently from others, to be unique, . . . to hold unconventional views), and for cognizance (to explore, to ask questions, to satisfy curiosity, to look, listen, inspect, to read and seek knowledge). Furthermore, Rokeach's personal values, a world of beauty (beauty of nature and the arts), freedom (independence, free choice), and wisdom (a mature understanding of life), Katz's value-expression motive (need for self-expression, self-development, and self-realization), and Kluckhohn's individualistic value orientation also qualitatively correspond with the Personal Growth consumer need.

The consumer needs typology provides the discipline of consumer behavior with its own classification of human needs specific to its domain of human behavior. Study of consumers' needs may now proceed with a need construct

developed specific to consumer behavior, rather than relying on the direct application of human need classifications which were conceptualized for the study of
behavior in other domains of human activity.

VI. IMPLICATIONS FOR THEORY AND RESEARCH

A. Motivational Bases of Consumer Attitude

The proposed typology of consumer needs has expanded knowledge of one of
the most central constructs in the comprehensive consumer behavior theories,
that of the non-specific motives, or fundamental consumer needs. In filling this
theoretical gap, it has in effect expanded knowledge of the total motive structure
underlying consumer behavior. Knowledge of the specific, or secondary level,
motives (relevant product attributes) is already well-developed in the marketing
and consumer behavior literature, especially as reported in the attitude formation
studies. With the new knowledge provided by the typology of fundamental
consumer needs and the present knowledge available on relevant product attributes, there is now some direction for investigating the theoretical link between
relevant product attributes and their underlying motivational bases—the fundamental consumer needs.

An illustration of a suggested theoretical link is shown in Table III where
relevant product attributes of an automobile, such as seat belts, gasoline economy, large size, and silver color, serve the means for satisfying fundamental
underlying consumer needs. The "means-end need chain" illustrates how, in the
choice to purchase an automobile, relevant product attributes are at a conceptually different level, and may be the means to satisfying more general or fundamental consumer needs.

In the example, a consumer may purchase an automobile with seat belts in
order to satisfy an underlying need for Physical Safety and perhaps a need to
Influence Others' use of seat belts. Or, a consumer may purchase an automobile
with good gasoline economy to meet his/her need for Material Security and/or
Acceptance by Others. A consumer may choose a large size automobile
because he/she perceives a large size auto will meet his/her needs for Physical
Safety, Material Comfort, and for Recognition from Others. Or finally, a consumer may buy an automobile that is silver color in order to satisfy a Personal
Growth need.

One will note that the same fundamental consumer need may be satisfied by
different product attributes, for example, need for Physical Safety in the choice
of an automobile may be satisfied by both seat belts and large size attributes. As
well, different fundamental consumer needs may be satisfied by the same product
attribute, for example, the large size attribute may satisfy all three consumer
needs, Physical Safety, Material Comfort, and Recognition from Others. This
would suggest a potential limitation in the application of multi-attribute attitude

Table III.   Example of "Means-End Need Chain" in Purchase of an Automobile

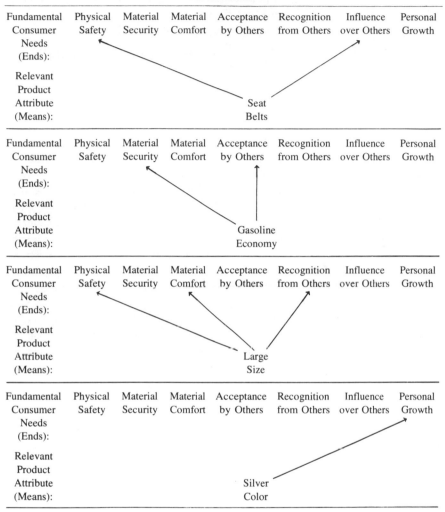

models. For when a single product attribute reflects two or more underlying consumer needs, the multi-attribute attitude formulation is limited in its explanatory power.

Further, on the theoretical link between non-specific fundamental consumer needs and "attitudes" toward brands, it would seem that since "choice criteria" is the importance ranking of relevant product attributes, and therefore the saliency component of "attitude" (Howard and Sheth, 1969), and since relevant product attributes derive from the underlying fundamental consumer needs which they satisfy, one may conclude that the effect of fundamental consumer needs on attitudes is mediated by the "choice criteria" mechanism. Choice criteria, because it is specific to a product class, may explain why one type of consumer need may be dominant in the choice within one product class and another type of consumer need may dominate the choice within another product class. Although Boote (1975) and Howard (1977) studied consumer values, rather than consumer needs, they have already taken the initial steps at establishing a theoretical link between consumer values and attitudes by way of choice criteria.

B. Sociology of Consumption

The inclusion of a discussion on societal implications (Mayer and Nicosia, 1977) of this study points out the need for viewing the study of consumer behavior beyond the marketing management perspective. The emphasis in this part of the discussion will focus on consumer behavior from a discipline perspective, suggesting implications of the typology for studying consumer behavior as a force in society.

The typology of consumer needs may serve as the theoretical basis for future research which asks questions about the *nature of consumption in a total society*. For example, longitudinal or cross-sectional studies using the consumer needs typology as a theoretical basis may be initiated to answer such questions as the following:

(1) Within a society, what is the extent, duration, and rate of change of the dominant consumer needs? Can this be predicted from changes in economic, demographic, and social structures in a society? Does this influence types and amount of goods consumed, and amount of time allocated to consumption activities?

(2) Would certain disadvantaged segments of a society have different consumer needs that dominate their choice behavior than the consumer needs of the mainstream of a society? For example, would it be more important for blacks, single women, single parents, or the aged to acquire a "quantity of life," that is, meet a Material Security or Material Comfort consumer need, rather than to reach for a "quality of life," to meet a Personal Growth consumer need?

(3) What are the differences in dominant consumer needs by cultures? To what extent are the differences due to their different stages in economic and social development? To what extent do the differences influence types and amounts of goods consumed, and amount of time spent on consumption activities?

FOOTNOTES

*The research reported here represents a portion of the author's doctoral dissertation completed at the University of Illinois, Champaign, Illinois, 1978. The author would like to thank her dissertation committee chairman, Professor Jagdish N. Sheth, for his guidance on this project, and also gratefully acknowledge the very useful comments of the reviewers.

1. "Want," "Need," and "Motive" will be used synonymously here. "Even though these terms tend to be used in slightly different ways in the psychological literature, treating them as synonyms facilitates discussion and does not result in serious ambiguity" (Howard and Sheth, 1969).

2. "Goal must be distinguished from goal-object" (Howard and Sheth, 1969). Whereas a goal may be to gain acceptance by others, a goal-object would be the product or brand consumed in order to attain that goal. For the goal, to gain acceptance by others, the goal-object may be, for a student, jeans or Levi brand jeans.

REFERENCES

Alderfer, Clayton P., "An Empirical Test of a New Theory of Human Needs." *Organizational Behavior and Human Performance* 4 (1969): 142-175.

Alderfer, Clayton P., *Existence, Related and Growth*. New York: The Free Press, 1972.

Andreason, Alan R., "Attitudes and Customer Behavior: A Decision Model," in Lee Preston (ed.), *New Research in Marketing*. Berkeley, California: Institute of Business and Economic Research, University of California, 1965.

Boote, A. S., "An Exploratory Investigation of the Roles of Needs and Personal Values in the Theory of Buyer Behavior." Unpublished doctoral dissertation, Columbia University, 1975.

Cofer, C. N., and Appley, M. H., *Motivation: Theory and Research*. New York: Wiley, 1964.

Cohen, Joel B., "An Interpersonal Orientation to the Study of Consumer Behavior." *Journal of Marketing Research* 4 (August 1967): 270-278.

Cohen, Joel B., Fishbein, Martin, and Ahtola, Olli T., "The Nature and Uses of Expectancy—Value Models in Consumer Behavior Research." *Journal of Marketing Research* 9 (1972): 456-460.

Dichter, Ernest, *A Strategy of Desire*. Garden City, New York: Doubleday, 1960.

Engel, James F., Kollat, David T., and Blackwell, Roger D. *Consumer Behavior*. Second ed. Hinsdale, Illinois: Dryden Press, 1968.

Evans, Franklin B., "Psychological and Objective Factors in the Prediction of Brand Choice." *Journal of Business* 32 (October 1959): 340-369.

Fennel, Geraldine, "Motivation Research Revisited." *Journal of Advertising Research* 15 (June 1975): 23-28.

Galbraith, John Kenneth, *The Affluent Society*. Boston: Houghton Mifflin, 1958.

Haire, Mason, "Projective Techniques in Marketing Research." *Journal of Marketing* 14 (1950): 649-656.

Hansen, F., "Psychological Theories of Consumer Choice." *Journal of Consumer Research* 3 (1976): 117-142.

Howard, John A., *Consumer Behavior: Application of Theory*. New York: McGraw-Hill, 1977.

Howard, John A., and Sheth, Jagdish N., *The Theory of Buyer Behavior*. New York: Wiley, 1969.

Jacoby, Jacob, "Consumer Psychology: An Octennium," in M. R. Rosenzweig and L. W. Porter (eds.), *Annual Review of Psychology*, pp. 331-358. Palo Alto, California: Annual Reviews, Inc., Vol. 27, 1976.

Katona, George, Strumpel, Burkhard, and Zahn, Ernest, *Aspirations and Affluence*. Toronto: McGraw-Hill, 1971.

Katz, Daniel, "The Functional Approach to the Study of Attitudes." *Public Opinion Quarterly* 24 (Summer 1960): 163-204.

Kluckhohn, Florence Rockwood, and Strodtbeck, Fred L., *Variations in Value Orientations*. Evanston, Illinois: Row, Peterson, 1961.

Koponen, Arthur, "Personality Characteristics of Purchasers." *Journal of Advertising Research* 1 (September 1960): 6-12.

Lutz, Richard J., "Changing Brand Attitude Through Modification of Cognitive Structure." *Journal of Consumer Research* 1 (March 1975): 49-59.

Maslow, A. H., "A Theory of Human Motivation." *Psychological Review* 50 (1943): 370-396.

Maslow, A. H., *Motivation and Personality*. New York: Harper, 1954.

Maslow, A. H., *Motivation and Personality*. Second ed. New York: Harper and Row, 1970.

Mayer, Robert Natham, and Nicosia, Francesco M., "New Contributions of Sociology to Consumer Research," in Barnett A. Greenberg and Danny N. Bellenger (eds.), *Contemporary Marketing Thought: 1977 Educators' Proceedings*, Series #41, pp. 239–242. Chicago: American Marketing Association, 1977.

Munson, J. M., "Personal Values: A Cross-cultural Assessment of Self Values and Values Attributed to a Distinct Cultural Stereotype," in H. Keith Hunt (ed.), *Advances in Consumer Research*, Vol. 5, pp. 160–166. Chicago: Association of Consumer Research, 1978.

Murray, Henry A., *Explorations in Personality*. New York: Oxford University Press, 1938.

Nicosia, F. M., *Consumer Decision Processes: Marketing and Advertising Implications*. Englewood Cliffs, New Jersey: Prentice-Hall, 1966.

Riesman, David, *The Lonely Crowd*. New Haven, Connecticut: Yale University Press, 1950.

Rokeach, Milton, *Beliefs, Attitudes and Values*. San Francisco: Jossey-Bass, 1968.

Rokeach, Milton, *The Nature of Human Values*. New York: The Free Press, 1973.

Rostow, W. W., *The Stages of Economic Growth: A Non-Communist Manifesto*. Cambridge: Cambridge University Press, 1961.

Schneider, Benjamin, and Alderfer, Clayton P., "Three Studies of Measures of Need Satisfaction in Organizations." *Administrative Science Quarterly* 18 (1973): 489–505.

Scott, Jerome, and Lamont, Lawrence M., "Relating Consumer Values to Consumer Behavior: A Model and Method for Investigation," in Thomas V. Greer (ed.), *Increasing Marketing Productivity*, pp. 283–288. Chicago: American Marketing Association, 1974.

Sheth, Jagdish N., "A Field of Study of Attitude Structure and the Attitude-Behavior Relationship," in Jagdish N. Sheth (ed.), *Models of Buyer Behavior: Conceptual, Quantitative, and Empirical*. New York: Harper and Row, 1974.

Sheth, Jagdish N., "A Psychological Model of Travel Mode Selection," in Beverlee B. Anderson (ed.), *Advances in Consumer Research*, Vol. 3, pp. 425–430. Cincinnati: Association for Consumer Research, 1976.

Sheth, Jagdish N., "A Model of User Behavior for Scientific and Technical Information (STI)." Faculty Working Paper #390, Urbana, Illinois: College of Commerce and Business Administration, University of Illinois, March 1977.

Sheth, Jagdish N., and Talarzyk, W. Wayne, "Perceived Instrumentality and Value Importance as Determinants of Attitudes." *Journal of Marketing Research* (February 1972): 6–9.

Sparks, David L., and Tucker, W. T., "A Multivariate Analysis of Personality and Product Use." *Journal of Marketing Research* 8 (February 1971): 67–70.

Tucker, W. T., and Painter, John, "Personality and Product Use." *Journal of Applied Psychology* 45 (October 1961): 325–329.

Vernon, Philip E., and Allport, Gordon W., "A Test for Personal Values." *The Journal of Abnormal and Social Psychology* 26 (Oct.–Dec. 1931): 231–248.

Vinson, Donald E., and Munson, J. M., "Personal Values: An Approach to Market Segmentation," in K. L. Bernhardt (ed.), *Marketing: 1776–1976 and Beyond*, pp. 213–317. Chicago: American Marketing Association, 1976.

Vinson, Donald E., Munson, J. M., and Nakanishi, M., "An Investigation of the Rokeach Value Survey for Consumer Research Applications," in William D. Perreault, Jr. (ed), *Advances in Consumer Research*, Vol. 4, pp. 247–252. Atlanta: Association for Consumer Research, 1977.

Vinson, Donald E., Scott, Jerome E., and lamont, Lawrence M., "The Role of Personal Values in Marketing and Consumer Behavior." *Journal of Marketing* (1977): 44–50.

Westfall, Ralph, "Psychological Factors in Predicting Product Choice," *Journal of Marketing* 26 (April 1962): 34–40.

Wilkie, William, and Pessemier, Edgar A., "Issue in Marketing's Use of Multi-Attribute Models." *Journal of Marketing Research* 10 (November 1973): 428–441.

CONSUMPTION OF MASS COMMUNICATION
CONSTRUCTION OF A MODEL ON INFORMATION CONSUMPTION BEHAVIOR

Preben Sepstrup, THE AARHUS SCHOOL OF
ECONOMICS AND BUSINESS ADMINISTRATION
AARHUS, DENMARK

I. INTRODUCTION

1. Background

It is a well-known fact that the consumer will not buy a product he or she does not care for somehow. It is also well-known that even the most perfect product will only be consumed if efforts are made to facilitate its way from producer to

Research in Marketing, Volume 3, pages 105–142
Copyright © 1980 by JAI Press Inc.
All rights of reproduction in any form reserved.
ISBN: 0-89232-060-5

consumer. The only way of finding out what facilitates the process is to study the consumer. Therefore, intensive studies have been made to develop consumer behavior theories, including works on motivation, cognition, attitude formation, information acquisition, brand preferences, buying intentions, product decisions, etc.[1]

Both theory and practice demonstrate that the basic product features may be perfect and yet nothing will be sold if the market does not know about them. The product itself can build up the necessary knowledge (demonstrations, exhibitions, shelves, etc.). However, to accomplish large-scale selling, it is necessary also to present the product features in symbolic form, that is, to produce a by-product consisting of information. Compared to previous attempts to explain the consumption of a product as such, very little has been done to investigate the consumption of the by-product. Of course, the great theories of consumer behavior have dealt with the topic, as they all include explanations of the consumer's use of information. Also many empirical studies have been made on the subject, without ever making it a central theme, though. There are only a few independent theoretical studies of the consumption of information, and the subject has never been treated independently of the consumption process or seen as part of the general behavior of the individual.

Consequently, the practicians of information processes have virtually been let down by consumer behavior theory. They have never been given a general theory of the consumption of mass media (information) on which to base their thinking and decisions.

The lack of such a theory is even more obvious in those cases where information is not a by-product but a main product, for example, consumer information, communication between authorities and citizens, communication on problems like traffic safety, drug problems, etc., and of course even more so in cases where the information is sold, that is, for the mass media industry, whether publicly or privately owned.

2. Purpose

The purpose of this paper is to introduce a general model on the consumption of information. The basic idea of the paper is to consider the output of the mass media—information—a product like other products, and to develop a model on the consumption of this special product by merging elements from consumer behavior theory and mass communication theory.

The purpose involves two problems. The first is to develop a general frame of reference for the understanding of the individual's information acquisition. The other is to develop a model which can be used to describe, explain, and predict needs for information, kinds of information wanted and consumed, and sources of information wanted and actually used.

3. Outline and Methodology

This paper is purely theoretical. First some assumptions about the individual and the way in which mass communication functions are presented. Then a general frame of reference is built up in Section II. In the light of this, the problems deriving from the purpose are further defined. Section III explains the need for information—when and how much. Section IV sets up a general explanation of how consumption of information takes place, and Section V develops a theory which explains how much information the individual will consume in relation to a certain need for information. Finally, Section VI deals with the question of the choice of information source.

It is important to emphasize that at the present stage of our understanding of consumption of mass communication, it is not helpful to concentrate especially on consumer behavior, even if understanding of consumer behavior is the ultimate goal. Consumer behavior is part of the individual's total behavior, and acquisition of product information is again an integrated part of the individual's total consumption of information and can only be understood in that context.

From the outset, we must focus on a general understanding of what leads the individual to use a given information source, also, if we want to understand the consumption of information in relation to buying processes. Once we have formulated a general theory, we can start building up more detailed and specific theories with special relevance to given subsets of behavior like, for instance, a consumer behavior. It is the idea of this paper to advance such a general understanding.

II. FRAME OF REFERENCE

1. Assumptions About the Individual

The purpose of this subsection is to stipulate some important features of human behavior. The first feature is the assumption that man's behavior is purposeful or goal-oriented. The goals are not given from birth, but determined, for instance, by consumed information, experience, social relations, and surroundings.

The goals directing human behavior are specific and not generalized, except for one very general rule, saying that the individual seeks a maximum of need satisfaction. This of course does not mean that the individual fulfills this purpose. Being a problem solver does not mean that all problems are solved. The individual behaves *as if* he tries to maximize the difference between utility and effort. Also, it is assumed that the individual basically is able to behave appropriately in relation to his goals. If the behavior seems inappropriate, the reason is to be found outside the individual.

These few assumptions are important to the development of the whole theory, and lie behind the very basic idea that information consumption is one among several functions leading to the achievement of the goals of the individual. Consumption of information substitutes and may be substituted by other activities. The individual seeks, applies, and rejects information as a means of achieving maximum need satisfaction with the least possible effort. The individual's use of information is instrumental in relation to need satisfaction, as is all consumption.

2. Assumptions About the Functioning of Mass Communication

The conception of information consumption being instrumental is identical with a functional approach to the understanding of the functioning and effect of mass communication. The model constructed in this paper belongs to the so-called "uses and gratifications" tradition.[2]

According to this tradition, it is not the media that affect people, but people that utilize the media, because they have problems (needs) and interests which make the use of different information sources necessary. Primarily it is not only the characteristics of information that condition the use of information, but also the characteristics of society, groups, and individuals.

It is further assumed as a principal rule that the individual does not want to perceive and is not consciously influenced by information *not* needed in some way. The receivers in the communication process are selective in their media contact. Use of information takes place because the individual expects some kind of need satisfaction. Competing information sources are all fulfilling certain functions for a goal-oriented individual.

3. The Concept of Information

In order to build the necessary frame of reference (purpose one of this paper), it is necessary to define the central concept of information.

Information is defined as knowledge about circumstances outside the individual which he receives through his sensory apparatus and is able to interpret meaningfully, which means that the individual gets an idea of what the knowledge can be used for.

The model concerns only information coming from what is normally called media, including other people, but excluding, for example, physical experience. This definition of the concept of information means that what is known beforehand is also considered information, but this does not necessarily mean that it has what is here termed information *value*. This concept of information value is further developed in Section VI.4.1. Suffice it here to state that information value is defined in relation to the individual's information storage or knowledge. The information storage consists of two components, viz. a content component and a probability component. Knowledge about circumstances outside the individual that is already inherent in the storage is still information, but it has no informational value unless the probability component is changed. The same information may involve different information value for different people. It depends on the individual whether something is information or not, and so does the value of information.

Consumption of information means receipt of information through the sensory apparatus, that is, acquisition of information, but *not* information processing.

4. Construction of a Frame of Reference

The use of mass media has been explained from many points of view. As stated in subsection I.2., information is here considered a product, and consequently the use of mass media is considered consumption of this product. This approach makes it possible to draw on consumer behavior theory. It therefore goes without saying that the frame of reference must refer to the basic features of the product and the consumption behavior.

It follows from subsection II.1. that an obvious point of departure for the construction of a frame of reference is consumer goals. The consumer has a goal if he is able to perceive a situation which is different from his present situation and wants to change to that situation. (I am able to imagine myself better trained and I want to be better trained, so I have a goal or problem or need.)

Consumption of information is one of many means of achieving different goals. This consumption of information (watching the news, reading a brochure) may be categorized in many ways. The most appropriate seems to be Schramm's distinction[3] between immediate and delayed reward, referring to the moment of the gratification. This distinction produces two categories. The first category includes consumption of information where the gratification, derived from the satisfaction of the information need, is related to the moment of consumption. The consumer does not intend to use the information beyond the moment of consumption. The usefulness of the information consumed is direct. (Examples are: watching a movie on TV, reading a novel, entertaining oneself with the glamorous pictures of magazine advertisement.) Normally, this category of information is called entertainment. For analytical purposes, we may call it directly instrumental consumption of information.

The second category includes consumption of information where the gratification derived from the satisfaction of the information need is not related to the moment of consumption. The consumer intends to use the information beyond the moment of consumption, the usefulness being indirect. (Examples are: going through the supermarket advertisements to find the best bargain, reading brochures to understand the advantages of different materials for rugs, or reading the TV program guide.) For analytical purposes, we call this category indirectly instrumental consumption of information.

A "behavioral episode" like shopping may relate solely to one of the two categories, but it is very likely that elements from both categories are involved. Also, the same "behavioral episode" may lead to consumption of information in relation to different goals (shopping, reading the newspaper). Therefore, consumption of information cannot be understood from the observable behavior alone. It is also obvious that a source of information is more attractive if it appeals to the motives behind both categories, and the more goals it is related to.

These multi-functional aspects in the use of mass media are a very complicating factor—especially in empirical investigations—but they are also an important factor in a realistic understanding of the consumption of media.

The multi-functional element has been the cause of much confusion in mass communication research. One of the reasons is that the starting point of most researchers has been the content of the media (the product offered) and not the needs of the consumers. This failure is avoided here, due to the influence from consumer behavior theory teaching us to start with the consumer and his social relations.

An important aspect of all kinds of consumer behavior is the behavioral routines. Information routines are a parallel to the multi-functional nature of mass media, because they are an adaption of the appropriateness of fulfilling several functions at the same time. Routines are necessary because of the combination of many needs and restricted resources. It is here hypothesized that the consumer tries to satisfy as many informational needs as possible through informational routines, which we also call the normal media use. Normal media use is the best combination of media the consumer can find to give him a satisfactory coverage of these normal informational needs compared to the effort of using the media. The routines are broken only when important problems cannot be solved in the ordinary way.[4] (A consumer in the market for a new car consults his friends and family or watches out for advertisements in the daily paper. If this is not enough, he will consider the trouble of contacting a less well-known person or perhaps the library for an issue of a consumer's journal, or of visiting a retailer.)

In the next section, our effort in this paper is restricted to building a model on consumption of indirectly instrumental information. This does not mean that direct use of information is of no interest. On the contrary, direct information is important for the understanding of indirect information, because consumption of direct information may lead the consumer to consumption of indirect information. Probably most consumption of indirect information is due to exposure to the medium because of routines or because the consumer will use the medium for direct purposes.

The probability of direct instrumental consumption leading to indirect instrumental consumption is higher for some media—e.g., the daily press and magazines—than for others like books or radio. The more heterogeneous the content of the medium, the more likely it is that one kind of consumption of information leads to another.

A few more concepts (analytical tools) are necessary to complete the frame of reference. First we shall distinguish between two kinds of attention. *Active attention* means that the perception of information is an important purpose of the behavior leading to the perception of information. Normally, this kind of behavior is characterized as seeking information. *Passive attention* means that the perception of information is due to some other kind of behavior. When a person looks for the TV program, he may be aware of an advertisement. This attention is passive.

Further, it will prove useful to distinguish between initial attention and continued attention.[5] *Initial attention* is the initial change from exposure to concentration of one or more senses on an element in the information source. *Continued attention* is the possible further concentration on more elements. (When the consumer reads his newspaper, initial attention tells him, for example, that here is an advertisement, perhaps that it is an advertisement for instant coffee. If he immediately moves his eyes to a picture showing the first snow in the streets, his attention has been initial only. If the consumer goes on reading the advertisement and notes the brand name and/or price and/or some arguments for purchasing the product, we call it continued attention.)

5. Delimitations

The purpose of this paper is to build a model on the consumption of information. Consumption of direct instrumental information is not covered by the theory, neither are the information processing and the *effects* of consumption of information.

6. Outline

The problem of constructing a model that can help us describe, understand, and forecast the information consumption behavior involves at least four problems:

(1) A WHAT problem, involving the size and kind of the information need (section III).
(2) A HOW problem, involving possible ways of satisfying the need for information (section IV).
(3) A HOW MUCH problem, involving the amount of information. The dependent variable will be formulated as the probability that consumption of information takes place in relation to a certain informational need (section V).
(4) A WHERE problem, involving the specific choice of information source, including the choice between routines and use of information outside

normal media use and the transitions from initial to continued attention (section VI).

III. THE WHAT PROBLEM: ON WHAT TOPICS DOES THE CONSUMER WANT INFORMATION, AND HOW MUCH?

In this section, we shall try to explain when the consumer will be interested in information, which—according to subsections II.1. and II.2—is a prerequisite of the establishment of communication processes. The section only deals with the need for information. The conditions for the fulfilment of the need are treated in sections IV–VI.

1. First Necessary Condition: Relevant Topic

The theoretical assumptions in II.1 and II.2 imply that the consumer will not seek (active, initial, and continued attention) information on topics that are not considered relevant (products/news that the consumer is not interested in). The consumer may get in touch with information on irrelevant topics through passive, initial attention, but normally there is only little probability that it will lead to continued attention.

This means that if a person considers a topic irrelevant, it is very difficult to reach such a person by mass communication on that subject. It is, however, not totally impossible. Consumption of information concerning an irrelevant topic may take place as a consequence of passive, initial attention. The possibility of this is greater the more direct instrumental information and the less cost the consumer expects as a consequence of the continued attention, but if a communicator tries to attract those not interested by adding direct instrumental information, he will often irritate those interested in the topic.

The main conclusion of the stipulations in section II is that the consumer is only interested in information dealing with a relevant topic (e.g., product or product characteristic). We have thus identified a necessary condition of consumption of information.

It is important to note that "topic" is not a broad category. A topic may be relevant (wanted), but this is not enough to ensure consumption of information. It is also necessary to communicate about the relevant features of the topic.

The author has investigated the question of relevant topic in relation to the planning of consumer information concerning color TV sets. The investigation included 889 households which had recently bought a color TV. The households were found in a country-wide Gallup poll based on area sampling of the cluster type with three stages, according to the so-called Deming plan. In this investigation, relevant topic was operationalized by the question: "Of these items, which

Table I. "Of these items, which were the two most important when you bought your color TV set?"

Choice Criteria	%
Quality of colors	56
Reliance of brand	50
Price	20
Dependability	19
Size of screen	11
Design	7
Easy to operate	6
Quality of sound	3
No answer	1
Total	173
N = 889	

were the two most important when you bought your color TV set?" Relevant topic is here the same as choice criteria. The result is shown in Table I. Table I shows that the first necessary condition is varyingly fulfilled for different choice criteria. According to the theory, this means that the chances of establishing a communication process with the consumers depend heavily on the communicator's choice of communication content.

2. Second Necessary Condition: Perceived Information Need

The question to be answered in this subsection is whether all relevant topics are equal as regards the consumer's interest in information. The consumer is, for example, interested in sports, food prices, cars, or in new boots for his children. Will he consume information about all of these topics?

Common sense tells us that a consumer would like to know more about some topics, and feels that he knows enough about others. The same common sense (and the stipulations in section II) tell us that it is an important (so important that we call it necessary) prerequisite of consumption of indirect instrumental information that the individual needs the information, which means that he wants to know more.

In order to describe this second condition, we use the concept of perceived information need. The term *perceived* indicates that information need is a subjective concept, the contents of which may very well differ from what various groups will call objective information needs.

The concept and function of information need can be derived almost solely from common sense. This, however, does not make the concept less important. The existing literature tries to establish a direct relationship between means (use of media) and goals. The use of the intervening variable information need (and relevance) makes it possible to reach a better understanding of the relationship. It might even be assumed that the attempt to establish a direct relation between media use and other needs than information needs has been an important reason for the lack of development in the understanding of the use of the mass media. One cannot solely explain the reading of newspaper A, or an article in this newspaper, by specific non-informational needs, or explain why a housewife goes through children's wear advertisements or visits retail outlets solely by the need for clothes for her children.

2.1. On Information Needs.   The empirical background for this section is a series of studies reported in Sepstrup (1973). The findings are not to be repeated here. It should be mentioned, however, that it was found out that the main reason why it is so difficult to make empirical investigations on consumption of information is that typically the information needs are not associated with relevant topics, but with specific dimensions of the topic, and that there are almost immense cost and value interrelationships.

Therefore, at the beginning, we must be satisfied with reliable, but simple models of the complicated reality.

A need may generally be understood as a difference between the way things are and the way the individual would like them to be. In order to determine and measure the concept of information need, we must therefore find out what constitutes the actual and the wanted situation. The actual situation is described through the variable "perceived actual knowledge" (K_a), defined as the knowledge the consumer thinks he possesses in relation to a certain topic (or dimension of a topic).

The wanted situation is described through the variable "perceived, necessary knowledge" (K_n), defined as the knowledge the consumer feels is necessary in order to be able to act/decide/feel secure/satisfied, etc., in relation to a certain topic.

If K_a is larger than or as large as K_n, there is no information need. If K_a is smaller than K_n, there is a need for information. The larger the difference between K_a and K_n, the larger the need for information. Consumption of information cannot only reduce but also increase a need for information.

Research on measurement of subjective information need has been scarce. The operationalizations of perceived risk[6] are much more complicated than those of subjective information need as defined here. Field research[7] indicates that very simple methods give reliable and valid results.

The basic theory presented here will, hopefully, be extended by determinants of K_a and K_n. For the time being, we shall only hypothesize that one variable plays a role, namely the perceived importance of the topic, which determines K_n. The determinants of the perceived importance depends on the topic. Possible determinants are experience, interests, use of information, income, and age.

The investigation referred to in subsection III.1. also tried to evaluate the need of information. According to the theory, it is useless to talk about the need of information in relation to color TV as such. The need is connected to the relevant topic. For practical purposes, we must therefore investigate the need of information for each choice criteria.

Table II shows the result of measuring information need in relation to four different choice criteria. Table II supports the idea that one cannot just talk about the need of information in relation to, for example, color TV. The need must be specified according to specific topics (choice criteria). For practical purposes, data such as those in Tables I and II point out which items to concentrate on if the communicator wants to reach the consumer's mind.

The consumer may objectively be wrong in his judgments or the communicator may want to talk about quite different things. However, knowledge of relevant topics and of needs of information is necessary to tell the communicator what topics must also be incorporated in the message to attract the attention of the consumer.

If we combine the two sets of figures in Tables I and II, we get a chart which tells partly about the communication potential, that is, the chances of getting in contact with the consumer, partly about what to talk about in the message.

Figure 1 shows four communication potential charts, giving us a quantitative tool which can be used for planning the content of the communication process.

We have now identified two necessary conditions to be fulfilled if the individual is to receive (consume) information. It is noteworthy that the two prereq-

Table II. "How much do you think you knew about dependability/quality of colors/design/price of different TV brands before you started to look for a new TV set?"

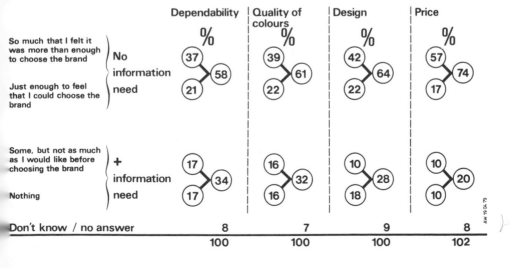

		Dependability %	Quality of colours %	Design %	Price %
So much that I felt it was more than enough to choose the brand	No information need	37	39	42	57
		58	61	64	74
Just enough to feel that I could choose the brand		21	22	22	17
Some, but not as much as I would like before choosing the brand	+ information need	17	16	10	10
		34	32	28	20
Nothing		17	16	18	10
Don't know / no answer		8	7	9	8
		100	100	100	102

AW 19 04. 79

Figure 1. Communication potential charts

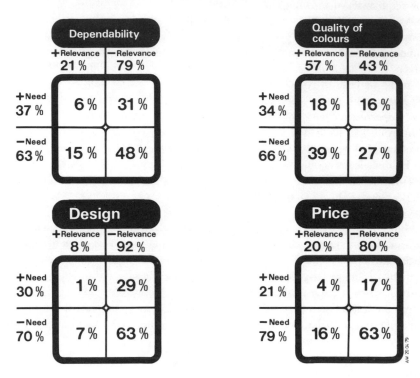

uisites are not fulfilled in many mass communication situations, such as news flow, public information, or advertising. Furthermore, most of the literature on communication and information management is devoted to an attempt to find ways to suspend the two necessary conditions (without stating the problem explicitly, of course).

The attempts in practice to work against the basic rules are the cause of much of the criticism of many kinds of mass communication. The model establishes a platform for a new practice in better accordance with common and individual interests.

IV. THE HOW PROBLEM: PROCEDURES FOR NEED SATISFACTION

This section forms an important background for the next two sections and widens the understanding of information consumption through an extension of the frame of reference as regards procedures for satisfaction of information needs.

It is an important element in the total model that there are four main procedures for acquisition of information.

As mentioned in II.4., the consumer is assumed to have a normal or routine consumption of media. This normal use of media is defined as regular use of the same media and is not motivated by a specific need. The normal use of media covers a need for direct instrumental information (it gives pleasure during the moment of consumption) and it is composed of media which, according to experience, on the average satisfies different needs of information (what is on TV, supermarket bargains, city council decisions, the knowledge that nothing dangerous has happened in the world). These needs cannot be specified be-forehand, but generally we know they will be there. Their satisfaction depends on indirect instrumental information.

This normal media use leads to passive, initial attention toward a lot of topics (the consumer sits down with his daily newspaper after work, and while relaxing he also registers that this is an advertisement for product A, this is an article on baking, this on Christmas habits, etc.). This way of getting in contact with information is the *first main procedure* for acquisition of information, if the initial attention is followed by continued attention (e.g., reading parts or all of the advertisement/article). We may call this procedure passive attention due to normal media use, and assume that the consumer primarily seeks to satisfy his information needs this way. In doing so, the consumer makes the most of the cost relations and information-value relations. There are no figures to support this hypothesis directly, but to the author it is an important conclusion from the totality of registrations on reading habits, information habits, media habits, and leisure habits.[8]

The *second main procedure* for acquisition of information is active, initial, and continued attention (information seeking) towards a specific topic inside normal media use. (The consumer is interested in information on color TV and looks for advertisements in his daily paper, but does not buy a consumer journal or go to a retail outlet.) We may call this procedure active attention due to normal media use, and assume that this is the most used way of information acquisition next to passive attention due to normal media use.

It may be impossible in empirical research to separate the two procedures—cf the joint treatment in the frame of reference and the next section—but the dif-ference is important, when we want to understand how people solve the problem of being informed.

The *third,* and less used, *main procedure* for acquisition of information is active, initial, and continuous attention outside normal media use in relation to a specific topic (going to a shop to ask for a brochure, phoning a consumer council for advice). Normally this implies higher costs than the two other procedures. We may call this procedure active attention outside normal media use.

Information consumption behavior does not necessarily escalate from the first to the third procedure. It may begin or end with each of the procedures.

Principally, there is a *fourth main procedure* for acquisition of information, namely passive, initial (followed by continued) attention outside normal media use. This means that the consumer is incidentally exposed to an information source, because of some other kind of behavior (waiting at the dentist's or driving home and as a consequence of this being exposed to information like a magazine in the waiting room or billboards along the road). The costs of information in such cases are rather low.

Whether the consumer tries to satisfy his needs for information inside or outside normal media use depends on his demands and expectations towards information value and costs compared with the size of the information need and the importance of the topic. The information need also explains whether passive or active attention is used in normal media use. The more important the topic and the greater the need for information, the more likely is active attention.[9]

V. THE HOW MUCH PROBLEM: GIVEN A NEED FOR INFORMATION, TO WHAT EXTENT IS IT SATISFIED?

Section III took up the so-called WHAT problem. We found that every consumer in relation to any topic will be in one of three situations: (1) the topic is irrelevant, or (2) the topic is relevant and (a) K_a is greater than or equal to K_n, which means that the consumer has no need for information, or (b) K_a is less than K_n, which means that the consumer has a need for information. We also saw that consumption of information is almost out of the question in the first two situations.

Section IV described the possible procedures for acquisition of information. Four variables were identified as important for need satisfaction.

In this section, we shall construct a model which tells us to what degree a need for information will be satisfied. The model must tell about the individual's motives, possibilities, and restrictions when it comes to consumption of information.

1. Basic Elements of the Model

Our starting point is a consumer who has a need for information (he wants to buy a TV set, but feels that he knows less than necessary on design, quality, and prices). What determines the extent to which this need is satisfied?

The first determinant to be mentioned is the costs of information. This variable is analyzed more closely in section VI. Suffice it here to say that information costs are the difficulties or the efforts like time, money, and various inconveniences related to the use of an information source.

Information costs are the most important limiting factor of consumption of information.[10] The model assumes that the consumer acquires information (relative to a certain topic) as long as it seems worth while. *The consumer behaves as if the difficulties (costs) and the importance of the topic are balanced against each other* (more time for seeking information on prices is acceptable for a family in the lower income brackets than in the higher income brackets; information on social security justifies much more effort than does the buying of a new record). The behavior normally does not lead to objective optimal decisions. The consumer is not an "economic man." He reacts to reality as perceived by him.

The model further assumes that the maximum cost is not only determined by the importance of the topic, but also by the expected possibility of acquiring the information wanted. (The consumer may want reliable information on the durability of TV sets and he may find this purchase an important topic. But if he expects that it is very difficult to find this information, he will only accept rather small costs of trying.) The probability of finding the information wanted is a determinant of the cost the consumer is willing to accept. This phenomenon is incorporated in the model through the variable "expected amount of information," which is defined as the portion of the need for information the consumer expects in order to be satisfied. "Expects" is a general evaluation based on the consumer's experiences. The term "expect" does neither here nor anywhere else imply anything about the level of consciousness of the process.

The assumptions stated of course hold true of all sizes of information need, but the model also assumes that the size of the need for information is a determinant for the amount of information consumed. In the model, this phenomenon is stated as follows: the larger the need for information, the higher the probability of consumption of information, other things being equal. (If the consumer plans his holidays, thinking that he knows the prices of charter flights to Spain, but knows little of the prices for renting a house at the coast, he will give priority to information on the latter issue.)

It is important to note that expected amount of information in many cases is only part of the expected utility of information consumption. Other expected gratifications may influence the use of information. This gives rise to information value and information cost interrelations, which may be able to explain behavior that cannot be understood solely from the assumptions made here. Such gratifications are not taken into account here, but it is important to integrate them in the theory, when it is further developed.

Five variables have now been identified as important determinants of the consumption of information: (1) the size of the information need, (2) the importance of the topic, (3) expected amount of information inside normal media use, (4) expected amount of information outside normal media use, and (5) expected costs of the perceived information source (the various relevant sources known to the consumer, which form the background for the expected amount of information).

Unfortunately, the exact formulation of the dependent variable in the model is rather difficult. The ideal is a variable expressing the amount of information consumed. This is, however, impossible because of the lack of a usable concept, expressing amount of information in this sense.

In the search of a definition of the dependent variable, the only realistic possibility to be found has been *the probability of consumption of information in relation to a certain need for information,* P(C), where P = probability and C = consumption. The consumer does not himself think in terms of P(C), but he can be brought to express expectations that are close to our understanding of P(C).

Figure 2 illustrates the model (on the HOW MUCH problem) as developed until now.

Other variables than the five registered in the figure may influence P(C), but it is hypothesized that they are the most important determinants, explaining most of the variations in P(C). How then, do these variables influence the consumption of information? Answers cannot be given in detail. Things are too complicated, and we know too little. What we can hope for is some main structure to help us understand and predict the consumption of information in broad outline.

The model describes the main structure in the relationship between P(C) and the independent variables in the following manner:

$$P(C) = f\left(a \cdot x_1 + b \cdot x_2 + c \cdot \frac{x_2}{x_5} + d \cdot x_3 + e \cdot \frac{x_3}{x_5} + f \cdot x_4 + g \cdot \frac{x_4}{x_5}\right),$$

where x_1 = the size of the need; x_2 = the importance of the need; x_3 = expected amount of information inside normal media use; x_4 = expected amount of information outside normal media use; x_5 = expected costs of perceived information sources.

The equation is only a tool of communication. It is *not* possible to measure the

Figure 2. Graphic illustration of the first version of the model

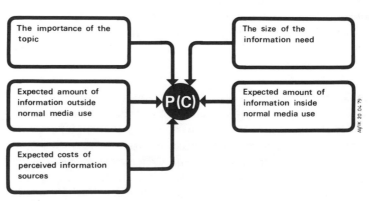

independent variables, and by use of the equation to determine P(C). The main reasons for this are scaling problems and the lack of knowledge about the coefficients (the relative strength of the variables). The equation is, however, not useless. It indicates the direction of the relationship between the dependent and independent variables, and we learn that not only the variables themselves but also certain relations between the variables are important.

To put it in a different way, we assume that the probability of consumption of information in relation to a certain information need is higher the greater the size of the information need is, the more important the topic is, the better the relation between the importance of the subject and the costs is, the greater the expectations of amount of information are, and the better the relations are between expected amounts of information and the costs.

2. Further Model Construction

It is obvious that the model needs further developing and improvement for several purposes. For the purpose of both understanding and empirical analysis, we need to identify the factors determining the value of the independent variables. These independent variables are broad categories, and for practical purposes, it is important to identify relevant easier-to-measure, easier-to-understand, and easier-to-operate-on variables. Also, it should be very interesting to find out where the often-used socio-economic data fit in.

The reader will recall that the purpose of this paper is to suggest a broad theory. Therefore a result like the following cannot be incorporated in the model: "the number of working hours have a limited effect on the reading of books and magazines, and (for females only) on the reading of newspapers—whereas an effect of this kind cannot be found when it comes to consumption of TV."[11] Instead, this finding is used to support an element in the model stating that "leisure time is a determinant of consumption of information." This statement then has to be specified according to different purposes.

In the following sections, the five independent variables listed in Figure 2 are treated as dependent variables, the purpose being to identify the variables they depend on.

2.1. The Importance of the Topic. The meaning of this variable has to be determined from case to case. Therefore it is not meaningful to talk about general determinants of this variable. We can formulate hypotheses on factors determining the importance only when knowing the topic: does the consumer risk much economically; is the product important in a social sense; is there a physical risk, and so on.

The "extended" model is illustrated in Figure 3.

Figure 3. Graphic illustration of the extension of the model: the importance of the topic.

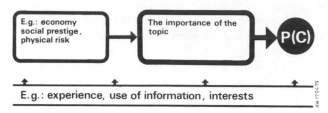

2.2. The Size of the Need. The extension of the model in relation to this variable illustrates the interaction between the main dimensions in information consumption behavior, as this extension is identical with the model developed in section III on information need. The extension is illustrated in Figure 4.

A comparison between Figures 3 and 4 shows that the importance of the topic has two functions. It may seem strange, but is just one of many indicators of the complexity of the problems dealt with.

2.3. Expected Amount of Information in Normal Media Use. The extension of the model in relation to this variable is illustrated in Figure 5.

Probably many factors influence the expected amount of information. At the present stage of knowledge, they cannot all be listed. Therefore the model is first extended through broad explanatory categories of variables (independent variables in relation to expected amount of information; see the third row in Figure 5). Thereafter, examples are given of factors influencing these categories of variables (row four in Figure 5). In order to prevent the reader from conceiving the theory as being more precise than it is, the relations between the two sets of independent variables are not specified.

"Expected amount of information" is defined as the portion of the need for

Figure 4. Graphic illustration of the extension of the model: the size of the need.

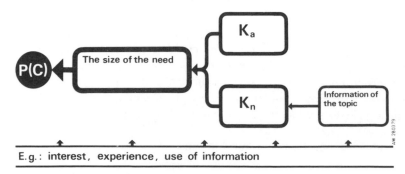

information which the consumer expects to be able to satisfy. This expectation is a general evaluation based on the consumer's experiences with the supply of information.

Even though it may be close to a tautology, these experiences must be included as an explanatory factor. This is done through the variable "experiences with information value."

The concept of information value will be discussed further in section VI as an important determinant in the choice of information source. The variable is a measure of the consumer's expectation of changes in K_a due to use of an information source. The model assumes, almost self-evidently, that experiences with this information value will influence the expected amount of information. (The consumer has an experience with several sources of information, which he uses when buying, for example, food. His evaluations of the chances of satisfying a new information need, of course, depend on this experience.)

Figure 5. Graphic illustration of the extension of the model: expected amount of information inside normal media use.

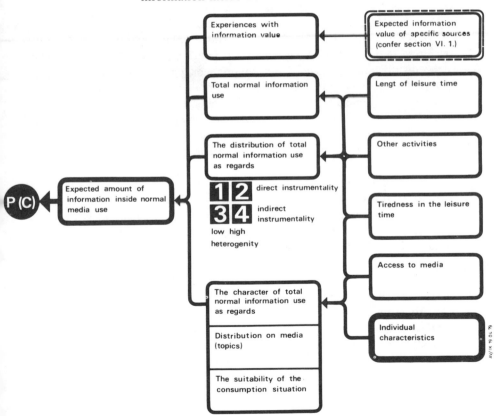

The next independent variable to be introduced is self-evident, too, namely "total consumption of information." The greater the total consumption, the higher the expected amount of information is, expected information value being equal. (A consumer wanting a dress has better chances of satisfying her need for information on fashion if she reads several magazines and newspapers than if she just reads the local paper.)

Other factors than experience with information value may also modify the relationship between total consumption of information and expected amount of information. The model stresses two main factors. The first factor is "the distribution of total consumption of information on direct and indirect instrumental consumption and between media with different degrees of heterogeneity as regards content."

A combination of the two factors (variables) gives (cf. Figure 5) four types of information consumption. A consumer having a relatively large consumption of information of type 1 (for example, he reads much fiction) will be low on expected amount of information inside normal media use. The higher proportions that types 2, 3, and 4 (in this order) compose of the total consumption of information, the higher the expected amount of information will be.

The other main factor is called the "character of information consumption." Of course this character has many dimensions (which can be used in further extensions of the model). In the model, relief is given to two characteristics. One is the distribution of the total consumption on concrete media (and thereby topics). The second is suitability of the consumption situation. "Suitable" means suitable for continued attention and active attention. The suitability varies according to whether a newspaper is read when going home from work, at home while the children are playing around, or late at night when the house is silent.

At a general level, it is not possible to specify the role of the character of the consumption. In concrete situations, however, it is possible to analyze the distribution on topics and the suitability of the consumption situation and from this to draw conclusions on the expectations about amount of information.

The above is not a detailed description of reality, of course. It is a proposal meant to bring about important dimensions of analysis and thinking in order to evaluate the probability of information consumption.

As already mentioned, the model could be more detailed at the present level. However, this is outside the scope of this paper and is to be left for another paper or practical situation. Here we shall concentrate on a further extension in our search for examples of variables which can be supposed to influence the main variables listed. They are (1) experience with information value, (2) the total consumption of information, (3) the distribution of the total consumption on direct and indirect consumption and on media with different degrees of content heterogeneity, and (4) the character of the media (topics) and the "suitability."

An extension of the model as regards information value is found in section VI.

Therefore, we can here focus on examples of variables, which can be hypothesized to determine or indicate the variables 2, 3, and 4.

Probably, the number of such variables is large and their interaction very complex. Therefore, only four variables of the kind sought are found in Figure 5. Supposedly, they are good examples. In concrete situations, it is necessary to think over whether it is possible from the examples to identify more or better factors to work with.

In brief, the variables in row four in Figure 5 can be commented upon as follows:

Length of leisure time:[12]   The period when the consumer does not sleep or work. The total consumption of information is supposed—other factors being equal—to be proportional with the length of leisure time. Presumably, length of leisure time also determines the distribution of information consumption. The amount of indirect instrumental consumption, for example, grows with the length of leisure time. (The more leisure time the consumer has, the less he needs to relax and "escape," and the more time he has for different interests causing information needs.)

Other activities:[13]   This variable refers to activities other than media consumption in the leisure time, be they either enforced or voluntary. The variable is important, but its role cannot be specified in general because of its strong dependence on the concrete situation.

Enforced activities will normally reduce the consumption of information and lead to a growing share of direct instrumental information. The influence of potential activities (carried out because they are attractive) can only be specified if we specify the activity. If it leads to increased use of information, it will normally lead to a growing share of indirect information.

Tiredness in the leisure time.   Obviously, the total consumption of information depends on how tired the consumer is in his leisure time, but it is doubtful whether general relations can be specified. If, however, the medium is specified, such relations can be formulated. Tired people, for example, have a relatively high consumption of TV. It is hypothesized that tiredness leads to a growing share of direct instrumental information.

Access to media.   Normally, access to media means physical and economic access. In this connection, we would recommend awareness of a social dimension of access, too. Social access then is a variable which informs us which media are acceptable and normal in the consumer's social relations.

It is self-evident that access to media is closely connected with the total consumption and its distribution.[14] A specification is only possible in actual situations.

Individual characteristics.   Figure 5 also has a box named "individual characteristics." This is a black box, meaning that psychological factors are supposed to influence the expected amount of information, but this influence will not be

Figure 6. Graphic illustration of the extension of the model: expected costs of
perceived information sources.

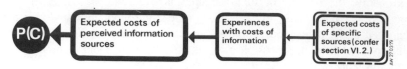

described here in order to draw certain limitations, and because considerable
space has been devoted to psychological variables in traditional communication
literature.

The extension of the model is graphically illustrated in Figure 5.

2.4. Expected Costs of Perceived Information Sources.   Expected costs of perceived information sources are based on the consumer's experience with costs of
information, which are based on the expected costs of specific sources. An
extension of the model is identical with the model on the information cost
variable presented in the next section on choice of information source.

The extension of the model is graphically illustrated in Figure 6.

2.5. Expected Amount of Information Outside Normal Media Use.   The extension of the model as regards expected amount of information outside normal
media use is not parallel to that of subsection 2.3. because, by definition, it is *not*
a normal, regular use, but a use which can be altered in the very short run.

Figure 7. Graphic illustration of the extension of the model: expected amount of
information outside normal media use.

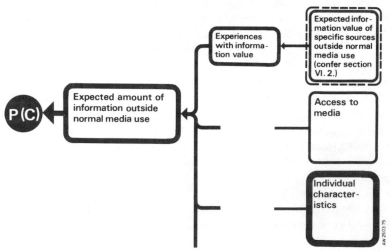

Therefore, the predominant determinant of the expected amount of information outside normal media use is the consumer's experience with information value outside normal media use (cf. section 2.3.). It is also obvious that both physical and social access to media must be important determinants. However, their role can be specified only in concrete situations. As in section 2.3., individual characteristics are considered a black box.

Total information use, its distribution and character can be seen as determinants of expected amount of information inside normal media use because these variables are unchanged in the short run, and their value is not dependent on immediate wants for information. The opposite is true as regards consumption of information outside normal media use.

Therefore, any further extension of the model is not possible at the present time. The "extension" of the model is graphically illustrated in Figure 7.

3. Socio-Economic Variables

Much empirical research shows certain relationships between several socio-economic variables and consumption of information.[15] The results have been achieved in a very mechanical way, and they are not unambiguous. Furthermore, socio-economic variables are registered in many situations. It is, therefore, worthwhile to try to understand the supposed relations especially between use of information and income, education, urbanization, and often age.

This section has demonstrated that it is possible to construct a model of consumption of information without involving socio-economic variables, not on purpose, but because they do not possess any explanatory power that calls for a central position in the model.

This seeming discrepancy between many empirical research findings and this model can, however, be explained by the model: the socio-economic variables do not themselves determine a consumption of information. The variables do not *explain* the consumption of information (cf. the fact that the results often differ in different investigations). The real explanations (determinants) are made up by the type of variables exemplified in this model. The correlation between consumption of information and socio-economic variables is found because these variables, to a certain degree, correlate with the aspects of the consumer's situation, which in the model are considered the real explanatory variables.

Therefore, from a theoretical point of view, the model will not be improved if we insert the socio-economic variables in it. The practical value depends on how well the socio-economic variables correlate with the explanatory variables. To establish this is one of the many projects suggested by the model.

Also sex, for example, has been demonstrated to determine the consumption of newspapers and magazines.[16] The reporting (and especially understanding) of such results has often involved a touch of female inferiority, which can now be set aside, as the model here tells that differences in the use of media is not due to

Figure 8. Graphic illustration of the model on P (C).

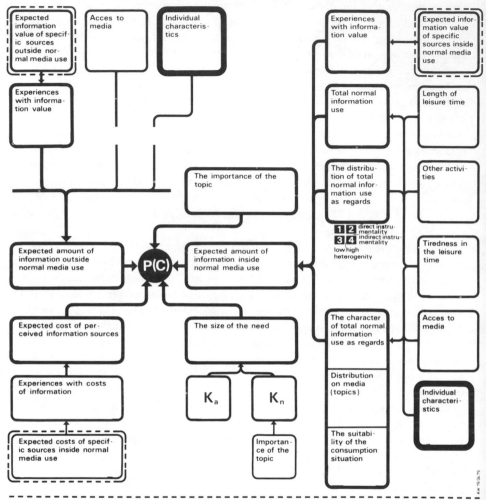

sex itself, but to the sex-related conditions. There are many other results where we can now move from description to understanding.

Figure 8 summarizes graphically the model(s) proposed in this section.

VI. THE WHERE PROBLEM: CHOICE OF SOURCE OF INFORMATION

In this section, we shall build up a theory which tells us *where* the consumer acquires information. This purpose includes three questions: (1) what determines whether initial attention is followed by continued attention or not, (2) what determines whether the consumption of information takes place inside or outside normal media use, and—most important for practical decisions—(3) what determines (inside or outside normal media use) the choice of specific sources of information.

The section also serves as an elaboration of section V as regards the variable information cost and information value.

Terms like *"choice* of information source" or "decision" do not imply any assumptions about the level of consciousness. What we mean is that the consumer behaves *as if* the processes described take place.

The first three subsections deal with the above-mentioned three questions and the last two with the variable information value and information cost, which are found to play an important role.

1. From Initial to Continued Attention

Assuming that the consumer has been brought to initial attention to information (an advertisement, an article, a TV program, a window display), what are the conditions of continued attention? Normally, this process is not considered a choice of information source. However, most consumption of information originates from passive attention inside normal media use (see section IV). The change from initial to continued attention therefore is a very important way of choosing information sources. The consumer sits down; reading his daily paper, he registers the presence of some kind of information (his attention is caught by the illustration of an advertisement for a new book) and has to decide whether or not his attention shall continue (i.e., use the source, consume the information, concentrate on further stimuli).

Section III said that the first necessary condition of continued attention is that initial attention gives the consumer the impression that the information is relevant (the consumer wants the product, is interested in the Middle-East situation).

This, however, is a necessary but insufficient condition. The consumer's resources are limited (e.g., time) and he cannot pay attention to all kinds of relevant information. What then—besides relevance—determines whether the consumer will continue his contact with the information source?

The problem is characterized by a consumer having a need for information, an idea about the importance of the topic to which the need relates, and the possibility of acquiring information if he accepts a certain inconvenience or effort (cost), which he perceives as rather realistic, because he is very close to the source of information. In this situation, we assume that the consumer behaves as if he considers two factors.

The first factor is a balancing of the expected cost x and the need y in relation to the topic z. (Is it worth the time and intellectual effort to go through a supermarket advertisement to find a bargain for tomorrow's dinner?)

The second factor is a balancing of the expected cost and the expected value of information.[17] The relevance of this second factor is due to the fact that the cost of reading an advertisement or newspaper article or a leaflet in the mail may be acceptable concerning the need of information and the importance of the subject, but not concerning the expected information value, for example, because the consumer too often has experienced that he learns nothing from advertisements for certain goods.

We may then conclude that if the initial attention makes the consumer suppose that the information is relevant, then the probability of continued attention depends on the importance of the topic and the size of the need for information, seen in relation to the expected costs of information and the relationship between expected value of information and expected costs of information. The probability is higher the better these relations are.

Presumably, the described processes are so interrelated (and often unconscious) that the consumer cannot describe them. However, this does not mean that the model is without theoretical or practical value. If we want to understand or forecast information consumption behavior, it brings us a step forward to think, analyze, and (partly) measure in accordance with the model proposed.

2. Active Attention Inside or Outside the Normal Use of Media?

We assume that a general evaluation of the relationship between value of information and information cost determines whether the use of information takes place inside or outside the normal use of media. The alternative preferred has the highest value of this relationship. The hypothesis is very logical, but perhaps not so important. It is even possible that this step in the choice of source is non-existent, which means that the consumer chooses directly between the individual sources. Therefore this short section may be more formal than important.

3. Choice of Specific Source of Information

If the consumer seeks information (active attention), how then will he decide what information sources to use?

In accordance with the above subsections, we assume that the consumer behaves as if he chooses the source of information (or combination of sources) that has the best relationship between expected value of information and the corresponding expected cost of information (as perceived by the consumer).[18] The level of consciousness may differ, and the consumer of course only chooses from among the sources known to him.

The basic ideas in a model on the consumer's choice of information source have now been presented in the above three subsections.[19] Even though only basic ideas are presented, we have obtained a more detailed and useful understanding than before because we have left the accepted method of combining media exposure and interest variables, as is common in most uses and gratifications studies. The variables "value of information" and "cost of information" have appeared to be extremely important. The building of a theoretically acceptable and useful model therefore demands a further analysis of these variables.

4. Expected Value of Information

There is no overall treatment of the concept of information value in the communication literature, excluding the mathematical information theory, which is of no use in a mass communication context. In this subsection, we shall define information value and formulate hypotheses on the determinants of the expected value of information as perceived by the consumer in relation to a specific information source.

4.1. What is Information Value? The term "information value" is often used in literature, but typically the concept is not defined, or the definitions are too broad to be of any use. The most important reason for the uncertainty in the analysis of information value in the communication literature is the mixing up of the value of information as such and the importance of the topic of the information.[20]

The approach in this paper makes it clear that the value of information and the importance of the topic are independent of each other and both separate, independent variables in relation to choice of information source. Both variables are important, but they should be kept separate.

The construction in this paper of an overall model on information consumption makes it easier to define the concept of information value. The model proposed in the preceding chapters and ordinary logic lead to a definition of the expected information value of an information source as the change in actual knowledge (K_a) due to the use of the source (initial and continued attention). Information changing actual knowledge to a higher level than necessary knowledge (K_n) is not regarded as having any information value. The perception of information value is subjective. Expected information value from the same source may vary with consumers of different backgrounds. Note that consumption of information does not necessarily diminish information need. It may also increase the need by influencing K_a or K_n.

4.2. Hypotheses on Determinants of Information Value. According to the model, the choice of information source is determined by expected value of information and information costs. Expected value of information is defined as expected changes in actual knowledge.

This seems relatively simple, but this may not be the case as far as reality is concerned. Among the complicating factors, it may be mentioned that K_a has at least two dimensions to which changes may refer, namely a quantitative dimension and a qualitative one. Therefore, and because we *know* too little, we shall concentrate on some basic assumptions which can (1) help understand and predict the consumer's choice of source, (2) tell the sender how to choose the right media, and (3) tell the media how to increase their attraction to the consumer.

It is not surprising that expected value of information is basically seen as a function of three factors: relevance, credibility, and comprehensibility. The consequence of this is that the consumer prefers a source of information that carries a new and useful (relevant) message which it is possible to comprehend and believe.

4.2.1. Expected relevance. Expected relevance is a comprehensive concept covering related variables, which are important because they influence the perception of the similarity between the content of the source and the information needed.

At least two basic factors influence the evaluation of the relevance. They are (1) the expectation that the source contains information different from actual knowledge, and (2) expected predictive value of information.[21] The higher these expectations are, the higher the value of expected relevance is, and consequently the value of information. (The difference between (1) and (2) is illustrated by a consumer who expects information on a loudspeaker in advertisements in his local paper to be different from his actual knowledge (the first variable), whereas he expects the predictive value of information to be low because he is interested in the sound and expects the information to be on the design.)

Possibly, expected relevance also depends on who else the consumer thinks will use the information.

4.2.2. Expected comprehensibility. Expected comprehensibility is a comprehensive concept covering several related variables, which are important because they influence the consumer's possibilities of perceiving and handling information. Among other factors, we expect comprehensibility to depend on expectations about the phrasing and presentation.

4.2.3. Expected credibility.[22] Expected credibility is a comprehensive concept covering several related variables, which are important because they determine the consumer's perception of the objectivity of the information.

Several variables presumably determine the consumer's evaluation of the credibility of the source. Three are incorporated in the model. They are (1) the expected intentions of the sender, (2) the expected expertness of the communicator, and (3) the expected topicality of the information.

The variable in the model relating to *intention* is formulated as the consumer's expectation to the degree of accordance between the consumer's motive to use the information and the sender's motive to send it. (The consumer may think that there is a better accordance between his and a retailer's intentions than between the intentions of a brochure and the consumer's intentions, because the retailer is not dependent on a single brand.) The higher the expected agreement, the higher the expected credibility is.

The variable in the model relating to *expertness* is formulated as the consumer's expectation from the competence/knowledge of the source. (The consumer may think that the expertness of the weather forecast is higher on TV than in a newspaper.) The higher the expected expertness, the higher the credibility is.

The variable in the model relating to *topicality* is formulated as the consumer's expectations from the ability of the source to carry the latest possible information. (A consumer may, for example, believe that advertisements are very topical, while this is not necessarily true as regards consumer magazines.) The higher the expected topicality, the higher the credibility is.

4.2.4. Socio-economic variables.   A number of investigations indicate a correlation between different socio-economic variables and choice of information source.[23] The explanation of this (and the relationship between these variables and the model) is the same as in subsection V.3.

The model of information value is graphically illustrated in Figure 9. It is a basic structure, which is to be extended or detailed in accordance with the user's need and the knowledge acquired through research and practice.

5. Expected Cost of Information

In this subsection, we shall define the concept of information cost and formulate hypotheses on the determinants of expected cost of perceived specific sources.

5.1. What is Cost of Information?   The literature of communication has no real analyses of the information cost concept. The expected information costs of perceived information sources are defined as the disutility (disadvantage) associated with the use of the information source.

The cost concept is related to a source, not an amount of information. If the consumer intends to use the "source" only partly (listen only to the weather forecast in the news, only read the classified advertisements in the newspaper, or only study the technical information in the brochure), this part is considered the information source. The costs of information are always the *additional* cost due to the specific consumption of information. (If a consumer intends to look for footwear-sale advertisements when reading his daily paper, the expected costs of information are only the costs added because of this activity, not the total cost associated with purchasing and reading the paper. The opposite is true if the newspaper is bought only for the sake of the shoe-sale advertisement. Confer the costs as a reason for consuming information inside normal media use.)

5.2. Hypotheses on Determinants of Costs of Information.   Basically, the costs of information consumption—according to the model—are determined by the

Figure 9. Graphic illustration of a model of information value

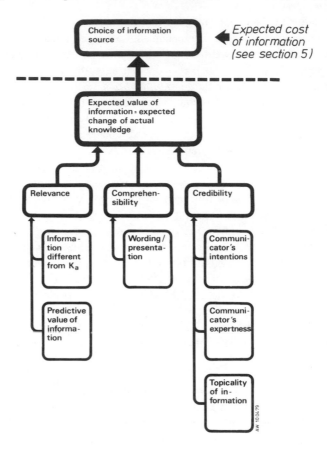

expected use of time, expected use of money, expected postponement of the behavior causing the information need, expected alternative use of time necessary for the information consumption, and expected physical and psychological strain. This basic model may be further developed through hypotheses on relations between these expectations and the consumers' individual characteristics and social situation. The variables use of time and use of money need no explanation. Postponement represents the disutility (inconvenience) of waiting. (The consumer may consider buying a percolator for a long time, but when he has decided to do so, the disutility of waiting another day because of lack of information may be enormous.) Physical and psychological strain represents the physical and emotional/intellectual effort that may be necessary in order to acquire the information.

These variables do not have the same relevance in relation to all sources or in different situations. But they are the basic variables from which to understand expected cost of information or to analyze or compare different sources of information.

It is very important to note that there are two steps in the formation of information costs. The first step is, for example, the time (minutes) the consumer expects the consumption of information to take. The next step is the (individual) transformation of this time to a cost (disutility). Therefore, expected cost is not a function of use of time, for example, but a function of the perception of the used time as a cost. This phenomenon has not been taken into consideration in existing empirical investigations. We can now incorporate the following relationship in our model:

$$
\begin{array}{l}
\text{Expected information} \\
\text{cost of perceived} \\
\text{information sources}
\end{array}
= f
\left\{
\begin{array}{l}
\text{The perception of expected use} \\
\text{of time as a cost} \\[6pt]
\text{The perception of expected use} \\
\text{of money as a cost} \\[6pt]
\text{The perception of expected} \\
\text{postponement as a cost} \\[6pt]
\text{The perception of the expected} \\
\text{utility of an alternative use of} \\
\text{time as a cost} \\[6pt]
\text{The perception of expected} \\
\text{physical and psychological} \\
\text{strain as a cost}
\end{array}
\right.
$$

There are several possible determinants of the perception of expected *use of time* as a cost. Some basic assumptions to be incorporated in the model are that the perception of expected use of time as a cost is a function of: (1) the consumer's (subjective) perception of length of leisure time—the more time, the less cost is involved in use of time; (2) alternative possibilities of activity—the more possibilities, the higher the cost associated with the use of time; (3) the extension of normal media use—the higher the normal consumption, the less extra time will normally be necessary to meet a need for information; and (4) the consumer's perceived ability to acquire and handle information—the higher the perceived ability, the less time is expected to be necessary.

The perception of expected *use of money* as a cost cannot be expressed as a specific amount. The question is whether the expected necessary amount is perceived as a small or large amount. The most obvious determinant of this is of course income.

Figure 10. Graphic illustration of a model of information cost.

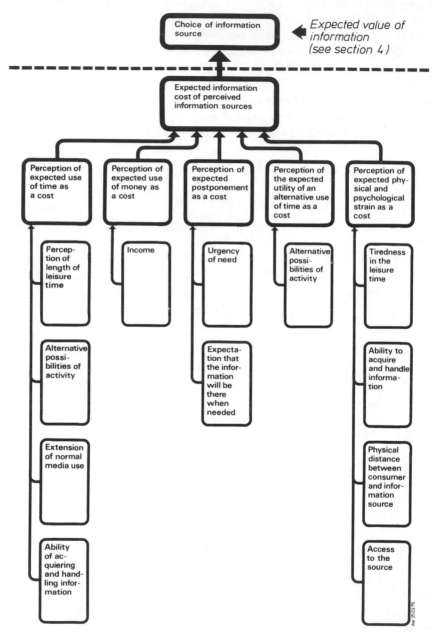

As a basic assumption, it is incorporated in the model that the perception of expected *postponement* as a cost is a function of (1) the consumer's perception of the urgency of the topic to which the information need is related (the more urgent, the higher the cost of postponement), and (2) the consumer's expectation that the information will be there when he needs it. The lower this expectation, the higher the expected cost of postponement is. (Food advertisements in the local newspaper have a high value of this variable, official consumer information on refrigerators a low one.)

The perception of the expected utility of an *alternative use of time* as a cost is difficult to determine. The perception may depend on many circumstances, which can only be specified in a concrete context. In a basic model, we may summarize these circumstances as the consumer's alternative possibilities of activity. The cost is higher the more and the better alternative possibilities the consumer has. As a basic assumption, it is incorporated in the model that the perception of expected *physical and psychological strain* is a function of: (1) the consumer's perception of tiredness in the leisure time—the more tired, the higher the cost is; (2) the consumer's abilities to acquire and handle information—the better the abilities, the less the cost is; (3) the physical distance between the consumer and the information source—the longer the distance, the higher the cost is;[24] and (4) access to the source the more difficult the access, the higher the cost is.

5.3. Socio-Economic Variables. No research demonstrates the relations between socio economic variables and expected cost of information. It should, however, be possible to argue that certain relations exist between the independent variables and, for example, education, income, age, and urbanization, the relationship being different for different sources. This should be further investigated.

As mentioned above, the purpose of this section has been to present a general model which can function as a platform for further theoretical and practical work. Undoubtedly, it is possible to be much more precise in the pinpointing of determinants when specifying the source.

The model on expected information cost of perceived information sources is graphically summarized in Figure 10.

VII. CONCLUSION

In the previous sections, we have formulated a large number of hypotheses, which together constitute a model on consumption of information. This has been done in the light of specified assumptions concerning the relationship between mass communication and individuals. The most important elements in the model are the pinpointing of the conditions necessary to the acquisition of information, the determinants of the probability of consumption of information in relation to an information need, and the explanation of how and where consumption of information takes place. Each of the dimensions of information consumption behavior are analyzed separately, but it is also obvious that the various dimensions are integrated elements with close interrelations and common determinants.

The model constructed in this paper does not cover all problems of information consumption behavior. It presents basic outlines, and is often more tentative than perfect. In spite of this, however, it does increase our understanding of the use of information (mass media) and does offer some help, whether the goal is a comprehensive theory of mass communication, the creation of profitable advertising campaigns, or a radical change of the media system.

The model may be said both to have been tested and not to have been so. The model has not been tested empirically, as it is presented here, but it has been tested in the sense that many of the components have an empirical reference. Almost all variables have been operationalized and the model has been used several times as a guide for collecting data to solve problems connected to the planning of information processes. It is, however, important to get a theoretical feedback before investing in large-scale empirical test of the model. This paper has been written to get this feedback, and because the model in its present form may hopefully offer inspiration for practicians as well as researchers.

FOOTNOTES

1. The literature is immense. Most findings can be found in either Nicosia (1966), Cox (1967), Engel, Kollat, and Blackwell (1968), Howard and Sheth (1969), Strumpel, Morgan and Yahn (1972), Bennet and Kassarjian (1972), Hansen (1972), Farley, Howard, and Winston (1974), or Sheth (1974).

2. For a description and analysis of the tradition, see, for example, Katz, Blumler, and Gurevitch (1973).

3. See Schramm (1949).

4. A further treatment of normal media use is to be found in section IV.

5. Cf. Ottesen (1977).

6. See Cox (1967).

7. See Sepstrup (1977).

8. A parallel assumption is briefly mentioned in Howard and Sheth (1969), p. 154.

9. This opens up for an alternative explanation of the many empirical results, which are normally explained as a result of selective processes; see, for example, Klapper (1963).

10. The concept of information cost is often used implicitly in the literature. Direct use of the concept is rare, but is found in Schramm (1954), Farley (1964), Downs (1961), Lanzetta and Kanereff (1962), Pruitt (1957), Green (1966), Irwin and Schmidt (1957), Bucklin (1965, 1966) Lundberg and Hultén (1968), and Atkin (1973).

11. See Augedal (1970).

12. Illustrations of the relationship between use of mass media and length of leisure time are found in Augedal (1970) Kleberg (1972), and Munk (1976).

13. The relationship between other activities and use of mass media is illustrated in Allart et al. (1958). See also Augedal (1970) and Wikmann (1974).

14. See Augedal (1970) or Edelstein (1974).

15. Examples of this research are found in Arndt (1972), Bennett and Mandel (1969), Berning, Jacoby and Jacoby (1974), Block (1972), Bucklin (1966), Chaffee and McLeod (1973), Staelin and Newman (1972), Thorelli (1971), Sepstrup (1976). A complete review up to 1971 is found in Sepstrup (1971).

16. See Augedal (1970), Rosvoll (1970), Dansk Media Index (1976).

17. The term ''value of information'' was introduced in V.2.3., and will be further defined and analyzed in subsection 4 of this section.

18. This is of course a logical assumption. The problem has only been dealt with to a limited extent in the literature. Support for the hypothesis is found in Farley (1964), Downs (1961), Irwin and Smith (1957), Bucklin (1965), Bucklin (1966), Lundberg and Hultén (1968) (all of information costs), and Farley (1964), Grønhaug (1972), Sears and Freedman (1967), Theil (1967), Tipton (1970), and Westley and Severin (1964) (all on information value).

19. Schramm (1954), Sepstrup (1971), and Atkin (1973) have similar hypotheses on selection of communication source, but their point of view lacks precision and is not developed further than to a black box level.

20. See Stigler (1961), Farley (1964), and Cox (1967).

21. The term is introduced in Cox (1967). Cox does not distinguish between predictive value of information and predictive value of the topic.

22. In the communication literature, credibility is often considered an independent variable influencing effect; see Westley and Severin (1964), Berlo, Lemmert, and Mertz (1969/70), Lundberg (1973), Maloney (1963), and Edelstein (1974).

23. See Westley and Severin (1964), Bostian and Ross (1965), Samuelsson, Carter, and Ruggels (1963), Augedal (1970), and Rosvoll (1970.

24. The importance of physical distance has often been illustrated. Quite different examples are Augedal (1970) and Bucklin (1969).

REFERENCES

Allart, Jyrhilä and Littunen, ''On the Cumulative Nature of Leisure Activities.'' *Acta Sociologica* III (1958).

Arndt, Johan, *Consumer Search Behavior. An Exploratory Study of Decision Processes among Newly-Married Home-Buyers.* Oslo: The Foundation of Market Research, Universitesforlaget, 1972.

Atkin, Charles, ''Instrumental Utilities and Information-Seeking,'' in P. Clarke (ed.), *New Models for Mass Communication Research.* London: Sage Publications, 1973.

Augedal, Egil, ''Eksponering for Massmedia blant Oslo-Folk (Exposure to Mass Media in Oslo).'' Institute of Press Research and Communication, University of Oslo, Mimeo No. 13, 1970.

Bennet, D. Peter, and Kassarjian, Harald H, *Consumer Behaviour.* Englewood Cliffs, N.J.: Prentice-Hall Inc., 1972.

Bennet, D. Peter, and Mandell, Robert M., ''Prepurchase Information Seeking Behavior of New Car Purchasers: The Learning Hypothesis. *Journal of Marketing Research* (November 1969).

Berg, Mie, Ekecrantz, Jan, Hemánus, Pertti, Mortensen, Frands, and Sepstrup, Preben (eds.), *Current Theories in Scandinavian Mass Communication Research.* Grenaa: GMT, 1977.

Berlo, K. David, Lemert, James B., and Mertz, Robert J., ''Dimensions for Evaluating the Acceptability of Messages Sources.'' *Public Opinion Quarterly,* No. 33 (1969/70).

Berning, A. Kohn, Jacoby, Carol, and Jacoby, Jacob, ''Patterns of Information Acquisition in New Product Purchases.'' *Consumer Research* 1, No. 2 (1974).

Block, E., Carl, ''Prepurchase Search. Behavior of Low-Income Households.'' *Journal of Retailing* 48, No. 1 (Spring 1972).

Bostian, J. E., and Ross, J. L., ''Functions and Meanings of Mass Media for Wisconsin Farm Women.'' *Journalism Quarterly* 42 (1965).

Bucklin, P. Louis, "Consumer Search, Role Enactment, and Marketing Efficiency." *Journal of Business* (Dec. 1969).
Bucklin, P. Louis, "Testing Propensities to Shop." *Journal of Marketing* (Jan. 1966).
Bucklin, P. Louis, "The Informative Role of Advertising." *Journal of Advertising Research*, No. 3 (1965)
Chaffee, H. Steven, and McLeod, Jack, "Individual vs. Social Predictors of Information Seeking." *Journalism Quarterly* (Summer 1973).
Clarke, Peter (ed.), *New Models for Mass Communication Research.* London: Sage Publications, 1973.
Cox, F. Donald (ed.), *Risk Taking and Information Handling in Consumer Behaviour.* Boston: Harvard University, 1967.
Dansk Media Index 1976 (The Danish Media Index 1976). Copenhagen: Danish Media Committee, 1976.
Downs, Anthony, "A Theory of Consumer Efficiency." *Journal of Retailing* (Spring 1961).
Edelstein, Alex, *The Uses of Communication in Decision-Making.* New York: Praiger, 1974.
Engel, E. James, Kallat, David T., and Blackwell, Roger D., *Consumer Behaviour.* New York: Holt, Rinehardt and Winston Inc., 1968.
Farley, U. John, "Brand Loyalty and the Economics of Information." *Journal of Business* (October 1964).
Farley, U. John, Howard, John A., and Ring, L. Winston, *Consumer Behavior. Theory and Application.* Boston: Allyn & Bacon, 1974.
Green, E. Paul, "Consumer Use of Information," in J. W. Newman (ed.), *On Knowing the Consumer.* New York: Wiley & Sons Inc., 1966.
Grønhaug, Kjell, "Utdannelse og kjøperatferd (Education and Consumer Behaviour)." *Tidsskrift f. samfunnsforskning* 1972, bd. 13.
Hansen, Fleming, *Consumer Choice Behaviour. A Cognitive Theory.* New York & London: The Free Press/McMillan, 1972.
Hovland, Carl J., Janis, Irving L., and Kelley, Harold H., *Communication and Persuasion.* New Haven: Yale University Press, 1953.
Howard, A. John, and Sheth, Jagdish N., *The Theory of Buyer Behavior.* New York: John Wiley & Sons Inc., 1969.
Irwin, F. W., and Smith, W. S., "Value, Cost and Information as Determiners of Decisions." *Journal of Experimental Psychology,* No. 54 (1957).
Katz, Elihu, Blumler, Jay G., and Gurevitch, Michael, "Utilization of Mass Communication by the Individual." Paper Prepared for Conference on Directions in Mass Communication Research. New York: Arden House, (May 1973).
Klapper, Joseph T., *The Effects of Mass Communication.* New York: The Free Press of Glencoe, 1963.
Kleberg, Madeleine, "Den potentielle publiken i Sveriges Radio (Potential Audience of the Swedish Broadcasting Corporation)." 1972.
Lanzetta, T. John, and Kanereff, Vera, "Information Cost, Amount of Payoff and Level of Aspiration as Determinants of Information Seeking." *Behavioral Science* 7 (1962).
Lundberg, Dan, *Medietrovärdighet och informationsanvändning. Ett experiment rörande informationsfunktionens betydelse för trovärdighetseffekter (Media Credibility and Application of Information).* The Economic Research Institute of the Business School of Stockholm, 1973.
Lundberg, Dan, och Hultén, Olof, *Individen och massmedia. (The Individual and Mass Media).* Stockholm: Norsted & Söner Förlag, 1968.
Maloney, C. Jacoby, "Is Advertising Believability Really Important?" *Journal of Marketing* (Oct. 1963).
McQuail, Denis (ed.), *Sociology of Mass Communication.* Harmondsworth: Penguin, 1972.
McQuail, Denis, Blumler, Jay G., and Brown, J. R., "The Television Audience: A Revised Perspec-

tive," in D. McQuail (ed.), *Sociology of Mass Communication*. Harmondsworth: Penguin, 1972.

Miller, G. A., "What is Information Measurement?" *American Psychologist* 8 (1953): 3-11.

Munk, Jens Kristian, "Anvendelse og forbrug af massemedier (Application and Consumption of Mass Media)." Unpublished dissertation, Copenhagen, 1976.

Newman, W. Joseph (ed.), *On Knowing the Consumer*, New York: Wiley & Sons Inc., 1966.

Nicosia, Francesco, *Consumer Decision Processes*. Englewood Cliffs, N.J.: Prentice-Hall Inc., 1966.

Ottesen, Otto, "The Response Function: A Theory of the Short Run Effect of Repetition of a Marketing Communication Message—Exemplified by Advertising," in E. Berg et al., *Current Theories in Scandinavian Mass Communication Research*. Grenaa: GMT, 1977.

Pruitt, D. G., "An Exploratory Study of Individual Differences in Sequential Decision Making." Unpublished Doctoral Dissertation, Yale, 1957.

Rosvoll, Berit, "Hvem leser ukeblad i Norge? Sociale faktorer og ukebladslesning. (The Audience of Weeklies in Norway. Social Factors and the Reading of Weeklies)." Institute of Press Research and Communication, University of Oslo, Paper No. 15, 1970.

Samuelson, M., Carter, R. F., and Ruggels, L., "Education, Available Time and Use of Mass Media." *Journalism Quarterly* (1963).

Schramm, Wilbur, "How Communication Works," in Wilbur Schramm (ed.), *The Process and Effects of Mass Communication*. Urbana: University of Illinois Press, 1954.

Schramm, Wilbur, "Information Theory and Mass Communication." *Journalism Quarterly* 17 (Spring 1955).

Schramm, Wilbur, "The Nature of News." *Journalism Quarterly*, No. 26 (1949): 259-69.

Schramm, Wilbur (ed.), *The Process and Effects of Mass Communication*. Urbana: University of Illinois Press, 1954.

Sears, D. O., and Freedman, J. L., "Selective Exposure to Information—A Critical Review." *Public Opinion Quarterly*, No. 31 (1967).

Sepstrup, Preben, "En studie af forbrugernes anvendelse af information i købsprocessen. (A Study of the Application of Information by the Consumers in the Buying Process)." Ph.D. dissertation, Institute of Marketing, The Aarhus School of Business Administration, Economics & Modern Languages, 1971.

Sepstrup, Preben, "Forbrugernes anvendelse af information. (The Consumers' Application of Information). "Paper prepared for the Conference on the Consumer's Role in Modern Society, Aalborg, 1976.

Sepstrup, Preben, *Individets erhvervelse af information—en empirisk analyse og en revideret model. (The individual's acquisition of information—empirical analysis and revised model)*. Aarhus: Institute of Marketing, 1973.

Sepstrup, Preben, *Måling af forbrugernes informationslager—en laboratorieundersøgelse. (Measurement of Actual Knowledge—Laboratory Experiment)*. Aarhus: Institute of Marketing, 1972.

Shannon, C. E., and Weaver, Warren, *The Mathematical Theory of Communication*. Urbana, 1949.

Sheth, N. Jagdish, *Models of Buyer Behavior. Conceptual, Quantitative, and Empirical*. New York: Harper & Row, 1974.

Staelin, Richard, and Newman, Joseph W., "Prepurchase Information Seeking for New Cars and Major Household Appliances." *Journal of Marketing Research* IX (Aug. 1972).

Stigler, J. George, "The Economics of Information." *Journal of Political Economy* (June 1961).

Strumpel, Burkhard, Morgan, James N., and Yahn, Ernest, *Human Behaviour in Economic Affairs*. New York: Elsevier Scientific Publishing Company, 1972.

Sveriges Radio (ed.), *Radio och tv möter publiken. (Radio and Television Meet the Audience)*. Stockholm: The Swedish Broadcasting Corporation, 1972.

Theil, H., *Economics and Information Theory*. Amsterdam: North Holland Publishing Co., 1967.

Thorelli, B. Hans, "Concentration of Information Power among Consumers." *Journal of Marketing Research* VIII (Nov. 1971).

Tipton, P. Leonard, "Effects of Writing Tasks on Utility of Information and Order of Seeking." *Journalism Quarterly,* No. 47 (1970).

Westley, H. Bruce, and Severin, Werner J., "Correlates of Media Credibility." *Journalism Quarterly* 41 (1964).

Wikmann, Anders, "Alternativa kvällsaktiviteter. (Alternative Evening Activities)." PUB/SR-35/74, Swedish Broadcasting Corporation, 1974.

WHAT CAN BE DONE ABOUT INTERVIEWER BIAS?

Donald S. Tull, UNIVERSITY OF OREGON

Larry E. Richards, UNIVERSITY OF OREGON

The effects of interviewers in biasing measurements obtained from respondents has been a recognized problem in conducting surveys since the classic study by Rice in 1929 (Rice, 1929). In that study two interviewers, one a prohibitionist and the other a socialist, were used to obtain data from homeless men in the Bowery in New York City. Rice found that the majority of the men interviewed by the prohibitionist reported that their difficulties were caused by liquor, while the downfall of those interviewed by the socialist was reported to be the result of industrial factors.

Bias can be caused by the interviewer by a variety of means. The interviewer is an important determinant of the refusal rate and so influences the biases arising from that source. Many respondents try subconsciously to please the interviewer by giving the response they think he or she "desires." The age, race, sex, and appearance of the interviewer may be taken as cues for "desired" responses, as well as his or her verbal and nonverbal behavior while the interview is being con-

Research in Marketing, Volume 3, pages 143–162

ducted. The interviewer may be an important determinant of how much of an effort the informant makes to remember or to determine otherwise the correct answers to questions. Interviewers may ask questions in such a way that they are
misunderstood. They may misinterpet responses or make consistent recording errors. All too frequently, biases are introduced by interviewers systematically
filling in information for items or entire questionnaires without benefit of having
obtained it from respondents.

While research findings suggest that interviewer-related variables are less
powerful than task variables (such as question form and question threat) in
causing response effects (Sudman and Bradburn, 1974). interviewers as a source
of response effects remain a significant problem. In the reinterview program
conducted by the Bureau of the Census on the Current Population Survey sample
respondents, for example, it was found that over an eight-year period, between
24 and 31 percent of the differences between the original and reinterview responses were errors chargeable to the original interviewer (U.S. Bureau of the
Census, 1968b).

A number of remedies have been developed for dealing with interviewer bias.
They can be categorized as falling within the general strategies of *designing to
avoid* bias induced by interviewers, and *ignoring, estimating,* or *measuring* the
bias that is present.

A brief discussion of these strategies follows. The major part of the chapter,
however, is devoted to a proposed method of measuring relative interviewer bias
and its application to data to which simulated biases have been added.

STRATEGIES FOR DEALING WITH INTERVIEWER BIAS: DESIGNING TO AVOID BIAS FROM INTERVIEWERS

The approaches that can be taken to reduce interviewer bias through design of the
survey include (1) designing to avoid interviewing, (2) designing the interviewing situation to minimize interviewer effects, (3) designing the sampling procedure to eliminate interviewer choice of respondents, (4) using a corroborative
design, (5) employing careful selection, training, and control procedures for
interviewers, (6) matching of interviewer and respondent characteristics, and (7)
selecting interviewers to produce compensating biases.

1. Avoiding Interviewer Bias by Avoiding Interviewing

The obvious first step in designing a study to avoid interviewer bias is to
consider whether interviewers should be used at all. Following an experiment to
determine interviewer effects in the 1950 censuses of population and housing, for
example, the Bureau of the Census was "greatly influenced" to introduce the use
of self-enumeration on a widespread basis in the 1960 census. A large scale
experiment was later conducted to evaluate self-enumeration effects in the 1960
censuses. The results of that study showed that the level of variability of re-

sponses was reduced to about one-fourth of the 1950 level (U.S. Bureau of the Census, 1968a).

Some studies have been designed to use interviewers to obtain part of the information desired and to have them leave a second questionnaire that is to be completed later by the respondent and mailed back. Interviews may be used for those questions where it would otherwise not be clear as to what constitutes an adequate response, but not used to ask sensitive questions where their presence might be a source of bias.

In one study, however, it was found that for a design of this type, interviewer effects carried over into the responses to the self-enumeration questionnaire. The study was concerned with the accuracy with which hospitalizations were reported. It was designed in such a way that interviewers were asked to obtain information on demographic characteristics, illnesses, other health related events, and hospitalizations for the past year from some respondents, and the same information except hospitalizations from others. The second group of respondents were asked to provide information on hospitalizations for the past year on a self-enumeration form provided them. It was found that those interviewers whose respondents had high underreporting rates in the interview tended to be those whose respondents had high underreporting of hospitalizations on the self-enumeration forms (Cannel and Fowler, 1964).

2. Design of the Interviewing Situation to Minimize Interviewer Effects

When it is necessary to use interviewers, the extent of the variance and bias they introduce can be reduced through the way the interview is designed. Some of the design features that, other factors being equal, will reduce bias due to the interviewer are the use of (1) structured rather than unstructured questionnaires (Cannell, 1954), (2) direct rather than indirect interviews (Human, 1954), (3) dichotomous or multiple choice rather than open-end questions (Collins, 1970; Guest, 1947; Sudman and Bradburn, 1974), (4) techniques with which the interviewer has experience, rather than new ones (Lansing, Ginsberg, and Braaten, 1961), (5) the randomized responses technique for sensitive questions (Campbell and Joiner, 1973), (6) avoiding disclosure to the interviewers of the hypotheses underlying the study (Rosenthal, 1976).

It will be recognized, of course, that these methods have effects on response that are unrelated to the interviewer. The method chosen should be the one that gives the best data overall.

3. Design of the Sampling Procedure to Eliminate Interviewer Choice of Respondents

The use of probability samples to eliminate selection biases is so well known that it does not need elaboration here. However, even when a probability sample of households is taken, the choice of respondents within the households is sometimes left to the interviewer. Such a procedure can lead to bias (Kish, 1949) and should be avoided when it is possible to do so.

4. Corroborative Designs

Choosing among candidate designs involves trade-off decisions concerning errors as well as time and cost considerations. For example, using a mail questionnaire will eliminate interviewer bias, but it will probably do so at the expense of substantially increasing nonresponse biases.

Webb and others have suggested using multiple designs in the same study as a means of dealing with nonsampling errors (Webb et al., 1966). They advocate using at least three different approaches to obtaining data on the same variable, or attributes. For example, a mail questionnaire, personal interviews, and observation might each be used in a particular study. If at least two of the three measurements are close enough to tend to corroborate each other, one can feel more confidence in the validity of the results than if only a single design had been used. Depending upon which measurements tended to corroborate each other, one might conclude either that interviewer bias was not a problem, or that it could be a problem for that measurement.

5. Selection, Training, and Control of Interviewers

If interviewers are to be used, it would seem apparent that the selecting promising interviewers, training them well, and supervising them carefully is one way of reducing interviewer effects.

Much has been written about each of these aspects of dealing with interviewers. (See, for example, Barioux, 1952; Boyd and Westfall, 1965; Case, 1971; Hansen and Steinberg, 1956; Hanson and Marks, 1958; Hyman, 1955; Ito, 1963; Kahn and Cannell, 1957; Parten, 1966; Sellitz et al., 1976; Sheatsley, 1951.) One would expect, however, that beyond a certain point the care exercised in selecting, training, and supervising interviewers contributes little to reducing interviewer effects. There is some empirical evidence to support this belief (Schyberger, 1967). Less investigation has been done on the relationship of extent of training and of supervision of interviewers to their performance than one would expect, however.

6. Matching of Interviewer and Respondent Characteristics

A finding reported in a large number of studies is that age, sex, race, and social class of interviewer can effect responses. (See, for example, Athey et al., 1960; Benny, Riesman, and Star, 1956; Colombotos, Elinson, and Loewenstein, 1968; Ehrlich and Riesman, 1961; Harding, 1947; Hatchett and Schuman, 1975/1976; Lenski and Legget, 1960; Schuman and Converse, 1971; Sudman and Bradburn, 1974; Trent, 1954.) It has therefore been suggested that interviewers be matched in the characteristics with the respondents they are assigned to interview.

After a careful review of the literature bearing on this issue, Sudman and Bradburn are unconvinced of the efficacy of matching as a means of reducing interviewer effects. They conclude that "... matching of interviewers has no effect on response unless the issues are highly related to the respondent and interviewer characteristics" (Sudman and Bradburn, 1974, p. 138), and that "... the best alternative would be to measure response effects by designing the survey such that respondent and interviewer characteristics are both matched and unmatched in random subsamples of the total sample" (p. 139).

7. Selection of Interviewers to Produce Compensating Biases

Parten (1966) and others have suggested that interviewers of both sexes of differing ages and with a range of views on the subject of the interview should be selected to produce compensating biases. In the late forties, it was believed that the use of predominantly middle class women of thirty to fifty years of age as interviewers was producing a favorable bias for Republican candidates in political polls. There has since been some effort by pollsters to reduce this source of bias by selecting interviewers of both sexes over a wider age range (and with roughly the same proportions being inclined toward voting for the Democratic and Republican candidates). (Even so, it is reported that some ninety percent of interviewers for pollsters are still women.)

IGNORING INTERVIEWER BIAS

The most common strategies for dealing with interviewer bias are, no doubt, to use one or more of the design features just discussed to reduce it and to ignore the unknown amount of bias that occurs despite the attempt(s) to avoid it.

As unscientific and ostrich-like as it may seem, the strategy of ignoring the interviewer biases that are present may not be a bad one when applied discriminately. There is a surprising degree of insensitivity of confidence level to bias. If the amount of bias is equal to one-fourth the standard error of the sampling distribution, for example, a bias-free confidence level of 95 percent erodes to only 94.1 percent. An increase in the bias present to one-half that of the standard error results in a reduction of the confidence level to only 92.1 percent. Beyond this point, however, the confidence level deteriorates rapidly. The relationship between confidence level and bias is shown in Figure 1.

The strategy of ignoring the interviewer bias present therefore becomes a viable one when it is judged to be relatively small when compared to the standard error of the sampling distribution. As sample size increases, the standard error decreases and the extent of the bias is unaffected. Thus, interviewer bias be-

Figure 1. Effects of Bias (From Interviewers or Other Sources) on 95% Confidence Level

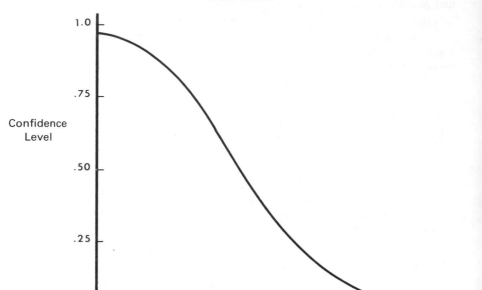

Bias Expressed as Number of Standard Errors

Source: Tull, D. S., and Albaum, G. S., *Survey Research: A Decisional Approach,* p. 67. New York: Intext Press, Inc., 1973.

comes relatively more important as sample size increases inasmuch as it results in greater distortion of confidence intervals and the results of hypothesis tests.

SUBJECTIVE ESTIMATION OF INTERVIEWER BIAS

The suggestion just made that the interviewer bias can be safely ignored if it is judged to be of a tolerable size indicates that estimation of a maximum level of the bias present is a necessary element of that strategy. We can extend the use of estimation beyond the decision of whether or not to ignore the bias; a subject estimate of the interviewer bias present can be used to adjust the data.

An example could be that of a pollster in the late forties who observed a continuing bias favorable to Republican candidates of two to three percentage points which was believed to be due to the age, dress, manner, and political leanings of interviewers. If he/she believed that such a bias were present in the (then) latest poll, an adjustment could have been made to the sample proportions of respondents reporting favoring the candidates of each party.

Brown (1969) and Mayer (1970) have been the chief advocates of such a strategy for nonsampling errors. They recommended that subjective estimates be made for nonsampling variable and systematic errors (including interviewer bias) and provide a scheme for incorporating them into a summary estimate of the nonsampling errors present.

There is much to recommend such a strategy when the measuring of nonsampling errors is not possible for economic or methodological reasons. Ignoring unmeasured nonsampling errors when they may be of a size beyond that which is tolerable places the burden of estimating the extent of the errors on the user of the information. He/she cannot possibly know as much about the circumstances under which the study was conducted as does the researcher and thus is almost certain to be less well equipped than the researcher to make such estimates. It would seem that the report of every empirical study should include estimates of the unmeasured nonsampling errors present, even if the estimates are presented in an appendix.

As desirable as the estimation of nonsampling errors in general, and interviewer bias in particular, may be, however, we have yet to see an instance of it being done in practice. This is no doubt due to the tenuous nature of making such estimates and to the tradition that research findings should be investigator-independent.

MEASUREMENT OF INTERVIEWER BIAS

The total mean square error of a survey measurement can be defined as consisting of the following components (Kallek, Nisselson, and Sturdevant, 1975):

$$\text{MSE(X)} = \text{sampling variance} + \text{nonsampling variance} + \\ \text{interaction between sampling and nonsampling deviations} \\ + (\text{bias})^2$$

This bias term is a collective for biases due to the questionnaire, the respondent, the interviewer, and those arising from the editing, coding, and tabulation of the data.

In order to measure interviewer bias, therefore, one must devise a method which permits eliminating the effects of the sampling and nonsampling variances (and the interaction between the two) and those due to questionnaires, the respondent, and data processing. There are two general methods of doing this. The first is to compare, for each interviewer, the recorded and the "true" values for a variable or an attribute, where the "true" value has been obtained from respondent reports. The second method is to use an experimental design in which each interviewer is considered to be a separate treatment.

1. Measurement by Comparison of Recorded and "True" Values

In this method of measurement, it is important that the "true" value be obtained from respondent reports. This permits the assumptions that the sampling and nonsampling variances individually balance out (the expectation of each is zero) and that the questionnaire, respondent, and data processing biases are present in the recorded and "true" values to the same degree. Given these assumptions, and the validity of the model for mean square error presented above, the difference between the recorded and "true" values for a sample of respondents interviewed by the same person is a measure of the bias induced by that interviewer.

"True" values for a measurement of interviewer bias by this method can be obtained in some instances from another survey conducted to obtain the same information and believed to have been done with little or no (or at least less) interviewer bias. (See, for example, Fay, 1975.) A more widely applicable method is to use better trained and more competent interviewers to reinterview a subsample of the respondents to the original survey (U.S. Bureau of the Census, 1975, 1968b).

There are some obvious problems with each of these methods of obtaining "true" values. Other surveys taken to obtain the same data are seldom available. If they were, and it was believed that the data from them were more accurate, the current survey would usually not have been necessary in the first place. Reinterviewing is expensive (the U.S. Bureau of the Census reports that its reinterviews cost up to seven times as much per interview as the original ones) and time consuming. Both methods, furthermore, share the problems of not providing an actual value for the comparison: at best, a measurement is obtained of the difference in bias between two interviewers.

2. Measurement by Experiment

A true experimental design for measuring interviewer bias requires, among other things, that either interviewers (treatments) be assigned to matched sets of respondents (subjects), or else that they be assigned randomly to respondents. Given the difficulties of insuring that sets of respondents are matched, the usual procedure is to make random assignments of interviewers whenever a true experimental design is used. This is known as an *interpenetrating subsample* design (Mahalanobis, 1946).

The interpenetrating subsample design requires that two or more interviewers conduct interviews on randomly selected subsamples or respondents from the population or the same subpopulations. *Fully interpenetrating subsamples* result when the subsamples of respondents assigned to each interviewer are drawn from the entire population. The use of a fully interpenetrating design is relatively inexpensive where the interviewers are graduate students and the respondents are undergraduate students in one or more of his or her classes. It is not inexpensive, however, when the interviewers are paid professionals and the respondents are from a sample taken from the entire country, state, or even a city, unless the interviews are to be conducted by telephone. (A fully interpenetrating subsample design used to measure interviewer bias in a telephone survey is described in Benson, 1969.)

It is not unusual to find examples of *partially interpenetrating subsamples* in practice, however. Such a design results when interviewers are assigned randomly to respondents within specified geographic areas, and the areas of two or more interviewers are designed deliberately to overlap.

An example of a partially interpenetrating subsample design is the one used by The Gallup Organization. Approximately 300 sampling locations are used in each national survey. When appropriate, the sampling locations are designed to overlap and different interviewers are used to interview randomly selected respondents within the same geographic area (Tull and Hawkins, 1976, pp. 175–176). (See Bailer, Bailey, and Stevens, 1977, and McKenzie, 1977, for other examples).

Even more common are *quasi-interpenetrating subsample* designs. Such a design occurs when a nonrandom (usually purposive) assignment of interviewers is made to respondents, but the assumption is made that the resulting assignments are indistinguishable in effects from those that would have occurred had the assignment been random. F values are then calculated for an analysis of variance for each of the major variables recorded by each interviewer for his or her set of respondents to test for the presence of bias (Cannell and Fowler, 1964, is an example). As pointed out by Kish (1962), this procedure in general results in an overestimate of interviewer bias.

The procedures discussed thus far for measuring interviewer bias, either by comparison with an externally determined "true" value or by experimental means, are generally not satisfactory due to reasons of expense or inaccuracy, or both. In the following section, we describe an alternative measurement procedure which is simple, inexpensive, and, judging from the results of the simulations in which it is used, promises to provide useful results in many sample survey situations.

MEASUREMENT OF RELATIVE INTERVIEWER BIAS

Suppose that one were fortunate enough to have the following set of conditions for a sample survey: (1) the variable of interest is perfectly correlated ($R^2 = 1.0$) with one or more predictor variables; (2) the values for the predictor variables are obtainable from the survey with no bias or variable error; and (3) the equation for the relationship between the variate of interest (the criterion variable) and the predictor variable(s) is known.

In such a situation, one would have a choice of two methods of obtaining information on the values for the criterion variable. One could obtain the values for the perfectly correlated predictor variable(s) and calculate the corresponding values for the criterion variable, or one could ask the respondents directly for the values of the criterion variable.

Suppose, however, that the responses concerning the values for the criterion variable are subject to interviewer and other biases, and to variable errors. The differences for each respondent between the recorded value (x_i) and the true value

(y_i) obtained from the known relationship with the predictor variable would be a measure of the algebraic sum of all biases and variable errors.

The mean of the sample values for the criterion variable obtained from using the known relationship with the predictor variable(s) would provide an unbiased estimate of the true population mean, μ_y. Unless there are counterbalancing biases, the mean of recorded values, μ_x, would not equal μ_y, the mean of the criterion variable.

So far as interviewer biases are concerned, the typical case is that they are not counterbalancing. In such case, $\mu_x = \mu_y$ and we cannot estimate $\mu_x - \mu_y$ solely based upon the sample data. Moreover, one must realize there are several components to the mean square error of an estimator. In our notation:

$$\text{MSE}(\bar{x}) = \text{var}(\bar{x}) + (\mu_x - \mu_y)^2.$$

If interviewers were homogeneous, equal biases, var $(\bar{x})$ would equal var$(\bar{y})$. But if the interviewers are heterogeneous, unequal biases, var$(\bar{x})$ will exceed var$(\bar{y})$, thus inflating MSE$(\bar{x})$. Since we can, we really should estimate the between-interviewer biases, or what we call *relative* bias.

If we let μ_{xi} denote the mean response interviewer i would obtain if he or she were to take a census of the finite population, the relative bias for interviewer i would be $\mu_{xi} - \mu_x$. Realizing that μ_x represents the average of all μ_{xi}-s, estimates of relative bias coupled with judgmental evaluation of the degree of counterbalancing interviewer biases could allow a researcher to estimate interviewer bias $(\mu_x - \mu_y)$ and perhaps reduce it by reducing relative bias. If, given the type, number, and amount of training of the interviewers, the researcher expects the interviewer biases approximately to counterbalance, then μ_x μ_y, and the overall effect of interviewer bias would be small. However, such biases will inflate the variance of the sampling distribution of the estimator of μ_x. If the relative biases can be adequately estimated, data revision could reduce the variance of the estimator, yielding more precise estimates.

We will examine two alternative approaches to estimating relative interviewer bias. We assume M interviewers, where M $>$ 2, and that each interviewer obtains more than one observation.

1. Estimation of Relative Interviewer Bias Using Interpenetrating Subsamples

With interpenetrating subsamples, we can calculate the mean response for each interviewer, $\bar{x}_i$, i = 1, 2, . . . , M. By weighing each $\bar{x}_i$ by its sample size and dividing the sum by the total number of sample observations, we obtain $\bar{x}$, and estimate of μ_x. It follows that $(\bar{x}_i - \bar{x}_i)$ is the estimate of the relative bias for interviewer i. If indeed subjects were randomly selected and randomly allocated to interviewers, and the response rate was 100 percent, $(\bar{x}_i - \bar{x})$ would provide us with an unbiased estimate of the relative bias for interviewer i. Recognizing that such conditions rarely if ever hold, this estimate is more than likely itself biased.

If the sampling design calls for some degree of clustering, be it single or multi-stage, we could expect $(\bar{x}_i - \bar{x})$ to include not only interviewer bias but also an inherent difference between the allocated subjects and the mean of the characteristic for all sampled subjects. Such inherent differences would be represented in the variance of the resulting $\bar{x}_i$'s, which would in turn inflate the variance of the appropriate estimator.

As an alternative approach to estimating relative interviewer biases, we propose a regression procedure.

2. Estimate of Relative Interviewer Bias Using Regression

The primary objective of the proposed technique is to account for inherent differences between subjects to estimate better relative interviewer biases. The procedure is to regress, via least squares, any and all variables believed to be related to the potentially biased quantitative characteristic. We would want to use any (quantitative or qualitative) variates that are believed to be independent of the interviewer bias on the characteristic of interest. If a variate is used that is correlated with the interviewer bias, the relative interviewer bias will be explained by the regression and therefore be masked, given the proposed procedure. The fit regression

$$\hat{y} = b_0 + b_1X_1 + b_2X_2 + \ldots b_kX_k$$

will provide an estimate of that portion of the potentially biased characteristic that can be explained by the predictor variates. The remainder, or residual ($y_i - \hat{y}$), would encompass both error in the regression model and relative interviewer bias. As the residuals will have a mean of zero, the mean of the residuals for interviewer i is an estimate of his or her relative bias.

Thus, the proposed procedure is to compute the mean residual for each interviewer and adopt these values as estimates of the relative interviewer biases.

COMPARISON OF PROCEDURES

In order to compare and contrast the above two procedures, two separate analyses were performed.

The first analysis utilized 1500 case observations on personal loan applications. The decision was made to add an interviewer bias component to the criterion variate, monthly take-home pay. Thirty cases were arbitrarily (not randomly) assigned to each of fifty hypothetical interviewers. Each "interviewer" was then assigned a bias for reported monthly take-home pay. The distribution of simulated interviewer biases was essentially uniform and ranged from -5% to $+5\%$.

The biased monthly take-home pay was then regressed on a set of variates believed to be related to actual monthly take-home pay such as age, occupation, number of dependents, and number of years on present job. The regression yielded an R^2 value of 0.8378. Table 1 shows the comparative results of the two methods. The second column represents the actual relative bias for each of the fifty interviewers. Note, these are the parameters we seek to estimate. Columns three and four give estimates of the corresponding actual relative biases based upon the interpenetrating and regression methods, respectivley.

Table 1. Comparison of Interpenetrating and
Regression Methods of Estimating Relative
Interviewer Biases for Personal Loan Data

Interviewer	Actual Rel. Bias	Int.	Reg.
1	14.75	101.07	15.37
2	19.18	− 68.86	10.99
3	−11.18	−103.89	−19.53
4	−10.68	90.71	6.90
5	−14.35	68.14	−13.32
6	− 9.18	75.97	− 9.98
7	18.98	− 47.19	19.14
8	−20.98	= 34.83	−25.36
9	−13.85	− 16.96	−16.60
10	21.62	88.81	38.57
11	13.82	36.47	11.99
12	19.95	− 52.69	12.16
13	−22.15	− 14.63	−25.15
14	24.92	143.77	26.66
15	− 4.48	51.47	− 6.14
16	22.68	94.51	20.68
17	− 9.52	55.67	− 8.97
18	15.02	− 15.29	12.92
19	4.78	− 0.49	5.11
20	−20.88	21.13	−19.58
21	4.25	21.19	5.25
22	0.15	− 33.03	6.08
23	17.67	28.41	16.26
24	9.05	23.67	10.00
25	−14.32	36.57	−13.46
26	−14.52	−117.69	−12.79
27	4.42	− 38.56	4.65
28	−14.22	− 72.56	−13.25
29	8.32	− 50.46	6.71
30	− 5.05	32.37	− 6.08
31	16.85	− 59.59	16.26
32	4.38	− 40.03	3.38
33	− 3.95	− 58.29	−10.02
34	−17.78	−129.69	−29.55
35	4.88	−207.69	13.70
36	− 2.52	−214.99	−14.62
37	−18.55	− 20.33	−16.71

Table 1. (continued)

38	20.58	255.14	19.81
39	−34.05	352.37	−33.24
40	25.47	405.54	22.92
41	18.18	− 2.26	16.78
42	− 8.72	− 35.49	− 8.38
43	− 8.88	− 31.03	− 8.51
44	10.18	44.31	12.92
45	21.42	85.37	19.60
46	− 4.25	− 19.56	− 6.26
47	−10.42	−129.96	− 8.55
48	10.58	−111.43	9.91
49	6.88	−123.13	6.24
50	−16.35	−157.66	−16.24

We can see that in only two instances (interviewer 20 and 37) is the quasi-interpenetrating method superior to the regression method. Thus, given this particular situation, the regression procedure is indeed the superior of the two methods of estimating relative interviewer biases. If we were to modify the sample data by subtracting the regression estimate of relative interviewer biases from the appropriate cases or observations, there are only four interviewers for which the modification would detract (interviewers 22, 33, 35, and 36). Note that all four of these interviewers have "small" actual relative biases. In the aggregate, the modification of survey data via regression estimates of relative interviewer biases would yield a substantial improvement in the precision of the estimate of μ_x. We would be replacing the actual relative biases, which have a variance of 236.1, with actual relative biases minus their regression estimate. These differences have a variance of 20.2, which is less than 1/10th that of the relative interviewer biases.

Recall that it is the mean square error (MSE) that we hope to reduce, where

$$\text{MSE} = \text{var } \bar{X} + (\mu_x - \mu_y)^2.$$

In the above simulation, var $\bar{X}$ components would be substantially reduced by using the proposed regression procedure.

There are really three reasons why the proposed regression procedure was so effective. First, we were able to identify predictor variates that collectively were highly correlated with actual monthly take-home pay. This was evidenced by the relatively large R^2 value. Clearly, the larger the R^2 value, the greater is our ability to explain inherent differences of subjects, thus the greater our ability to detect and estimate relative interviewer biases.

Second, the predictor variates were uncorrelated with the interviewer biases. Had the auxiliary variates been correlated with the relative interviewer biases, such biases would have been explained by the regression and we would not have been able to detect them.

Third, the cases were not randomly assigned to interviewers and, although not contrived, some degree of clustering existed in the data. This is evidenced by the fact that interpenetrating estimates ranged from a low of -214.99 to a high of 405.54, which suggests that some interviewers were assigned cases with relatively small monthly take-home pay while others were assigned cases with substantial monthly take-home pay.

The second analysis was performed on 6,900 observations from the Public Use Samples of Basic Records, 1970 census. This analysis was performed in order to examine the properties of the proposed regression technique under "less favorable" conditions. Two hundred thirty sequential cases, which certainly includes a clustering effect, were assigned to each of thirty hypothetical interviewers. Annual household income was chosen as the variable of interest and a variety of demographic variables were used as the predictor variables. Each of the thirty interviewers was assigned a bias component that ranged from $-\$4,300$ to $+\$4,900$. The assigned biases are shown in Table 2.

As the number of observations per interviewer was held constant and the mean of the assigned biases was $+\$487$, the actual relative bias per interviewer was equal to the difference between the interviewer bias and \$487.

Table 3 shows both actual relative interviewer bias and the corresponding regression estimates. In this case, R^2 for the regression was only 0.33. Note that in only three instances (interviewers 4, 6, and 21) would the proposed modification yield an increase in the relative bias. And we can see that this occurred in cases where the actual relative biases were small.

By the proposed modification, we would be replacing the actual relative bias by the difference between the actual relative bias and the regression estimate of it. In this simulation, the values for these components of variance were, respectively, 8,199,810 and 332,017. This substitution translates into a 95.95 percent reduction. Again this reduction would directly affect the magnitude of var $\bar{X}$, the variance component of MSE.

Although the strength of the regression was fairly low, $R^2 = 0.33$, the proposed technique for estimating and reducing relative interviewer bias was quite effective. This was partially a result of the relatively large sample size per "interviewer." While in the first analysis "interviewers" were assigned thirty observations, in this analysis each "interviewer" was assigned 230 observations.

Clearly, the relative magnitude of interviewer biases, the sample size per interviewer, and the strength of the regression all affect our ability to detect and estimate relative interviewer biases. Therefore, the performance of the proposed technique is dependent on all three of these factors. However, it is worth noting that the one contributing factor under the control of the researcher, sample size, can compensate for either of the other two.

Note that to this point the suspect variable (the one believed to be potentially biased) has been quantitative. Qualitative variables could of course also be biased by the interviewers.

Table 2. Biases Assigned to Hypothetical
Interviewers in Public Use Sample Data Simulation

Interviewer	Bias
1	800
2	0
3	2700
4	1000
5	− 100
6	600
7	4700
8	−4000
9	−4300
10	4900
11	200
12	−4100
13	3000
14	− 900
15	3400
16	400
17	4600
18	2700
19	−2100
20	1200
21	0
22	3300
23	− 800
24	−1300
25	2700
26	−4200
27	−1100
28	4200
29	3300
30	−3800

If we restrict our discussion to dichotomous qualitative variables, our problem remains basically the same as that for quantitative variables. That is, the reported sample proportion per interviewer can be viewed as the mean of a dichotomous quantitative variable which can assume only the values zero or one. We can then again regress the potentially biased qualitative variable on any and all variables believed to contain information relative to whether the element does or does not possess the given characteristic. The quantitative variable in question would be coded as 1 if the element were recorded as possessing the characteristic and 0 if it were not. In this case, the predicted value for the dependent variable would be an estimate of the probability that the given element was indeed a 1 (possessed the specified characteristics). The regression is performed in order to estimate and thus isolate the inherent differences in elements or subjects in order to detect more accurately relative interviewer biases.

Table 3.   Evaluation of the Regression Estimation of Relative Interviewer Biases and Proposed Modification for Public Use Sample Data

Interviewer	Actual Relative Bias	Reg. Est. of Rel. Bias	ARB-RERB
1	313	497	− 184
2	− 487	− 506	+ 19
3	2213	2030	183
4	513	1169	− 656
5	− 587	− 612	25
6	113	95	208
7	4213	3549	664
8	−4487	−5063	576
9	−4787	−4372	− 415
10	4413	4692	− 279
11	− 287	− 131	− 156
12	−4587	−3619	− 968
13	2513	3694	−1181
14	−1387	−1396	9
15	2913	2076	837
16	− 87	− 99	12
17	4113	3288	825
18	2213	2336	− 123
19	−2587	−1508	−1079
20	−1687	−2567	880
21	− 487	−1359	872
22	2813	2343	470
23	−1287	−2039	752
24	−1787	−2224	437
25	2213	2533	− 320
26	−4687	−4830	143
27	−1587	−1210	− 377
28	3713	4047	− 334
29	2813	3033	− 220
30	−4287	−3828	− 459

The residuals again contain both error and relative interviewer bias. Under the assumption that the error term in the regression model has mean zero, the average of the residuals for those observations reported by a specific interviewer would be an estimate of that interviewer's relative bias.

Therefore, the proposal is to modify the reported proportions for the M interviewers by subtracting the mean residual for interviewer i from his or her reported sample proportion. The only real difference in the case where the potentially biased variable is qualitative rather than quantitative is that the R^2 value will be relatively small, given the dichotomous dependent variable. This will in turn necessitate a larger sample size per interviewer in order to obtain a specific level of efficiency.

IMPLICATIONS OF THE REGRESSION PROCEDURE

The objective of this research has been to derive estimates of the relative interviewer biases. There are several implications of this procedure.

1. *The estimated relative interviewer biases can help in implementing the measurement strategy technique of reinterviewing by indicating to the researcher the potential outlines within the set of interviewers.* When a reinterviewing program is being contemplated, the regression estimates may be very useful in helping to identify the respondents of which interviewers need to be reinterviewed. From the results of the two simulations, the regression procedure is clearly superior to the quasi-interpenetrating subsample method for this purpose.

2. *Knowledge of the estimated relative interviewer biases may help in implementing the strategy of subjectively estimating the bias.* The variance of the estimated relative interviewer biases will provide an indication of the homogeneity or heterogeneity of interviewers. Given the survey variables and the experience and training of the interviewers, the researcher may be able to formulate a better judgment of the magnitude of $\mu_x - \mu_y$.

3. *The proposed regression procedure gives the researcher the option of adjusting the data by algebraically subtracting each interviewer's estimated relative bias.* The effect is to convert the x_{ij} values into $(x_{if} - (b_j - \hat{\mu}_b))$ values. Under the condition that each interviewer obtains the same number of responses, the average value of $(b_j - \hat{\mu}_b)$ will be zero. Thus, the mean of x_{ij} will equal the mean of $(x_{ij} - (b_j - \hat{\mu}_b))$ and the point estimate of $\hat{\mu}_y$ will not change.

However, under certain conditons, the variance of $(x_{ij} - (b_j - \hat{\mu}_b))$ will be less than for x_{ij}. Since

$$\text{var} (x_{ij} - (b_j - \hat{\mu}_b)) = \text{var} (x_{ij}) + \text{var} (b_j - \hat{\mu}_b)$$
$$- 2\text{cov} (x_{ij}, (b_j - \hat{\mu}_b)),$$

it follows that

$$\text{var} (x_{ij} - (b_j - \hat{\mu}_b)) < \text{var} (x_{ij})$$

when

$$\text{cov} (x_{ijo} (b_j - \hat{\mu}_b)) > 1/2 \text{ var} (b_j - \hat{\mu}_b).$$

Clearly both var $(b_j - \hat{\mu}_b)$ and cov $(x_{ijo} (b_j - \hat{\mu}_b))$ can be estimated from the survey data. One might adopt as a decision rule the adjustment of the reported values whenever estimated var $(b_j - \hat{\mu}_b)$/estimated cov $(x_{ij} (b_j - \hat{\mu}_b))$ is less than two. As this ratio approaches zero, the var $(x_{ij} - (b_j - \hat{\mu}_b))$ approaches var (y_i), which is the lower limit for the variance component of the MSE $(\hat{\mu}_y)$.

4. *If the regression procedure is to be used, thought should be given to including questions in the survey that will provide data on one or more predictor variables that are expected to be highly correlated with the variable(s) of interest and*

uncorrelated with the potential interviewer bias. Actually, one would want to include as many questions as practicable that are designed to provide data on variables believed to be related to the potentially biased variable(s) of interest. In the simulations described earlier, for example, it would have been useful to have had data on the value of the housing unit of the respondent (if owned), or the rent paid, and other variables correlated with income as their addition as predictor variables in the regression would very likely have significantly increased the value of R^2.

There is, of course, a tradeoff between the number of these types of questions used and the effects that the added length and complexity of the questionnaire will have on respondent cooperation and on response accuracy.

One final point. As was the case in this study, a check should be made to insure that the regression assumptions are met. In particular, an analysis of residuals should be made to detect model bias. The "better" the regression, the greater will be the researcher's ability to detect and estimate relative interviewer bias.

REFERENCES

Athey, K. R., Coleman, J. E., Reitman, A. P., and Tang, J., "Two Experiments Showing the Effect of the Interviewer's Racial Background on Responses to Questionnaires Concerning Racial Issues." *Journal of Applied Psychology* 44 (1960): 244–46.

Bailar, B. A., *Some Sources of Error and Their Effect on Census Statistics,* Washington, D.C.: U.S. Bureau of the Census.

Bailar, B. A., Bailey, L., and Stevens, J., "Measures of Interviewer Bias and Variance." *Journal of Marketing Research* 14 (August 1977): 337–343.

Barioux, Max, "A Method for the Selection, Training, and Evaluation of Interviewers." *Public Opinion Quarterly* 26 (Spring 1952): 128–130.

Benney, M., Riesman, D., and Star, S. A., "Age and Sex in the Interview." *American Journal of Sociology* 62 (1956): 143–152.

Benson, P. H., "A Paired Comparison Approach to Evaluating Interviewer Performance." *Journal of Marketing Research* 6 (1969): 66–70.

Boyd, H. W., Jr., and Westfall, Ralph, "Interviewer Bias Revisisted." *Journal of Marketing Research* 2 (1965): 58–63.

Brown, R. V., *Research and the Credibility of Estimates.* Boston: Harvard University Press, 1969.

Campbell, C., and Joiner, B. L., "How to Get the Answer Without Being Sure You've Asked the Question." *The American Statistician* 27 (December 1973): 229–231.

Cannell, C. F., "A Study of the Effects of Interviewers Expectations Upon Interviewing Results." Ph.D. Thesis, Ohio State University, 1955.

Cannell, C. F., and Fowler, F. J., Jr., "A Note on Interviewer Effect in Self-Enumerative Procedures." *American Sociological Review* 29, No. 1 (February 1964): 270.

Case, B., "How to Catch Interviewer Errors." *Journal of Advertising Research* 11, No. 2 (April 1971): 39–43.

Collins, W. A., "Verbal Idiosyncracies as a Source of Bias." *Public Opinion Quarterly* 34 (Fall 1970): 416–422.

Colombotos, J., Elinson, J., and Loewenstein, R., "Effect of Interviewer's Sex on Interview Responses." *Public Health Reports* 83 (1968): 685–690.

Ehrlich, J. S., and Riesman, D., "Age and Authority in the Interview." *Public Opinion Quarterly* 25 (1961): 39–56.

Fay, R. E., III, "Problems of Nonsampling Error in the Survey of Income and Education: Content Analysis." U.S. Bureau of the Census, 1977.

Fay, R. E., III, Memorandum to H. Nisselson, both of the U.S. Bureau of the Census, "Some Previous Experience in Evaluating the Measurement of Poverty." September 16, 1975.

Franzen, R., and Williams, R., "A Method of Measuring Error Due to Variance Among Interviewers." *Public Opinion Quarterly* 20 (1956): 587–592.

"The Gallup Organization: Design of a National Probability Sample," Case study appearing in D. S. Tull and D. I. Hawkins (eds.), *Marketing Research: Meaning Measurement, Method.* New York: Macmillan Publishing Co., Inc., 1976.

Graham, D., U.S. Bureau of the Census, "Comparative Analysis of the Number of Crime Incidents Reported on the Original and Reinterview Survey, For Identical Persons (National Crime Survey Eight Impact and Five Largest Cities 1975)." October 31, 1975.

Guest, L., "A Study of Interviewer Competence," *International Journal of Opinion and Attitude, Research* Vol. 1 (December 1947): 17–30.

Hansen, M. H., and Steinberg, Joseph, "Control of Errors in Surveys." *Biometrics* 12 (1956): 462–474.

Hanson, R. H., and Marks, E. S., "Influence of the Interviewer on the Measuring of Survey Results." *Journal of the American Statistical Association* 53 (1958): 635–55.

Harding, J., "Refusals as a Source of Bias," in H. Cantril (ed.), *Gauging Public Opinion.* Princeton: Princeton University Press, 1947.

Hatchett, S., and Schuman, H., "White Respondents and Race of Interviewer Effects." *Public Opinion Quarterly* 39 (Winter 1975/76): 523–528.

Hyman, H. H., *Interviewing in Social Research.* Chicago: University of Chicago Press, 1954.

Ito, R., "An Analysis of Response Errors: A Case Study." *Journal of Business* 36 (October 1963): 440–47.

Kahn, R. L., and Cannell, C. F., *The Dynamics of Interviewing Theory, Technique and Cases.* New York: Wiley, 1957.

Kallek, S., Nisselson, H., and Sturdevant, T. R., "Evaluation Studies of the United States Economic Censuses." Paper presented at the 40th Session of the International Statistical Institute, Warsaw, Poland, 1975.

Kish, L., "A Procedure for Objective Respondent Selection Within the Household." *Journal of the American Statistical Association* 44 (1949): 380–387.

Kish, L., "Studies of Interviewer Variance for Attitudinal Variables." *Journal of the American Statistical Association* (1962): 92–115.

Lansing, J. B., Ginsberg, G. P., and Braaten, B., *An Investigation of Response Error.* Urbana: University of Illinois Bureau of Economic and Business Research, 1961.

Lenski, G. F., and Leggett, J. C., "Caste, Class, and Difference in the Research Interview." *The American Journal of Sociology* 65 (1960): 463–467.

Mahalanobis, P. C., "Recent Experiments in Statistical Sampling in the Indian Statistical Institute," *Journal of the Royal Statistical Society* 109 (1946): 325–370.

Mayer, C., "Assessing the Accuracy of Marketing Research." *Journal of Marketing Research* 3 (1970): 285–291.

McKenzie, J. R., "An Investigation into Interviewer Effects in Market Research." *Journal of Marketing Research* 14 (August 1977): 330–336.

Parten, M., *Surveys, Polls, and Samples: Practical Procedures.* New York: Cooper Square Publishers, Inc., 1966.

Rice, S. A., "Contagious Bias In The Interview: A Methodological Note." *American Journal of Sociology* 35 (1929): 420–423.

Rosenthal, R., *Experimenter Effects in Behavioral Research,* Chapter 8. New York: Irvington Press, 1976.

Schuman, H., and Converse, J. M., "The Effects of Black and White Interviewers on Black Responses in 1968." *Public Opinion Quarterly* 35 (1971): 44-68.

Schyberger, B. W., "A Study of Interviewer Behavior." *Journal of Marketing Research* 4 (February 1967): 32-5.

Selltiz, C., Jahoda, M., Deutsch, M., and Cook, S. W., *Research Methods in Social Relations,* 3rd. ed. New York: Dryden Press, 1976.

Sheatsley, P. B., "An Analysis of Interviewer Characteristics and Their Relationship to Performance, Part III." *International Journal of Opinion and Attitude Research* 5 (1951): 193-197.

Sudman, S., and Bradburn, N. M., *Response Effects in Surveys.* Chicago: Aldine Publishing Company, 1974.

Sudman, S., Bradburn, N., Blair, E., and Stocking, C., "Modest Expectations: The Effects of Interviewers' Prior Expectations on Responses." *Sociological Methods and Research* 6, No. 2 (November 1977): 177-182.

Tella, A., "Cyclical Behavior of Bias Adjusted Unemployment." Methods for Manpower Analysis No. 11, the W. E. Upjohn Institute for Employment Research, 1976.

Trent, R. D., "The Color of the Investigator as a Variable in Experimental Research with Negro Subjects." *Journal of Social Psychology* 40 (1954): 281-287.

Tull, D. S., and Albaum, G. S. *Survey Research: A Decisional Approach.* New York: Intext, Inc., 1973.

Tull, D. S., and Hawkins, D. I., *Marketing Research: Meaning, Measurement, Method.* New York: Macmillan Publishing Company, 1976.

U.S. Bureau of the Census, *Accuracy of Data for Selected Housing Characteristics as Measured by Reinterviews, 1970 Census of Population and Housing.* Washington, D.C.: U.S. Government Printing Office, January, 1975.

U.S. Bureau of the Census, *Evaluation and Research Program of the U.S. Censuses of Population and Housing, 1960: Effects of Interviewers and Crew Leaders.* Series ER60 No. 7, Washington, D.C.: U.S. Government Printing Office, 1968a.

U.S. Bureau of the Census, *The Current Population Survey Reinterview Program, January, 1971 through December, 1966—Technical Paper 19.* Washington, D.C.: U.S. Government Printing Office, December, 1968b.

Veroff, J., Atkinson, J. W., Feld, S. C., and Gurin, G., "The Use of Thematic Apperception to Assess Motivation in a Nationwide Interviewer Study." *Psychological Monographs: General and Applied* (Fall 1960): 1-32.

Webb, E. J., et al., *Unobtrusive Measures: Nonreactive Research in the Social Sciences.* Chicago: Rand McNally and Company, 1966.

TEMPORAL DIMENSION OF CONSUMER BEHAVIOR: AN EXPLORATION WITH TIME BUDGET

M. Venkatesan, UNIVERSITY OF OREGON

Johan Arndt, NORWEGIAN SCHOOL OF BUSINESS AND ECONOMICS

CONCEPTUAL APPROACHES TO TIME USE

Temporal dimension of consumer behavior is receiving increasing attention. In a recent review article on time and consumer behavior, Jacoby, Szybillo, and Berning (1976) pointed out that no major conceptual treatment or systematic empirical effort has been focused on the subject of time.

Even in the social sciences, use of time as a basis for studying social behavior in households is a development of the 20th century (Chapin, 1974). Economic view of time use has suggested (Becker, 1965) treating time as a resource that

Research in Marketing, Volume 3, pages 163–234

Copyright © 1980 by JAI Press Inc.

All rights of reproduction in any form reserved.

ISBN: 0-89232-060-5

can be traded off with money. Thus, this approach viewed activity choice as a function of trade offs among constraints. That such a view is taken by many for all areas of human activities is evidenced by Hagerstrand (1969), who argued that time use and spatial behavior may best be understood in terms of constraints rather than incentives and the like. Cullen (1972) viewed the average weekday as tied up in routines over which individuals have little control, and in general activities are organized around "key structuring episodes," such as work, homemaking, eating, and the like. He uses a concept of "stress links" between activity and environment and thus activities are undertaken, not as a choice, but as a result of stress responses. Chapin (1974) rejects both the utility-maximizing concepts and explaining behavior in terms of preference analysis. His approach to human time use conceives of an individual's activities "as the result of a complex and variable mix of incentives and constraints serving to mediate choice" (p. 9).

In the consumer behavior literature, time has been viewed both as an independent variable by some and as a dependent variable by others. For example, Howard and Sheth (1969) seemed to have recognized the importance of time in the consumer choice processes and thus their model of buyer behavior explicitly indicates "time pressure" as one of the exogenous variables.

> Time Pressure is the inverse of the amount of time the buyer has available to perform the behavior required for the acts of purchasing and consumption. It is the amount of time required to perform these acts in relation to the time he has allocated to himself for doing them. It incorporates momentary instead of long-term changes in the time available for purchasing.

Foote (1966) conceptualized that certain purchases are occurring at very different points in the career as a consumer. Thus, in his view, the product will be classified in the career of the consumer. He will make the career of the consumer rather than the purchase, the unit of study, and so the movement in time by the consumer becomes the focal point.

Schary (1971), in an insightful article, recognized the interaction of time with consumer behavior. His conceptual model visualized time utilization in the consumption process as part of the consumer's choice process. Such a view emphasized the importance of time use by consumers in gathering product information and in the act of consumption itself. He clearly recognized that it is not the "objective time" spent by consumers that matters, but the consumers' perception of that time which may influence both the produce choice and the way the product is used. He considered the act of consumption as a production process performed by the consumer (designated as an "activity"), and thus time along with goods and services become inputs to that activity. He saw the relevance of time to marketing strategy when he observed (Schary, 1971, p. 54) that:

> ... the key to understanding the consumers may well lie in measuring his time use. The market segments which are created by his time choices could be more meaningful than many

currently used measures. Marketing management may have to invest in a greater understanding of time use in order to measure its implications for market segmentation.

Schary's framework is presented in Figure 1. Such a framework has attempted to identify the most directly relevant dimension of consumer time allocation. His categorizations seem explicitly to recognize that time plays different roles in work and nonwork related activities and that its role is dependent on the nature of chosen activities. Finally, his framework considers attitudinal dimensions which create consumers' evaluation of time.

A somewhat different but directly applicable schematic model of factors affecting the use of time is provided by Robinson (1975). His schematic (Figure 2) considers four sets of antecedent factors affecting time use; those factors are: environmental, personal, role, and resource. Robinson has not provided any data to substantiate this schematic model. However, the Survey Research Center is continuing its collection of time use by Americans. Robinson indicated that while little change is seen in the gross allocation of time devoted to work, housework, and leisure, there is increasing evidence that Americans tend to spend more time traveling and shopping than they had done in the last ten years.

Arndt and Gronmo (1977) provided a scheme for looking at time use by consumers with regard to "shopping" activity and provided a scheme, which is shown in Figure 3. Their scheme envisions time as a dependent variable, with a variable called "orientation to shopping" as intervening between time spent on shopping and a set of antecedent variables. The antecedent variables are specified as follows:

A. *Structural Conditions*
   1. Distance to nearest grocery store
   2. Centrality of municipality of residence
   3. Occupational structure of municipality of residence
B. *Possession of Strategic Products*
   1. Ownership of car
   2. Ownership of refrigerator
   3. Ownership of freezer
C. *Social Position*
   1. Sex
   2. Health
   3. Employment status of respondent and of spouse
   4. Time spent on work
   5. Number of children
   6. Stage in family life cycle
   7. Education of respondent and of spouse
   8. Total household income

Figure 1. A Structure of Consumer Time Allocation

I. The Role of Time

   A. Work and Income-related Activity

      1. Compensated time.

      2. Necessary nonwork, noncompensated time; e.g., do-it-yourself activities.

   B. Leisure

      1. Daily patterns of available time.

      2. Extended intervals of leisure.

II. The Sequence and Complementarity of Activity

   A. Simultaneity -- Whether activities by their nature are exclusive, or whether they are more appropriate together.

   B. The Social Role -- Whether activities are chosen in a singular social setting, or whether they require a larger set of activities involving group interaction.

   C. Relationship among Activities -- Whether activities are unique in themselves, or are related sequentially or otherwise to other activities.

III. The Schedule of Time Values

   A. Diurnal Patterns -- How do time values differ for successive intervals during the day?

   B. Longer Cycles -- Weekly, monthly, and seasonal patterns.

   C. Noncyclic Time -- Vacation and retirement.

IV. Attitudinal Dimensions

   A. Conflict -- Potential competition between activities for the available time.

   B. Urgency -- Whether a general underlying attitude toward the uses of time governs the uses of time.

   C. Perception of Duration of Activity.

   D. Substitution -- Whether time in a particular situation is regarded as a substitute for other resources, e.g. physical energy.

Figure 2. Schematic Model of Factors in Time Use

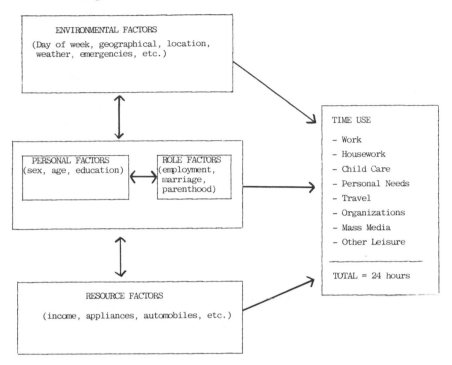

Based on Robinson [1975], p. 849.

On the basis of their prior research, Arndt and Gronmo also distinguished between two different classes of orientations to shopping: (1) supply-need orientation, and (2) noneconomic orientation. The first category essentially is an economic orientation; they believed that the time spent on shopping varies with the need of supply from retailers. "The Elasticity of activities refers to the fact that certain activities being mandatory or structurally determined are less amenable to contraction (and to expansion) than to others given an autonomous change in another activity" (Arndt and Gronmo, 1977, p. 231). It should be noted here that Arndt and Gronmo indicated that they constructed this scheme based on the analysis of the time use data obtained in the time budget survey conducted by the Norwegian Central Bureau of Statistics in 1975. The data were not explicitly collected for explaining variations in the time spent in shopping.

Taken together, these frameworks/schemes suggest that consumers' use of time is dependent upon the demographic variables, situational and environmental variables which affect consumer choice processes. What is important in these frameworks is that they clearly are concerned with consumers' perception of

Figure 3. Schematic Overview of Proposed Relationships Between Time Spent
on Shopping and Antecedent and Consequent Conditions

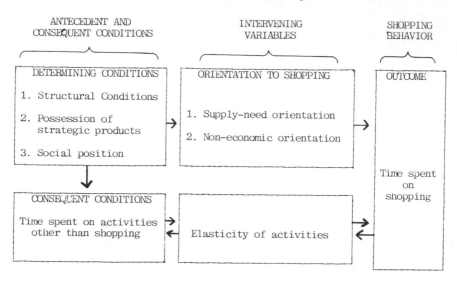

time; thus their allocation of time to alternate activities yields some measure of
consumers' priorities and/or preferences. Suffice it to point out here that no
cogent explanation on the determinants of time use is available, as the present
state of scant research in this area is unable to provide any more than a description of mere allocation of time to "shopping" activities.

TIME USE STUDIES

Interesting patterns of social life have been uncovered by sociologists and others
when they have examined how people spend their time in various human activities. This line of research, which has gained wide acceptance by sociologists in
Europe, is based on the concept of "time budget." This concept is primarily
concerned with how different kinds of people allocate different amounts of time
to various activities, such as doing work, shopping, taking meals, listening to the
radio, visiting friends, watching television, and the like. This method, thus, aims
to rank activities by the length of time spent in particular activities. Since there
are only 24 hours in a day, the focus has been on the proportion of time claimed
to have been allocated by people to the various activities either within the course
of a day (daily time budgets) or within some other frame of reference, such as
weekly time budgets (7 × 24 hours), and the like. As Szalai (1972, p. 1) aptly
observed, "... it is not time itself, either as a physical or as a subjectively
perceived entity, but rather the use people make of their time which is the real

subject of time budget studies.'' The conventional time budget studies were concerned with the day-long activities of select groups (workers, a particular social class, urban segments, and the like) of people. Much of the time budget studies by sociologists have primarily been devoted to leisure time expenditure. Other time use studies (such as Chapin, 1974; Robinson, 1975; Szalai, 1972) have focused their attention on living patterns of rural and/or urban residents and the way they allocate their time to varying activities in the course of a day.

An ambitious undertaking by Szalai and his associates (1972) investigated the use of time in 12 countries in order to study and compare the temporal distribution of everyday activities. They investigated the allocation of time by individuals in these countries to 96 activity categories. The activities were divided into 10 main groups: work, housework, child care, shopping, personal needs, education, organizational activities, entertainment, active leisure, and passive leisure. Each of these major groups were further divided into detailed activities within the groups. For example, the "shopping" group of activities was further broken down as follows (Szalai, 1972, p. 562): (1) purchasing of everyday consumer goods; (2) purchasing of durable consumer goods; (3) personal care outside home (e.g., hairdresser); (4) medical care outside home; (5) administrative services, offices; (6) repair and other services; (7) waiting for the purchase of goods and services; (8) other services; (9) traveling connected to the above mentioned activities (including waiting for means of transport). The results obtained based on a sample of 1,243 in 44 cities of the United States in the aforementioned 12 countries time budget study, is shown in Table 1. The data shown is for the total sample. Unfortunately, this is the only glimpse we have of time spent in consumption-related activities, as the researchers' concerns were with time spent in other activities, interactions, and social relations. Therefore, the original list of 96 activities were collapsed into 37 activities, and thus the time spent by con-

Table 1. Findings of Time Budget Study Re. USA (in average minutes per day)

	44 Cities–USA	Jackson–USA
Sample Size	1243	778
Time Spent in		
1. Marketing	14.0	15.9
2. Shopping	1.1	2.0
3. Personal care	1.6	2.2
4. Medical care	1.2	1.0
5. Administrative Services	0.7	0.3
6. Repair service	2.4	3.3
7. Other service	12.3	10.4
8. Travel	18.6	18.3

Based on Szalai (1972), p. 576.

sumers in the activities shown in Table 1 was reduced to one single category called "marketing." Such a loss of consumption-related time information from this cross-cultural time budget study, though understandable, is unfortunate.

Foote (1966) related the time budget research that was conducted in connection with consumer acquisition of appliances. While the intended use was for obtaining information regarding appliances in the "career" of the consumer, the information obtained related to the activities/episodes concerning food-related activities, clothing-related activities, housing-related activities, personal care activities, education, recreation, transportation, and other activities. The people in this research were instructed to "record the hour you went to bed, the hour you got up, and all the activities from the time you got up until the time you went to bed" (Foote, 1966, p. 42). In other words, information was obtained in the logs on a 24 hour basis, which would account for every moment of the full day. As is clear from the direction and type of data that seemed to have been obtained, and as seen from the sample findings presented by Foote and shown in Table 2, this time budget study provided little information about consumption-related activities.

Chapin (1974) has studied how individuals go about their everyday lives in the Washington, D.C. metropolitan area. A series of five studies conducted by him to research urban activity systems utilized activity analysis, eliciting time spent on various activities. Two hundred twenty-five activities were identified, which were grouped into 40 classes of activities, for which information on time use was obtained. One of the activity groups identified was "shopping." This category

Table 2.   Preference Ratings and Minutes Spent per Day on the Most
Time-Consuming Activities (Sleep and Work Omitted)

	Minutes per Day		Preference Rating	
	Men	Women	Men	Women
Watch television	115	142	29	30
Listen to radio	39	95	10	11
Talk with family	79	85	21	20
Visit, talk with friends	29	60	59	69
Smoke cigarette	38	44	20	29
Wash, dry dishes	3	38	−28	−2
Cook, specific operation	4	34	21	16
Read paper	30	32	29	36
Drink coffee	12	20	16	35
Clean	4	25	−22	−5
Cook dinner	1	21	40	6
Games and hobbies	20	17	56	74
Get ready for sleep	17	20	4	6

Based on Foote (1966), p. 43.

included shopping for goods, (convenience, shopper, and consumer durables) retail services, personal services, and repair services. His results indicated that individuals spent 1.59 (mean) hours during weekdays, 2.27 (mean) hours during Saturdays and 0.94 (mean) hours on Sundays in the "shopping" activity category. About 31% of his sample of 1667 seemed to have engaged in the "shopping activity."

Hawes (1975, 1977) employed a "weekly time budget" concept to obtain information regarding the number of hours in a week spent in leisure time pursuits by a sample of adult males and females, who were members of a Mail Panel of the Market Facts. This study had found that male respondents averaged 5.2 hours of leisure or free time per day, as compared to female respondents who averaged 5.7 hours per day. Table 3 summarizes the findings of this study. As is apparent, and as in the Szalai (1972) study, very little information regarding consumption-related activities have been forthcoming from the list of activities

Table 3. Mean Hours per Week Spent by Respondents in Indicated Activities

	Females (N=603)		Males (N=512)	
	Mean	% of 168 hrs.	Mean	% of 168 hrs.
Sleeping, napping	51.4	30.5	51.1	30.5
Eating meals (breakfast, lunch, dinner)	11.7	7	11.5	7
Personal care	8.2	5	6.7	4
Working at your job (including *all* paid employment)	15.6	9.5	41.0	24.5
Commuting to and from work	1.9	1	4.6	2.5
Other work-related activity (meetings, reading, study, "homework")	2.7	1.5	3.3	2
Housework, necessary home maintenance and lawn care	22.8	13.5	5.7	3.5
Shopping	4.2	2.5	1.9	1
Playing with or helping your children	10.2	6	5.0	3
Reading newspapers and magazines	5.1	3	5.1	3
Watching television	15.7	9.5	14.3	8.5
Hobbies, games, crafts, etc.	5.6	3.5	4.1	2.5
Visiting with friends or relatives	6.0	3.5	4.7	3
Participating in sports or	1.3	1	1.9	1
Attending sporting events as a spectator	.7	.5	.9	.5
Entertainment outside the home (*other than* sporting events)	3.2	2	3.2	2
Other major activities	2.2	1.5	2.2	1.5

listed in Table 3. Some interesting findings emerge from this study in analyzing the answers of the consumers about what would the respondent do with an extra two hours in her/his day and what would the respondent do with a three day weekend every week. Among the responses given to both of these questions, their answers indicate that they would spend some of the increased (hypothetical) time in shopping, in window shopping, and on personal business and errands.

Arndt and Gronmo (1977) presented findings based on a time budget survey conducted by the Norwegian Central Bureau of Statistics in 1971–2. Based on the time data obtained in a "diary" format, they indicate that their sample reported that average shopping time per week day was 25 minutes, of which 16 minutes represented in-store shopping activities, and 9 minutes were spent in traveling to and from the store. Sixteen out of the 25 minutes seemed to have been allocated to the purchasing of convenience goods. They have also attempted to examine the relationship between some of the antecedent factors (structural condition variables, possessions, demographics, and the like) and shopping time.

A study conducted by the Norwegian Central Bureau of Statistics (1975) indicated that all persons in their sample spent on the average of 0.3 hours/day in the purchase of all goods and services. However, an average of 0.5 hours each is indicated for those engaged in purchase of grocery goods and for those engaged in purchase of clothes and shoes; 0.8 hours (average) is indicated for those was engaged in other unspecified purchases.

In reviewing these studies, one thing becomes clear, that is, purchase-related activities utilize some of the available time during the day and that a major share of people engage in this activity daily. Because some of these studies were interested in activity pattern for the day as a whole and because others of these studies were interested more in leisure time activities, all the information collected regarding individuals' shopping activities were reduced to one activity group and thus information was combined to present the time spent in these activities. The category "shopping" itself has been narrowly conceived to include only time use information relating to purchasing activity (purchase of some goods and services) by consumers. Such a narrow orientation did not focus on the use of time as part of the consumers' choice process, nor did it encompass such activities as information-seeking, travel, postpurchase trial of products, conversations regarding satisfaction/dissatisfaction, and the like. Some studies, such as Chapin's (1974), include window shopping as part of walking activity and some explicitly gather data on total travel time related to the shopping activity (Arndt and Gronmo, 1977; Chapin, 1974). At this point, it is clear that no study has explored the time use patterns of consumers in all phases of consumption-related activites.

SOME METHODOLOGICAL CONSIDERATIONS

The major reason for lack of information on the use of time related to consumption activities, apart from secondary importance assigned to these set of activities by researchers with other concerns, is the problem of obtaining time use information from consumers and the problems of measurement of time. Foote (1966, p. 39) explained the problem (many years ago) as follows:

> Of the many who have thought this would be a good thing, only a few have attempted it. Fewer yet have ever completed a study and virtually no one has published results. There are certain reasons for this other than the difficulty of just getting to the point of publication. One is the problem in field work of getting people to make a record of their behavior. Many studies have foundered on this and their failures have not been reported. It is a matter of shame to the researcher to have to admit to the low rate of response and cooperation. When we talked with people who have attempted such studies, we discovered that they all have run into this problem. The head of one market research corporation told me that they got only about 25 percent of the people to keep an actual record of their purchases. He felt better when we told him that we got only about 15 percent on our first try. This is one of the problems of this kind of research and we have found no easy way of solving it.

There are essentially two research approaches to gather information on activity patterns from people. They are survey research methods and ethnographic study methods. Much of the data collection for time use information has come from survey method; to our knowledge, only one study had employed ethnographic study method (Chapin, 1974). In the survey approach, activity information is obtained by structured interviews from a sample of predetermined subjects. This is done in one of the following or a combination of three ways: (1) By a field listing of activities performed by the subjects on the previous day. Respondents are asked to list the activities and the sequence for these activities from their memories; (2) By a check list approach in which respondents are asked to identify, from a precategorized list of activities, those in which the respondent engaged in a typical day or week and indicate the allocation of time to each activity; and (3) By a "diary" method, in which respondents are asked to keep a diary for the day ("tomorrow") following the interview, in which the respondent is briefed on the type of activities and other aspects relating to their time allocation to activities. The interviewer revisits the respondent to pick up the "diary" (usually for a 24–hour period), and checks it for completeness and correctness of information.

Szalai (1972) utilized the "yesterday" activities recall procedure with 10% of their sample, and then a diary was provided to them to record the subsequent day's activities. However, most of their sample were provided with a "diary" and "fresh" (yesterday) interviews were used only if the respondent was unwilling or unable to furnish a self-recorded "diary." Thus, the information obtained in this study was for 24 hours a day. Foote (1966) indicated that they had asked their respondents to keep a log on a 24–hour basis to account for all of their activities for the full day. Chapin (1974) has used mostly "yesterday" listings and one-day ("tomorrow") diaries. Hawes (1977) obtained his information through mailed questionnaires to a sample of households of the Consumer Mail Panel of Market Facts. The Norwegian Central Bureau of Statistics (1975) obtained their information through the "diary" method. Each respondent was asked to keep a diary for 2 or 3 days; the period covered was Sept. 1, 1971 to Aug. 31, 1972. Thus, by assigning different proportions of samples to different 2 or 3 day time periods, their procedure was intended to provide a picture of time use patterns for the year. As is apparent, to obtain any information to indicate pattern variations and sequences, some form of "diary" procedure for longer periods is required from respondents.

The second problem of data collections deals with "units of recall" for which records are kept. For example, the Norwegian data collection procedure in 1975 has been to break up the time units into 15 minute segments in the recording sheets. Chapin (1974) asked for the "starting time" for each activity listed by the respondent. The Survey Research Center (Robinson, 1975) asks two questions to get at the "unit of recall," viz. what time the activity began and what time it ended. Szalai (1972) and his researchers had found that "the duration of an activity tends to be the type of information that is most seriously affected both by the procedure employed and by the ability of the respondent to observe himself (p. 72).

The third problem concerns the nature and extent of grouping of primary and secondary activities. It is generally recognized that time as a metric can overemphasize the activities in which the respondent was engaged. In asking the respondent to recall in chronological order all the activities in which he/she was engaged and to indicate the time allocated for such activities or indicating the beginning time for each activity, the aim is to get as accurate a time allocation picture as possible. Since individuals engage in activities concurrently (talking while watching television, etc.), it is necessary to make sure that both activities are counted and the time allocation recorded. In the chronological recall procedure, secondary or parallel activities may tend to be omitted or can result in biased accounts of the amount of time spent in primary activities. In cases where check lists are provided, both primary and secondary or parallel activities must be listed in order to elicit information.

Which procedure will give better information for time allocation to activities connected with consumption? First of all, all the procedures currently employed result in "self-reported" measures of time usage and thus time budget studies contain data of widely varying reliability and validity. Secondly, it is known that routinized behavior (such as "shopping") of short duration is very sensitive to differences in data collection procedures (Szalai, 1972). Thirdly, self-recording seemed more accurate for types of behavior that call for some planning in advance and for most of the regularly recurring activities. It would seem that the data for basic research may need respondent's own categorization and the format may need to remain somewhat unstructured with regard to type of activities. For research in consumer's use of time, an applied research area, prior designations of activity and preestablished classification systems may need to be introduced at the time of the interview to obtain useful results. Such incidental activities as seeking some information from salespersons, window shopping, or travel to a store for purchase of products (on the way to work, for example), and the like, will not easily be recalled. In addition to preestablishing categories, the type of information obtained from consumers needs to be broadened so as to be useful for explanations of consumer choice behavior. All the studies which have obtained time use patterns for individuals have obtained information (or categorized obtained information) into a classification called "shopping" or "marketing" activity, which only includes "purchasing" related time information; that is, time spent in purchasing convenience and other goods and services, and sometimes the travel time associated with these purchasing activities. Such a view of consumption-related activities is much too narrow. To be useful, time use data must relate to prepurchase, purchase, postpurchase, and consumption activities. Since many of the consumption-related activities can be performed while engaged in doing other activities, it is necessary to list the type of activities for which time allocation information is being elicited. Since any technique attempting to elicit consumer time use information employs self-reported measures, and since the key to understanding the consumers' time use is in obtaining his/her perception of time allocated to particular activities relevant to their decision-making processes (and not necessarily the "objective" data on time spent), consumers must be specifically asked to indicate the time that they estimate to have spent on these activities. Such information can be actual or estimated, as the amount of time allocated to differing consumption-related activities may indicate consumers' preference for those activities or at best may indicate the need or importance. Also, as our emphasis is on personal behavior in nonobligatory activities, where the individual is expected to have considerable latitude in the exercise of his/her choice, perceived measurement of time may well depend on clear specification of the type of activities included in the activity categories. Finally, Foote (1966) had noted that consumers tend to define the activity unit in episodic manner, viz. with a beginning, a middle, and an end, and that the day consists of series of connected episodes. If they tend to recall in this episodic manner, we can presume that consumers may tend to remember consumption-related episodes, such as complaining to the salesperson, returning an appliance, or even asking for specific information about a particular product and the like. However, to date no research study on time use asked respondents about these activities and we believe ours to be the first study to ascertain time allocation information for all phases of consumption-related activities.

THE EXPLORATORY STUDY

Our exploratory study in consumers' time allocation to various phases of consumer decision processes was conducted in Bergen, Norway.

We were interested in setting up a "panel" and collect time allocation information for a longer period of time than 24 hours. As no one has collected data, in a time budget sense, on the phases of consumer decision-making in which this project was interested, we had to test our instruments. The instructions and the self-recording activity forms were first prepared in English, then translated to Norwegian and translated back to English to check the earlier translation. Our aim was to make it as easy as possible for the respondent to understand the activity for which she was asked to indicate the amount of time spent on a given day.

A short questionnaire and instructions were prepared. This first version was tested with five volunteer subjects, and they were unable to complete the questionnaire. The respondents were not sure whether to include only the time spent by themselves in the activities specified or to include the estimated times spent by the respondent's spouse and children in these activities. Other questions which posed difficulties related to "information-seeking" activities—the test subjects were unsure whether to report only those times spent on acquiring information and which later culminated in a purchase. Because of these difficulties, a second self-recording questionnaire was developed. The questions were more specific and to the point. The instructions were clear and made simple. The respondents were instructed to indicate times spent only for their own activities. There were still some misunderstandings regarding the postpurchase phase. The example we had provided in the first questionnaire related only to "trying out" a product that had been purchased and we had hoped the respondents would generalize to other postpurchase situations. Because of the difficulties still encountered by the respondents in our pilot tests on these questions, we changed our questions to specific postpurchase activities. The finalized questionnaire and instructions were prepared in seven colors—one for each day of the week. The self-recording questionnaire contained, besides the instructions, three parts: Part I contained questions on the respondent's characteristics (household size, age of respondent, income, education, and the like); Part 2 asked questions about their regular shopping activities and attitudes; and Part 3 was aimed to ascertain time allocation information on prepurchase information-seeking activities (general and specifically relevant to one or more purchase), purchasing activities, the number of stores visited, travel time, and finally activities relating to the postpurchase phase (trial and trying out of newly purchased products, conversations, and other expressions of complaints or satisfaction with purchases).

Sample Selections

Because of time and budget constraints and because of the distances involved in collecting from the residential communities, which were widespread around Bergen (Norway), it was decided to choose a sample in three locations which were easily accessible. The aim in our sample selection was to recruit adult women reflecting low, medium, and high income households. The three residential areas were chosen because they represented the desired (three) income levels. Our objective was to recruit a "panel" of women who would be willing to cooperate to maintain the self-reporting "activity and time records." We also desired a sample size of at least 100 households to maintain such records. Therefore, a sample scheme was devised to contact 170 households. Within each area, the first household to be chosen was designated (by street and house number), and thereafter a "skip rate" was provided to the interviewer to choose the next household. The "skip rate" was based on the number of houses in that income level in a particular residential area. Such a rate was devised so as to be proportional to the total number of houses in the blocks and to obtain the desired number of households (adult women respondents) from these three areas. This sampling procedure yielded a sample of 120 women who were willing to cooperate with the study and who agreed to maintain the records for the next *seven* days. The 120 willing respondents came from the three income levels as follows: high income 36, medium income 54, and low income 30. Due to illness or unexpected travel, 26 respondents did not complete the "diaries," and 4 that were completed were "unusable" because they did not follow the instructions; therefore our usable data came from a sample of 90 women. The background characteristics are shown in Table 4.

Each respondent was given a pen as a token of our appreciation for participating in the study. The respondents were given the instruction sheet and all seven recording sheets (one for each day). They were asked to start record keeping from the next day. On the second day, two research assistants were assigned to phone each respondent to see whether she had any problem or difficulty and if there were any questions, they were fully answered and any problems were "solved" so that recording would proceed smoothly. If a respondent was unavailable for telephone contact after several "tries," or if she had no telephone in the household, a letter was sent to "explain and encourage" their participation. By this time, the respondents had been repeatedly impressed to fill out the record form for each day, including Sunday, even if there were no activities for that particular day. At the end of the seven-day period, the recorded diaries were collected and the respondents were thanked for their cooperation.

CONSUMER TIME ALLOCATION PATTERNS

The analysis of the results is intended to give us a perspective and description on the allocation of time by consumers during the three phases of consumption-related activities. Because our sample was judgmental (convenience) and because the study is exploratory in nature, only mean-time allocation statistics were developed. The aim was not to infer about time budgets for the population of Norway as a whole, nor did we desire a comparison of this segment with others. Past studies have presented results both in terms of per capita (based on the total sample size) expenditure of time on activities, and the time spent by those who engaged in those activities. For example, in the U.S. portion of the Szalai study (1972), the participation rates for the marketing activities ranged from a high of

Table 4.   Background Characteristics of the
Sample (in percentage)

Sample Size (N = 90)	100
Age Group of Respondent	
20–29	27
30–39	12
40–49	25
50–59	20
60+	16
Household Size	
1	9
2	30
3	23
4	23
5+	15
Age of Youngest Child	
No Child	46
Under 5 Years	20
6–12 Years	20
13–19	14
Working Status of Respondent	
Full-time	40
Part-time	20
Not Working	40
Education Level of Respondent	
Primary Schools	44
Vocational Schools	26
Secondary Schools	18
Between Secondary and Univ.	8
University and Equiv.	4

Income Level	Respondent	Husband
No Income	30	4
Less than NKR. 15,000	9	7
15,000–19,999	9	3
20,000–29,999	17	7
30,000–39,999	10	0
40,000–49,999	9	15
50,000–59,999	8	18
60,000–69,999	6	11
70,000–79,999	2	14
80,000–89,999	—	5
90,000+	—	16

34% for "marketing" activities to a low of 2.4 % for medical services, and in the Chapin (1974) study, the participation rate was 36% for the weekdays and 48% for Saturdays. In our study, with the exception of postpurchase activities, the participation rate in the prepurchase and purchasing phase activities ranged from 56% (low) to a high of 91%. Under the circumstances, the data is presented only for the participants of these activities, as time spent in these activities on a per capita basis does not add to any explanation. It should also be reemphasized that all of our sample respondents are female adults and the analysis relates only to the time spent by them in the consumption-related activities. Also, data for Sunday is not included in our analysis, as only a negligible percentage participated in any activities, as all the stores (with the exception of a few small corner tobacco stores) are closed on Sunday and there is no major Sunday newspaper in Bergen. Also in our analysis, time spent on Thursdays is shown separately, as all the stores and shops are open late (9 p.m.) on Thursdays, and much of the advertising for specials come out in Thursday's newspaper, particularly for grocery stores and department stores.

Information-Seeking Activities

It is clear from Table 5 that a substantial number of people report engaging in general information-seeking (not related to any specific purchase) activities. Table 11 supports the fact that the individuals in this sample tend to spend more time in information-seeking activities than in purchasing and/or postpurchase activities. There is more variation in the amount of time spent in seeking general than in the case of specific information. (See Tables 5 and 6.) It is also clear from these two tables that the sample respondents seem to spend more time on Thursdays in these activities (see also Table 10) than on weekdays and/or Saturdays. This observation is borne out by the mean duration of time spent in overall information-seeking activities, which is as follows: weekdays (mean) 30 minutes, Saturday (mean) 32 minutes, and Thursdays (mean) 43 minutes. In addition, Table 7 makes it clear that people tend to spend more time in general information-seeking activities than in specific information-seeking activities. In fact, respondents seem to have spent 2.5 times more time in general information-seeking activities as compared to the time spent in specific information-seeking. Also, for the duration for which time allocation information is obtained, it appears that more participants utilize newspapers, magazines, and journals as sources of information than any other source that were listed for them. It also appears that they seem to spend more time with this source (see Table 7) than with other sources.

Since no other study obtained time allocation information on the prepurchase phase, there are no findings against which to compare our results. Suffice it to point out that based on the time spent in this phase of consumption-related activities by our respondents, one can conclude future time budget studies must

Table 5. Time Spent in General Information Seeking Activities

	Weekday*		Thursday		Saturday	
	% engaging in activity	Mean minutes	% engaging in activity	Mean minutes	% engaging in activity	Mean minutes
1. Newspaper, magazines and journals	36	17	40	15	36	20
2. Brochures and catalogs	9	14	16	14	10	17
3. Discussions/Conversations with:						
1. Members of household	11	16	12	17	9	10
2. Friends and acquaintances	6	20	4	25	3	9
3. Store personnel	8	15	10	16	6	12
4. Window shopping and at store premises	10	14	12	21	11	17
5. Other sources	3	15	2	7	—	—

*Excluding Thursdays.

180

Table 6. Time Spent in Specific Information Seeking Activities

Sources	Weekday		Thursday		Saturday	
	% Engaging in Activity	Mean Minutes	% Engaging in Activity	Mean Minutes	% Engaging in Activity	Mean Minutes
1. Newspapers, magazines and journals	15	14	12	10	13	16
2. Brochures and catalogs	6	10	10	10	8	8
3. Discussions/Conversations with:						
3.1 Members of household	8	14	8	7	7	10
3.2 Friends and acquaintances	1	6	3	13	1	5
3.3 Store personnel	7	10	9	6	12	9
4. Window shopping and at store premises	7	10	6	14	8	10
5. Other sources	—	—	1	120	—	—

Table 7. Time Spent in Information Seeking Activities by Participants

Source	General Information Seeking	Specific Information Seeking
	(Average for the week in minutes)	
1. Newspapers, magazines, journals	39	12
2. Brochures and Catalogs	10	5
3. Conversation with		
a. Members of Household	11	6
b. Friends and Acquaintances	6	1
c. Store Personnel	8	5
4. Window shopping and Store Premises	12	5
5. Other Sources	2	1
All Sources	88	35

ascertain more and accurate information for this activity from consumers. In our recording procedure, the distinction between general information-seeking and specific information-seeking activity may have caused some problems. In the post-recording sessions, some respondents indicated they had some difficulty in assigning their information-seeking activities into these two categories. Also, this survey was considerably helped by the absence of commercials in the Norwegian television and radio. Introducing broadcast medium as another source for information-seeking activity may well change the rate of participants and the amount of time spent in information activities from these two sources. If there were Sunday editions of newspapers similar to some of the Sunday papers of major American metropolitan areas, the time allocated to newspapers may be considerably different. Finally, nonpersonal sources seem to have been more utilized than personal sources. This may have more to do with national characteristics.

Time Spent in Purchasing Activities

Among the purchasing activities, time allocated to the purchase of grocery products dominates for the weekdays, Thursdays, and Saturdays, in terms of participation in this activity. It is also clear from Table 8 that the amount of time spent in purchasing activities, particularly for grocery products and shoes and clothes, appear to be higher on Thursdays and Saturdays. This is consistent with the late closings of shops on Thursdays and free time available on Saturdays, particularly for those (60% in our sample) who were fully or partly employed. Purchasing grocery products is an obligatory activity pattern and sufficiently widespread participation therefore should not be surprising. Again, the variation and more than average level activity on Thursdays and Saturdays for all purchasing-related activities can be seen in Tables 10 and 11. Not surprisingly, mean travel times are also higher for Thursdays and Saturdays (see Table 10). Among the "discretionary" forms of purchase activities (such as nongrocery

Table 8. Time Spent in Purchasing Activities

Purchasing Activity for	Weekday		Thursday		Saturday	
	% Engaging in Activity	Mean Minutes	% Engaging in Activity	Mean Minutes	% Engaging in Activity	Mean Minutes
1. Grocery Products	72	14	80	17	69	22
2. Shoes and Clothes	12	22	27	35	17	25
3. Cosmetics	4	7	4	5	3	4
4. Consumer Durables	4	13	7	12	2	23
5. Leisure Goods	7	10	10	16	7	16
6. Other Articles	12	16	20	17	17	26

purchases), purchasing time for shoes and clothes and for leisure goods seem to be the activities on which time is spent (see Table 8).

Since many of the other time budget studies have obtained data for "shopping" (or marketing) activities, it may be worthwhile to compare our findings with others. For example, Szalai's (1972) findings indicated that for purchasing of everyday consumer goods, an average of 4.8 minutes per week were allocated by a Belgian sample, 41 minutes (mean) for France, 30 minutes (mean) for Hungary, 35 minutes for Poland, and 41 minutes for the United States. The present study found that for the week, our sample spent an average of 2 hours in purchasing activities. Chapin (1974) found that his Washington, D.C. sample spent on the average 1.02 hours (mean) on weekdays, 0.72 hours on Saturday, and 0.50 hours for Sundays by participants in the "shopping activity." Our comparable data are as follows: 82 minutes for weekdays, 102 minutes on Thursdays, and 116 minutes for Saturdays. However, our findings corroborate the findings from the Norwegian Central Bureau of Statistics (1975), which are as follows:

	Norwegian Central Bureau Sample (Sample: Men & Women)	Our Study (Sample: Women Only)
	(Average minutes/day)	
Groceries	10	11.7
Shoes and Clothes	1	4.2
Other	5	4.4
Total	16	20.3

It should be noted here that telephone buying of groceries and other products is not included in our time allocation. However, our time data appears to include some of the preparation time for purchase lists before engaging in purchasing activities, particularly for grocery products.

Postpurchase and Other Activities

Interpretation of the data obtained for this phase of the consumption process requires considerable *caveat*. It was revealed in our post data collection sessions that most of our respondents did not include any "trying out" of new grocery products (as it involves considerably more time), but that they included time spent in testing new shoes, hi-fi's and the like. Also, it was felt by the researchers that some of the postpurchase activities relative to the use of the product, such as complaints or dissatisfaction and the like, might well develop after a period of

Table 9. Time Spent in Postpurchase Activities

Activity	Weekday		Thursday		Saturday	
	% Engaging in Activity	Mean Minutes	% Engaging in Activity	Mean Minutes	% Engaging in Activity	Mean Minutes
1. Trial and/or Examination	9	17	13	22	6	9
2. Complaints and Expressions of Dissatisfaction	5	8	4	2	7	12
3. Expressing Satisfaction	9	9	18	12	8	15
4. Other Postpurchase Activity	2	14	—	—	—	—

time and our data collection duration of one week may not have been adequate to "pick up" such activities.

As Table 9 indicates, the overall postpurchase activity level and therefore the time allocated to it appear very low compared to other phases of the activities. The only findings of significance here is that such activity and the time spent appear to be somewhat higher on Thursdays and Saturdays (as compared to Monday and Tuesday), the same two days in which purchasing activity level was high. It may be that not much postpurchase activity takes place on which appreciable time is spent. Much of such activities may take place only at the cognitive level or it may mean the type of purchase situations covered during the period of this study did not involve items or purchases sufficiently important to generate or warrant postpurchase activities of the type that were presented to them for recording purposes.

Table 10 generally confirms the pattern of heavier purchasing and travel time activities during Thursdays and Saturdays. The table also indicates the variations by day of the week for all of these activities. Table 11 presents the participants' allocation of time for these activities by the characteristics of the participants. The time use pattern shows variations due to age. For example, the time spent on information-seeking activities is low in the age categories 20-29 and 30-39 and increases thereafter, reaching a maximum for the age group 50-59. While there is some reduction in time spent in this activity for people 60 years and older, still the activity level appears to be much higher than that of the youngest group. The time spent in purchasing activities follows similar patterns. Household size does not seem to have any visible effect on the time used for information-seeking activity. The time spent for purchasing activity, however, is increasing with increasing size of the household.

The study by Norwegian Central Bureau of Statistics (1975) has previously found that employment status was important. In particular, it found that there was a negative relationship between time spent on work and purchasing activities. In our sample, 40% of the respondents are employed full-time and another

Table 10.   Time Spent by Participants by Days of the Week
(in mean minutes per day)

Activity

Days of the Week	Information Seeking	Purchasing	Postpurchase	Travel
Monday	21	18	14	27
Tuesday	28	19	13	26
Wednesday	36	22	27	32
Thursday	43	32	17	35
Friday	29	25	18	31
Saturday	32	33	15	36

Table 11.   Time Spent by Participants by Their Characteristics
(Average for the week in minutes)

Characteristics	Information Seeking	Purchasing	Postpurchase	Travel
For all Participants	133	120	34	148
A. *Age*				
20–29	73	104	31	110
30–39	97	105	24	157
40–49	167	137	33	181
50–59	174	123	43	153
60+	166	125	34	144
B. *Household Size*				
1	163	86	22	84
2	126	115	34	133
3	153	124	42	165
4	109	127	39	158
5+	136	134	35	171
C. *Working Status*				
Full-Time	139	111	29	134
Part-Time	117	119	48	142
Not Working	133	129	34	164
D. *Education*				
Primary School	132	116	37	153
Vocational School	140	138	48	163
Secondary School	134	125	14	140
Other School	118	95	38	136
University	120	75	5	63
E. *Total Household Income*				
Below (NKR) 15,000	51	63	—	102
15,000–19,999	25	89	—	24
20,000–29,999	139	133	34	143
30,000–39,999	120	108	73	111
40,000–49,999	14	91	20	59
50,000–59,000	87	99	8	120
60,000–69,000	66	93	71	102
70,000–79,000	98	147	26	187
80,000–89,000	88	119	13	169
90,000+	198	129	35	172

20% of the respondents are employed part-time. Therefore, we analyzed the time spent in purchasing activities by respondents categorized by their working status. The χ^2 values were not significant for any of the working status classification of the respondents. While there are no statistically significant relationships between working status and time spent in purchasing activities, some interesting findings did emerge, as seen in Table 11. For example, time allocated for information-seeking is the greatest for full-time working women, greater for the unemployed, and low for those working part-time. On the other hand, time allocated for purchasing activities shows a clear pattern of full-time working status women spending less time, partly employed seeming to spend somewhat more in their time spent for purchasing, and "not working" spending the greatest amount of time. One plausible explanation for this interesting phenomenon may be that in trying to compensate for the limited availability of purchasing time, the full-time working women allocate more time for information-seeking activities in order to be updated and to be somewhat well-informed in their purchasing activities.

The education levels of the respondents and the allocation of time for these varying activities did not generally show any relationships. However, there appears to be a drop in the usage of time, beyond secondary school level, for information-seeking activities. Similar but somewhat stronger tendencies seem to occur for purchasing activities. Also, the life cycle classification of the respondents did not relate to any of the time allocation data. The Norwegian Central Bureau Study (1975) had reported finding that total household income affected the shopping time positively. In our analysis, we used the husband's income, wife's income, and the total household income to relate to the time spent in any of the three major activity areas of our interest. No relation was found with any of the income classifications.

Finally, the travel patterns were not analyzed extensively because of the smallness of our sample (in terms of participants) and since travel data was not given by most of the respondents. In addition, the location of our judgmental sample may not be representative of the travel pattern of residents in other parts of town. The only finding of any practical significance is that the travel time seems to vary with the time allocation for purchasing activities as may be expected.

CONCLUSIONS

This study, which appears to be the first of its kind, has made the attempt to elicit time budget information as it relates to important activities of consumers. The study indicates that it is possible to get time allocation information for all phases of consumption-related activities. The study elicited only limited demographic information from its respondents. Other variables such as ownership of consumer durables, the amount expended, and the product groups for which the activity was being undertaken might have been more helpful. Other findings may have emerged if the field setting included television and radio as sources of information (commercials) for consumers. The prospects for undertaking time budget studies to ascertain the temporal dimensions of consumer behavior appear brighter. The role of time in consumer decision-making process may therefore become increasingly amenable for research.

REFERENCES

1. Arndt, Johan, and Gronmo, Sigmund, "The Time Dimension of Shopping Behavior: Some Empirical Findings," in William D. Perreault, Jr. (ed.), *Advances in Consumer Research,* Vol. 4, pp. 230–235. Atlanta, Georgia: Association for Consumer Research, 1977.

2. Becker, Gary S., "A Theory of the Allocation of Time." *The Economic Journal* 75 (1965): 493-517.
3. Chapin, F. S., *Human Activity Patterns in the City: Things People Do in Time and Space*. New York: John Wiley & Sons, 1974.
4. Cullen, Ian G., "Space, Time and The Disruption of Behavior in Cities." Paper presented to the Research Group on Time Budgets, Brussels, 1972.
5. Foote, N. N., "The Time Dimension and Consumer Behavior," in J. W. Newman (ed.), *On Knowing the Consumer*, pp. 38-46. New York: John Wiley and Sons, 1966.
6. Hagerstrand, Torsten, "What About People in Regional Science." Paper of the Regional Science Association, 23, 1969.
7. Hawes, Douglass K., Talarzyk, W. Wayne, and Blackwell, Roger D., "Consumer Satisfactions from Leisure Time Pursuits," in Mary Jane Schlinger (ed.), *Advances in Consumer Research*, Volume 2, pp. 817-836. Atlanta, Georgia: Association for Consumer Research, 1975.
8. Hawes, Douglas K., "Time Budgets and Consumer Leisure Time Behavior," in William D. Perreault, Jr. (ed.), *Advances in Consumer Research*, Vol. 4, pp. 221-229. Atlanta, Georgia: Association for Consumer Research, 1977.
9. Howard, John, and Sheth, Jagdish N., *The Theory of Buyer Behavior*. New York: John Wiley & Sons, 1969.
10. Jacoby, Jacob, Szybillo, G. J., and Berning, C. K., "Time and Consumer Behaviour: An Interdisciplinary Overview." *The Journal of Consumer Research* 2 (March 1976): 320-339.
11. Norwegian Central Bureau of Statistics, *Tidsymttingsundersokelsen* 1971-72. Oslo: Statistisk Sentralbyra, 1975 (Hefte 1.)
12. Robinson, John P., "Time As An Indicator of Social Change and the Quality of Life," in Mary Jane Schlinger (ed.), *Advances in Consumer Research*, Vol. 2, pp. 847-850. Atlanta, Georgia: Association for Consumer Research, 1975.
13. Schary, P. B., "Consumption and the Problem of Time." *The Journal of Marketing* 35 (April 1971): 50-55.
14. Szalai, Alexander, *The Use of Time: Daily Activities of Urban and Suburban Populations in Twelve Countries*. The Hague: Mouton, 1972.
15. Voss, Justin L., and Blackwell, Roger D., "Markets for Leisure Time," in Mary Jane Schlinger (ed.), *Advances in Consumer Research*, Volume 2, pp. 837-846. Atlanta, Georgia: Association for Consumer Research, 1975.

MARKETING MIX DECISION RULES FOR NONPROFIT ORGANIZATIONS

Charles B. Weinberg*, UNIVERSITY OF BRITISH

COLUMBIA

ABSTRACT

What price should a nonprofit organization charge users and how much effort should the organization devote to developing, delivering, and communicating its services to users and to attracting contributions from donors? A review of current practice in these areas illustrates some of the problems that arise from currently employed decision rules. A formal structuring of the nonprofit organization's marketing mix problem leads to the determination of optimal decision rules. In many cases, these rules suggest that a nonprofit organization should charge lower prices and devote more of its resources to marketing than a similarly situated business should. In addition, the relationship between donations and fund raising expenditures is estimated empirically for one organization.

Until the late 1960s, marketing was considered to be a function or activity primarily of profit making businesses. Since then, however, there has been

Research in Marketing, Volume 3, pages 191–234

increasing recognition that marketing applies to a wide range of nonprofit organizations and government agencies (Lovelock and Weinberg, 1978).

Originally, most public and nonprofit organizations viewed marketing primarily as advertising (and perhaps, personal selling as well) to obtain people's support for a cause ("Fight Forest Fires") or to raise funds ("Give the United Way"). This misperception is, of course, understandable since advertising is the most visible and intrusive component of marketing. This emphasis on advertising was probably reinforced by the recognition achieved by a number of successful public service advertising campaigns.

Marketing, however, is a complex managerial activity covering a broad range of actions. A useful way of examining this complexity is to look at the elements of the marketing planning process. Webster (1974) provides a very helpful conceptualization of this planning process by dividing it into seven stages:

1. Definition of the mission and objectives of the firm based on an assessment of the organization's strengths and weaknesses.

2. Development of a market orientation by careful assessment of the firm's environments to develop specific market opportunities.

3. Development of a positioning strategy of differential advantage for selected market segments.

4. Design of specific marketing policies and tactics for competing in the market place, that is, specification of the marketing mix—goods and services, price, communication, and distribution—in light of the chosen positioning strategy.

5. Integration of marketing policies and tactics into a synergistic whole designed to produce maximum impact in the marketplace.

6. Execution and monitoring of market plans and adjustment when necessary.

7. Evaluation by periodic, systematic measurement of results against specific standards.

Focus of the Article

This article concentrates on step 4, the specification of the marketing mix. Within the marketing mix, the primary focus is on determining price and setting levels of resource effort for marketing activities, for example, deciding how many outreach centers to have, specifying the amount of money to be devoted to advertising, selecting the number of volunteers to employ on a fund raising campaign, and determining prices and discounts to offer. There are, of course, other significant aspects of marketing mix decisions. For example, marketing communication (advertising, personal selling) decisions include specification of communication goals, definition of the role of different communication modes, choice of message strategy, and determination of the message distribution plan as well as the expenditure level. Although this article concentrates on budget levels and price, this concentration does not imply that other factors are not significant as well.

The focus of this paper is on the marketing mix because, as will be seen, there are fundamental differences between businesses and nonprofit organizations with regard both to selecting the optimal price and to setting the optimal levels of effort for the other elements of the marketing mix. These differences arise from two main sources. First, nonprofits do not follow an objective of profit maximization across the full range of marketing decisions. And second, nonprofits must simultaneously determine a marketing mix both for resource attraction (e.g., money and time) from donors and also for the marketing of services to users.

This article is divided into five major parts. First, we present a conceptualization of the American economy as consisting of three primary sectors—business, government, and nonprofit. We then examine some implications of this trichotomy. Particularly important is the fact that many nonprofits raise a significant proportion of their funds from government agencies and private contributions. In many cases, only a small portion of a nonprofit's total income is earned from consumers of the organization's goods and services. This section concludes by suggesting that usage maximization—of the services that the organization chooses to provide—is an appropriate objective function for many nonprofits.

Second, we review the ways that nonprofit organizations make marketing mix decisions. In contrast to the marketing planning framework offered above, many nonprofits make marketing mix decisions on a piecemeal basis, and often without a considered evaluation of what the spending level should be on each marketing mix element.

Third, employing usage maximization as the objective function for nonprofit organizations, we formulate the marketing mix problem analytically and solve it for the optimal price to charge users and optimal level of effort to devote to marketing services and to attracting donations. The formulation, in particular, includes the interrelationship between usage of the service and the response by contributors to the organization's fund raising efforts. In contrast to profit maximizing institutions facing identical demand and cost curves, the nonprofit should usually charge a lower price and devote more effort to the marketing of its services. The former result is often posited; the latter is not.

Fourth, using a major private university as an example, we employ regression analysis to estimate the relationship between fund raising expenditures and donor contributions. This allows us to estimate the elasticity of contributions received to fund raising effort, and to utilize the empirical results with the model developed in the previous section.

Finally, we conclude the article with a brief summary.

THE THREE SECTOR ECONOMY

As Ginsberg *et al.* (1965) describe in *The Pluralistic Economy,* the American economy is increasingly being recognized as composed of three major sectors: (1) private-for-profit, that is, the business or profit maximizing sector; (2) the public or government sector, including federal, state, and local governments and their agencies; and (3) the nonprofit sector, which includes religious organizations, many hospitals, arts institutions, museums, charitable organizations, family planning agencies, environmental and wildlife preservation groups, social welfare organizations, and numerous others. In this article, our attention will focus on the nonprofit sector.

The terminology "nonprofit" refers primarily to the organization and not necessarily to the industry in which the organization participates. Industries such as hospitals, the arts, and education contain participants from all three sectors. For example, private nonprofit colleges compete both with state universities and profit-making vocational schools. As another example, although some television stations are funded primarily by state or city governments, and others are community supported, the majority are owned by profit-making companies. On the other hand, some areas of activity, such as religion, consist virtually entirely of nonprofit institutions.

The legal category of nonprofit is too broad for our purposes, since it includes some organizations such as mutual insurance companies and savings and loan associations, which seem more similar to businesses than to the voluntary, charitable, or philanthropic organizations, which seek to achieve communal goals, with which we are concerned. Nonprofit status can carry a number of significant advantages, including exemption from such levies as property taxes and also the ability to collect tax deductible contributions. Although some nonprofit institutions are in reality profit maximizers, our concern is not with those groups. Our concern is with what some call the "voluntary nonprofit" sector, although we will occasionally use illustrative examples from the public sector.

Implications of the Deficit Nature of Nonprofit Organizations

A critical difference between nonprofit organizations and businesses is that many nonprofits incur substantial deficits and thus require either government grants or private benefactions. Some nonprofits, such as performing arts groups and hospitals, charge a price for their services so that users bear some of the costs of the provided services. Other organizations, such as libraries and religious groups, make no direct charge for their services, and consequently financial support for the organization is not directly tied to usage.

The proportional relationship among user charges, government grants, and contributions for nonprofit organizations can be seen in a study of nonprofits which conduct operations in New York (McLenithan, 1976). By state law, all non-exempt organizations which receive more than $25,000 in contributions must file an annual financial statement. Religious organizations, accredited educational institutions, and certain types of membership organizations are exempt. As shown in Table 1, each organization is classified into one of nine categories (health, social welfare, civic, cultural, environmental, fraternal and political, fundraising, hospital, and other). The data are from 2488 organizations which

Table 1. Average Public Support, Government Grants, and Revenue Expressed in Percentages by Type of Organization

Percent of Total Public Support, Government Grants, and Revenue From Each Source

	Health	Social Welfare	Civic	Cultural	Environment	Fraternal & Political	Fund Raising	Hospital	Other
Public Support									
Contributions	33%	28%	38%	27%	68%	76%	68%	3%	52%
Indirect public support	27	6	7	1	1	2	14	1	1
Total public support	60	34	45	28	69	78	82	4	53
Government fees and grants	11	13	14	22	1	—	4	2	3
Revenue: Program service fees	24	47	32	40	22	1	5	88	29
Other revenue	5	6	9	10	8	21	9	6	15
Total revenue	29	53	41	50	30	22	14	94	44

Source: G. J. McLenithan, "Public Disclosure Requirements of Charitable Organizations." *The Philanthropy Monthly* (September 1976). Note: The data are based on reports filed with the State of New York for 2488 nonprofit organizations in the years 1973, 1974, and 1975.

filed with New York for the years 1973, 1974, and 1975, and represent a three year average.

As can be seen, aside from hospitals, no group as a whole earned as much as 50% of its total revenues from program service fees. And hospitals are a special case, since a substantial portion of hospital fees are paid by third parties, for example, Blue Cross/Blue Shield, insurance companies, and Medicare. The median level of government support as a percentage of total receipts is 7%; the median level of contributions, 35%. The two major groups excluded from this study—religious organizations and educational institutions—are heavily dependent on contributions (and government support in the latter case) for financial survival. For example, *Giving USA 1977* (1977) lists religion (at $12.8 billion) and education (at $4.1 billion) as the first and third largest recipients of contributions in 1976.

The marketing task of the nonprofit is more complex than that of the business or commercial organization, which generally prospers if it can satisfy consumer needs better than the competition. The nonprofit organization must not only provide goods and/or services (generically referred to as "products") which meet user needs, but it also must satisfy the donors from whom it attracts resources. For some nonprofits, this often means that the products offered to donors must appeal to the donors' intuitive appraisals of client needs and may limit the range of services provided.

> The United Methodist Church, to illustrate, found that many of its members (donors who provide much of its financial support) were not pleased by its growing interest in helping blacks who were not parishioners (Shapiro, 1973, p. 124).

Table 2.   Sources and Recipients of Contributions
(1976)

Sources	Amount (in Billions)	
Living Individuals	$23.58	(80%)
Bequests	2.36	(8%)
Foundations	2.13	(7%)
Corporations	1.35	(5%)
Total:	$29.42	100%

Recipients	Amount (in Billions)	
Religion	$12.84	(44%)
Health and Hospitals	4.37	(15%)
Education	4.07	(14%)
Social Welfare	2.67	(9%)
Arts and Humanities	2.08	(7%)
Civic and Public Affairs	.97	(3%)
Other	2.42	(8%)
Total:	$29.42	100%

Source: *Giving USA 1977 Annual Report,* New York: American Association of Fund-Raising Counsel, 1977.

Another example is the limitations that some donors place on the counseling and educational services that family planning agencies can offer to their clientele.

In many cases, an organization's success in serving clients will lead to success in raising funds from benefactors. For example, a manager of one performing arts series explained that he turned to an aggressive marketing policy to build an audience for several reasons, including the observation that it is easier to raise money for a performing arts series that is sold out at half price than one which is half empty at full price. Nevertheless, some organizations appear to be successful at attracting donations without necessarily satisfying market needs. As noted by Shapiro (1973), a 1972 *Time Magazine* article suggested that Father Flanagan's Boys Town was, at that time, better at raising money than raising boys.

Objective Function

Specification of the objective function for making marketing mix decisions is of course, crucial. In the business sector, the objective function for determining the optimal marketing mix is usually based on profit maximization. (See, for example, Kotler, 1971.) Although the definition of profit in an actual organizational setting is never as straightforward as theoretical treatments would suggest and few would suggest that a firm will make *every* decision based on profit maximization, most will agree that

> profit is sure to be a goal of nearly every [business] enterprise—probably the predominant goal. Profit is a universal measure of business performance; invariably, financial statements of firms focus upon the amount of profit. Few businessmen deliberately pursue policies which they think will in the long run yield profits far below what otherwise could be earned. Nonetheless, some firms are almost certain to evidence more profit-conscious and profit-oriented behavior than others (Thompson, 1977, p. 316).

Among the alternatives to profit maximization are satisficing behavior, sales maximization, market share maximization, long run survival, personal goals of managers, and growth.

By definition, nonprofit organizations are not profit maximizers. In order to achieve insights into the nature of the marketing mix decision for nonprofits and to be able to compare their decisions to those of businesses, we need to specify an objective function that captures the distinctiveness of the nonprofit sector and is broad enough to cover a range of nonprofit organization as well. Consequently, in this article we assume that the objective function for a nonprofit organization when making marketing mix decisions is *maximization of the amount of its products or services which are consumed or utilized,* subject to the amount of *revenues and donations* being at least equal to the cost of providing the service. If revenues and donations are fixed and consequently independent of any marketing efforts by the organization, then the objective leads to a resource allocation problem. The more general case is the one in which revenues and donations are conditional on the marketing mix.

Although this objective does not include all nonprofit organizations, it appears to be representative of such organizations as universities and other educational institutions, health maintenance organizations (HMO), museums, performing arts organizations, religious groups, family planning and other social agencies, legal aid societies, and libraries. In considering maximization of usage, it should be kept in mind that we are referring to the products and services which the organization chooses to offer—presumably based on market analysis and the organization's charter—and not necessarily the products or services which are "easiest" to market. The usage to be maximized sometimes also must be restricted to only portions of the organization's product line or to certain market segments. For example, a health maintenance organization (HMO) in which users prepay for medical care probably wants to maximize utilization of its preventive health care services and not its emergency room. A university may wish to maximize applications from qualified applicants, not from anyone with a high school diploma. Or a university may want to increase applications to its undergraduate school but not its graduate school.

Some nonprofit organizations do not provide any direct services to users, but primarily attempt to motivate changes in awareness, attitudes, and behavior patterns; for example, environmentalist organizations work to promote wilderness preservation, groups concerned with health issues try to increase the number of non-smokers, and safety councils attempt to promote defensive driving and obedience to the 55 MPH speed limit. For these types of organizations, maximum adoption of the advocated idea or behavior seems to be an appropriate objective.

The marketing mix objective of maximization of usage focuses on one of the critical differences between profit and nonprofit organizations. In addition, it provides a rationale for providing services beyond the point of marginal revenue maximization, and when the ability to attract donations is included, to set price below marginal cost in certain situations.

Several other objective functions can be postulated. For example, one objective function is producer self-satisfaction, in which the members of the organization do what pleases them most. This might hold particularly for artistic organizations. As we discuss below, this objective function does not appear to be applicable when an organization is making such marketing mix decisions as prices to charge, number of different offerings or services to provide, and amount of advertising to do. However, the strategic choice of product-market in which the organization chooses to participate is often heavily influenced by the desires of the organization members.

Another possible objective function is that nonprofit organizations are identical in goals to business organizations, but only use the nonprofit form as a means to solicit contributions and to reduce or avoid taxes. Such a notion may imply that the "owner-managers" are rewarded with high salaries and benefits, rather than profits and capital gains. As discussed previously, although this objective is surely pursued by some organizations, it is not the focus of this study.

Still another possible objective function is a more refined version of the usage maximization objective in which a manager places different weights upon usage by different market segments or of different components of the product line. For example, the manager of a performing arts series at a university may weight more heavily attendance by the university's students than attendance by community residents. Similarly, the manager may place a higher value on attendance at concerts by young, relatively unknown artists than on attendance at concerts by well-known, established performers. We can extend the model developed below to include these differential weightings. However, before using a weighted model, an organization needs to have established a procedure for setting weights.

In summary, we assume that a nonprofit organization, when making marketing mix decisions, is seeking to maximize consumption or utilization of its services, subject to meeting costs. In addition, as discussed in the previous section, we allow the amount of donations received to be influenced not only by marketing effort, but also by the level of utilization of the organization's services.

SOME APPROACHES TO DETERMINING THE MARKETING MIX

In this section, we review and critique different approaches to the problem of determining the marketing mix for nonprofit organizations. (See Table 3.) We begin by briefly reviewing the public sector economics literature, which focuses primarily on price and pays little attention to other elements of the marketing mix. The public sector model is not directly applicable to nonprofit organizations. However, many managers are familiar with the basic result: set price equal to marginal cost. Consequently, it is useful to discuss this literature here.

Next, we examine the notion of producer self-satisfaction as the dominant

Table 3. Approaches to Determining the Marketing Mix for Nonprofit Organizations

A. Public Sector Economics
B. Self-Satisfaction (Producer Satisfaction)
C. Rules of Thumb
   1. Professional (or Production) Approach
   2. Price Rules
      2.1 Cost Plus or Minus Pricing
      2.2 Minimal and Free Pricing
      2.3 Fair Pricing
      2.4 Ability to Pay
   3. Marketing Communication
      3.1 Use Available Free Goods
      3.2 Announcement Only
      3.3 Demand Oriented
   4. Fund Raising as a Separate Activity

motive when a nonprofit organization determines its marketing mix. Although self-satisfaction is an important component in an organization's choice of product-market to serve and can influence marketing mix decisions, we show it is limited as an overall model. The final and major portion of this section classifies and analyzes the major rules of thumb that nonprofit managers appear to be using in making marketing mix decisions.

Public Sector Economics

A portion of the economics literature focuses on price setting in government agencies for which user charges can be assessed. The decision rule that this literature generally presents is for the agency to set price equal to marginal cost per unit. In most cases,[1] this rule will leave some fixed costs not covered by user fees. The usual prescriptions for meeting the fixed expenses are either to cover the fixed cost by revenues from the general taxing authority of the government or to levy a charge which varies per user as opposed to per unit. The per user charge does not affect the number of units consumed by a user, but it can influence the number of users.

The major argument offered for the price equal to marginal cost rule is one of economic efficiency. It can be shown that if all other markets are efficient, then setting price equal to marginal cost is optimal from a global viewpoint. The price equal to marginal cost rule is also attractive because if the government, as a monopoly supplier, were to be replaced by a set of perfectly competitive suppliers, then price would be equal to marginal cost. Although the perfect competition and complete external efficiency conditions are seldom observed, the notion of charging the user only marginal cost is an intuitively appealing one.[2] It is consonant with the belief that those who benefit from public services should pay for them. Presumably, only if there are social benefits (positive externalities) that would not otherwise be available to society at large should a government agency be willing to price below marginal costs.

When the effects of marketing variables such as advertising are also included, the public sector economics model has some difficulty in specifying an optimal course of action. In particular, the model does not allow for advertising to affect "taste" (preferences) and even viewing advertising purely as information also causes difficulty. In brief, if the relationship between demand and price can be affected by advertising and other marketing variables, then the rule of setting price equal to marginal cost does not uniquely determine the quantity marketed. For example, if the marginal cost of production is assumed to be constant at $2.00 per unit, and the effect of increasing advertising expenditures by 20% is to increase demand by 10% above the current level, then setting price equal to marginal cost does not determine whether utilization will be at its current level or at 10% above its current level. If marginal cost is not constant, then the advertising level partially, albeit indirectly, determines the marginal cost to which price is set equal. Furthermore, the marginal cost is influenced by whether advertising is treated conceptually as a fixed or variable cost.[3]

Finally, the public sector economics model views fund raising as exogenous. Presumably, no valuable resources are used in raising funds to cover operating deficits, and the public sector manager cannot take actions to market his or her organization and alter the amount of funding it receives. Yet, at least some of the time that officials of state and local governments and even of federal agencies spend testifying before the U.S. Congress and its committees and meeting formally and informally with Congressional staff assistants must be classified as fund raising.

Self-Satisfaction (Producer Satisfaction)

Etgar and Ratchford (1974) propose a dual market structure similar to the one discussed earlier. The perspective is that of the management of a nonprofit organization which controls three variables—price, advertising to users, and advertising to benefactors. However, an additional variable, producer satisfaction, is also introduced. The authors claim that the primary objective of most nonprofit organizations is producer satisfaction: that is, the

> product is created mainly for the satisfaction of producers themselves. . . . The organization will modify its product away from the one which gives its own members the most satisfaction only insofar as is necessary to obtain enough revenue from these customer groups to survive financially (Etgar and Ratchford, 1974, p. 259).

A philharmonic orchestra which plays classical music rather than rock music is used to exemplify this argument. Although it is certainly true that in most professional organizations the members derive personal satisfaction, the focus on maximization of personal interests seems limited as a general model. Furthermore, in the operationalization of the model, Etgar and Ratchford define satisfaction as a variable independent of the quantity of the product consumed. Thus, orchestra members would be indifferent between a one-performance and twenty-performance season at the same satisfaction level and between one person in the audience and an auditorium filled to capacity.

However, this criticism is not meant to suggest that producer satisfaction can be neglected, especially in the case of artistic organizations. For example, Adizes (1975) argues that:

> The purpose of the not-for-profit artistic institution is to enable artists to create and communicate their output to the society at large according to their artistic consciences. The organization should develop the needs of the audience so that the audience will be able to absorb its product, rather than developing a product that is dictated by the needs of the existing market. The purpose of the artistic organization is to expose an artist and his message to the widest possible audience, rather than to produce the artist and the message which the largest audience demands (Adizes, 1975, p. 80).

An artistic organization which neglects the needs of its artists in order to meet current market needs will often find that its artistic vitality declines. Yet, on the other hand, audience needs cannot be neglected if the artist is to have an audience. There is obviously no simple solution for this dilemma. However, as Adizes implies, attempts at solutions should not be static but rather concerned about the dynamics of audience development over time.

For example, Ryans and Weinberg (1978) examined the process of development over time of a subscription audience for the American Conservatory Theatre (ACT), a major repertory theatre in San Francisco. The study indicated that almost one-third of the new subscribers to ACT had not attended an event at ACT for up to five years previous to the year they first subscribed. From a product-market standpoint, the challenges to ACT include continuing to attract this new audience, finding ways to develop the tastes of these "sudden subscribers" so that they will appreciate the range of plays that ACT produces, and designing a season series which can appeal to both sudden subscribers and long-term attenders.

We have focused here on the relationship between self-satisfaction and the organization's product. However, self-satisfaction can also affect other aspects of the organization's marketing program. For example, with regard to distribution, a number of welfare agencies locate their offices at a distance from the low income areas in which their clients live in order to meet the desires of their own employees. As another example, in the area of communications, some advertisements appear to be more concerned with the (ego gratifying) needs of the sponsors than the needs of the clients.

Rules of Thumb

Many nonprofit managers, faced with a lack of formal analytic decision rules and difficult problems in measurement of response functions, have generated rules of thumb for making marketing mix decisions. These rules tend to treat each of the elements of the marketing mix as independent decisions. In this section, we review some of these rules and illustrate them with examples. No formal surveys of the decision rules employed have been taken, so the results are suggestive and impressionistic. In addition, the rules are chosen to illustrate points on a spectrum and many managers may use blends of these rules in practice. Some of these rules are as follows:

1. Professional (or Production) Approach. The organization provides the best possible services as it sees them and believes enough people will make use of those services to justify their existence. This approach is known as "minimal" or "no-sell" marketing.

> Organizations practicing minimal marketing do not consciously perform a marketing function and assume that demand will grow for their product simply because they are offering it, or offering it well. Many hospitals assume that there will be an adequate number of patients for

their beds simply because of the growing population and the availability of their services. Many universities assume that there will be an adequate number of student applicants for the same reasons. They think "Why should one have to sell a worthwhile service?" (Kotler, 1975, p. 8).

Often organizations taking this approach face markets characterized by increasing demand and limited competition and are thus able to adopt a product policy and marketing approach which is not based on responsiveness to market needs. During the 1970s, as many colleges encountered problems in student recruitment and hospitals faced financial difficulties, administrators at these institutions, often belatedly, turned to marketing approaches to help understand problems and develop comprehensive marketing-oriented solutions. As the following excerpts from an article in *Hospitals* about the Methodist Hospital in Marion County, Indiana indicate, rather than passively accepting a decrease in demand, a marketing approach can lead to the development of a product policy and marketing program in which the organization can prosper,

A study written by the hospital's administrative resident provided a framework for a comprehensive, detailed marketing plan for the hospital. . . .

Where to market. First, the study recommended that, in order to best compete for Marion County patients, the hospital market its emergency department services. The hospital has the largest and most comprehensive emergency department in the state, it is the most centrally located hospital in relation to all of the major interstate highways, and it has the largest and most sophisticated intensive care unit. Moreover, emergency patients contributed heavily to inpatient days. For these reasons, the development of the emergency department as a trauma center was undertaken. . . .

Second, the study recommended that the hospital market inpatient services to patients outside Marion County by emphasizing the hospital's sophisticated specialty services and the availability of specialists located close to the hospital. Reaching the outlying markets was deemed worthwhile, because their expanding populations needed to be served and because their hospitals were small. . . .

Which services to market. The study's recommendations emphasized the hospital's highly specialized services and de-emphasized its primary care services. It seemed logical that patients should receive care at their local hospitals whenever possible. Consequently, the hospital chose not to aggressively market routine services, such as obstetrics, even though it had a declining obstetrical volume. . . .

How to reach the market. The study recommended building rapport with the outlying hospitals through shared service programs. These programs would help develop the relationships between hospitals and between medical staffs that would be necessary to groom these markets for patient referrals (Seaver, 1977, p. 60).

2. Price Rules

2.1. Cost plus or minus pricing.
Price is related primarily to cost with relatively little attention paid to demand effects. The cost base varies by organization and may include only marginal costs or may include all fixed overhead costs. Demand effects are sometimes considered in the sense that the organization wants to break even on its cost base.

The Red Cross Blood Bank program provides an example of this approach. As discussed below, the program has recently been converted into one for which there are no donor credits and all users pay only a processing fee. The processing fee, or price, varies by region of the country, but, according to a Red Cross brochure, is based on the "irreducible cost of recruiting, processing, collecting, and distributing the blood to the hospitals."

2.2. *Minimal and free pricing.* The organization believes that price should not be an obstacle to usage and consequently tries to offer its services free or at a token price which bears little relation to cost. The organization implicitly is assuming that benefactors will cover costs.

Ginsberg puts this type of pricing strategy into historical perspective as follows:

> Since the aim of philanthropy is to make useful goods and services available to the poor who could not otherwise secure them, many nonprofit organizations long followed the practice of offering their services free of charge or at a price far below cost. As a consequence, their pricing policy was frequently so haphazard that it did not even justify the term "policy." Recently, however, several forces have been operating to alter the situation and to force many nonprofit organizations to rationalize their pricing structure. Many middle- and even high-income groups increasingly desire to obtain the services of nonprofit organizations, such as universities, hospitals, symphony orchestras. However, philanthropy has not been able to provide subsidized services for all. Moreover, there is no reason why wealthy persons should give large sums away so that others in the middle-income brackets can obtain services free of charge or substantially below cost.
>
> The transition from the old to the new approach to pricing has left many anomalies. Room rates for private patients in many nonprofit hospitals still cover only current expenses; in these hospitals wealthy patients may continue to receive a subsidy with respect to the capital costs of hospital care.
>
> Many hospitals, colleges, and other nonprofit institutions continue to price their services at or below cost, and some continue to provide services to certain groups without charge. Nonprofit agencies have a personal approach and a welfare orientation which is lacking in profit-seeking enterprises. They are often overtly discriminatory, such as when they make special efforts to attract those who cannot pay their regular rates. This is true of colleges which offer scholarships to deserving students.
>
> The process of costing is not the same in profit-seeking and nonprofit enterprises. The latter are only slowly coming to consider cost accounting systems, which charge interest on invested capital and depreciation on plant and equipment. Because these expenses are so often neglected in computing costs, tuition at nonprofit colleges and the charges made by many hospitals bear even less relation to true costs than the public generally assumes to be the case (Ginsberg, Hiestand, and Reubens, 1965, p. 77–8).

2.3. *Fair pricing.* The organization sets what it believes to be a fair price for its services based either on an intuitive feeling of what "fair" means or on a review of what other organizations offering similar services are charging. Fair pricing rules often include segmentation factors. Many nonprofit organizations offer discounts if an individual is a member of an appropriate age or occupational group.

For example, a student report summarized one zoo's pricing policy as follows:

Admission is $2.00 for adults and does not include parking. Discounts are given to children, groups, members, and college students. No real research has been done on pricing, although questionnaires and suggestion cards have revealed some complaints about the price and parking. The guideline in setting prices is what comparable recreational and educational institutions charge.

Of course, what is "fair" is often difficult to determine. Historically, British Rail, like most railways charged passengers in proportion to the distance traveled. However, in 1968, British Rail converted to a selective pricing system in which route fares were based on quality of product, strength of market, and degree of competition, an approach which reflected much more of a marketing orientation than the previous one. One objection to the new system was that "the concept of a 'fair fare' would disappear—no longer would the cost per mile for each ticket type be the same for everyone ("Pricing a Ticket to Ride," 1977, p. 302).

2.4. Ability to pay. Some nonprofits base their prices on the individual user's ability to pay. As noted above, these pricing policies are often overtly discriminatory, such as when a college offers a scholarship to a deserving, needy student, but reflects the welfare orientation of these organizations.

Several museums have adopted an ability to pay approach to admissions pricing. Faced with the dilemma of needing to increase revenues from visitors but wanting to broaden the socio-economic mix of their audience, museums have turned to a policy of "pay-what-you-like-but-pay-something" as a compromise solution. Under this system, an admission charge is "suggested," and a minimum of $.25 or so may also be established. The Metropolitan Museum in New York City, for example, received an average of $.82 per visitor when it suggested a general admission fee of $1.25 and $.50 for students.

An ability to pay approach is a pricing system which is segmented on an individual basis. When this approach is used for expensive items like a college education, the school should ideally develop a very careful system for setting the price. When the item is relatively low in cost, such as with museum admissions, the organization needs to develop a pricing system that will motivate people to pay what they can, in fact, afford to pay. In the case of museums, the suggested price can be a very critical component in determining total revenue.

3. Marketing Communication Rules

3.1. Use available free goods. Nonprofit organizations generally have access to free advertising and free volunteer (personal selling) help and some organizations, rather than budget for a specific quantity of communication effort, employ whatever is available. There are dangers in this approach because free advertising cannot always be directed specifically at chosen target segments; moreover, the management of a volunteer organization can be expensive and time consuming.

Many of the problems with the use of volunteer help relate to the issue of *control* of the amount, duration, and quality of the volunteer's effort. Volunteers in fund raising programs often are embarrassed to ask friends to increase their monetary donations from previous levels and will not aggressively pursue recalcitrant donors. Also, volunteers may not find it convenient to adjust their time schedules to the needs of the organization. Perhaps even more important than control of the amount of effort are the problems involved in directing the volunteers' efforts into the areas that the organization wishes to pursue. Volunteers often have strong preferences for the activities in which they are willing to partake. One social service agency found it difficult to develop an outreach program for alienated, "anti-social" senior citizens because the volunteers mainly wanted to work with well-adjusted seniors similar to those whom the agency was already serving. At times, volunteers may greatly affect the organization's product. For example, the after school programs at Y's and community centers often depend largely on the talents and interests of the volunteers who lead the activities.

The problems of control are often compounded because many nonprofits do not realize the difficulty of managing a part-time, unpaid volunteer organization. In contrast, many businesses devote considerable time and attention to the management of their paid, full-time field sales force consisting primarily of career employees. The nonprofit's management often naively assumes that since the "volunteers are here because they want to be here," the volunteers will all be highly motivated towards achieving a common goal.

Finally, the increasing participation of women in the labor force suggests that nonprofits will find it increasingly more difficult to attract volunteers and thus may be compelled to conduct their operations with fewer volunteers than in the past. In brief, volunteer help is a scarce resource and costly in terms of the money and effort required to train, motivate, and manage this apparently free good.

Many of the problems relating to the use of public service advertising also are based on the loss of control. An organization committed to not paying for advertising must restrict its choice of advertising agencies to those willing to work for free or for out-of-pocket expenses only. In addition, it cannot specify the scheduling of its advertisements. If, for example, the advertisement is to be broadcast on television, the organization has no control over the time of day when it will be broadcast, the TV stations on which it will be shown, and what the time interval between commercials will be. Of course, there have been some very successful public service campaigns, but many organizations have been disappointed by the results achieved.

Another problem with public service campaigns is that they often must be non-controversial in order to satisfy the sensitivities of the multiple parties involved in providing a free campaign. For example, a report on an advertising campaign developed for Planned Parenthood noted that

> it took two years to get our campaign approved. Whenever our campaign was presented to a reviewing committee (and we had more reviewing committees than I could possibly re-

member), some surgical action was always inevitable . . . our campaign falls a good deal short of the objectives . . . hoped for. But compromise is a fact of life'' (Manoff, 1973, p. 114).

Again, the Red Cross Blood Bank program illustrates the difficulty of working under a no paid advertising stricture. Until 1977, donors and their families received free blood in case of need while non-donors had to pay a replacement fee for blood utilized and sometimes had to replace the blood as well. In 1977, the Red Cross, which supplies the majority of the blood used in the United States, switched to a volunteer no credit system in which any person in a Red Cross supplied hospital receives all the blood needed with only a processing fee and not a replacement fee being charged. The Red Cross's ban on paid advertising has prevented Red Cross Blood Banks from informing people about this new system, its overall benefits, and, in particular, from communicating with potential donors who may feel that they have lost something because they no longer receive replacement credits. The problem is particularly acute in areas such as Northern California where nearby nonprofit blood banks still offer replacement credits. The result of the advertising prohibition is that other elements of the marketing mix, for example, paid donor recruitment personnel, have to bear a disproportionate share of the overall marketing communication task with consequent inefficiencies for the total system.

3.2. Announcement only. Marketing communication is used primarily to announce the availability of services and other functional attributes of the service. Little effort is made to describe comprehensively the services offered, to provide persuasive information about the service, and to motivate trial and repeat usage of the service.

The difficulty encountered by Health Maintenance Organizations (HMO) which offer prepaid medical care by a group of doctors illustrates the effects of being confined to the announcement only type of advertising. Because many Americans are accustomed to a fee-for-service individual practitioner medical service, becoming a member of an HMO often involves substantial changes in people's attitudes and behaviors. Although some individuals may convert based on only a limited marketing campaign, quite often a substantial membership base is required for the HMO to be financially viable. As with other consumer goods and services, an effective way to help develop a substantial market in a short period of time is often a marketing program which includes extensive advertising to persuade the potential consumer to become informed about or try the service and to remind triers to become regular users or, in this case, members. Yet, one of the reasons that ''Prepaid Health Plans Run into Difficulties as Enrollment Falters'' (Lublin, 1975)—as a 1975 *Wall Street Journal* headline summarized the situation—is that many have confined themselves to very limited types of advertising.

3.3. Demand oriented. Some public sector organizations appear to have carefully analyzed the relationship between marketing communication and demand and are using what might be classified as an ''objective and task approach.'' For example, the Baptist General Convention of Texas conducted a major campaign based on market research results and assessments of the possible accomplishments of mass media and personal communications to motivate more people to attend church (Martin, 1977).

4. Fund Raising as a Separate Activity.   Most public sector organizations seem to view fund raising as a distinct and separate activity, although it often requires the time of key organizational members. In some organizations, fund raising budgets are based on the results of a careful study of the response of donations to fund raising effort (see, for example, ''Stanford University: The Annual Fund,'' 1977); in other organizations, the budget setting process is more intuitive. There appears to be a general notion of setting marginal revenue equal to marginal cost, especially when individual elements of a fund raising program are being evaluated. A constraint on employing the marginality rule is that some donors— especially foundations—expect fund raising costs to be a small fraction of funds raised. However, as shown in Table 4, many nonprofit organizations, especially smaller ones, have fund raising costs which exceed 20% of funds raised. These, of course, are averages and the marginal cost of the last dollar raised is almost surely higher. Even large organizations may find that particular components of their overall fund raising are costly. For example, the Stanford University Annual Fund (''Stanford University: The Annual Fund,'' 1977, p. 80) which seeks

Table 4.   Fund Raising Expenses as Related to Contributions for 920 New York Nonprofit Organizations

Fund Raising Expenses as a Percentage of Contributions	Voluntary Health and Social Welfare Organizations		All Other Organizations*	
	Number	Contributions	Number	Contributions
>50%	17	$ 9.3 million	13	$ 3.1
40–50%	13	6.3	16	24.1
30–40%	27	7.5	36	23.8
20–30%	53	26.8	51	55.9
<20%	241	244.7	453	477.3
Total	351	$294.5	569	584.2
Fund Raising Expenses as Percentage of Contributions	16.5%		12.4%	

*Includes civic, cultural, fraternal, and fund raising (e.g., United Way) organizations.
Source: M. Gross, ''A New Study of the Cost of Fund Raising in New York.'' *The Philanthropy Monthly* (April 1976).
Notes: These data are based on financial reports filed with the State of New York by nonprofit organizations which received contributions exceeding $100,000. Of the 1202 such organizations which have filed as of August 1975, 282 reported no fund raising expenses and are excluded.

yearly contributions primarily from alumni, has a cost to funds raised ratio of 12%. This ratio, which is generally regarded by professional fundraisers as low, is higher than the cost to funds raised ratio for other Stanford University giving programs. For some organizations, the critical question is how to allocate a given fund raising budget, while, for others, the critical question is specification of the budget size.

DETERMINATION OF THE OPTIMAL MARKETING MIX

In the previous section, we classified and discussed a number of the approaches that nonprofit managers have used to make marketing mix decisions. As can be seen, many of these approaches are casual and fail to take full account of the complexity involved in developing a marketing program. The approaches employed tend to focus on one element at a time rather than looking at the interactions among marketing mix elements. Even within an element, the approaches do little to examine the relationship between different levels of that variable and results. Yet, the notion that there is a causal link between marketing effort and demand is fundamental for a manager who wishes to develop effective and efficient marketing programs. This relationship between effort and demand, often termed a "response function" and used to develop a "conditional sales forecast," can help provide the basis for deciding such questions as the price to charge, the amount of money to spend for advertising, and the intensity of the distribution system to design.

The advantages of viewing the marketing mix problem from the perspective of a conditional sales forecast are both conceptual and practical. From a conceptual viewpoint, this approach forces a manager to state explicitly what the major determinants of demand are and, to the extent possible, what the nature of the relationship between demand and these determinants is. This helps the manager to understand what the impact of different marketing plans will be. When the manager can actually provide numerical estimates of the response relationship between the marketing mix variables and demand, then he or she has the basis for a practical tool to help make decisions. The most sophisticated use of response functions occurs when they are formally included in a marketing model.

Nature and Role of Marketing Models

Historically, the use of marketing models as an aid to managers in determining the marketing mix has been confined largely to packaged goods businesses, although applications in other consumer and capital goods industries have been reported as well. Most recently, some nonprofit organizations have also adopted marketing models. For example, Weinberg and Shachmut's (1978) ARTS PLAN modeling system was implemented by the manager of a performing arts series. The overall system aided the manager by relating performance type (e.g., dance, chamber music, and jazz), season of the year, and promotion level to seats sold at a given performance and for the total series.

Marketing models can be divided into two major classes (Aaker and Weinberg, 1975; Montgomery and Weinberg, 1973), descriptive models and decision models. Descriptive models are ones which take a given set of inputs and then produce a conditional sales forecast based on the estimated response function. These are often termed "what-if" models because they report *what* will happen *if* these actions are taken. Decision models go further; they include an algorithm which suggests an optimal solution to the marketing mix problem. To do this, a decision model needs a specification of what the objective function is. Because the model is only an approximation to the real world, its answer is rarely a "true" optimal. But it does provide a reasonable guide for managers. In the only controlled "real world" experiment we have been able to locate in the literature, United Airlines salespersons who used a marketing model to plan the number of sales calls they made on accounts had 8% higher sales than a matched sample of salespersons who did not have access to the model (Fudge and Lodish, 1977). This difference is statistically significant, and is also substantial in dollar terms. We believe that both descriptive and decision models can be of considerable help to the nonprofit marketing manager.

In this section, we develop a framework for making marketing mix decisions in nonprofit organizations. This framework is based on the response function approach we have advocated above; that is, we state explicitly the relationships between marketing variables and results. We then employ this framework to determine the optimal levels at which different elements of the marketing mix should be set for nonprofit organizations.

There are two major purposes to be accomplished by determining this optimal solution. The first is so that a methodology and solution will be available for use in building marketing decision models for nonprofit organizations. The second, and perhaps more important purpose, is so that the optimal behavior for nonprofit organizations can be compared to that for profit maximizing organizations. As can be inferred from the discussion in the previous section, many nonprofits appear to be reluctant to market their services aggressively. Yet, as will be shown below, this reluctance to devote substantial efforts to marketing, at least as compared to profit maximizing firms, is inappropriate. In many cases, a nonprofit firm facing identical demand and cost curves to a profit maximizing organization should not only spend more money on marketing and charge lower prices, but should also spend money to attract donations.

In the sections that follow, we discuss a nonprofit's operations in terms of dollar expenditures. Dollars, however, are not the only resource that an organization has. It may find, for example, that the demand for the service is dependent upon the number of volunteers it can allocate to that service. This can occur, perhaps, because the quality of the service is altered or because the volunteers serve as the sales force. The analysis that follows can readily be extended to include non-monetary resources.

Framework and Model Specification

In order to specify the model mathematically, the following notation is needed:

p — the price per unit of consumption
x — marketing expenditures to users
y — marketing expenditures to donors
$q=f(p,x)$ — quantity of services used by clients
$s=g(q,y)$ — subsidies raised
$c=h(q)$ — cost of producing q units (total cost)

The functions f, g, and h are assumed to have all necessary derivatives. The symbols x and y represent variables, but the model can be extended to include x and y as vectors.

It should be noted in particular that the subsidies or donations function, $s=g(q,y)$, is dependent on the quantity q. This is included to capture two effects. First, organizations which have larger user bases may be perceived as being more worthy of support by donors. Foundations often require that organizations indicate the level of community support they have as part of the grant application. An organization which provides food and shelter for the needy, for example, might expect that the more needy people it serves, the more likely it is to attract donations. The second reason for including q is that it affects the size of the target market for many organizations. Thus, for example, the results of a fund raising campaign for a university should be dependent on the number of graduates of the school. Or, as a final example, a performing or visual arts institution may find its attenders a primary target for fund raising efforts. The model formulated here does not explicitly account for multiperiod effects, such as the carry-over of advertising. However, similar comparative conclusions to those developed below about optimal marketing mix decisions for profit maximizing and nonprofit organizations will hold in the multiperiod and the single period cases.[4]

The marketing mix problem for the nonprofit organization can be stated as follows:

$$\text{Max } q = f(p,x) \tag{1}$$

subject[5,6] to

$$p\,f(p,x) - h(q) - x + g(q,y) - y = 0 \tag{2}$$

The optimal solution to this problem will be denoted p*, x*, and y*. Writing (1) and (2) in the Lagrangian format yields

$$\text{Max } L = q - \lambda[pq - c - x + s - y] \qquad (3)$$

where λ is the Lagrange multiplier.

The first order conditions for a maximum can be stated as:

$$\frac{\partial L}{\partial p} = \frac{\partial q}{\partial p} - \lambda\left[q + p\frac{\partial q}{\partial p} + \frac{\partial s}{\partial q}\frac{\partial q}{\partial p} - \frac{\partial c}{\partial q}\frac{\partial q}{\partial p}\right] \qquad (4)$$

$$= \frac{\partial q}{\partial p}\left[1 - \lambda\left(p + \frac{\partial s}{\partial q} - \frac{\partial c}{\partial q}\right)\right] - \lambda q = 0$$

$$\frac{\partial L}{\partial x} = \frac{\partial q}{\partial x} - \lambda\left[p\frac{\partial q}{\partial x} + \frac{\partial s}{\partial q}\frac{\partial q}{\partial x} - \frac{\partial c}{\partial q}\frac{\partial q}{\partial x} - 1\right] \qquad (5)$$

$$= \frac{\partial q}{\partial x}\left[1 - \lambda\left(p + \frac{\partial s}{\partial q} - \frac{\partial c}{\partial q}\right)\right] + \lambda = 0$$

$$\frac{\partial L}{\partial y} = \lambda\left[\frac{\partial s}{\partial y} - 1\right] = 0 \qquad (6)$$

$$\frac{\partial L}{\partial \lambda} = pq + s - c - x - y = 0 \qquad (7)$$

$$\text{Define } m = p + \frac{\partial s}{\partial q} - \frac{\partial c}{\partial q}. \qquad (8)$$

The term m ("augmented margin") has an interesting interpretation. The portion $p + \partial s/\partial q$ represents the revenue from the user and donor markets respectively of the last unit sold at a given price. Thus when the marginal cost $\partial c/\partial q$ is subtracted out, m (which may be negative) is then seen to be the margin from the last unit sold augmented by the marginal revenue gained from the donor market. If subsidies were not dependent upon usage, ($\partial s/\partial q = 0$), then m would be the margin on the last unit.

Substituting (8) into (4)–(5) yields, after algebraic manipulation,

$$(\lambda m - 1)\left(-\frac{\partial q}{\partial p}\right) = \lambda q \qquad (9)$$

$$(\lambda m - 1)\frac{\partial q}{\partial x} = \lambda \qquad (10)$$

and (6) becomes, after algebraic manipulation,

$$\frac{\partial s}{\partial y} = 1 \qquad (11)$$

Along with (7), the nonprofit or no-deficit constraint, (9), (10), and (11) are the necessary conditions for an optimal marketing mix. In the usual manner, define the elasticity of quantity sold to p and x respectively as

$$
e_p = - \frac{\partial q}{\partial p} \cdot \frac{p}{q} \left.\vphantom{\begin{array}{c} \\ \\ \\ \\ \\ \end{array}}\right\} \tag{12}
$$

and

$$
e_x = \frac{\partial q}{\partial x} \cdot \frac{x}{q}
$$

Then, combining (9) and (10) and using the definitions of elasticity in (12) yield the equivalent of the Dorfman-Steiner (1964) conditions which state a relationship among the marketing mix variables for the profit maximizing organization.

$$
e_p = e_x \frac{pq}{x} \tag{13}
$$

Obtaining the Dorfman-Steiner conditions was not obvious because the specified goal is usage maximization subject to a constraint, not revenue or profit maximization. Further, it should be noted that (13) does not uniquely specify the optimal value of p and x but only a necessary condition on their optimal values. Non-optimal values may also satisfy the Dorfman-Steiner conditions.

Equation (11) indicates that the optimal expenditure on marketing to the donor market is achieved where marginal revenue, $\partial s/\partial y$, equals marginal cost, 1. If s were independent of q, then the MR = MC rule could be applied to the donor market. This result follows from observing that s (q,y) − y in (3) would be separable if either s were independent of q or q were assumed constant for purposes of setting y.

It should be noted, however, that nonprofit organizations cannot always use this marginality rule (11) for donations, because of an explicit or implicit practice which requires that fund raising expenses not exceed a certain fraction of donations. This restriction could be accommodated by adding a constraint of the form

$$
\frac{y}{s(q,y)} \leq r \tag{14}
$$

to the problem stated in (1) and (2). The term r represents the maximum ratio of fund raising expenses to donations. Whether or not this constraint is binding depends upon the value of r and the marginal returns ($\partial s/\partial y$). If the constraint is binding, then the Lagrange multiplier can be used to indicate the cost of imposing this constraint. However, the primary managerial question is more likely to be what should the ratio be, and consequently the approach taken here is to solve (1) and (2) without including (14).

We now wish to contrast solution (4)–(7) to that which would be obtained under two other conditions: (A) profit maximizing firm and (B) nonprofit organization which cannot raise funds from donors. To make this comparison, we need to characterize the returns to scale properties of f(p,x), g(q,y), and c(q). With regard to response to marketing efforts, although there has been some support for a convex-concave of S-shaped response function, many empirical studies support diminishing returns to scale, at least in the relevant range for decision making (Freeland and Weinberg, 1977). Consequently we assume that q = f(p,x) is a decreasing return to scale function of x and p. Marginal costs are assumed to be either linear or decreasing in accordance with the results of most empirical studies. Although it can be argued theoretically that marginal cost will increase as an organization nears its capacity, empirical evidence does not support this contention, at least in the relevant range for decision making. As summarized in Johnston's classic work, "over substantial ranges of output . . . it [marginal cost] is probably constant" (Johnson, 1960, p. 192).

First we examine the nonprofit firm which cannot raise outside funds, or for which s is independent of y. By definition, we have [g(q,y*) − y *] ≥ [g(q,0)]. Thus, from (2), the effect of making donations sensitive to marketing input y is to increase the amount by which costs, h(q) + x, exceed revenues, pq, while the organization remains at breakeven. This outcome can occur only if there is either an increase in marketing expenditures to users (x) or a decrease in price (p), or both.

Now we consider the case of a profit maximizing firm with demand function f(p,x) and cost curve h(q). At the optimum, an operating profit maximizing firm will have pf(p,x) − h(q) − x > 0; a nonprofit organization however, will have pf(p,x) − h(q) − x ≤ 0. Given the stated returns to scale assumptions, the change of pf(p,x) − h(q) − x from positive to nonpositive can only occur if either or both p* is lower and x* is greater than the optimal price and marketing expenditures for the profit maximizing firm. In the next section, it is shown that when f(p,x) is assumed to be a power (constant elasticity) function, then an optimally behaving nonprofit organization will both charge less and spend more on marketing efforts than a profit maximizing firm facing the same demand function. It is generally accepted that nonprofit organizations might charge lower prices; it is not generally accepted that they should devote more resources to marketing than the profit maximizing firm facing identical demand and cost functions. Current practice is for nonprofit firms to spend relatively small amounts on marketing. These results suggest that this decision is probably based more on historical precedent and inertia than on an analytical study of the implications of the demand model the organization faces. The actual optimal allocation, of course, will depend upon the responsiveness of demand and donations to marketing variables and the costs.

Power (Constant Elasticity) Function Model

The previous section derived the necessary conditions for the optimal marketing mix for nonprofit organizations. To illustrate the optimal solution, it is necessary to assume functional forms for f(p,x) and g(q,y). We will use the power or constant elasticity function denoted by

$$f(p,x) = \alpha_0 p^{-\alpha_1} x^{\alpha_2} \qquad (\alpha_0, \alpha_1, \alpha_2 > 0) \qquad (15)$$

$$g(q,y) = \beta_0 q^{\beta_1} y^{\beta_2} \qquad (\beta_0, \beta_1, \beta_2 > 0) \qquad (16)$$

There are a number of reasons for the choice of this function. With the possible exception of the linear model, which gives unreasonable answers when used in an optimizing context, the power function is probably the most frequently used form for representing the marketing mix problem. The power function (15) is extremely flexible and can represent a variety of relationships between q, p, and x according to the values of the parameters. The function is also called a constant elasticity model because $e_p = \alpha_1$ and $e_x = \alpha_2$ for all values of p and x. Because of the multiplicative structure of (15), the model also can take account of interactive effects. For example, the impact of a simultaneous 5% price decrease and 10% advertising increase will be greater than the sum of the effects of each marketing action taken separately.

The power function lends itself well to parameter estimation. If historical or experimental data are available, after taking logarithms of both sides of (15), regression can be employed to estimate the parameters. If only subjective judgment data are available or a "decision calculus" procedure is to be utilized, then α_1 and α_2 can be directly estimated by answers to such questions as "What % sales increase will result from a 25% (say) increase in advertising?" Without effecting the values of α_1 and α_2, p and x can be indexed by reference or base case values.

In summary, the power function model is generally suitable and is frequently used to represent the relationship between demand and marketing mix variables. However, some limitations of the model should be stated. Zero values of p and x generally do not emerge. The variable p's negative coefficient $(-\alpha_1)$ implies division by zero when p = 0. A zero value of x results in no demand because of the multiplicative nature of (15). However, it would be rare for the optimal solution to include x = 0, although some organizations charge no price. Another difficulty is that (15) does not include an upper limit or saturation level for sales.

Although (15) can represent decreasing returns to scale, the saturation effect will not be modeled directly. Finally, constant elasticity may be questionable in some cases.

All these criticisms can be dealt with by using a more complex functional form such as the following:

$$f(p,x) = \gamma_0 e^{-\gamma_1 p} [\gamma_3 + (1-\gamma_3)(1-e^{-\gamma_2 x})] \quad (\gamma_0, \gamma_1, \gamma_2, \gamma_3 \geq 0) \quad (17)$$

$$\left.\begin{array}{l} \text{At } p = 0, f(p,x) = \gamma_0[\gamma_3 + (1-\gamma_3)(1-e^{-\gamma_2 x})]; \\[6pt] \text{at } x = 0, f(p,x) = \gamma_0\gamma_3 e^{-\gamma_1 p}; \text{ and} \\[6pt] \text{as } x \to \infty, f(p,x) = \gamma_0 e^{-\gamma_1 p} \end{array}\right\} \quad (18)$$

However, using (17) or a similar function will add considerably to the complexity of the algebraic development of the optimal marketing mix without a comparable gain in insight. The interested reader can pursue a development parallel to the one below for (17) or any other well behaved function.

In summary, (15) and (16) provide a representative and convenient model for the marketing mix problem. More complex models can be developed, especially when examining a particular organization; however, they are not necessary for the problem examined here and their inclusion would obfuscate further an already complex algebraic development. As discussed earlier, most empirical evidence supports the use of decreasing returns to scale; to implement this condition we require

$$\alpha_1 > 1$$
$$0 < \alpha_2, \beta_1, \beta_2 < 1 \quad (19)$$

The functional form of the cost function will be assumed to be linear, that is,

$$h(q) = c_f + c_v q \quad (c_f, c_v \geq 0) \quad (20)$$

If (20) were to be replaced by a cost function which included decreasing marginal costs as a function of q, the effect on the results that follow would be to further separate the optimal marketing mixes of profit maximizing firms and nonprofit organizations. For many nonprofit organizations, for example, mass transit agencies and performing arts groups, many costs do not vary per person served.

Optimal Marketing Mix for Power Functions

Using the response functions (15) and (16), and the linear cost function (20), the optimal marketing mix is developed in the Appendix for the profit maximizing firm and for nonprofit organizations which may accept price donations from benefactors. The results and some of their implications will be summarized here and then illustrated by a numerical example.

We first show, using (15), that a nonprofit organization has both lower price and higher marketing expenditures than a profit maximizing firm does. We have already seen that at least one of these conditions must occur. For both profit and nonprofit organizations, the Dorfman-Steiner equation (13) holds as a necessary condition. For (15), we have price elasticity $(e_p) = \alpha_1$ and marketing effort elasticity $(e_x) = \alpha_2$. Consequently, (13) becomes

$$\alpha_1 = \alpha_2 \frac{pq}{x} \tag{21}$$

After replacing q by $\alpha_0 p^{-\alpha_1} x^{\alpha_2}$, we obtain

$$x^{1-\alpha_2} \, p^{\alpha_1 - 1} = \frac{\alpha_0 \alpha_2}{\alpha_1} \tag{22}$$

The right hand side of (22) is a positive constant. Because $\alpha_1 > 1$ and $0 < \alpha_2 < 1$, x and p are both raised to positive powers. As compared to a profit maximizing organization, a nonprofit organization must have either lower prices or higher advertising. However, the equality in (22), which is a necessary condition in both the profit and nonprofit cases, can only be maintained when a nonprofit organization both lowers price and raises marketing expenditures as compared to a profit maximizing firm.

In addition, (21) can be restated to show that at the optimum, the ratio of user marketing expenses to user revenue (p^*q^*) is a constant:

$$\frac{x^*}{p^*q^*} = \frac{\alpha_2}{\alpha_1} \tag{23}$$

This constant provides a means of determining whether the organization's actual pricing and marketing strategies are in balance. The conditions for a decreasing returns to scale function require that $\alpha_2/\alpha_1 < 1$, so that marketing expenses should be less than revenues.

Similarly, the ratio of donor marketing expenditures (y^*) to contributions is, from (A17), a constant:

$$\frac{y^*}{s^*} = \beta_2 \tag{24}$$

As with the user market, this constant provides a means of determining whether donor marketing activities are in balance with contributions. If there is a constraint r (see 14) on the ratio of y^* to s^*, then a comparison of β_2 and r will indicate whether the constraint is binding. Unfortunately, the optimal ratio of funds from the user and donor markets cannot be reduced to a constant.

Summary of Solution

The optimal solution to the marketing mix problem is stated in general form in the Appendix. However, to provide a more compact representation, it is convenient to assume that

$$\alpha_1 + \alpha_2 = 2$$

$$2\beta_1 + \beta_2 = 1$$

The optimal price strategies (p*) for the profit maximizing firm and for usage maximizing organization which cannot obtain contributions and those which can are given in Table 5.

The optimal marketing effort to users, x*, can be stated in terms of p* in all three cases by use of (23)

$$x^* = \left[\frac{\alpha_0 \alpha_2}{\alpha_1} \right]^{1/1-\alpha_1} p^{*-1} \tag{25}$$

Table 5.   Optimal Price Strategies
(Assuming $\alpha_1 + \alpha_2 = 2$, $2\beta_1 + \beta_2 = 1$)

Profit Maximizing Firm

$$p^* = \frac{c_v \alpha_1}{\alpha_1 - 1}$$

Nonprofit Firm Without Donations

A. Fixed Costs = c_f

$$p^* = \frac{(k_2 - k_1) - \sqrt{(k_2 - k_1)^2 - 4c_f c_v k_2}}{2c_f}$$

B. No fixed costs ($c_f = 0$)

$$p^* = \frac{c_v k_2}{k_2 - k_1}$$

Nonprofit Firm With Donations

A. Fixed Costs = c_f

$$p^* = \frac{(k_2 - k_1 + k_3) - \sqrt{(k_2 - k_1 + k_3)^2 - 4c_f c_v k_2}}{2c_f}$$

B. No Fixed Costs ($c_f = 0$)

$$p^* = \frac{c_v k_2}{k_2 - k_1 + k_3}$$

Notation:

$$k_1 = \left[\frac{\alpha_0 \alpha_2}{\alpha_1} \right]^{1/1-\alpha_2} \qquad\qquad k_2 = \frac{\alpha_1}{\alpha_2} k_1$$

$$k_3 = \frac{2\beta_1}{\beta_2} (\beta_0 \beta_2)^{1/2\beta_1} k_2^{1/2}$$

Further, for nonprofit organizations which can obtain donations, the optimal marketing expenditures are given by

$$y^* = \left[\frac{\alpha_1}{\alpha_2} \left(\frac{\alpha_0 \alpha_2}{\alpha_1} \right)^{1/1-\alpha_1} (\beta_0 \beta_2)^{1/\beta_1} \right]^{1/2} p^{*-1} \qquad (26)$$

If there are fixed costs ($c_f > 0$), then both the profit and nonprofit organizations would not operate if those costs could not be met from revenues and contributions.

Illustrative Example

In order to illustrate the implications of the marketing mix decision rules, a numerical example is developed in this section. The parameter values chosen are hypothetical, although they would appear to be representative of at least some nonprofit organizations. The numerical examples are summarized in Table 6.

In particular, demand for service is given by

$$q = \alpha_0 p^{-\alpha_1} x^{\alpha_2}$$

$$= 1000 p^{-1.6} x^{.4} \qquad (27)$$

Table 6. Numerical Example of Optimal Decisions

	p*	x*	y*	Gross User Revenue	Profit From Users
Profit Maximizing					
No fixed costs	$2.67	$3720	—	$14,882	$5581
Fixed costs = $5000	$2.67	$3720	—	$14,882	$581
Usage Maximizing, No Donations					
No fixed costs	$1.33	$7441	—	$29,764	0
Fixed costs = $5000	$2.02	$4921	—	$19,682	0
Usage Maximizing, Donations					
No fixed costs					
$\beta_0 = 10$	$1.25	$7915	$ 378	$31,659	−$1512
$\beta_0 = 50$	$ .90	$10,984	$3922	$43,934	−$15,687
Fixed costs = $5000					
$\beta_0 = 10$	$1.72	$5763	$ 275	$23,051	−$1101
$\beta_0 = 50$	$1.02	$9705	$3466	$38,823	−$13,862

Constants for Numerical Example
$\alpha_0 = 1000$, $\alpha_1 = 1.6$, $\alpha_2 = .4$
$\beta_1 = .4$, $\beta_2 = .2$
$c_v = \$1.00$

Figure 1. Optimal Decisions

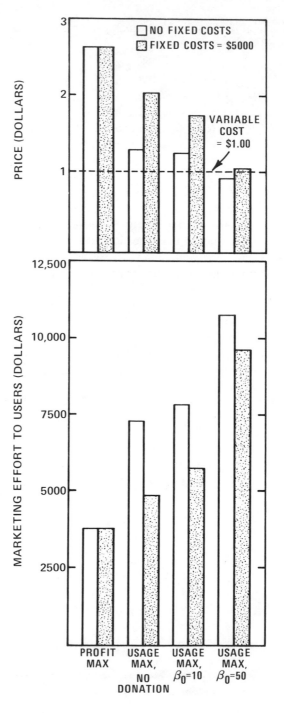

and the contribution market is described by

$$s = \beta_0 q^{\beta_1} y^{\beta_2}$$
$$= 50q^{.4} y^{.2} \tag{28}$$

The coefficients of price ($\alpha_1 = 1.6$) and marketing effort ($\alpha_2 = .4$) represent a moderate degree of sensitivity of demand to the price and marketing variables. Similarly, contributions are moderately sensitive to total usage of the service ($\beta_1 = .4$), but somewhat less sensitive to effort devoted to the benefaction market ($\beta_2 = .2$). In other words, a 50% increase in usage would increase donations by 20% ($1.5^{.4} = 1.2$); a 50% increase in effort devoted to the benefaction market would increase donations by 10% ($1.5^{.2} = 1.1$). The α_0 and β_0 are scale values; Table 6 provides an alternative value of β_0 (10) which provides 80% less contribution dollars at any value of q and y.

In order to show the effect of fixed costs on the optimal solution, Table 6 shows the optimal values of the decision variables for the cases of zero fixed costs and for $c_f = 5000$.

As can be seen in Figure 1, the usage maximizing organization not only charges a lower price than the profit maximizing firm, but also spends more money on marketing ($10,984 vs. $3720). For the nonprofit organization, the loss from users is exactly equal to the amount by which donations (e.g., $19,509) exceed the marketing expenditures to the donor market (e.g., $3922). Both the price and the marketing expenditures for the nonprofit organization which cannot raise donations are intermediate between the other two organizations. By definition, the nonprofits show no deficit. When the potential of the benefaction market is reduced ($\beta_0 = .10$), the optimal price is increased from $0.90 to $1.25 in the case of no fixed costs.

The effect of fixed costs on the level of service offered differs for the profit and nonprofit firms. For the profit maximizer, assuming that fixed costs are covered by revenues so that the firm remains in business, there is no effect on the optimal values of p* and x*. The nonprofit firm, however, because it cannot incur a deficit, must increase p* (from $.90 to $1.02) and decrease x* (from $10,984 to $9,705) as compared to the case of no fixed costs. Nevertheless, output is still higher than for the profit maximizing firm.

In summary, the numerical examples illustrate the degree to which a nonprofit organization should optimally charge lower prices and spend more on marketing than a profit maximizing firm facing identical demand and cost functions.

RESPONSIVENESS TO MARKETING EFFORTS

Utilization of the marketing mix decision rules depends upon being able to measure the parameters. In addition to intuitive judgments as to what the effect of a marketing program will be, there are a number of other available techniques including survey research, historical analysis, decision calculus, and experimentation which may be used singly or in combination. We first review estimation approaches for the responsiveness of users to marketing efforts and then examine resource attraction. The focus will be on historical analysis as a means to estimate response coefficients. In particular, we estimate the elasticity of contributions to fund raising expenditures for a major private university.

Demand Estimation

Because demand estimation in the business, nonprofit, and public sectors is similar, an extensive set of published studies which estimate the sensitivity of market response is available. For example, Clarke (1976) provides a review of published studies which estimate the relationship between current and lagged advertising and sales or market share. There have been a number of studies which examine simultaneously several elements of the marketing mix, for example, Lambin's (1972) study of service station market share, and Montgomery and Silk's (1972) study of the effect of journal advertising, direct mail, and sampling on sales of prescription drugs. In addition, there have been a few studies of the effect of marketing mix variables on use in public and nonprofit settings. For example, Blattberg and Striver (1970) find that transit promotion in Pittsburgh significantly increases ridership in the off-peak but not the peak hours. Another example is Epp's (1973) analysis of the U.S. Army's 1971 paid advertising campaign which, he concludes, had a positive effect on short term recruitment. As discussed previously, Weinberg and Shachmut (1978) examine the relationship of attendance at performing arts events to performance type, seasonality, and other factors. There are an increasing number of studies which examine the applicability of marketing to nonbusiness settings or which use market research data to design services and to determine benefits to offer (see Lovelock and Weinberg, 1978, for a review). Nevertheless, there are still relatively few published empirical studies which relate marketing mix components to utilization for services of nonbusiness organizations.

In summary, there has been extensive analysis of the relationship of demand to marketing effort in the private sector. These studies can be used to provide guidance in determining demand sensitivity for nonprofit organizations but there is a need for substantial empirical work in this area. This is especially true because most public sector organizations offer services and many of the demand estimation studies are concerned with goods.

Resource Attraction

Although authors such as Mindak and Bybee (1971) show that a fund raising program can be structured as a marketing problem, little empirical work is generally available in this area. An exception is a recent econometric study by Helmer, who finds a positive relationship between number of direct mailings to Ohio State alumni and their willingness to contribute to alumni clubs or funds.

One of the main reasons that there has been such limited study of fund raising responsiveness is the lack of data. Although many organizations report the amount of contributions received, until recently the accounting records of many organizations did not segregate fund raising costs.[8] Some organizations can separate out the cost of a particular one-time campaign but not the ongoing costs of the fund raising efforts.

Because there is limited published empirical research which shows the sensitivity of contributions to fund raising efforts, we shall measure this effect for an educational institution. In particular, we seek to estimate the elasticity of contributions to marketing effort i.e., the β in (16). We define and measure two marketing mix variables—the total costs of fund raising and whether or not a special campaign or promotion is being run. (See below for a further definition of the variables.) The underlying hypothesis can be quite simply stated—funds raised are dependent on the fund raising effort and that relationship can be measured.

Fund raising efforts may be divided into three categories. The first category includes the salaries and expenses of the organization's employees who are primarily concerned with fund raising and also the costs of brochures, advertising, meetings, and other materials used in fund raising. These are readily measurable quantities, although records are not always as clearly segregated as would be desirable. The second category consists of the volunteer time provided by faculty and other university employees who assist from time to time in fund raising, for example, entertaining potential donors. The third category is the time donated by volunteers, who are usually alumni. The magnitude of the effort contributed by those in the last two categories is operationally difficult to measure accurately. However, it seems reasonable to assume that the amount of volunteer efforts is correlated with the measurable expenditures in the first category for many organizations.

Nonprofit organizations often have periodic special campaigns. For example, a university may have a 50th Anniversary campaign, a museum may have a campaign to raise funds to purchase a particular collection, and a temple may hold a new building fund campaign. These campaigns presumably have an effect both through increasing the efforts of those doing the fund raising and also on the willingness of people to donate. An analogy between campaigns and promotions of frequently purchased consumer goods can be drawn. In deciding upon a schedule of promotions, the brand manager needs to decide how long each promotion should last and the time interval between promotions. A brand manager whose product is frequently promoted may find that consumers perceive the promotion as the usual state for that brand. Another factor to be considered in scheduling consumer promotions is the extent to which the promotions displaces future sales of the product. Similar concerns exist for the manager of a nonprofit organization in scheduling the frequency and duration of campaigns. For example, public television has recently been criticized because of the frequency and duration of its membership campaigns.[9]

Thus, two marketing mix variables—fund raising expenses and whether a campaign was in progress in a given year—are available.

The dependent variable is total funds raised. Although total funds can include contributions from corporations and foundations as well as individuals, we did not examine each category separately because gifts by corporations, for example, may often be the results of fund raising efforts to individuals.

Twenty-one years of annual data are available. (See Table 7.) Ideally we would like additional observations. However, although one could possibly extend the data further back in history, data from the too distant past are suspect in light of the major changes that have taken place in educational institutions. Because almost all contributors make only one contribution per year, an annual time period is the appropriate one to use. Shorter time periods would not be meaningful and, in any case, data are not available on a more frequent basis.

There are a number of external factors that may influence the relationship

Table 7. Deflated Contributions and Fund Raising Expenses

Year	Deflated Contributions*	Deflated Fund Raising Expenses*	Campaign Year
1	.14	.10	No
2	.19	.12	No
3	.27	.12	No
4	.35	.14	No
5	.70	.31	Yes
6	.29	.19	No
7	.55	.22	No
8	.59	.27	No
9	.75	.56	Yes
10	.67	.70	Yes
11	1.19	.84	Yes
12	1.10	.64	Yes
13	.80	.54	Yes
14	.62	.62	No
15	.61	.63	No
16	.81	.62	No
17	.76	.66	No
18	.74	.67	No
19	.69	.76	No
20	.74	.89	Yes
21	1.00	1.00	Yes

*Stated in index number form to protect confidential data.

between fund raising expenditures and donations. Although the data set is limited, we wish to take account of some of these factors. One reason that both contributions and fund raising expenses are increasing over time is due to inflation. To correct for this effect, we have restated the data in constant dollars by using a GNP deflator.

An important factor in explaining donations is the number of people who have used the service. As we discussed earlier when defining the function $s=g(q,y)$, the contributions received may be related directly or indirectly to the number of users, in this case represented by the number of living alumni of the university.[10] In fact, the count of alumni is limited to those who had graduated at least ten years earlier in order to provide time for the graduate to complete additional schooling and become "established." (Use of other time periods has minimal effects on the results.)

As expected, number of alumni is strongly positively correlated (.72) with contributions. However, number of alumni is also positively correlated with deflated fund raising expenditures. Although not surprising, this provides a dilemma with regard to estimation by use of regression of the elasticity of fund raising expenditures because collinearity in the independent variables increases the standard errors of the estimates of the coefficients. To help break this collinearity deadlock, annual fund raising expenses and contributions are divided by number of living alumni in each year to yield "per capita" data.

In view of the limited number of observations, no additional external variables are included in our analysis. However, it should be noted that the percentage of games won by the football team has a small positive correlation ($r^2 < .10$) with total gifts. However, there is probably a stronger relation with some more specialized funds. Helmer, for example, finds a positive relationship between the results of the Ohio State football season and membership in an alumni organization.

Estimation of Elasticity

In order to estimate the elasticity of contributions to fund raising expenditures, three different models are estimated:

A. A power function model with two predictor variables—per capita fund raising expenditures and whether or not a campaign is conducted in a given year, that is,

$$s = \gamma_{A0} \, y^{\gamma_{A1}} \, e^{\gamma_{A2}D}$$

where s — contributions per capita

y — fund raising expenditures per capita

D — a 0,1 dummy variable, in which 1 represents a campaign year, and 0 a year in which a campaign is not being conducted.

B. A power function model with per capita fund raising expenditures as the predictor variable, that is,

$$s = \gamma_{B0}\, y^{\,\gamma_{B1}}$$

C. A linear model with per capital fund raising expenditures and whether or not a campaign year as the predictor variables, that is,

$$s = \gamma_{C0} + \gamma_{C1}\, y + \gamma_{C2}\, D$$

The estimation results are given in Table 8.

Model A is the most direct analog to the illustrative example in the previous section; however, because the t-value (1.60) of the campaign dummy variable is slightly below that required for significance at the .05 level, model B was tested without that variable. In comparing the elasticities of fund raising expenditures, which are given directly by the γ_1 coefficients, we see that the coefficient is higher (.61 vs. .52) in model B. However, this increment probably occurs because fund raising expenditures are being given credit for the special efforts associated with a campaign. Furthermore, for model B the Durbin-Watson statistic of 1.16 is significant at the .05 level, which suggests that there is (mild) positive autocorrelation. Thus, in terms of estimating elasticity, the .52 estimate of model A, which controls for the campaign effect, is more appropriate.

Table 8. Estimation Results

Model A—power function, two predictors
$R^2_{adj} = .69$, Durbin-Watson Statistic = 1.21

Variable	β	B	Standard Error (B)	t
Fund Raising Expenditures (per capita)	.69	.52*	.11	4.63
Campaign Year	.24	.22	.14	1.60

Model B—power function, one predictor
$R^2_{adj} = .66$, Durbin-Watson Statistic = 1.16*

Variable	β	B	Standard Error (B)	t
Fund Raising Expenditures (per capita)	.82	.61*	.10	6.36

Model C—linear function, two predictors
$R^2_{adj} = .62$, Durbin-Watson Statistic = 1.41

Variable	β	B	Standard Error (B)	t
Fund Raising Expenditures (per capita)	.52	9.83*	3.20	3.07
Campaign Year	.38	.11*	.05	2.26

Notes: Sample size = 21
*Significant at the .05 level.

The power function model assumes that elasticity is constant for all spending levels. In order to examine the range of elasticities that might have held at different spending levels, we also estimate a linear model (model C). In this model, both y and D are statistically significant at the .05 level. Elasticity at any given value of s and y is given by

$$\gamma_{C1} \frac{y}{s}$$

The elasticity is computed at the mean value of y, and at $y \pm 1\sigma$. To control for the effect of campaigns, we assume that D = 0 in calculating the elasticity. Thus, the following three elasticity estimates are obtained:

Value of y	Elasticity
$\bar{y} - 1\sigma$	.32
$\bar{y}$	.47
$\bar{y} + 1\sigma$	.57

As can be seen, these elasticity values are all within the 2σ level (95% confidence level) of the constant elasticity estimate of .52 achieved in the power function. In summary, contributions appear to be highly responsive to fund raising expenditures.

Earlier, using the power function as the response function, the optimal ratio of fund raising expenditures to contributions was shown to be equal to the coefficient of y, in this example, .52. For the university being studied here, the value of y/s is less than .1. The university can clearly increase its fund raising expenditures with a consequent improvement in total funds raised. However, it seems that at a certain point, probably much below the value of .52, the ratio of expenditures to contributions would become too high and would have an adverse effect on the university's image. Thus, the university must be placing an implicit or explicit constraint on the amount of money it wishes to devote to fund raising efforts. Nevertheless, the university appears to have considerable potential for increasing both its fund raising expenditures and contributions. For example, if fund raising expenditures are doubled, then contributions would increase by 40% and the ratio of expenditures to contributions would still be less than 15%.

Finally the effect of campaigns should be noted. Although not quite significant in the power function model, the dummy variable for campaign is significant in the linear model. This is, of course, in line with the apparent beliefs of many university administrators who periodically announce special fund raising campaigns. In fact, given the substantial returns to campaigns, the critical questions are how frequently can the university declare new campaigns and what should the duration of a campaign be, not whether a campaign approach should be used.

In summary, there appears to be a substantial return to fund raising expenditures for the university studied. More generally, nonprofit organizations should attempt to use econometric and other techniques to understand better the relationship between fund raising efforts and contributions and consequently, to set fund raising budgets.

SUMMARY

Nonprofit organizations are increasingly adopting marketing concepts and approaches. In particular, these organizations are beginning to use the framework of a marketing mix to make decisions. To determine the marketing mix, decision rules are needed which reflect the objective function of a nonprofit and the dual markets that it faces. These were developed in general and illustrated in the particular case of power function models. As compared to business organizations facing identical demand and cost functions, nonprofit organizations should charge lower prices and devote more money to marketing. In some circumstances, a nonprofit should price below marginal cost.

To implement decision rules, estimates of response coefficients need to be made. To date, there has been limited published empirical work in the nonprofit sector, but the analyses carried out in the private sector context provide a useful starting point for demand estimation. For the resource attraction or fund raising problem, we demonstrated the effectiveness of special campaigns and fund raising expenditures in one organization, a private university.

Additional research is needed to clarify the nature of the objective function in public and nonprofit organizations, to determine the appropriate form of response functions to be used, and to estimate the coefficients of the selected response functions in both the donor and user markets.

FOOTNOTES

*Charles B. Weinberg is Associate Professor of Marketing and Public Management in the Faculty of Commerce and Business Administration, University of British Columbia. This research was partially supported by a grant from TRW, Inc. The helpful comments of Professors C. H. Lovelock, V. R. Rao, and J. N. Sheth, and of Imran Currim and Tsuneo Yahagi, doctoral students at Stanford University, on a previous draft of this paper are gratefully acknowledged. The empirical work in the last section is partially based on a paper by Shelby McIntyre.

1. The only exceptions would be unusual cases, such as constant marginal costs and no fixed costs.

2. Many public utilities (e.g., electric, gas, and water) have a price structure of fixed fee plus a charge per unit consumed. The per unit charges, however, are often above the marginal costs. This has been demonstrated when California water agencies have found themselves unable to meet costs as users reduced water consumption in response to the drought of 1977.

3. Furthermore, in some cases advertising can increase price sensitivity. Thus Eskin (1975) found that for a new consumer food product, the company should choose between a higher advertising, low price strategy and a low advertising, high price strategy.

4. The reader not interested in the mathematical development of the optimal solution may wish to go directly to Table 5 and the section "Summary of Solution."

5. The non-negativity constraints on p, x, and y will not be stated and will be assumed to be met.

6. Depending upon the time frame being utilized, a nonprofit organization may have a target of maintaining a certain specified surplus at the end of each planning period. If the target surplus is the same surplus the nonprofit holds at the start of the period, then (2) can remain as stated. However, if there is to be change in the level of surplus, then the right hand side of (2) should be replaced by the amount of that change, and possibly expressed as an inequality as well. The analytical results that follow essentially hold under this modification, although the phraseology and some of the equations would need slight restatement. One way to handle this modification would be to restate the cost function, $c = h(q)$, to include the desired change in surplus position and treat the desired change in surplus as a fixed cost.

7. The empirical portion of this section is partially based on an unpublished paper on fund raising by Shelby H. McIntyre.

8. Even with New York's requirement that organizations file an annual return of fund raising costs and contributions, 282 organizations of a total of 1202, which received contributions of \$100,000 or more reported no costs of fund raising (see Table 3).

9. In winter 1978, the San Francisco public television station, KQED, offered its viewers the following "benefit:" no more "pledge night" campaigns until August 1978 if the contribution goal is met. The goal was met, although the importance of this benefit is not known.

10. Number of donors was not used because, in the framework developed earlier, q represents the number of users of the service which is distinct from number of people who contribute.

REFERENCES

Aaker, D. A., and Weinberg, C. B., "Interactive Marketing Models." *Journal of Marketing* (October 1975).

Adizes, I., "The Cost of Being an Artist." *California Management Review* (Summer 1975).

Blattberg, R. C., and Stivers, S. R., "A Statistical Evaluation of Transit Promotion *Journal of Marketing Research* 8 (August 1970).

Clarke, D. G., "Econometric Measurement of the Duration of Advertising Effect on Sales." *Journal of Marketing Research* (November 1976).

Dorfman, R., and Steiner, P. O., "Optimal Advertising and Optimal Quality." *American Economic Review* (December 1964).

Epps, T. W., "An Econometric Analysis of the Effectiveness of the U.S. Army's 1971 Paid Advertising Campaign." *Applied Economics* (December 1973).

Eskin, G., "A Case for Test Market Experiments." *Journal of Advertising Research* (April 1975).

Etgar, M., and Ratchford, B. T., "Marketing Management and Marketing Concept: Their Conflict in Non-Profit Organizations." *1974 Proceedings,* American Marketing Association.

Freeland, J. R., and Weinberg, C. B., "Implications of S-Shaped Response Functions for Decision Making," Research Paper No. 394, Stanford Business School, July 1977.

Fudge, W. K., and Lodish, L. M., "Evaluation of the Effectiveness of a Model Based Salesman's Planning System." *Interfaces* (November 1977): Part 2.

Ginsberg, E., Hiestand, D. L., and Reubens, B. G., *The Pluralistic Economy.* New York: McGraw Hill, 1965.

Giving USA 1977 Annual Report. New York: American Association of Fund-Raising Counsel, 1977.

Gross, M., "A New Study of the Cost of Fund Raising in New York." *The Philanthropy Monthly* (April 1976).

Helmer, R. M., personal communications.

Johnston, J., *Statistical Cost Analysis.* New York: McGraw Hill, 1960.

Kotler, P., *Marketing Decision Making, A Model Building Approach.* New York: Holt, Rinehardt, and Winston, 1971.

Kotler, P., *Marketing for Nonprofit Organizations*. Englewood Cliffs: Prentice Hall, 1975.

Lambin, J. J., "A Computer On-Line Marketing Model." *Journal of Marketing Research* (May 1972).

Lovelock, C. H., and Weinberg, C. B., "Public and Nonprofit Marketing Comes of Age," in T. Bonoma and G. Zaltman (eds.), *Annual Review of Marketing*. Chicago: American Marketing Association, 1978.

Lublin, J. S., "Prepaid Health Plans Run into Difficulties as Enrollment Falters." *Wall Street Journal* (February 11, 1975).

Manoff, R. K., "The Mass Media Family Planning Campaign for the United States," in *Using Commercial Resources in Family Planning Programs*. Honolulu: East West Center, 1973.

Martin, W., "The Baptists Want You!" *Texas Monthly* (February 1977).

McLenithan, G. J., "Public Disclosure Requirements of Charitable Organizations." *The Philanthropy Monthly* (September 1976).

Mindak, W. A., and Bybee, H. M., "Marketing Applications to Fund Raising." *Journal of Marketing* (July 1971).

Montgomery, D. B., and Silk, A. J., "Estimating Dynamic Effects of Marketing Communication Expenditures." *Management Science* (June 1972).

Montgomery, D. B., and Weinberg, C. B., "Modeling Marketing Phenomena: A Managerial Perspective." *Journal of Contemporary Business* (Autumn 1973).

"Pricing a Ticket to Ride," *Modern Railways* (August 1977).

Ryans, A. B., and Weinberg, C. B., "Consumer Dynamics in Nonprofit Organizations." *Journal of Consumer Research* (September 1978).

Seaver, D. J., "Hospital Revises Role, Reaches out to Cultivate and Capture Markets," *Hospitals* (June 1, 1977): 59-63.

Shapiro, B. P., "Marketing for Nonprofit Organizations." *Harvard Business Review* (September–October 1973).

"Stanford University: The Annual Fund," in Lovelock, C. H., and Weinberg, C. B., *Cases in Public and Nonprofit Marketing*. Palo Alto: Scientific Press, 1977.

Thompson, A. A., *Economics of the Firm*. Englewood Cliffs: Prentice Hall, 1977.

Webster, F. E., *Marketing for Managers*. New York: Harper & Row, 1974.

Weinberg, C. B., and Shachmut, K. M., "ARTS PLAN: A Model Based System For Use in Planning a Performing Arts Series." *Management Science* (February 1978).

APPENDIX

Optimization of Power Function
(Constant Elasticity) Models

In this appendix, we derive the optimal values of price (p), marketing effort to users (x), and, where applicable, marketing effort to donors (y), for three optimization conditions:

(A) Profit Maximization
(B) Usage Maximization subject to no deficit, *with* Contributions
(C) Usage Maximization subject to no deficit, *without* Contributions.

These results are derived assuming that response is modeled by a power function (constant elasticity) and cost by a linear function.

Thus, we have the following relationships:

$$q = f(p,x) = \alpha_0 p^{-\alpha_1} x^{\alpha_2} \tag{A1}$$

$$s = g(q,x) = \beta_0 q^{\beta_1} y^{\beta_2} \tag{A2}$$

$$c = h(q) = c_f + c_v q \tag{A3}$$

where α_0, α_1, α_2, β_0, β_1, β_2, c_f, and c_v are non-negative constants. To preserve decreasing returns to scale for q and s, we also require

$$\alpha_1 > 1$$
$$\alpha_2, \beta_1, \beta_2 < 1 \tag{A4}$$

The power function structure allows us to state the partial derivatives of q and s as follows:

$$\frac{\partial q}{\partial p} = -\alpha_1 \frac{q}{p}$$

$$\frac{\partial q}{\partial x} = \alpha_2 \frac{q}{x}$$

$$\frac{\partial s}{\partial q} = \beta_1 \frac{s}{q} \tag{A5}$$

$$\frac{\partial s}{\partial x} = \beta_2 \frac{s}{x}$$

Because the Dorfman-Steiner equation (13) holds for all the objective functions investigated in this appendix, we can substitute (A1) and (A5) into $e_p = e_x (pq/x)$ to express x* as a function of p*,

$$x^* = k_1 p^{*\, 1-\alpha_1/1-\alpha_2} \tag{A6}$$

where

$$k_1 = \left[\frac{\alpha_0 \alpha_2}{\alpha_1} \right]^{1/1-\alpha_2} \tag{A7}$$

(A) Profit Maximization. The objective function is to maximize Z_π, where

$$Z_\pi = pq - c - x \tag{A8}$$

Using (A1) and (A3), (A8) becomes

$$Z_\pi = p(\alpha_0 p^{-\alpha_1} x^{\alpha_2}) - c_f - c_v(\alpha_0 p^{-\alpha_1} x^{\alpha_2}) - x \tag{A9}$$

Setting first derivatives with respect to p and x equal to 0 yields, after algebraic manipulation,

$$p^* = \frac{c_v \alpha_1}{\alpha_1 - 1} \tag{A10}$$

$$x^* = \left[\frac{\alpha_0 \alpha_2}{\alpha_1} \right]^{1/1-\alpha_2} \left[\frac{c_v \alpha_1}{\alpha_1 - 1} \right]^{1-\alpha_1/1-\alpha_2} \tag{A11}$$

Provided that Z_π is positive, p* and x* are the optimal solution. (A11) is equivalent to (A6), of course.

B. Usage Maximization with Contributions. The objective is to maximize usage subject to not incurring a deficit including contributions. Algebraically, the problem may be stated as follows:

$$\text{Max } q = \alpha_0 p^{-\alpha_1} x^{\alpha_2} \tag{A12}$$

subject to
$$pq - (c_f + c_v q) - x + \beta_0 q^{\beta_1} y^{\beta_2} - y = 0 \tag{A13}$$

The general solution to this problem was developed in the text, so we can proceed by substituting (A1) to (A3) and the appropriate derivatives into the equations already established. From (A6), we already have x* as a function of p*. Substituting (A6) into $q = \alpha_0 p^{-\alpha_1} x^{-\alpha_2}$, allows us to state q* as the following function of p*:

$$q^* = \frac{\alpha_1}{\alpha_2} \left(\frac{\alpha_0 \alpha_2}{\alpha_1} \right)^{1/1-\alpha_2} p^{*\alpha_2-\alpha_1/1-\alpha_2} = k_2 p^{*\alpha_2-\alpha_1/1-\alpha_2} \tag{A12}$$

where
$$k_2 = \frac{\alpha_1}{\alpha_2} k_1 \tag{A13}$$

Further, it can readily be seen that

$$\frac{x^*}{p^* q^*} = \frac{\alpha_2}{\alpha_1} \tag{A14}$$

The necessary condition $\partial s / \partial y = 1$ from (11) in the text leads to

$$\beta_0 \beta_2 q^{*\beta_1} y^{*\beta_2-1} = 1$$

or
$$y^* = (\beta_0 \beta_2)^{\beta_1/1-\beta_2} q^{*\beta_1/1-\beta_2} \tag{A15}$$

and after substitution into (A2)

$$s^* = \frac{1}{\beta_2} (\beta_0\beta_2)^{\beta_1/1-\beta_2} q^{*\beta_1/1-\beta_2} \tag{A16}$$

Dividing (A15) by (A16) yields

$$y^*/s^* = \beta_2 \tag{A17}$$

and

$$s^* - y^* = \left(\frac{1-\beta_2}{\beta_2}\right) y^*. \tag{A18}$$

The expressions for y^* and s^* can be further specified in terms of p^*. Thus all the terms in the nonprofit or no deficit constraint (A9) can be expressed in terms of p^* and then solved for p^* as follows

$$p^*q^* - (c_f + c_v q^*) - x^* + s^* - y^* = 0 \tag{A19}$$

$$p^*\left(k_2 p^* \frac{\alpha_2-\alpha_1}{1-\alpha_2}\right) - c_f - c_v k_2 p^* \frac{\alpha_2-\alpha_1}{1-\alpha_2} - k_1 p^{*1-\alpha_1/1-\alpha_2}$$

$$+ \left(\frac{1-\beta_2}{\beta_2}\right)(\beta_0\beta_2)^{1/1-\beta_2} (k_2)^{\beta_1/1-\beta_2} p^{*(\alpha_2-\alpha_1/1-\alpha_2)(\beta_1/1-\beta_2)}$$

$$\times (k_2 - k_1)p^{*1-\alpha_1/1-\alpha_2} - c_v k_2 p^{*\alpha_2-\alpha_1/1-\alpha_2} + k_3 p^{*(\alpha_2-\alpha_1/1-\alpha_2)(\beta_1/1-\beta_2)}$$

$$- c_f = 0 \tag{A20}$$

where

$$k_3 = \left(\frac{1-\beta_2}{\beta_2}\right) (\beta_0\beta_2 k_2{}^{\beta_1})^{1/1-\beta_2} \tag{A21}$$

Equation (A20) can be solved for p^* by analytic or numeric methods depending upon the values of the constants. For example, if $2\beta_1 + \beta_2 = 1$ and $\alpha_1 + \alpha_2 = 2$, (A20) becomes quadratic in p^*, such that

$$p^* = \frac{(k_2 - k_1 + k_3) - \sqrt{(k_2 - k_1 k_3)^2 - 4c_f c_v k_2}}{2c_f} \tag{A22}$$

If there are no fixed costs, $c_f = 0$, then it can be shown that

$$p^* = \frac{c_v k_2}{(k_2 - k_1 + k_3)} \tag{A23}$$

Interestingly, if $k_3 > k_1$, then the optimal price is *below* the variable cost.

Using (A6) and (A22) and noting that $\alpha_1 + \alpha_2 = 2$ implies that $\dfrac{1-\alpha_1}{1-\alpha_2} = -1$

and $\dfrac{\alpha_2 - \alpha_1}{1-\alpha_2} = -2$ yields.

$$x^* = k_1 p^{*-1} = \frac{k_1}{k_2} \left(\frac{k_2 - k_1 + k_3}{c_v} \right) \tag{A24}$$

Further

$$y^* = \frac{k_2^{1/2}(\beta_0\beta_2)^{1/1-\beta_2}}{p^*} \tag{A25}$$

C. Usage Maximization Without Contributions.   The formal development of this case is parallel to the previous one except that all terms involving y are omitted. For example, the Lagrangian is stated as

$$\text{Max } L = q - \lambda[qp - (c_f + c_v q) - x] \tag{A26}$$

Thus, the relationships between x^*, p^*, and q^* given in (A6) and (A12) hold, and all that remains is to solve for p by substitution into

$$pq - c_f - c_v q - x = 0 \tag{A27}$$

which yields

$$(k_2 - k_1)p^{*\,1-\alpha_1/1-\alpha_2} - c_v k_2 p^{*\alpha_2 - \alpha_1/1-\alpha_2} - c_f = 0 \tag{A28}$$

As with (A20), if $\alpha_1 + \alpha_2 = 2$, then (A28) becomes a quadratic equation. If it is further assumed that there are no fixed costs (c_f - 0), then

$$p^* = \frac{c_v k_2}{(k_2 - k_1)} = \frac{\alpha_1}{\alpha_1 - \alpha_2} c_v \tag{A29}$$

$$x^* = k_1 p^{*-1} = \frac{\alpha_1 - \alpha_2}{\alpha_1} \frac{k_1}{c_v} \tag{A27}$$

Numerical examples for the three objective functions are given in the text.

TESTING STOCHASTIC MODELS OF CONSUMER CHOICE BEHAVIOR: A METHODOLOGY FOR ATTACKING THE MANY-TO-ONE MAPPING PROBLEM*

R. Dale Wilson, THE PENNSYLVANIA STATE UNIVERSITY

I. INTRODUCTION

In the twenty-year period that has elapsed since stochastic modeling techniques were initially applied to marketing data, much effort has been expended to portray consumer brand choice behavior as a stochastic process. Following Kuehn's (1958) innovative doctoral dissertation, a plethora of models has been developed and fitted to choice behavior data for the purpose of determining the statistical underpinnings of the brand choice process. In short, these models posit

Research in Marketing, Volume 3, pages 235–272
Copyright © 1980 by JAI Press Inc.
All rights of reproduction in any form reserved.
ISBN: 0–89232–060–5

235

that choice behavior can be represented by statistical formulations that explicitly allow for the probabilistic (but not necessarily random) nature of human choice processes (cf. Kuehn and Day, 1964). Because of these efforts, stochastic modeling research has emerged as a popular, and sometimes controversial, mode for representing consumer behavior processes.

Despite the success of stochastic modeling ventures, critics have pointed out that methodological problems exist in this area which could jeopardize the future applicability of stochastic models to marketing data. It has recently become clear that these problems must be attacked to assure that the future growth and development of stochastic models in a marketing context can be realized. Without this evidence of scientific maturity, future gains from stochastic modeling methods may simply not materialize.

It is with these concerns in mind that this article can be justified. In a broad sense, the objective of the paper is to propose a methodological environment for dealing with one of the problems which plagues much of the existing stochastic modeling research—the "many-to-one mapping" problem. The cornerstone of the methodology is a statistical test which was developed by the author (Wilson, 1977) for the purposes of model comparison and evaluation. This formalized, objective procedure would seem to offer improvement over the method of subjectively comparing goodness-of-fit statistics and their probability values, which has become the traditional method of model evaluation in the stochastic modeling literature. Further, this improvement incorporates a parameter estimation method that deviates only slightly from the conventional chi-square estimation procedure suggested by Morrison (1966). The methodology proposed here is applicable to those modeling situations where certain models are constrained versions of other models. Four sets of empirical brand choice data are used to illustrate the methodology.

II. LITERATURE REVIEW

A. Brand Choice as a Probability Process

A review of the marketing and consumer behavior literature provides several different and, in some cases, competing explanations of how brand choice behavior can be conceptualized as probabilistic. These approaches, which seem to have been developed independently from one another, illustrate the growing realization on the part of behavioral researchers that there are theoretical and empirical grounds for viewing a set of specific behaviors as having various probabilities of occurrence. These grounds include response uncertainty notions (Coleman, 1964a, 1964b) and their application (Montgomery, 1969b; Jones, 1971), the concept of evoked set (Howard and Sheth, 1969), evidence of multi-brand loyalty (Cunningham, 1956; Ehrenberg and Goodhardt, 1970; Jacoby,

1971), and attempts to control "noise" in research data (Bass, 1975, 1977; Hinich and Rosenthal, 1975).

The portrayal of specific human behavior processes such as brand choice as probabilistic has desirable properties from a noise-reduction point of view. This is especially true since the difficulties inherent in predicting and explaining specific brand choice are now widely known. As illustrated by Bass's (1975, 1977) discussion of studies in which researchers have had little success in explaining variance in studies of brand choice, "noise" or error problems are particularly bothersome in highly disaggregate settings where the purpose is to explore individual choices or purchases. Situational influences on consumer choice are now recognized as having an important influence on brand choice (Hansen, 1972), thus complicating investigations of consumer choice processes. Whether the lack of success in predicting specific patterns of human behavior is caused by consumers' inabilities or unwillingness to express their cognitive structures, novelty seeking attempts, the operation of some cerebral mechanism which generates random behavior, shortsightedness on the part of researchers, or some other reason, remains unknown. Regardless, the study of consumer behavior as a stochastic process takes the possible occurrence of these factors into account.

B. Alternative Stochastic Theories and Supporting Research

The stochastic models that have appeared in the marketing literature have portrayed the brand choice process in a variety of ways and have found numerous applications. Models have been developed which consider consumer choice as a zero-order (i.e., stationary) process (e.g., Bass, 1974b; Herniter, 1973, 1974; Kalwani and Morrison, 1977), as a first order Markov process (e.g., Morrison, 1966; Herniter and Howard, 1964; Maffei, 1960), as a higher-order learning process (e.g., Carman, 1966; Haines, 1964; Kuehn, 1962; Wierenga, 1974), and as a function of external time effects (Montgomery, 1969b; Jones, 1971). These models have been adapted, or similar models have been built, to account for the adoption of new products (Aaker, 1971; Haines, 1964, 1969), to include responses to various pricing policies (Lilien, 1974a, 1974b), to interpret Twedt's (1964) emphasis on the "heavy-half" consumer segment (Morrison, 1968), and to combine simpler models to form "composite" models (Jones, 1970b, 1973). In addition, articles have appeared in the literature (e.g., Morrison, 1970) that are critical of attempts to show the influence of past brand choices without considering the inclusion of a stochastic element (e.g., May, 1969). Zero-order models proposed and tested by Bass (1974a, 1974b) and Herniter (1973, 1974) represent macro-market behavior as a stationary process and differ in their level of aggregation than previously-discussed models.[1] Recently, the focal behavior of stochastic modeling studies has been broadened to include store choice (Aaker and Jones, 1971; Wilson, 1977) and media choice (Zufryden, 1976). Model comparisons are provided by Kalwani and Morrison (1977), Massy, Montgomery, and Morrison (1970), Montgomery (1969a), Wierenga (1974), and Wilson (1977) among others.

Using a slightly different perspective, stochastic brand choice models have also been used in conjunction with models of purchase incidence to form "comprehensive" models of consumer behavior. This approach incorporates the multidimensions of consumer purchase behavior such as brand choice, purchase timing and frequency, and/or store choice. Examples of this approach can be found in the work of Herniter (1971; Herniter and Cook, 1970) and Zufryden (1977, 1978). For example, Zufryden combined a Condensed Negative Binomial Distribution of aggregate product class purchases, a Beta-based distribution of individual brand choice probability for the population of consumers, and a Linear Learning Model of individual brand choice behavior in order to investigate brand choice and purchase timing behavior. Zufryden's model, referred to by the acronym CNBL, is found to provide an accurate fit to consumer diary panel data. The relationship between brand choice and purchase incidence has also been the subject of other recent empirical investigations by Bass, Jeuland, and Wright (1976), Jeuland (1977), and Shoemaker et al. (1977).

The uses of stochastic models of consumer purchasing activity have been many and varied. Stochastic models have been found to be useful in describing, understanding, and predicting aggregate market behavior (Bettman and Jones, 1972) by providing summary measures of market activity, long-run market share, and market structure (Aaker and Jones, 1971; Montgomery and Ryans, 1973). But Bennett (1977) and Howard (1977) have recently stressed that stochastic models may be more useful for prediction purposes than for diagnostic purposes, especially at the individual consumer level. These comments by Bennett and Howard are supported by recent stochastic modeling research, most of which has stressed the *predictive* efficacy of the models instead of their ability to provide an accurate *understanding* of brand choice processes. Other approaches, such as information-processing models (e.g., Bettman, 1970; Ray and Ward, 1976) and comprehensive theories of buying behavior (e.g., Howard and Sheth, 1969; Engel, Blackwell, and Kollat, 1978), no doubt provide better mechanisms for more accurately describing and understanding human choice behavior. But when the purpose of a brand choice investigation is prediction, a stochastic modeling venture is likely to provide fewer errors, especially if the analysis is performed at the aggregate level (Bass, 1974b, 1977; Hinich and Rosenthal, 1975; Bettman and Jones, 1972).

C. The Many-to-One Mapping Problem in Stochastic Modeling Efforts

The theories and empirical work in stochastic choice modeling have by no means been free of methodological problems. Several problematic issues are inherent in various degrees of intensity in every attempt at building and testing stochastic models. Montgomery (1967; Montgomery and Ryans, 1973; Montgomery and Urban, 1969) has summarized several factors that complicate the interpretation and usefulness of the models. Of these problems, the "many-to-one mapping" problem seems to be the most severe. This problem is related to the structure of specific stochastic choice models and is concerned with the common finding that two or more structurally different stochastic models may be consistent with the same consumer choice data. Because of the extent of the many-to-one mapping problem, a theoretical model which yields seemingly accurate predictions for observed brand choice data should not necessarily be accepted as the model that is most useful in a particular situation. This problem is particularly disturbing when researchers attempt to evaluate only one model in isolation, but careful consideration must also be given to the many-to-one mapping problem when one model is evaluated vis-a-vis other models.

Because the many-to-one mapping problem has had substantial impact on stochastic modeling research, several previous attempts have been made to solve it.[2] For example, Morrison (1966) has made some headway in reducing the severity of the problem by suggesting that model parameters be estimated by the minimum chi-square procedure. This procedure provides both an objective function for estimating parameters and a goodness-of-fit measure between model-generated theoretical data and overt consumer choice data. Competing models may then be judged on the basis of their relative closeness-of-fit. Unfortunately, when the many-to-one mapping problem occurs (as it does quite often), Morrison's procedure is deficient because of its imprecision in discriminating among competing models. Specifically, the task of interpreting the goodness-of-fit of two or more alternative models is quite subjective since criteria for model performance are not specified. The same concern exists when two or more models are evaluated via a procedure suggested by Aaker (1970), who advocates the use of the models' mean value function in determining the predictive ability of the models across time. These methods simply do not provide objective a priori criteria for evaluating the relative fit of competing stochastic models.

III. MODELING CONCEPTS

The purpose of this section is to provide the details of a methodology designed to counter the many-to-one mapping problem. Several modeling concepts are proposed that, when used in unison, provide an objective environment for evaluating model fit. Although a specific methodology is proposed and tested here, the procedure is flexible enough so that other researchers may change certain elements of the methodology to meet their own requirements. Such components as the specific mechanism used for incorporating statistical heterogeneity and the models used in the analysis may be changed without forfeiting the crucial aspects of the methodology.

A. Model/Embedded-Model Relationships

One of the most interesting aspects of many stochastic brand choice models is the interrelationship that exists among the models' parameter structures. For these models, it is possible to show that one model is "embedded" in (or, alternatively, is "nested" in or is a subset of) another model. Thus, the parameter structure of a general model can be restricted so that the restricted version of the general model becomes the equivalent of a simpler model having an unrestricted parameter vector. In this type of model/embedded-model relationship, the general model is designated as "Model A" and the simpler model is designed as "Model B." More formally, a model/embedded-model relationship exists if all of the parameters of Model B are contained in Model A and if it is possible to constrain the parameters of Model A in such a way that will cause the probability generating mechanism of the two models to be the same.

The interrelationship among some existing models of consumer choice has been briefly mentioned by several authors (Wierenga, 1974; Jones, 1973; Massy, Montgomery, and Morrison, 1970; Blattberg and Sen, 1973; Srinivasan and Kesavan, 1976). For example, it is clear that since Jones (1970) combines the Linear Learning Model and the Probability Diffusion Model (Montgomery, 1969b) to form his Dual-Effects Model, both of the simpler models are embedded in the more complex Dual-Effects Model. A similar, albeit not so noticeable, relationship exists between the Linear Learning Model and two of its embedded models—a simple homogeneous Markov Model and the heterogeneous Bernoulli Model. The Markov Model is achieved by constraining the Linear Learning Model parameter λ to zero, and the Bernoulli Model is attained by constraining parameters α, β, and λ to zero, zero, and one, respectively.

The fact that one stochastic choice model may be construed as a subset of another stochastic choice model is an appealing property. If it is possible to specify a class of alternative stochastic models in which this relationship holds, the task of uncovering the true nature of the brand choice process is simplified. To illustrate how consumer choice models may be constructed in a model/embedded-model relationship and to preview the more detailed discussion that follows, consider the relationship that exists among the following stochastic models:

Bernoulli Model $\subseteq$ Single Response Function Model $\subseteq$ Linear Learning Model $\subseteq$ Linear Learning-Brand Loyal Model, and

Bernoulli Model $\subseteq$ Brand Loyal Model $\subseteq$ Brand Loyal Model with an Intercept Term $\subseteq$ Linear Learning-Brand Loyal Model

where $\subseteq$ indicates the existence of an embedded relationship as previously defined. The salient characteristics of each of the models are outlined in Table I, and Figure 1 illustrates the parameter constraints necessary to achieve the model/embedded-model relationships for these models.

Table 1. Characteristics of Brand Choice Models

	Bernoulli Model	Brand Loyal Model (Without Intercept)	Brand Loyal Model With Intercept	Single Response Function Model	Linear Learning Model	Linear Learning-Brand Loyal Model
Heterogeneity?	Yes	Yes	Yes	Yes	Yes	Yes
Nonstationarity (i.e., does the model allow for choice occasion feedback?)?	No	Yes	Yes	Yes	Yes	Yes
Number of Values the Model May Attain?	One	Many	Many	Many	Many	Many
Directions it May Change?	No Change	Two	Two	One	Two	Two
Number of operators affecting the probability change?	None	Two	Two	One	Two	Two
Parallel Operators?	N.A.[a]	No	No	N.A.[a]	Yes	No
Existence of an identity operator (i.e., is it possible for the probability to remain constant from t to t+1?)?	Yes	Yes	No	No	No	No
Number of parameters estimated from the data (assuming arbitrary heterogeneity)?	Four	Five	Six	Six	Seven	Eight
Degrees of freedom $(v - q - 1)$?	Eleven	Ten	Nine	Nine	Eight	Seven
Number of times that the model appears as a subset of other models?	Five	Two	One	Two	One	Zero

[a]N.A. = Not Applicable.

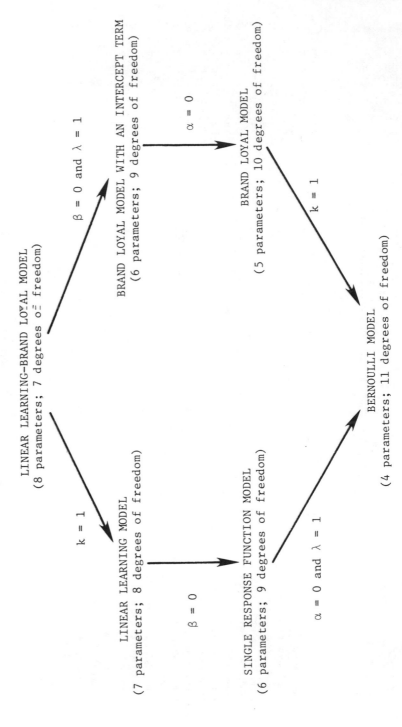

Figure 1. Model/Embedded-Model Relationships

B. Models of Consumer Choice

This section provides a discussion of the stochastic models that are used to illustrate how models may be embedded in more general versions. The models developed here are designed to represent the nature of choice processes via alternative probability mechanisms (each of which has theoretical, empirical, and/or intuitive support) and to use the model/embedded-model relationships for more consistent estimation, interpretation, and evaluation of model parameters.

1. The Linear Learning-Brand Loyal Model (LL-BRLOYAL). Among the models to be considered, the Linear Learning-Brand Loyal Model has the most parameters and, therefore, is the most general. This model results from combining the probability mechanism of Morrison's (1966) Brand Loyal Markov Model with that of the Linear Learning Model. LL-BRLOYAL, which results in a highly flexible model containing several interesting subset models, is specified as:[3]

$$\Pr[\Delta_{t+1} | \Delta_t = \delta, f(p_t)] = \alpha + \delta[\beta + \lambda f(p_t)] + (1 - \delta)[k\lambda f(p_t)], \quad (1)$$

$$-1 \leq \beta \leq 1, \quad \alpha, k, \lambda \geq 0, \quad \alpha + \beta + \lambda \leq 1, \quad \alpha + k\lambda \leq 1$$

where Δ_{t+1} signifies the choice of Brand 1 at purchase occasion $t+1$;

$\Pr(\Delta_t) = p_t$ and the $f(\cdot)$ notation indicates that p_t is a distributional parameter;
δ represents the brand chosen at occasion t ($\delta = 1$ if Brand 1 was chosen and $\delta = 0$ otherwise); and
α, β, λ, k, and the first n raw moments of $f(p_t)$ are parameters to be estimated from the data.

The most important assumptions of the model include population heterogeneity, n^{th}-order feedback, nonstationary behavior over time, and either increasing or decreasing probabilities of choosing Brand 1 depending on the sequence of past events.

Theoretical and empirical support for the model can be found in the mathematical psychology literature in that class of models which contains both non-equal intercept terms and non-parallel operators. Except for Wierenga's (1974) work, the marketing and consumer behavior literature has ignored this type of model in investigations of brand choice. Notwithstanding the better mathematical tractability obtained by imposing an equal-slope condition (as in the Linear Learning Model, for example), there is no reason to overlook this type of probability-generating mechanism as a potential model for research in complex choice behaviors. As Wierenga (p. 140) points out, it seems important to look into the possibility that the equal-λ condition imposes a serious limitation on the modeling of consumer choice processes. Thus, the non-equal slope parameters of the Linear Learning-Brand Loyal Model are a positive step in the building and testing of models representing brand choice processes. Section IV.C.5 of this article illustrates that the structure of LL-BRLOYAL yields model parameters and goodness-of-fit measures that are the equivalent of a non-parallel operator Linear Learning Model. A further illustration of this point is provided by Wilson (1977).

The flexibility and generality of the Linear Learning-Brand Loyal Model causes it to be the most complex in interpretation of the models to be discussed here. However, interpretation is aided because this model is the equivalent of the Linear Learning Model except for the slope parameter, $k\lambda$, in the rejection operator.[4] The interaction between the k and λ parameters causes the rejection operator to be non-parallel to the purchase operator as long as $k \neq 1$. If $k\lambda > \lambda$ (i.e., if $k > 1$), the slope of the rejection operator is greater than the slope of the purchase operator. The opposite holds, of course, if $k < 1$.

2. The Linear Learning Model (LINLEARN).

One of the models embedded in the Linear Learning-Brand Loyal Model is the well-known Linear Learning Model, which was first applied in a marketing context by Kuehn (1958, 1962). This model typically does an adequate job of representing consumer choice processes and is specified as:

$$\Pr[\Delta_{t+1}|\Delta_t = \delta, f(p_t)] = \alpha + \delta[\beta + \lambda f(p_t)] + (1 - \delta)[\lambda f(p_t)], \quad (2)$$

$$-1 \leq \beta \leq 1, \quad \alpha, \lambda \geq 0, \quad \alpha + \beta + \lambda \leq 1,$$

where $\delta = 1$ if Brand 1 was chosen at t and $\delta = 0$ otherwise.

Equation (2) points out that the purchase operator contains the parameter β, which can be interpreted as the incremental feedback caused by choosing Brand 1 that is not present from buying Brand 0. If $\beta > 0$, positive feedback is associated with choosing Brand 1; negative feedback is implied if $\beta < 0$. If β is large, then $\Pr(\Delta_{t+1})$ is greatly affected by past choices of Brand 1. The parameter α is the intercept term that helps to determine the lower limit of the probability of choosing Brand 1. The slope parameter, λ, can be interpreted as the effect of past shopping experiences on the probability of choosing Brand 1 without regard to specific brand choices.

The impetus of the Linear Learning Model came from the area of mathematical learning theory (Bush and Mosteller, 1955); but the particular model structure chosen by Kuehn seems to have been motivated by the following factors: (1) by specifying the model as he did, Kuehn could explicitly incorporate the appealing assumptions of incomplete learning and incomplete extinction; and (2) by specifying the model as he did, Kuehn could make the model more mathematically tractable in that the long-run expected value of the probability of selecting Brand 1, $E[p_\infty]$, could be calculated. The usual interpretation of this value is the long-run market share for Brand 1 under stable market conditions. However, two critical points should be made here. First, one may question the explicit inclusion of incomplete learning and incomplete extinction. It may be argued that a model of choice behavior should be specified so that the incomplete learning-incomplete extinction property will appear if it is warranted by the data but will not appear only because of the explicit requirement of an inflexible model. Secondly, the use of $E[p_\infty]$ as a long-term market share measure is questionable at best, since it measures market share trends only under stable competitive conditions. These two points indicate that two of the major attributes of the Linear Learning Model may not be as positive as was once thought.

Another difficulty with the model is the assumption that the choice of a particular brand (Brand 1) is *always* a reinforcement (Wierenga, 1974; Kotler, 1971). Wierenga discusses this problem as follows:

> [In the Linear Learning Model] . . . every time brand 1 is purchased the probability of buying brand 1 again is increased, while each brand 0 purchase has the effect of decreasing the probability. This is a rather rigid assumption because it can be imagined that after a brand 1 purchase the probability of buying that brand again will not increase at all. . . . Generally, every brand 1 purchase will not always constitute a 'reward' for every customer (p. 145).

Despite the problems noted above, as well as the occasional criticisms which appear in the literature (Srinivasan and Kesavan, 1976; McConnell, 1968; Lawrence, 1969, 1975), two especially positive features of the Linear Learning Model are evident. First, a review of the current literature in mathematical learning theory indicates that even though the Linear Learning Model was originally developed over twenty years ago (Bush and Mosteller, 1955), it is still in vogue. The current literature in this area seems to be concerned with applying the model to a wide range of situations—such as short-term and long-term memory storage and forgetting, recognition resulting from the presentation of cues, and stimulus-response theory—and does not appear to be drifting away from the original theory of statistical learning as developed by Bush and Mosteller (Greeno and Bjork, 1973). In their recent review article, Greeno and Bjork (1973) consider recent applications to be completely continuous with the development of mathematical learning theory in the 1950's. In the judgment of Greeno and Bjork, ''. . . what we are reporting is *not* a paradigm shift, whatever that may be'' (p. 81, emphasis theirs).

Second, mathematical learning theory is completely consistent with those situations in which behavior is considered to be more or less habitual. Examples of this ''habit persistence'' class of behavior from marketing include the frequent purchase of existing products and brands over lengthy time spans. Estes's (1972) interpretation of this point is that individuals are continually assessing probabilities of future events based on past events. He points out that mathematical learning theory

... accounts for probability learning in terms of the accumulation in memory of weighted ensembles of associations between recurring situations and subsequent events.

[These models] ... provide vehicles for applying theoretical interpretations of probability learning to the problems of choice and decision making in social and economic contexts (p. 81).

According to this view, consumers are continually reassessing their behaviors' ability to satisfy their needs and wants. Past experiences resulting from brand choice decisions thus are thought to influence present and future choice since consumers engage in adaptive behavior based on purchase event feedback. Consumers utilize feedback from their past behavior in a Bayesian-like fashion by continually updating their probabilities of brand choice as new information is processed. Theoretically, adaptive behavior takes place regardless of whether or not the situation represents "pure" learning, as in the case of purchasing a new product innovation.

With this last point in mind, it is not surprising that the research by Lawrence (1975) and Srinivasan and Kesavan (1976) found that Kuehn's (1962) application of linear learning theory produces results that are quite close to the results generated by the moving average methods of Box and Jenkins (1970) and the exponential smoothing model. This is because all three of these methods update current brand choice probabilities based upon consumers' previous brand choices. In a sense, all three models employ what might be termed "moving average" methods as the cornerstone of their analyses.

Above and beyond the popularity of the Linear Learning Model, its flexibility is indicated by the model's wide application in the area of brand choice and its limited application in store choice and television selection situations. Zufryden (1973, 1975a, 1975b) has even found the linear learning framework to significantly contribute to an understanding of consumers' responses to advertising exposures. But even though this model is an attractive representation of consumer choice processes, alternative probability mechanisms should be investigated as potential contributors to a more complete understanding of consumer choice processes. This is the role that is played by the various other stochastic models developed here.

When the parameter k in the Linear Learning-Brand Loyal Model is restricted to a value of one, the Linear Learning Model results. Consequently, the Linear Learning Model is a subset model of the Learning-Brand Loyal Model with k = 1.

3. *The Single Response Function Model (ONERESP).* The Single Response Function Model is specified as:

$$\Pr[\Delta_{t+1}|\Delta_t = \delta, f(p_t)] = \alpha + [\delta\lambda + (1 - \delta)\lambda]f(p_t), \qquad (3)$$

$$\alpha, \lambda \geq 0, \quad \alpha + \lambda \leq 1,$$

where $\delta = 1$ if Brand 1 was chosen at t and $\delta = 0$ otherwise. This formulation constitutes the same model event regardless of whether Response 1 or 0 was chosen at the previous choice occasion. Thus, this intuitively appealing model allows for the feedback effects of the overall brand choice experience across time without the confounding effects of specific-brand feedback. Theoretically, the Single Response Function Model is similar to Montgomery's (1969b) Probability Diffusion Model since it does allow for changing probabilities over time, but not in response to the specific brand chosen at choice occasion t.

In the terminology of mathematical psychology, the type of probability mechanism used by the Single Response Function Model is referred to as a "single-operator linear model" (Atkinson, Bower, and Crothers, 1965). First developed in a paper by Bush and Sternberg (1959), the single-operator linear model views the probability mechanism as a simple linear transformation in brand choice probabilities from one response trial to the next. The probability is, however, only allowed to change in one direction. This model is important because it measures the stability of the probability process; that is, it measures the degree to which equilibrium has been achieved in the probability process without deference to the influence of differential responses. Therefore, $\Pr(\Delta_{t+1})$ is a function of "satisfaction" with past product category experience. The influence of a past choice of Brand 1 is no stronger than the influence of a past choice of Brand 0, and vice versa. The combined effects of parameters α and λ provide an indication of how fast the market is adjusting to its equilibrium.

Like the other models discussed thus far, the Single Response Function Model is a heterogeneous n^{th}-order model. The probability-generating mechanism of ONERESP is a constrained version of: (1) the Linear Learning-Brand Loyal Model with $\beta = 0$ and $k = 1$, and (2) the Linear Learning Model with $\beta = 0$.

4. The Brand Loyal Model (BRLOYAL).

4. The Brand Loyal Model (BRLOYAL). The Brand Loyal Model, which is specified as

$$\Pr[\Delta_{t+1}|\Delta_t = \delta, f(p_t)] = [\delta + (1 - \delta)k]f(p_t), \quad k \geq 0 \qquad (4)$$

where $\delta = 1$ if Brand 1 was chosen at t and $\delta = 0$ otherwise, is an interesting model since the choice of Brand 1 will not alter the probability of selecting Brand 1 in the future. However, the choice of Brand 0 *will* alter the probability of selecting Brand 1 at the next choice occasion. The past choice of Brand 0 can have either a positive or negative effect, depending upon the magnitude of the parameter k.[5] The Brand Loyal Model features the same sort of probability mechanism as does Morrison's (1966) Brand Loyal Markov Model except that, as a constrained version of the Linear Learning-Brand Loyal Model, it retains higher-order properties. This structure of choice probabilities has also received support from Jones's (1970b) work which proposes this type of feedback mechanism as an alternative to a linear learning one in his Dual-Effects Model of brand choice.

The purchase operator in BRLOYAL is termed an "identity operator" by Atkinson, Bower, and Crothers (1965) in that the choice of Brand 1 at purchase occasion t does not alter $\Pr(\Delta_{t+1})$. The parameter k determines the nature of the feedback from Brand 0 on $Pr(\Delta_{t+1})$, and this reverses the situation from the Linear Learning Model since LINLEARN is primarily concerned with the degree of positive or negative feedback from purchasing Brand 1. If $k > 1$, there is negative feedback from buying Brand 0 since it increases $Pr(\Delta_{t+1})$. Likewise, $k < 1$ implies positive feedback from buying Brand 0 and would reduce the probability of buying Brand 1 on the next trial. If $k = 1$, the entire process (not only the purchase operator) becomes an identity operator, and the experience of purchasing Brand 0 has no different impact than the experience of purchasing Brand 1.

Like the previous models discussed in this paper, a subset relationship exists between BRLOYAL and other models. The Brand Loyal Model is a constrained version of: (1) the Linear Learning-Brand Loyal Model with $\alpha = 0$, $\beta = 0$, and $\lambda = 1$; and (2) the Brand Loyal Model with an Intercept Term with $\alpha = 0$.

5. The Brand Loyal Model with an Intercept Term (BRLOYINT).

The structure of the Brand Loyal Model with an Intercept Term is equivalent to the Brand Loyal Model except that it allows for a constant term. BRLOYINT is specified as:

$$Pr[\Delta_{t+1}|\Delta_t = \delta, f(p_t)] = \alpha + [\delta + (1 - \delta)k]f(p_t), \quad k \geqslant 0, \tag{5}$$

where $\delta = 1$ if Brand 1 was chosen at t and $\delta = 0$ otherwise.

Equation (5) is similar to the probability mechanism of (4), but the purchase operator is no longer an "identity operator." It is not possible for the probability of choosing Brand 1 to remain constant from one trial to the next if $\alpha \neq 0$. The α parameter is responsible for determining the extreme lower limit of the probability of choosing Brand 1. BRLOYINT is a heterogeneous, n^{th}-order model and is a constrained version of the Linear Learning-Brand Loyal Model with $\beta = 0$ and $\lambda = 1$.

6. The Bernoulli Model (BERN).

Considered by some to be only a naive model that can be used only as a benchmark for comparison purposes, the Bernoulli Model can be used to gain a great deal of insight into consumer choice processes. The Bernoulli Model is specified as:

$$Pr[\Delta_{t+1}|\Delta_t = \delta, f(p_t)] = [\delta + (1 - \delta)]f(p_t) \tag{6}$$

where $\delta = 1$ if Brand 1 was chosen at t and $\delta = 0$ otherwise. By featuring probabilistic behavior according to some statistical distribution (in which the possible responses do not necessarily have an equal chance of occurrence), the Bernoulli Model explicitly assumes that the choice process under consideration has achieved an equilibrium state.

The Bernoulli Model is a heterogeneous, first-order model. In other words, different consumers are allowed to have different probabilities of choosing Brand

1; but previous choices of Brand 1 are not allowed to change the current or future probabilities of selecting Brand 1. By definition, the process is stationary since consumers' probabilities of choosing Brand 1 do not change over time. The probability mechanism for the Bernoulli Model consists of a stable-probability identity operator since $Pr(\Delta_t)$ is identical to $Pr(\Delta_{t+1})$ for all t.

It is interesting to note that the Bernoulli Model is embedded in all of the models discussed heretofore. It is a constrained version of: (1) the Linear Learning-Brand Loyal Model with $\alpha = 0$, $\beta = 0$, $\lambda = 1$, and $k = 1$; (2) the Linear Learning Model with $\alpha = 0$, $\beta = 0$, and $\lambda = 1$; (3) the Single Response Function Model with $\alpha = 0$ and $\lambda = 1$; (4) the Brand Loyal Model with an Intercept Term with $\alpha = 0$ and $k = 1$; and (5) the Brand Loyal Model with $k = 1$.

C. Estimating Parameters Via Minimum Chi-Square Procedures

Stochastic modeling macrotheory requires that model parameters be estimated and that goodness-of-fit measures of the models' abilities to describe a series of brand choice decisions be obtained. A minimized chi-square statistic fulfills both of these needs and has been the most popular procedure for both parameter estimation and goodness-of-fit. Morrision (1966) provides a detailed analysis of this point.

Minimum chi-square methods are applicable in situations where response observations are frequencies of a finite number n of mutually exclusive events categorized dichotomously. The v possible behavior sequences (i.e., $v = 2^n$) by which the consumer can be categorized are indexed by i, $i = 1,2,\dots, v$. For example, consider a brand decision string of length four by a particular diary panel. In this case, there are 16 possible behavior patterns ($v = 2^n = 2^4 = 16$) in which the panel members' behavior could be categorized; these possibilities are indexed by i, $i = 1,2,\dots, 16$. For each possible sequence, i, there is an observed number of sample respondents, N_i, whose actual brand choice string matches that of each sequence. The total sample size is

$$N = \sum_{i=1}^{v} N_i \tag{7}$$

We now have a set of observed frequencies, $N_1, N_2, \dots, N_v$, each of which has a hypothetical probability of occurring, $\Pi_1, \Pi_2, \dots, \Pi_v$, as a function of a unique vector of model parameters, θ. The theoretical probabilities of occurrence as a function of the parameter vector are symbolized by $\Pi_i(\theta)$ for each of the v possible brand choice sequences.

In order to measure the goodness-of-fit of the model and to determine the optimal vector of parameters, θ^*, we need to define a measure of discrepancy between the observed frequencies $N_1, N_2, \dots, N_v$ and their respective hypothetical expectations $N\Pi_1(\theta), N\Pi_2(\theta), \dots, N\Pi_v(\theta)$. Several measures of discrepancy have been suggested (cf. Rao, 1973), but two measures stand out as prime candidates: (1) the conventional Pearson chi-square statistic, and (2) the modified Neyman chi-square statistic. The conventional Pearson chi-square statistic,

$$\chi^2 = \sum_{i=1}^{v} \frac{[N_i - N\Pi_i(\theta)]^2}{N\Pi_i(\theta)} \tag{8}$$

has been suggested by Morrison as an appropriate measure of discrepancy and has been used almost exclusively in stochastic model applications since then. If the model is viable and if brand choice decision sequences are independent, then the parameter estimates obtained in this way are BAN (best asymptotically normal) and have the appealing properties of consistency, asymptotic normality, and asymptotic efficiency. The Pearson chi-square has $v - q - 1$ degrees of freedom, where q is the total number of parameters to be estimated from the data for a particular stochastic model of consumer choice.

Neyman (1949) has also shown that a modified version of the conventional Pearson chi-square statistic,

$$\chi^2 = \sum_{i=1}^{v} \frac{[N_i - N\Pi_i(\theta)^2}{N_i} \tag{9}$$

is also distributed as chi-square with $v - q - 1$ degrees of freedom and produces estimates that are BAN. Thus, the denominator of the conventional chi-square, the expected number of consumers appearing in each sequence, $N\Pi_i(\theta)$, can be replaced with the actual number of consumers appearing in each sequence, N_i, while retaining the BAN properties of the conventional Pearson chi-square statistic.

While the asymptotic properties of the Pearson chi-square and the Neyman chi-square are equivalent, it is clear that the finite sample properties of the two statistics differ since the expected frequency in the denominator term of the Pearson chi-square is replaced with the observed frequency in the Neyman chi-square. A search of the statistics literature revealed no discussion of the finite sample properties of the Neyman modification of the chi-square goodness-of-fit test. But since (1) Pearson's statistic is distributed as *approximately* chi-square for finite sample sizes under the null hypothesis that the data were generated by the model under consideration, and (2) a null hypothesis that is true will yield a near equivalence between the denominator terms of the Pearson chi-square and the Neyman chi-square, $N\Pi_i(\theta)$ and N_i respectively, it can be assumed that the Neyman version is approximately equal to the original Pearson chi-square under the null hypothesis. Clearly, Neyman's modified version of Pearson's chi-square assumes that none of the observed values is equal to zero (Neyman, 1949), but this potential problem can easily be solved by replacing N_i with unity if its observed value is zero (Rao, 1973).

Theoretically, the analytical procedure for estimating parameters via the minimum chi-square technique consists of differentiating the function with respect to θ, setting the derivatives equal to zero, and solving. Unfortunately, even in the simplest cases these equations are difficult to solve (Bishop, Fienberg, and Holland, 1975) because of the problems in finding closed-form expressions for θ as functions of the sample statistics. Even replacing the $N\Pi_i(\theta)$ of the conventional Pearson chi-square with the N_i of the modified Neyman chi-square does not allow enough simplification for an analytical solution to be useful (Massy, Montgomery, and Morrison, 1970).

With these difficulties fresh in mind, it is easy to appreciate the numerical procedures that are available to circumvent the problem. For example, Massy, Montgomery, and Morrison (1970) used a non-linear programming (NLP) solution which combines a modified second-order Newton's procedure with a pattern search routine for the purpose of parameter estimation. This combined approach seems to provide a powerful technique for estimating the parameters of stochastic models of consumer choice and purchase incidence.

D. Contribution of the Neyman Chi-Square Estimation Method

While the Neyman modification of the conventional chi-square has been suggested in the stochastic modeling literature as a viable candidate for a goodness-of-fit measure (Massy, Montgomery, and Morrison, 1970), to date it has never been used in published stochastic applications. But since the models which were proposed earlier in this paper are constructed so that some models are subsets of other models, the Neyman chi-square statistic makes a valuable contribution to the strategy of attacking the many-to-one mapping problem. When model comparisons are made across models using the same data set, the denominator and the N_i term in the numerator of the Neyman modified chi-square remain stationary for all models. It is then possible to test the relative fit of one model over another without the confusion of having the denominator terms in the chi-square statistic fluctuate from model to model. In addition, Wilson (1977) has shown that parameter estimates and chi-square values that are generated under the Pearson and Neyman criteria usually deviate only slightly for the same data base.

Referring to our prior discussion, it was noted that the following model/embedded-model relationships exit:

BERN $\subseteq$ ONERESP $\subseteq$ LINLEARN $\subseteq$ LL-BRLOYAL; and
BERN $\subseteq$ BRLOYAL $\subseteq$ BRLOYINT $\subseteq$ LL-BRLOYAL.

It should be clear that the more flexible the model (i.e., the more parameters that are unconstrained), the better the accuracy of the fit of the model. The greater flexibility of the Linear Learning-Brand Loyal Model will allow less total deviation between actual and expected cell frequencies than will the more constrained Linear Learning Model. Likewise, the Linear Learning Model will allow less total deviation than the more constrained Single Response Function Model, and so on. Since the denominator term of the Neyman modified chi-square remains stationary across models, it can be concluded that the following weak ordering of Neyman chi-squares exists:

$$\chi^2_{\text{BERN}} \geq \chi^2_{\text{ONERESP}} \geq \chi^2_{\text{LINLEARN}} \geq \chi^2_{\text{LL-BRLOYAL}} \text{ and} \qquad (10)$$

$$\chi^2_{\text{BERN}} \geq \chi^2_{\text{BRLOYAL}} \geq \chi^2_{\text{BRLOYINT}} \geq \chi^2_{\text{LL-BRLOYAL}} \qquad (11)$$

However, this claim can only be made in a global sense; that is, it ignores the potential problem of local optima in the numerical parameter estimation procedure.

E. Tests of Hypotheses and Methods of Evaluation Across Models

Although reference has been made to formal tests of hypotheses in previous sections of this paper, hypothesis testing issues have not yet been discussed in detail. Now that the models, parameter estimation techniques, and goodness-of-fit issues have been treated, a discussion of hypotheses tests is in order.

1. Traditional Goodness-of-Fit Hypotheses. In the past, by far the most popular method of evaluating the goodness-of-fit of stochastic choice models has been by inspection of the chi-square statistic. In other words, the hypotheses

$$H_0 : \chi^2 = 0$$
$$H_1 : \chi^2 > 0$$

can be tested by comparing the calculated chi-square statistic against the theoretical value for any given level of statistical significance. An alternative way to state this set of hypotheses is as follows:

H_0 : The model is a perfect representation of the consumer choice process that generated the data;

H_1 : The data were generated by some other (unspecified) model.

Recently, the trend has been to present the probability value (or p-value) associated with the chi-square value to indicate the closeness of fit between the observed data and the theoretical data generated by the model under scrutiny. The p-value indicates that probability of finding a chi-square of equal or higher magnitude than the value actually found if the model is a perfect representation of the process that generated the data. For example, an observed chi-square of 15.51 with 8 degrees of freedom would indicate that a chi-square of 15.51 *or more* should occur in a random sampling process in the long-run only about five times per hundred under the null hypothesis that the model under scrutiny generated the data. The interpretation of a low p-value (.05 in the example above) is that the model is not a viable representation of the situation under investigation. In the stochastic modeling literature, a p-value of .10 is generally considered to be the minimally acceptable level of statistical significance. Because the p-value adjusts for varying degrees of freedom across models, it has been used as the major (and, in many cases, the sole) measure of how well the model fits the data in stochastic applications (see, for example, Montgomery, 1969a).

Although p-values associated with the conventional Pearson chi-squares have enjoyed a great deal of popularity in the stochastic modeling literature, an analysis of p-values alone hardly seems adequate to deal with the issue of how much better one model fits than another. Fortunately, the Neyman modification of the conventional Pearson chi-square may be useful in gaining insight into the relative goodness-of-fit for alternative models.

2. The Importance of Model Parsimony. The many-to-one mapping problem raises the following question: What criteria should be used to determine the "best" model for a given data base when two or more stochastic models having quite dissimilar structures provide goodness-of-fit statistics that are very nearly equal? More often than not, researchers have simply chosen the model having the highest p-value as the one "best" model regardless of the structure of the competing models.

The inherent weakness in merely inspecting p-values can be illustrated by examining goodness-of-fit values for hypothetical (but typical) brand choice data. Suppose, for example, that Model Y (df = 7) yields a chi-square value of 3.13 (p > .80) while Model Z (df = 10) yields a chi-square of 6.64 (p > .75). Would the p-value of .80 for Model Y indicate that it better represents the actual process that generated the data? Or should the researcher conclude that the two models fit the data about the same with the difference in chi-squares attributable solely to the three additional parameters in Model Y? Depending upon the structure of the models in question, these additional parameters may allow for a more flexible model (and thus a closer fit) without providing additional insight into the choice process itself.

The determinative point of the previous paragraph revolves around the issue of model parsimony. A principle that is well-founded in the general philosophy of science (e.g., Popper, 1959), in scientific methodologies such as statistics (e.g., Box, 1976), in applications of social research (e.g., Smith, 1975), and in marketing modeling and information system design (Little, 1970; Montgomery, 1973), parsimony refers to the simplicity of a theory. This criterion argues that relative to other theoretical models of the same phenomenon, the one with the most economy of specification is best (Smith, 1975). Indeed, the idea of parsimony forms the basis for Montgomery's (1967; Montgomery and Urban, 1969) statement that stochastic models of consumer choice behavior are more parsimonious than deterministic models of the same behavior and, consequently, may be preferable. In a recent philosophical article, Box (1976) also makes an intriguing plea for parsimony. Box argues that since all scientific models are wrong anyway, the scientist will not be able to obtain a "correct" model by excessive elaboration and, therefore, should seek an economical description of a natural phenomenon.

3. Tests of Hypotheses for Embedded Models. Given the importance of model parsimony, an appealing way to view the hypotheses related to an evaluation of the improvement in fit achieved across models is to consider the existence of model subset relationships. If these model interrelationships are explicitly considered, it becomes possible to test model hypotheses concerning closeness-of-fit in a way that approximates the generalized likelihood ratio test.[6] The series of hypotheses to be tested is:

$$H_0 : \chi_A^2 = \chi_B^2$$
$$H_1 : \chi_A^2 < \chi_B^2$$

where Model B is a constrained version of Model A. The null hypothesis suggests that the embedded model fits as well as the more general model having one or more additional parameters. On the other hand, the alternative hypothesis expects that the additional parameter(s) of the more general model will allow for a better fit than the constrained, and thus more inflexible, model having fewer parameters. It is also possible to deduce hypotheses from the more specific, embedded models concerning the constrained values of certain parameters in the more general models. For instance, when comparing LL-BRLOYAL (the general model) with LINLEARN (the embedded model), the implicit hypothesis concerning the LL-BRLOYAL parameter k is $H_0 : k = 1$ versus $H_1 : k \neq 1$; when comparing LL-BRLOYAL with ONERESP, the implicit hypothesis is $H_0 : k = 1$ and $\beta = 0$ versus $H_1 : k \neq 1$ and/or $\beta \neq 0$; and so on.

By specifying the series of hypotheses in this fashion, it is possible to construct an F-test to evaluate the incremental difference between any pair of Neyman chi-squares. The following test statistic is appropriate:

$$\text{computed } F = \frac{(\chi_B^2 - \chi_A^2)/(df_B - df_A)}{\chi_A^2/df_A} \tag{12}$$

where χ_A^2 and χ_B^2 are the Neyman chi-square values associated with Model A (the general model) and Model B (the embedded model) respectively, and df_A and df_B are the respective degrees of freedom for Model A and Model B. This statistic, which can be used as a stepwise test to determine how well one model fits the data relative to an embedded model for a particular data set, is distributed approximately as F with degrees of freedom corresponding to $(df_B - df_A)$ and df_A. Equation (12) makes use of the following statistical principles:

1) the independence of the numerator and denominator which comes about

because the incremental value of the difference between χ_B^2 and χ_A^2 could not be contained in χ_A^2 alone;

2) the additive property of the chi-square distribution (Freund, 1971; Lancaster, 1969; Winkler and Hays, 1975);

3) the F-distribution which results when the ratio of two independent chi-square variables, each divided by its degrees of freedom, is formed (Freund, 1971; Rao, 1973; Winkler and Hays, 1975); and

4) the assertion that the BAN chi-square estimates used in this research have basically the same asymptotic properties as maximum likelihood estimates (Neyman, 1949).

It is interesting to note that the test statistic in (12) avoids the problem of potential bias caused by dependence between chi-squares. This problem, discussed by Massy, Montgomery, and Morrison (1970) and Atkinson, Bower, and Crothers (1965) is evident in the statistic

$$\text{computed } F = \frac{\chi_B^2/df_B}{\chi_A^2/df_A} \tag{13}$$

when it is used to compare the fit of Model A relative to Model B for a given set of data. In this case, χ_A^2 and χ_B^2 are dependent since χ_A^2 is fully contained in χ_B^2, thus violating a major assumption of the F-test. Since the numerator and denominator of the stepwise procedure of (12) are independent, it is possible to use this test to explore the significance between the fit of two models, one of which is embedded in the other.

To date, stepwise methods of model evaluation such as that of (12) have not been fully implemented in the stochastic modeling literature. Though it is very common to find references to the existence of subset relationships in this body of literature, this advantageous model/embedded-model structure has not been exploited in empirical applications. When mentioned, this relationship is usually included only in authors' discussions of models to be empirically tested and is not treated again when the models are evaluated as to their relative goodness-of-fit.[7]

It is interesting to note that the philosophy of model testing suggested in this paper has also been suggested in the econometrics literature to assist with the selection of the most appropriate model. For instance, Kendall and Stuart (1973) have proposed an F-test to aid in solving the specification problem in econometric research, which occurs when the true theoretical model of the underlying physical process is misrepresented either by omitting a relevant variable from the matrix of independent variables or by including an irrelevant variable in the matrix of independent variables (Johnston, 1972; Pindyck and Rubinfeld, 1976). The Kendall-Stuart approach embeds interesting alternative models within one general model and then tests hypotheses about the values of certain parameters contained in the general model by using a likelihood ratio test. In short, an

F-statistic is proposed that tests the difference between the sums of squares for the nested and generalized econometric models. As in (12), the Kendall-Stuart method also rejects the nested model if the computed F-value is greater than the theoretical F-value at the specified level of significance. Parameter restrictions and a resulting F-test are also used by Chow (1960), who provides a methodology for identifying structural changes in data gathered across time. In the marketing literature, the specification problem, the model structure problem, and the respective Kendall-Stuart and Chow solutions are discussed by Parsons and Schultz (1976).

In the stochastic modeling literature, a suggested procedure for model evaluation which closely resembles the stepwise procedure of (12) is one suggested by Blattberg and Sen (1973). Blattberg and Sen describe a chi-square test developed by C. R. Rao (1961, 1973) in which a constrained model can be evaluated relative to a more general one. The major advantage that (12) holds over Rao's method is that of simplicity. In short, the data requirements for Rao's procedure are the expected and observed sample proportions for each behavioral sequence in both the constrained and more general model. Equation (12) uses only the aggregate chi-square values and their respective degrees of freedom for the two models and is, therefore, computationally simpler than Rao's method.

Even though Rao's method could be applied to a stochastic modeling situation that uses actual recorded choice behavior, Blattberg and Sen did not do so, however, since the primary purpose of their article was to use *simulated* brand choice data in an investigation of the small sample size properties of chi-square estimates. The Blattberg and Sen paper, as well as their later article (1975) which proposes a Bayesian method for discriminating between alternative stochastic models at the individual consumer level in cases where lengthy purchase histories are available, provides more evidence of the need for improved methods of model comparison.

4. Tests of Hypotheses for Non-Embedded Models.   While prior discussion has centered on model subset relationships and a stepwise evaluation procedure for such models, it will also be necessary to evaluate the differences in fit between models that are not embedded in one another (e.g., BRLOYAL and LIN-LEARN). In this case, the null hypothesis is the same as before, but the alternative hypothesis must be changed to reflect the non-existent subset relationship. More specifically, the hypotheses are:

$$H_0 : \chi^2_A = \chi^2_C$$
$$H_1 : \chi^2_A \neq \chi^2_C$$

where Model C is not embedded in Model A. The alternative hypothesis now suggests that the two models will differ in their fit, but no a priori prediction can be made with regard to which of the two models should fit better. Because no subset relationship exists, a two-tailed hypothesis must be specified and tested by calculating the following problematic statistic:[8]

$$\text{computed } F = \frac{\chi_A^2/df_A}{\chi_C^2/df_C} \tag{14}$$

As noted before, (14) violates the independence requirement of the F-test and should therefore be used with caution. The p-value associated with each minimized chi-square should also be carefully inspected to determine the relative fit of Model A versus Model C.

IV. AN EMPIRICAL ILLUSTRATION OF THE METHODOLOGY

The purpose of Section IV is to provide an illustration of the model testing framework proposed in Section III. Empirical results are given for four sets of brand choice data.

A. Incorporating Population Heterogeneity

As noted previously, one of the elements of the methodology which lends itself to change by individual researchers is the method used to incorporate population heterogeneity into the specific choice models. The focal point of the heterogeneity issue is the intuitively appealing assumption that consumers vary in their probabilities of choosing a particular brand. The importance of the heterogeneity assumption was brought to the forefront by Frank's (1962) criticism that the statistical effects of homogeneity allowed for the occurrence of spurious "learning" in Kuehn's (1958) original linear learning application. Because of Frank's argument and because of the intuitive appeal of statistical heterogeneity as indicated above, the heterogeneity feature has become the hallmark of theoretical and empirical research in stochastic models of consumer brand choice behavior. Massy (in Massy, Montgomery, and Morrison, 1970) is responsible for providing a convenient method for incorporating population heterogeneity in stochastic models. This method, which defines a prior distribution of initial brand choice probabilities, is used in the empirical analysis which follows. For the models tested in this paper, the distribution of choice probabilities, denoted $f(p_0)$, is defined as an arbitrary distribution. The assumption of an arbitrary distribution of initial choices has flexibility as its main advantage. The parameters of an arbitrary distribution can be found by estimating the moments around the origin as in most other statistical distributions, but the complete relationship among the moments of the distribution remains unspecified.

Because of the flexibility of the arbitrary distribution, it was chosen over other distributions that have been suggested as possible candidates to represent the dispersion of initial choice probabilities. For example, research by Jones (1970a, 1974) has indicated that of the intuitively appealing alternatives to the arbitrary distribution, the two-parameter beta distribution most adequately represents the initial choice probabilities. The flexibility of the beta distribution is limited, however, in that the relationship between the first two moments about the origin and higher-order moments is completely specified. Even though the prior specification of a beta distribution would save two degrees of freedom in the parameter estimation process, the arbitrary distribution was chosen because of the precedent set by other researchers as well as its unmatched freedom from restrictions. An example of the increased flexibility (and thus improved fit) of the arbitrary distribution when compared to the beta distribution is provided in Chapter 4 of Massy, Montgomery, and Morrison (1970). These data show a rather large mean difference between the chi-squares for the Brand Loyal Markov Model under arbitrary heterogeneity and under beta heterogeneity for ten data sets.

B. Data Description

The "Favorite Brand" Coffee data, first analyzed by Massy, Montgomery, and Morrison (1970), were used to estimate the parameters of the models proposed in Section III.B. These data were chosen because they were readily available and because the findings reported here can be contrasted with the findings of Massy, Montgomery, and Morrison. The data were originally obtained from the *Chicago Tribune* Consumer Panel, and each family's coffee purchases were reduced to binary form.[9] For each family, "Brand 1" represents a purchase of the family's favorite coffee brand, while "Brand 0" represents a purchase of any of the remaining coffee brands in the market. For the purpose of model input, a brand choice string of length four was calculated. Complete details of the experimental design are available in Massy, Montgomery, and Morrison (1970).

For the empirical analysis reported here, four data segments were selected. These include those families who purchased more than the median amount of coffee (designated as HEAVY users), those families who purchased less than the median amount of coffee (LIGHT users), those families who remained loyal to their favorite brand across the three-year period (LOYAL users), and those families who switched favorite brands within the three-year period (NON-LOYAL users). Each of the four consumer segments are analyzed independently in the empirical results which follow.

C. Results

Each of the four data sets was applied to each of the six brand choice models discussed earlier. Parameter estimates for each model were obtained by using the numerical procedures developed by Massy, Montgomery, and Morrison (1970). In short, Massy, Montgomery, and Morrison use a combination of two nonlinear programming algorithms to minimize the goodness-of-fit measure. For each model and each data set, model parameters were estimated twice—once using the conventional Pearson chi-square as the minimization criterion and once using the Neyman chi-square as the minimization criterion.

1. Parameter Estimates and Goodness-of-Fit Statistics. The results of the parameter estimation process are presented in Table II. In this table, only the parameter estimates obtained by minimizing the Neyman chi-square are presented. Although the Pearson chi-square parameter estimates are not presented here, their values correspond closely to the values of the Neyman chi-square estimates. For comparison purposes, both the Pearson chi-square statistic and the Neyman chi-square statistic are reported. As would be expected, there are slight differences between the two goodness-of-fit measures, but these differences are not large enough to merit special attention.

As can be seen from Table II, the more general models seem to provide a much closer fit to the data than the simpler models. Using .10 as the minimum p-value for accepting the hypothesis that a model fits the data, only LL-BRLOYAL is accepted for all four data segments. LINLEARN is accepted for three of the four data sets, BRLOYINT is accepted for two data sets, and BRLOYAL is accepted only for the LIGHT user segment. Both BERN and ONERESP are rejected in all four tests.

2. BERN, BRLOYAL, BRLOYINT, and LL-BRLOYAL Model Comparisons. The formal model comparisons carried out via (12) are summarized in Table III for the BERN, BRLOYAL, BRLOYINT, and LL-BRLOYAL series of model/embedded-models. Table III presents the results of the incremental-difference F-test for all four sets of Neyman chi-square values. Degrees of freedom are also given for each pairwise comparison.

In the interpretation of Table III, one problem that cannot be taken lightly is that of determining the point at which a ..lore parsimonious model should be rejected in favor of a more complicated model that does a better job of fitting the data. This issue is, of course, reflected in the level of statistical significance to be adopted for the test. The maximum probability of a Type I error chosen for the empirical test should depend upon the importance given to the concept of model parsimony. Because of the importance of the idea of parsimony in the philosophy of science as well as in applications-oriented methodologies (as discussed in Section III.E.2), the traditional level of .05 is used to evaluate the model comparisons. This rather strenuous level of statistical significance is also justified on the grounds that stochastic brand choice models are not intended to provide a general theory of consumer behavior. These models seem to be much more useful in the area of prediction (Bennett, 1977; Howard, 1977), where the need for parsimony in model building is greater. As a consequence, a relatively large difference between chi-squares should occur before the null hypothesis of equality between the two chi-squares is rejected.

The data in Table III provide more support for the Linear Learning-Brand

Table II. Parameter Estimates and Goodness-of-Fit Data

Data Segment	Model	df	Neyman Chi-Square	P-Value for Neyman Chi-Square[a]	Pearson Chi-Square	Parameter Estimates[b]							
						α	β	λ	k	μ_1	μ_2	μ_3	μ_4
1. HEAVY USERS	BERN	11	30.25	<.010	30.68	0.0[c]	0.0[c]	1.0[c]	1.0[c]	.7373	.6014	.5163	.4566
(Sample size = 2660)	BRLOYAL	10	26.58	<.010	27.70	0.0[c]	0.0[c]	1.0[c]	.9732	.7421	.6049	.5173	.4550
	BRLOYAL	9	22.02	<.010	21.58	.0081	0.0[c]	1.0[c]	.9611	.7323	.5889	.4965	.4302
	ONERESP	9	29.16	<.010	29.81	.0267	0.0[c]	.9745	1.0[c]	.7214	.5836	.4984	.4391
	LINLEARN	8	6.61	.500	6.02	.1206	.2234	.6195	1.0[c]	.7256	.5613	.4551	.3754
	LL-BRLOYAL	7	4.85	.600	4.74	.1039	.3499	.4911	1.2095	.7250	.5440	.4360	.3568
2. LIGHT USERS	BERN	11	24.06	<.010	25.22	0.0[c]	0.0[c]	1.0[c]	1.0[c]	.6952	.5377	.4451	.3835
(Sample size = 2650)	BRLOYAL	10	14.23	.100	14.85	0.0[c]	0.0[c]	1.0[c]	.9626	.7029	.5437	.4482	.3841
	BRLOYINT	9	10.02	.300	9.62	.0077	0.0[c]	1.0[c]	.9498	.6939	.5290	.4296	.3624
	ONERESP	9	23.54	<.010	24.83	.0024	0.0[c]	1.0000	1.0[c]	.6915	.5328	.4397	.3778
	LINLEARN	8	5.62	.600	5.78	.0915	.2177	.6525	1.0[c]	.6913	.4950	.3835	.3088
	LL-BRLOYAL	7	5.43	.600	5.34	.0867	.1726	.7118	.9600	.6916	.5025	.3922	.3172
3. LOYAL USERS	BERN	11	33.08	<.010	31.10	0.0[c]	0.0[c]	1.0[c]	1.0[c]	.7940	.6745	.5947	.5357
(Sample size = 3600)	BRLOYAL	10	31.31	<.010	28.60	0.0[c]	0.0[c]	1.0[c]	.9728	.7961	.6749	.5927	.5313
	BRLOYINT	9	28.53	<.010	25.01	.0030	0.0[c]	1.0[c]	.9821	.7910	.6692	.5876	.5270
	ONERESP	9	33.08	<.010	30.52	.0117	0.0[c]	.9920	1.0[c]	.7805	.6557	.5732	.5125
	LINLEARN	8	15.75	.025	13.22	.1114	.2047	.6582	1.0[c]	.7867	.6425	.5407	.4515
	LL-BRLOYAL	7	9.32	.200	9.81	.0711	.4516	.4225	1.4412	.7855	.6133	.4956	.3623
4. NONLOYAL USERS	BERN	11	30.75	<.010	31.25	0.0[c]	0.0[c]	1.0[c]	1.0[c]	.5518	.3484	.2409	.1773
(Sample size = 1710)	BRLOYAL	10	19.70	.025	20.71	0.0[c]	0.0[c]	1.0[c]	.9519	.5675	.3595	.2455	.1765
	BRLOYINT	9	9.17	.400	9.25	.0211	0.0[c]	1.0[c]	.9149	.5469	.3313	.2147	.1455
	ONERESP	9	29.75	<.010	30.57	.0055	0.0[c]	1.0000	1.0[c]	.5437	.3396	.2326	.1696
	LINLEARN	8	3.84	.800	3.80	.1762	.1952	.4938	1.0[c]	.5439	.3008	.1793	.1110
	LL-BRLOYAL	7	3.84	.750	3.80	.1749	.1802	.5180	.9681	.5440	.3040	.1817	.1088

[a]Probability of a larger chi-square value if the data were generated by the model under consideration.
[b]All parameter estimates presented here were generated by minimizing the Neyman chi-square.
[c]Value is a fixed constant.

260

Table III. F-Tests for BERN, BRLOYAL, BRLOYINT, and LL-BRLOYAL Model Comparisons[a]

Embedded Model	Less Restricted Model		
	BRLOYAL	BRLOYINT	LL-BRLOYAL
BERN			
HEAVY USERS	1.381	1.682	9.165[c]
LIGHT USERS	6.908[b]	6.305[b]	6.004[b]
LOYAL USERS	0.565	0.718	4.461[b]
NONLOYAL USERS	5.609[b]	10.590[c]	12.264[c]
df	(1, 10)	(2, 9)	(4, 7)
BRLOYAL			
HEAVY USERS		1.864	10.454[c]
LIGHT USERS		3.781	3.781
LOYAL USERS		0.877	5.505[b]
NONLOYAL USERS		10.335[b]	9.637[c]
df		(1, 9)	(3, 7)
BRLOYINT			
HEAVY USERS			12.391[c]
LIGHT USERS			2.959
LOYAL USERS			7.214[b]
NONLOYAL USERS			4.858[b]
df			(2, 7)

[a] All F-statistics were calculated via (12).
[b] $p < .05$.
[c] $p < .01$.

Loyal Model than the other models. Reading down the LL-BRLOYAL column in the table, it is clear that the simpler models are rejected when compared to LL-BRLOYAL in ten of the twelve pairwise tests. The results indicate that LL-BRLOYAL provides the best representation of the brand choice process for the HEAVY, LOYAL, and NONLOYAL consumer segments. For the LIGHT users of "Favorite Brand" Coffee, however, the Brand Loyal Model emerges as the most accurate model. This model is retained when evaluated against LL-BRLOYAL, and BERN is rejected in favor of BRLOYAL in the LIGHT user test. Further, the formal comparison between BRLOYAL and BRLOYINT indicates that BRLOYAL is not rejected in favor of BRLOYINT although the difference between the Neyman chi-squares is 4.21 (14.23 minus 10.02).

3. BERN, ONERESP, LINLEARN, and LL-BRLOYAL Model Comparisons. The results of the incremental-difference F-test of (12) for BERN, ONERESP, LINLEARN, and LL-BRLOYAL are presented in Table IV. For the four data segments analyzed here, these model comparisons provide overwhelming support for the Linear Learning Model at the .05 level of significance. Except

Table IV.   F-Tests for BERN, ONERESP, LINLEARN, and LL-BRLOYAL
Model Comparisons[a]

	Less Restricted Model		
Embedded Model	ONERESP	LINLEARN	LL-BRLOYAL
BERN			
HEAVY USERS	0.168	9.537[c]	9.165[c]
LIGHT USERS	0.099	8.750[c]	6.004[b]
LOYAL USERS	0.000	2.934	4.461[b]
NONLOYAL USERS	0.151	18.687[d]	12.264[c]
df	(2, 9)	(3, 8)	(4, 7)
ONERESP			
HEAVY USERS		27.292[d]	17.543[c]
LIGHT USERS		25.509[d]	11.673[c]
LOYAL USERS		8.803[b]	8.923[b]
NONLOYAL USERS		53.979[d]	23.616[d]
df		(1, 8)	(2, 7)
LINLEARN			
HEAVY USERS			2.540
LIGHT USERS			0.245
LOYAL USERS			4.829
NONLOYAL USERS			0.000
df			(1, 7)

[a] All F-statistics are calculated via (12).
[b] $p < .05$.
[c] $p < .01$.
[d] $p < .001$.

for one model comparison involving LINLEARN and its embedded models, the embedded models are rejected in favor of LINLEARN. However, when LIN-LEARN is tested against the more general Linear Learning-Brand Loyal Model, the simpler LINLEARN is never rejected.

Table III clearly indicates that, when the models evaluated here are viewed in a model/embedded-model relationship, no support is forthcoming for BERN, ONERESP, or LL-BRLOYAL. This statement is warranted even though the non-parallel operators of LL-BRLOYAL allow the reduction of the Neyman chi-square for the HEAVY, LIGHT, and LOYAL data segments.

4. Non-Embedded Model Comparisons.   As noted previously, it is necessary in some cases to evaluate the relative performance of models not contained in a model/embedded-model structure. For the models proposed and tested in this paper, such non-embedded model comparisions are presented in Table V. These results are a product of (14) and, consequently, should be interpreted cautiously.

The F-tests for the non-embedded models test the null hypothesis of equality between the two chi-square statistics. Since none of the data segments yield

Table V. F-Tests for Non-Embedded Model
Comparisons[a]

	ONERESP	LINLEARN
BRLOYAL		
HEAVY USERS	1.219	0.311
LIGHT USERS	1.838	0.494
LOYAL USERS	1.174	0.629
NONLOYAL USERS	1.678	0.244
df	(9, 10)	(8, 10)
BRLOYINT		
HEAVY USERS	1.324	0.338
LIGHT USERS	2.349	0.631
LOYAL USERS	1.159	0.621
NONLOYAL USERS	3.244	0.471
df	(9, 9)	(8, 9)

[a]All F-statistics are calculated via (14). None of the F-ratios are
significant at the .05 level.

significant results for the four model comparisons at the .05 level of significance,
the null hypothesis must be accepted in every case.

5. A Check on the Efficacy of LL-BRLOYAL.   Earlier statements in this article
(Section III.B.1) claimed that the Linear Learning-Brand Loyal Model is the
empirical equivalent of a Linear Learning Model with non-parallel operators.
Consequently, it is important to compare results obtained from the two models.
Recall from (1) that the structural form of LL-BRLOYAL is

$$\Pr[\Delta_{t+1}|\Delta_t = \delta, f(p_t)] = \alpha + \delta[\beta + \lambda f(p_t)] + (1 - \delta)[k\lambda f(p_t)] \quad (1)$$

As we have seen, the resulting interaction between the k and λ parameters in the
rejection operator allows for non-parallel operators, except in the case where k =
1. Thus, this model purports to provide the same results as a Linear Learning
Model with non-parallel operators of the form

$$\Pr[\Delta_{t+1}|\Delta_t = \delta, f(p_t)] = \alpha + \delta[\beta + \lambda_1 f(p_t)] + (1 - \delta)]\lambda_2 f(p_t)], \quad (15)$$
$$-1 \leq \beta < 1, \quad \alpha,\lambda_1,\lambda_2, \geq 0, \quad \alpha + \beta + \lambda_1 \leq 1, \quad \alpha + \lambda_2 \leq 1,$$

where $\delta = 1$ if Brand 1 was chosen at occasion t and $\delta = 0$ otherwise, as long
as $\lambda_1 \neq \lambda_2$.

If the models of (1) and (15) are equivalent, they should provide the same
results when the parameter vectors of both models are estimated from the same
set of data and invoke the same minimum chi-square criterion. As a check on the
efficacy of LL-BRLOYAL, the parameters of both models were estimated for the
four data sets. The results of the comparison for the NONLOYAL consumer
segment, which are typical of the data studied here, are presented in Table VI.
These results serve as strong evidence that the two models are equivalent. Esti-

mated parameters α, μ_1, μ_2, and μ_3 for the two models are exactly the same, while the values for the β and μ_4 parameters differ by only .0002 and .0001, respectively. For the purchase operator (λ versus λ_1), the difference in estimated parameter values is .0002. The estimated slope parameters for the rejection operator are virtually identical, even though they take different computational forms in LL-BRLOYAL ($k\lambda = .5015$) and in the non-parallel operator Linear Learning Model ($\lambda_2 = .5014$). Given this close corespondence between the two vectors of model parameters, we would expect the same results from the chi-square statistic. A comparison of the results confirms this expectation; the Neyman chi-square statistics are exactly alike ($\chi^2 = 3.84$; p > .80). When the model parameters were reestimated using the Pearson chi-square as the minimization criterion, the two sets of parameter estimates were quite similar and the chi-square values were exactly the same ($\chi^2 = 3.80$; p > .75).

The purpose of the model comparison for (1) and (15) is to add credence to the Linear Learning-Brand Loyal Model and its contribution to the methodology. The results are non-trivial because nuances are often found in NLP estimation techniques. The results of Table VI show that, as an empirical issue, no estimation problems are encountered in the parameter structure of LL-BRLOYAL. It can now be concluded that the two models are equivalent, both theoretically and empirically. The LL-BRLOYAL version was chosen for detailed analysis since it offers the advantage of permitting a model/embedded-model relationship among the models.

6. *Summary of Empirical Results.* When the empirical results presented in Tables II–VI are considered jointly, two major conclusions must be drawn. The first conclusion deals with the possible differences in interpretation between the

Table VI. Parameter Estimates and Chi-Square Statistics for LL-BRLOYAL and the Linear Learning Model with Non-Parallel Operators (for NONLOYAL USERS)[a]

	Non-Parallel Operator Linear Learning Model	LL-BRLOYAL
α	.1749	.1749
β	.1804	.1802
Purchase Operator	$\lambda_1 = .5178$	$\lambda = .5180$
Rejection Operator	$\lambda_2 = .5014$	$k\lambda = .5015$
μ_1	.5440	.5440
μ_2	.3040	.3040
μ_3	.1817	.1817
μ_4	.1087	.1088
Neyman Chi-Square Value	3.84	3.84
	(p > .80)	(p > .80)
Pearson Chi-Square Value	3.80	3.80
	(p > .75)	(p > .75)
df	7	7

[a]All parameters were estimated by minimizing the Neyman chi-square statistic.

formal model comparison method of (12) and the subjective model comparison method of judging the magnitude of the chi-squares and p-values as suggested by Morrison (1966). As an illustration of these differences in interpretation, consider the results of the parameter estimation process of LINLEARN and LL-BRLOYAL in the HEAVY user segment. The data in Table II indicate that when using a subjective interpretation of the chi-squares, LL-BRLOYAL ($\chi^2 = 4.85$; p > .60) would be judged to provide a better fit to the data than would LINLEARN ($\chi^2 = 6.61$; p > .50). In contrast, the data from the incremental-difference F-test reported in Table IV for the LL-BRLOYAL/LINLEARN comparison indicate that the model representing the null hypothesis (LINLEARN) must be accepted as the more appropriate representation of the HEAVY user data.

Such differences in interpretation would seem to be common in stochastic modeling applications where the many-to-one mapping problem occurs. Other examples appear in the LIGHT user segment (BRLOYAL versus BRLOYINT), the LOYAL user segment (LINLEARN versus LL-BRLOYAL), and the NON-LOYAL user segment (LINLEARN versus LL-BRLOYAL). It should be noted, however, that the degree of differences in interpretation is often a function of the level of statistical significance adopted for the F-test of (12).

The second conclusion that must be drawn from the empirical results concerns the overall efficiency of the Linear Learning Model. As noted before, LINLEARN emerges as the best representation of all four data sets summarized in Table IV; and LL-BRLOYAL fits the data best in three of the four data segments summarized in Table III. However, Table IV also shows that in the LL-BRLOYAL/LINLEARN comparison LINLEARN must be judged to provide the most accurate fit to the data at least for three of the four segments. For the LIGHT user data, however, the same conclusion is not forthcoming since BRLOYAL emerges as the most appropriate model in the Table III comparisons.

It is interesting to note that the results presented by Massy, Montgomery, and Morrison (1970) also provide overall support for the Linear Learning Model. In their more subjective analysis, Massy, Montgomery, and Morrison concluded that LINLEARN provided a better fit to the ''Favorite Brand'' Coffee data than the Brand Loyal Markov Model (Morrison, 1966), the Customer Loyal Markov Model (Morrison, 1966), and the Bernoulli Model. Since the findings reported earlier in this article parallel the findings reported by Massy, Montgomery, and Morrison, it is clear that the Linear Learning Model provides an effective structure for predicting brand choice probabilities for the ''Favorite Brand'' Coffee data.

V. SUMMARY AND CONCLUSIONS

Previous research in the area of stochastic choice models suggests that this class of models may provide insight into the nature of human choice processes in a variety of social and economic contexts. Unfortunately, the many-to-one mapping problem has made the task of model comparison and evaluation nearly impossible for many consumer choice data sets. With this in mind, this paper presented an approach designed to reduce the severity of the many-to-one mapping problem.

In the methodology presented here, several modeling concepts are combined to create a formal model evaluation method that is objective and is based upon an F-test which evaluates the incremental differences in model fit. The statistical methods are based on the interesting property that some well-known stochastic models have other models embedded in them and that other interesting stochastic models can be developed which have this property. Another positive feature of the methodology is that it utilizes a parameter estimation procedure (the minimum Neyman chi-square method) which contains only a slight modification to the conventional Pearson chi-square method of parameter generation. Two series of brand choice models which take advantage of model/embedded-model relationships were presented. As an illustration of the methodology, "Favorite Brand" Coffee data were used to estimate the parameters of the six stochastic models. For the data examined here, the Linear Learning Model emerged as the best overall representation of the brand choice process.

The methodology presented in this article suggests the need for further research in stochastic modeling. Such issues as situational differences in brand choice decisions, differences in choice behavior across stimulus objects (e.g., brands, stores, media, etc.) and competitive environments, and differences in decision-making across market segments are prime targets for future studies. Speculating on where such a research program would ultimately lead, one might expect an objective model evaluation procedure to yield more insight into the true nature of human choice behavior than previous subjective methods of model evaluation. At one extreme, the viability of the zero-order (i.e., stationarity) assumption used by some researchers (Bass, 1974a, 1974b; Herniter, 1973; Shoemaker et al., 1977) could be rigorously evaluated. At the other extreme, models that proposed complex probability mechanisms (Jones, 1970b, 1973) may also be evaluated, thus identifying those model parameters that are superfluous to the correct modeling of the brand choice process.

FOOTNOTES

*The methodology presented in this article was developed in the author's doctoral dissertation (Wilson, 1977). Thanks are in order to the members of the dissertation committee for their guidance: David J. Curry (co-chairman), Gerald J. Eskin (co-chairman), Peter C. Riesz, Mark Moriarty, and J. Frank O'Connor. J. Morgan Jones (UCLA) kindly provided the nonlinear programming computer algorithm used for parameter estimation in the empirical stage of the research. The author also thanks Jagdish N. Sheth and two anonymous reviewers for their useful comments on an earlier draft of this article.

1. The work by Bass and Herniter explains macro-market behavior with inferences drawn to the individual level. For most of the brand choice models mentioned thus far, the theory is designed for

explanation at the micro-level with inferences being drawn to the aggregate-marketing level. It remains to be seen which approach offers more to the understanding of marketing phenomena, but it is clear that the selection of a research strategy for a particular investigation of loyalty/switching behavior should depend upon the questions to be answered by the research and the stability of brand choice probabilities across time. The methodology to be proposed in this paper could be used as a check on the stationarity of purchase probabilities in any given market prior to a macro-market study such as those proposed by Bass and Herniter.

2. Although the major attempts at solving the many-to-one mapping problem are briefly mentioned here, a much more detailed discussion of the possible solutions to this important problem is available elsewhere (Wilson, in press).

3. A note regarding notation is in order here. In this paper, the notation that is used is more succinct than that usually found in the marketing literature. The notation is designed to more clearly communicate the idea that the probability of choosing Brand 1 is conditional on the sequence of past behavior *and* the initial probability of choice. The $f(\cdot)$ notation is consistent with that adopted by Wierenga in his discussion of stochastic model parameters. This notation, designed to point out that p_t is a distributional parameter which varies according to some probability density function, is more explicit than the more conventional notation used by Massy, Montgomery, and Morrison and others. In conventional stochastic modeling notation, the Linear Learning-Brand Loyal Model is specified as:

$p_{t+1} = \alpha + \beta + \lambda p_t$ if Brand 1 was chosen at t
$p_{t+1} = \alpha + k\lambda p_t$ if Brand 0 was chosen at t.

4. The traditional stochastic modeling terms, "rejection operator" and "purchase operator," are used to differentiate the two forms of alternative model equations. Simply put, when $\delta = 1$, the "purchase operator" portion of the equations is activated; when $\delta = 0$, the "rejection operator" segment is brought to life.

5. In a strict sense, one might expect k to be constrained to lie in the (0,1) interval (i.e., $0 \leq k \leq 1$). Such a restriction would, however, disallow the very interesting type of feedback that occurs when $k > 1$. The author has found this type of feedback to occur for store choice data (Wilson, 1977). These violations were not severe enough to cause model interpretation problems and may even contribute to an understanding of the behavioral processes underlying consumer choice by uncovering response patterns that may not be otherwise evident. As an aside, some researchers (e.g., Massy, Montgomery, and Morrison, 1970; McConnell, 1968) have detected violations of basic probability tenets which were severe enough to allow for the conclusion that the stochastic model should be rejected as a reasonable representation of choice processes.

6. See Chapter 2 in Massy, Montgomery, and Morrison (1970) or Wilkes (1962) for a discussion of the generalized likelihood ratio test. This test requires maximum likelihood parameter estimates; but, as noted earlier, maximum likelihood estimates are difficult to obtain for the class of models discussed in this paper. As a consequence, most researchers have used search procedures or other numerical methods to minimize the conventional chi-square statistic *a la* Morrison (1966).

7. An exception is provided by Aaker (1971). Aaker uses the generalized likelihood ratio test to evaluate two simpler models which are embedded in his New-Trier Model of brand choice. Chi-square estimates are also generated in this application.

8. The details for calculating the confidence intervals for such a two-tailed F-test are provided by Winkler and Hays (1975). In the case of (12), where an ordered relationship between the two chi-squares is clearly defined, a traditional one-tailed F-test is appropriate.

9. Although most stochastic models require that brand choice data be reduced to a 0–1 process, Bieda (1974) has proposed and tested a "multi-brand" Linear Learning Model which permits feedback from the purchase of many different brands in a given product category. In light of Kesavan and Srinivasan's (1976) finding that binary models possibly introduce a bias which causes the true order of the process to be underestimated, additional research attention should be focused on higher-order, multi-brand models.

REFERENCES

Aaker, David A., "A New Method for Evaluating Stochastic Models of Brand Choice," *Journal of Marketing Research*, 7 (August 1970), 300–6.

Aaker, David A., "The New-Trier Stochastic Model of Brand Choice," *Management Science*, 17 (April 1971), 1027–36.

Aaker, David A. and J. Morgan Jones, "Modeling Store Choice Behavior," *Journal of Marketing Research*, 8 (February 1971), 38–42.

Atkinson, R. C., G. H. Bower, and E. J. Crothers, *An Introduction to Mathematical Learning Theory*. New York: John Wiley, 1965.

Bass, Frank M., "An Empirical Analysis of the Theory of Stochastic Preference," Paper No. 455, Institute for Research in the Behavioral, Economic, and Management Sciences, Krannert Graduate School of Industrial Administration, Purdue University, April 1974a.

Bass, Frank M., "The Theory of Stochastic Preference and Brand Switching," *Journal of Marketing Research*, 11 (February 1974b), 1–20.

Bass, Frank, M., "Unexplained Variance in Studies of Consumer Behavior," in *Control of "Error" in Marketing Research Data*, John U. Farley and John A. Howard (eds.). Lexington, Mass.: Lexington Books, 1975, 11–36.

Bass, Frank M., "Analytical Approches in the Study of Purchase Behavior and Brand Choice," in *Selected Aspects of Consumer Behavior: A Summary from the Perspective of Different Disciplines*, Robert Ferber (ed.). Washington, D.C.: U.S. Government Printing Office, 1977, 491–514.

Bass, Frank M., Abel Jeuland, and Gordon P. Wright, "Equilibrium Stochastic Choice and Market Penetration Theories: Derivations and Comparisons," *Management Science*, 22 (June 1976), 1051–63.

Bennett, Peter D., "Theory Development in Consumer Buying Behavior," in *Consumer and Industrial Buying Behavior*, Arch G. Woodside, Jagdish N. Sheth, and Peter D. Bennett (eds.). New York: North-Holland, 1977, 3–15.

Bettman, James R., "Information Processing Models of Consumer Behavior," *Journal of Marketing Research*, 7 (August 1970), 370–6.

Bettman, James R. and J. Morgan Jones, "Formal Models of Consumer Behavior: A Conceptual Overview," *Journal of Business*, 45 (October 1972), 544–62.

Bieda, John C., "A Heterogeneous (Multi-Segment) Vector (Multi-Brand) Linear Learning Model for Consumer Choice Behavior," unpublished Ph.D. dissertation, University of California, Los Angeles, 1974. [Cited in *Marketing Doctoral Dissertation Abstracts, 1974–75*, Donald L. Shawver (ed.). Chicago: American Marketing Association, 1977, 31–2].

Bishop, Yvonne M. M., Stephen E. Fienberg, and Paul W. Holland, *Discrete Multivariate Analysis: Theory and Practice*. Cambridge, Mass.: M.I.T. Press, 1975.

Blattberg, Robert C. and Subrata K. Sen, "An Evaluation of the Application of Minimum Chi-Square Procedures to Stochastic Models of Brand Choice," *Journal of Marketing Research*, 10 (November 1973), 421–7.

Blattberg, Robert C. and Subrata K. Sen, "A Bayesian Technique to Discriminate Between Stochastic Models of Brand Choice," *Management Science*, 21 (February 1975), 682–96.

Box, George E. P., "Science and Statistics," *Journal of the American Statistical Association*, 71 (December 1976), 791–9.

Box, George E. P. and G. M. Jenkins, *Time Series Analysis: Forecasting and Control*. San Francisco: Holden-Day, 1970.

Bush, Robert R. and Frederick Mosteller, *Stochastic Models for Learning*. New York: John Wiley and Sons, Inc., 1955.

Bush, Robert R. and Saul H. Sternberg, "A Single-Operator Model," in Robert R. Bush and William K. Estes, (eds.), *Studies in Mathematical Learning Theory*. Stanford, Calif.: Stanford University Press, 1959, 204–14.

Carman, James M., "Brand Switching and Linear Learning Models," *Journal of Advertising Research,* 6 (June 1966), 23-31.

Chow, Gregory C., "Tests of Equality Between Sets of Coefficients in Two Linear Regressions," *Econometrica,* 28 (July 1960), 591-605.

Coleman, James S., *Introduction to Mathematical Sociology.* New York: Free Press, 1964a.

Coleman, James S., *Models of Change and Response Uncertainty.* Englewood Cliffs, N.J.: Prentice-Hall, 1964b.

Cunningham, Ross M., "Brand Loyalty—What, Where, How Much?", *Harvard Business Review,* 34 (January–February 1956), 116-28.

Ehrenberg, A. S. C. and G. J. Goodhardt, "A Model of Multi-Brand Buying," *Journal of Marketing Research,* 7 (February 1970), 77-84.

Engel, James F., Roger D. Blackwell, and David T. Kollat, *Consumer Behavior,* 3rd Ed. Hinsdale, Ill.: Dryden Press, 1978.

Estes, William K., "Research and Theory on the Learning of Probabilities," *Journal of the American Statistical Association,* 67 (March 1972), 81-102.

Frank, Ronald E., "Brand Choice as a Probability Process," *Journal of Business,* 35 (January 1962), 43-56.

Freund, John E., *Mathematical Statistics,* 2nd Ed. Englewood Cliffs, N.J.: Prentice-Hall, 1971.

Greeno, James G. and Robert A. Bjork, "Mathematical Learning Theory and the New 'Mental Forestry'," in Paul H. Mussen and Mark R. Rosenzweig (eds.), *Annual Review of Psychology,* Vol. 24. Palo Alto, Calif.: Annual Reviews, 1973, 81-116.

Haines, George H., Jr., "A Theory of Market Behavior After Innovation," *Management Science,* 10 (July 1964), 634-58.

Haines, George H., Jr., *Consumer Behavior: Learning Models of Purchasing.* New York: Free Press, 1969.

Hansen, Flemming, *Consumer Choice Behavior: A Cognitive Theory.* New York: Free Press, 1972.

Herniter, Jerome D., "A Probabilistic Market Method of Purchase Timing and Brand Selection," *Management Science,* 18 (December 1971), 102-13.

Herniter, Jerome D., "An Entropy Model of Brand Purchase Behavior," *Journal of Marketing Research,* 10 (November 1973), 361-75.

Herniter, Jerome D., "A Comparison of the Entropy Model and the Hendry Model," *Journal of Marketing Research,* 11 (February 1974), 21-9.

Herniter, Jerome D. and Victor J. Cook, "A Multidimensional Stochastic Model of Consumer Purchase Behavior," Marketing Science Institute Research Program, Technical Report, 1970.

Herniter, Jerome D. and Ronald A. Howard, "Stochastic Marketing Models," in *Progress in Operations Research,* Vol. II, David B. Hertz and Roger T. Eddison (eds.). New York: John Wiley, 1964, 33-96.

Hinich, Melvin J. and Howard Rosenthal, "Summary and Conclusions," in *Control of "Error" in Market Research Data,* John U. Farley and John A. Howard (eds.). Lexington, Mass.: Lexington Books, 1975, 313-26.

Howard, John A., *Consumer Behavior: Application of Theory.* New York: McGraw-Hill Book Company, 1977.

Howard, John A. and Jagdish N. Sheth, *The Theory of Buyer Behavior.* New York: John Wiley, 1969.

Jacoby, Jacob, "A Model of Multi-brand Loyalty," *Journal of Advertising Research,* 11 (June 1971), 25-31.

Jeuland, Abel P., "Relationships Between the Purchase Timing Process and the Choice Process," in *1977 Educators' Proceedings,* Barnett A. Greenberg and Danny N. Bellenger (eds.). Chicago: American Marketing Association, 1977, 176-80.

Johnston, J., *Econometric Methods,* 2nd Ed. New York: McGraw-Hill, 1972.

Jones, J. Morgan, "Distribution of Probability of Purchase in Models of Consumer Brand Choice Behavior." Paper presented at the 11th American Meeting of the Institute of Management Science, Los Angeles, Calif., October 1970a.

Jones, J. Morgan, "A Comparison of Three Models of Brand Choice," *Journal of Marketing Research,* 7 (November 1970b), 466–73.

Jones, J. Morgan, "A Stochastic Model for Adaptive Behavior in a Dynamic Situation," *Management Science,* 17 (March 1971), 484–97.

Jones, J. Morgan, "A Composite Heterogeneous Model for Brand Choice Behavior," *Management Science,* 19 (January 1973), 499–509.

Jones, J. Morgan, "Testing Probability of Purchase Distributions and Ad Hoc Market Segmentation Schemes," in *1973 Combined Proceedings,* Thomas V. Greer (ed.). Chicago: American Marketing Association, 1974, 246–9.

Kalwani, Monohar U. and Donald G. Morrison, "Estimating the Proportion of 'Always Buy' and 'Never Buy' Consumers: A Likelihood Ratio Test with Sample Size Implications," *Journal of Marketing Research,* 14 (November 1977), 601–6.

Kendall, Maurice G. and Alan Stuart, *The Advanced Theory of Statistics: Volume 2,* 3rd Ed. New York: Hafner Publishing Company, 1973.

Kesavan, R. and V. Srinivasan, "Bias in Stochastic Binary Models of Brand Choice," in *1976 Educators' Proceedings,* Kenneth L. Bernhardt (ed.). Chicago: American Marketing Association, 1976, 115–9.

Kotler, Philip, *Marketing Decision Making: A Model Building Approach.* New York: Holt, Rinehart and Winston, 1971.

Kuehn, Alfred A., "An Analysis of the Dynamics of Consumer Behavior and Its Implications for Marketing Management," unpublished Ph.D. dissertation, Carnegie Institute of Technology, 1958.

Kuehn, Alfred A., "Consumer Brand Choice as a Learning Process?", *Journal of Advertising Research,* 2 (December 1962), 10–17.

Kuehn, Alfred A. and Ralph L. Day, "Probabilistic Models of Consumer Buying Behavior," *Journal of Marketing,* 28 (October 1964), 27–31.

Lancaster, H. O., *The Chi-squared Distribution.* New York: John Wiley, 1969.

Lawrence, Raymond J., "Patterns of Buyer Behavior: Time for a New Approach?", *Journal of Marketing Research,* 6 (May 1969), 137–44.

Lawrence, Raymond J., "Consumer Brand Chocie—A Random Walk?", *Journal of Marketing Research,* 12 (August 1975), 314–24.

Lilien, Gary L., "Application of a Modified Linear Learning Model of Buyer Behavior," *Journal of Marketing Research,* 11 (August 1974a), 279–85.

Lilien, Gary L., "A Modified Linear Learning Model of Buyer Behavior," *Management Science,* 20 (March 1974b), 1027–36.

Little, John D. C., "Models and Managers: The Concept of a Decision Calculus," *Management Science,* 16 (April 1970), B-466–85.

Maffei, Richard B., "Brand Preferences and Simple Markov Processes," *Operations Research,* 8 (March–April 1960), 210–18.

Massy, William F., David B. Montgomery, and Donald G. Morrison, *Stochastic Models of Buying Behavior.* Cambridge, Mass.: M.I.T. Press, 1970.

May, Frederick E., "Adaptive Behavior in Automobile Brand Choices," *Journal of Marketing Research,* 6 (February 1969), 62–5.

McConnell, J. Douglas, "Repeat-Purchase Estimation and the Linear Learning Model," *Journal of Marketing Research,* 5 (August 1968), 304–6.

Montgomery, David G., "Stochastic Modeling of the Consumer," *Industrial Management Review,* 8 (Spring 1967), 31–42.

Montgomery, David G., "Stochastic Consumer Models: Some Comparative Results," in *Applications of Management Science in Marketing,* David B. Montgomery and Glen L. Urban (eds.). Englewood Cliffs, N.J.: Prentice-Hall, 1969a, 99–113.

Montgomery, David B., "A Stochastic Response Model with Application of Brand Choice," *Management Science,* 15 (March 1969b), 323–37.

Montgomery, David B., "The Outlook for MIS," *Journal of Advertising Research,* 13 (June 1973), 5–11.

Montgomery, David B. and Adrian B. Ryans, "Stochastic Models of Consumer Choice Behavior," in Scott Ward and Thomas S. Robertson (eds.), *Consumer Behavior: Theoretical Sources.* Englewood Cliffs, N.J.: Prentice-Hall, 1973, 521–76.

Montgomery, David B. and Glen L. Urban, *Management Science in Marketing.* Englewood Cliffs, N.J.: Prentice-Hall, 1969.

Morrison, Donald G., "Testing Brand-Switching Models," *Journal of Marketing Research,* 3 (November 1966), 401–9.

Morrison, Donald G., "A Stochastic Interpretation of the Heavy Half," *Journal of Marketing Research,* 5 (May 1968), 194–8.

Morrison, Donald G., "Adaptive Behavior in Automobile Brand Choices: A Reply," *Journal of Marketing Research,* 7 (February 1970), 117–9.

Neyman, J., "Contribution to the Theory of the χ^2 Test," in Jerzy Neyman, (ed.), *Proceedings of the Berkeley Symposium on Mathematical Statistics and Probability,* Vol. 1. Berkeley, Calif.: University of California Press, 1949, 239–73.

Parsons, Leonard J. and Randall L. Schultz, *Marketing Models and Econometric Research.* New York: North-Holland, 1976.

Pindyck, Robert S. and Daniel L. Rubinfeld, *Econometric Models and Economic Forecasts.* New York: McGraw-Hill, 1976.

Popper, Karl R., *The Logic of Scientific Discovery.* New York: Science Editions, 1961.

Rao, C. Radhakrishna, "A Study of the Large Sample Test Criteria Through properties of Efficient Estimates," *Sanhyā: The Indian Journal of Statistics,* Series A, Part 1, 23 (February 1961), 25–40.

Rao, C. Radhakrishna, *Linear Statistical Inference and Its Application,* 2nd Ed. New York: John Wiley, 1973.

Ray, Michael L. and Scott Ward, *Communicating with Consumers: The Information Processing Approach.* Beverly Hills, Calif.: Sage Publications, 1976.

Shoemaker, Robert W., Richard Staelin, Joseph B. Kadane, and F. Robert Shoaf, "Relation of Brand Choice to Purchase Frequency," *Journal of Marketing Research,* 14 (November 1977), 458–68.

Smith, H. W., *Strategies of Social Research: The Methodological Imagination.* Englewood Cliffs, N.J.: Prentice-Hall, 1975.

Srinivasan, V. and R. Kesavan, "An Alternative Interpretation of the Linear Learning Model of Brand Chocie," *Journal of Consumer Research,* 3 (September 1976), 76–83.

Twedt, Dik Warren, "How Important to Marketing Strategy is the 'Heavy User'?", *Journal of Marketing,* 28 (January 1964), 71–2.

Wierenga, B., *An Investigation of Brand Choice Processes.* Rotterdam: Rotterdam University Press, 1974.

Wilks, Samuel S., *Mathematical Statistics.* New York: John Wiley, 1962.

Wilson, R. Dale, "Generalized and Embedded Versions of heterogeneous Stochastic Models of Consumer Choice Behavior: An Empirical Test and Statistical Evaluation in a Dynamic Store Selection Context," unpublished Ph.D. dissertation, University of Iowa, 1977.

Wilson, R. Dale, "Advances in Discriminating Among Competing Stochastic Models of Consumer Brand Choice Behavior," in *1978 Educators' Proceedings,* Subhash C. Jain (ed.). Chicago: American Marketing Association, in press.

Winkler, Robert L. and William L. Hays, *Statistics: Probability, Inference, and Decision,* 2nd Ed. New York: Holt, Rinehart and Winston, 1975.

Zufryden, Fred S., "Media Scheduling: A Stochastic Dynamic Model Approach," *Management Science,* 19 (August 1973), 1395–1406.

Zufryden, Fred S., "A Methodology for Measuring Response to Media Effects," *Operational Research Quarterly,* 26 (October 1975a), 641–7.

Zufryden, Fred S., "A Model of Dynamic Response to Advertising," in *1974 Combined Proceedings,* Ronald C. Curhan (ed.). Chicago: American Marketing Association, 1975b, 401–5.

Zufryden, Fred S., "Patterns of TV Program Selection," *Journal of Advertising Research,* 16 (December 1976), 43–7.

Zufryden, Fred S., "A Composite Heterogeneous Model of Brand Choice and Purchase Timing Behavior," *Management Science,* 24 (October 1977), 121–136.

Zufryden, Fred S., "An Empirical Evaluation of a Composite Heterogeneous Model of Brand Choice Purchase Timing Behavior," *Management Science,* 24 (March 1978), 761–73.

A MULTIVARIATE STOCHASTIC MODEL OF BRAND CHOICE AND MARKET BEHAVIOR

Fred S. Zufryden, UNIVERSITY OF SOUTHERN CALIFORNIA

INTRODUCTION

Marketing decision variables play the central role in a firm's marketing programming. The setting of a firm's marketing mix requires an appropriate allocation of marketing effort in view of objectives and policies. The primary guide to marketing decision-making is based on a firm's assumptions of probable market response as a function of its marketing mix over time. Unfortunately, a firm's knowledge of the nature of the expected market response to settings of the marketing mix is limited due to the complex nature of the consumer behavior process.

In retrospect, most past stochastic model studies have not attempted to for-

Research in Marketing, Volume 3, pages 273–303

mulate (nor apply) models that include significant aspects of the marketing mix. The primary difficulty stems from the fact that the market response phenomenon is complicated greatly by the nature of individual consumers who are heterogeneous with respect to aspects such as purchase incidence and brand choice behavior (e.g., Bass, Jeuland, and Wright, 1976; Chattfield and Goodhardt, 1973; Ehrenberg, 1965; Zufryden, 1976). Moreover, consumers are likely to react differentially with respect to their brand choices, in response to particular marketing mix influences (e.g., Blattberg and Sen, 1976). Despite these difficulties, scholars are currently in agreement that mathematical models such as stochastic models must become more managerially oriented if they are to gain wider practical use (Blattberg, 1976). Thus, models including marketing mix variables that are considered here should become a high priority research direction in the future.

This paper focuses on a new mathematical model framework which combines ideas of brand choice and purchase incidence models. However, in contrast to the past studies that have appeared in the literature, it also introduces a comprehensive framework which allows the incorporation of *any* type and number of external variables or factors that may be found to be relevant to consumer and market response behavior. An overwhelming advantage of the model is that it lends itself to simple but yet powerful parameter estimation methods.

Despite the abundance of studies that deal with market response behavior models found in the literature, this area of research remains in its infancy in terms of the limited contributions made to date towards explaining marketing mix influences. For example, brand choice models—such as Zero-Order (Frank, 1962), Markov (Ehrenberg, 1965; Harrary and Lipstein, 1962; Jeuland, 1976; Styan and Smith, 1964), Linear Learning (Carmen, 1966; Jones, 1970b; Kalwani and Morrison, 1977; Massy, Montgomery, and Morrison, 1970, Ch. 5), and Entropy models (Herniter, 1973; Bass and Wright, 1976)—have examined the behavior of individual buyers and aggregate markets through stochastic frameworks by considering the undifferentiated sum total of exogenous factors that may impinge upon consumers' brand purchase probabilities. Therefore, these models exclude the specific consideration of marketing mix aspects as well.

Recently, a pioneering research thrust has involved the development of composite stochastic models through the integration of component stochastic models of behavior. For example, Bass and Wright (1976), Herniter (1971), and Zufryden (1975b, 1977) have respectively combined Zero-order, Markov, and Linear Learning models of brand choice and models of purchase incidence within unified composite model structures. These models have been shown empirically viable. Although marketing mix variables are not specifically considered, these models suggest a useful integrative approach for potential extensions. Indeed, the present study extends the framework of the Herniter (1971) and Zufryden (1975b, 1977) models with the addition of purchase explanatory variables.

Several past stochastic models have been extended to include *one* aspect of the marketing mix. For example, the author has shown how advertising media effects can be incorporated within a stochastic structure (Zufryden, 1975, 1973). Lilien (1974), in a similar vein, has developed an extension of the Linear Learning model which incorporates price as a determinant of brand choice behavior. Prasad (1972) has shown how the distribution decision-related aspect of store selection can be handled within a similar framework. Aside from these latter studies, few other stochastic models have included any specific marketing mix aspects. Hence, to date, these models have had limited managerial impact.

The proposed model framework includes the strengths of stochastic models. It considers both the brand choice and purchase incidence behavior phenomena from both an individual consumer and aggregate market standpoint. Thus, many of the results that these models provide can be obtained from the model. For example, such measures of market performance as the time patterns of market share, the market penetration, trial and repeat purchase patterns within a market can all be derived. Moreover, the model, unlike its predecessors, provides a comprehensive structure for incorporating *any* explanatory variables that may be relevant to a market situation of interest. This is accomplished through the use of a Logit model formulation which is tied to a first-order Markov process. The explanatory variables are then linked to the measures of market performance. This paper provides both the theoretical development of the model as well as an illustration of its application on the basis of data from a consumer panel study.

MATHEMATICAL MODEL STRUCTURE

The model structure includes two basic submodel components. One of these components examines consumer brand choice behavior through a Logit-Markovian structure which is expressed as a function of relevant explanatory variables. The other component examines consumer and market purchase incidence behavior for the product category of the particular brand that is studied.

The overall model is based on the following structural assumptions:

1. Individual consumer purchase behavior is a function of explanatory variables *including* the last brand purchased. The explanatory variables may include marketing mix, purchase situational, or consumer segmentation aspects that are found to relate to brand choice behavior. In general, the explanatory variables are represented by a vector x which incorporates either categorical variables through the use of 0/1 vector components or continuous variables.

2. A Logit model formulation is used to derive a first-order Markov process of brand choice behavior as a function of x. It is assumed that the same transition matrix is appropriate for all consumers subject to a *given* setting of explanatory variables. Moreover, it is assumed that the transition matrix is stationary *given* a particular setting of explanatory variables.

3. An individual consumer's initial brand choice probability P_o is assumed to be distributed according to an arbitrary probability distribution $f(P_o)$ with mean m_o at time $t=0$ over the population of consumers (or defined market segments).

4. Two alternative stochastic models, leading to two model versions, are used to characterize individual product class purchase incidence: (a) the Poisson Distribution and (b) the Condensed Poisson Distribution.

5. The individual mean product class purchase rate (μ) is assumed to vary over the population of consumers (or within defined market segments) according to the Gamma Distribution.

6. Given the alternative assumptions of (4) and that of (5) above, the aggregate product class purchase distribution is given by either a Negative Binomial Distribution (NBD) or a Condensed Negative Binomial Distribution (CNBD) (i.e., see Ehrenberg, 1950, and Chattfield and Goodhardt, 1973).

Figure 1 presents a flow chart summary of the basic overall model framework. Note that the brand choice and purchase incidence model components are inte-

Figure 1. Summary or Overall Model Framework

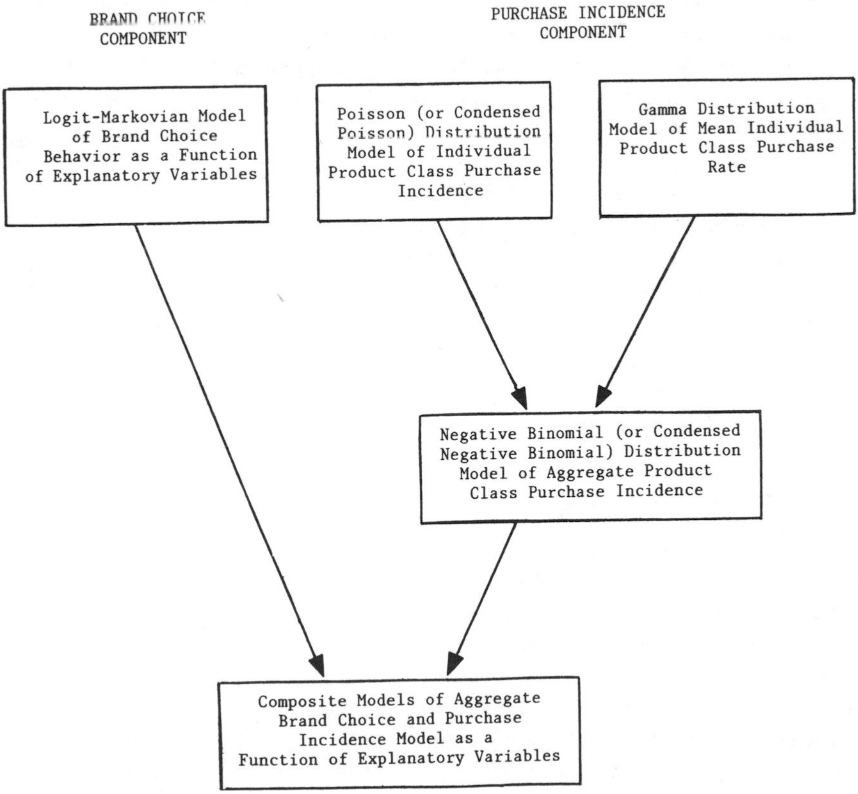

grated within one analytical structure to provide composite models of aggregate brand choice *and* purchase incidence behavior models as a function of explanatory variables of interest.

BRAND CHOICE BEHAVIOR

In the developments that follow, consider a vector x of explanatory variables. In the interest of generality, the specific number of elements of the vector or the nature of the explanatory variables are not specified. However, it is emphasized that the model provides a general structure whereby any relevant variables (e.g., consumer demographics, geographics, product price, promotions, etc.) that influence individual brand choice decisions may be included. The determination of the best set of explanatory variables to include in the model is considered an empirical issue which pertains to the particular marketing problem being considered. The model provides a means for developing this best set of variables within its general framework by means of a parameter estimation methodology which is discussed in a subsequent section. It should be noted that the proposed methodology could also be used to test a priori hypotheses concerning the relevance of potential purchase explanatory variables. In this sense, the determination of the best set of variables to include in the model may be a theoretical issue as well.

The basic Logit model formulation described by Green, Carmone, and Wachpress (1977) is utilized to relate x to consumer brand choice probability at a particular purchase occasion. However, it is modified and extended in an important way. Additional consideration is given to the non-stationarity of the consumer brand choice process by allowing the dynamic change of brand choice probability as a function of the last brand purchase, which is included as an explanatory variable as well.

Consider the Logit functioning $\psi(x)$ given by

$$\psi(x) = \ln \left[\frac{P(A|x)}{1-P(A|x)} \right] \tag{1}$$

where $P(A|x)$ is the individual consumer choice probability for a particular brand A, given the explanatory variable vector x. The linear-Logit function is used, hence $\psi(x)$ may also be written as

$$\psi(x) = b_0 + \sum_{i=1}^{I} b_i x_i + \epsilon, \tag{2}$$

where b_0 is the value of $\psi(x)$ when all variables x_i are set at their lowest levels, the other b_i's represent the incremental contributions of setting the variables at other than their lowest levels, and ϵ denotes an error term. In the case of continuous variables, the corresponding b_i coefficients are defined analogously to those of a linear regression equation. In the case of categorical ones, the x_i's are coded as 0 or 1 (e.g., Green, Carmone, and Wachpress, 1977) such that b_i denotes the incremental contribution of the corresponding discrete variable *level*).

In the above model, the last variable index I is defined at each product class purchase occasion, n, such that[1]

$$x_I = \begin{cases} 1 & \text{if brand A was purchased at the previous purchase occasion} \\ & (n-1); \\ 0 & \text{if another brand (O) was purchased at the previous purchase} \\ & \text{occasion } (n-1). \end{cases}$$

Hence, combining (1) and (2) above, the following conditional probabilities are defined:

$$P(A_n|A_{n-1}, x) = \frac{1}{1 + e^{-\psi_A(x)}}, \tag{3}$$

where

$$\psi_A(x) = b_0 + \sum_{i=1}^{I-1} b_i x_i + b_I$$

and $P(A_n|A_{n-1},x)$ is the conditional probability of purchasing brand A at purchase occasion n *given* that A was purchased at occasion n-1. The vector, for notational convenience, now represents explanatory variables *excluding* x_I.

Similarly, the conditional probability of purchasing brand A at purchase occasion n given that brand 0 (one of the competing brands) was purchased at occasion n−1 and x prevails may be stated as:

$$P(A_n|O_{n-1}, x) = \frac{1}{1 + e^{-\psi_O(x)}}, \tag{4}$$

where

$$\psi_O(x) = \psi_A(x) - b_I.$$

Since it is assumed that consumers abide by a homogeneous and stationary first-order Markov process (e.g., Herniter, 1971) given a particular setting of x, the following transition matrix represents the dynamic brand choice process:[2]

Purchase at occasion n

$$
\text{Purchase at occasion } n-1 \quad
\begin{array}{c}
A \\[2pt]
O
\end{array}
\begin{bmatrix}
A & O \\[4pt]
\dfrac{1}{1 + e^{-\psi_A(x)}} & \dfrac{e^{-\psi_A(x)}}{1 + e^{-\psi_A(x)}} \\[16pt]
\dfrac{1}{1 + e^{-\psi_o(x)}} & \dfrac{e^{-\psi_o(x)}}{1 + e^{-\psi_o(x)}}
\end{bmatrix}
\tag{5}
$$

Thus, it is observed that the Logit-based first-order Markovian transition matrix (5) characterizes brand loyalty and switching behavior as a function of the vector x of explanatory variables. The basic form of this model was chosen essentially because of its inherent flexibility in handling purchase explanatory variables, of either continuous or categorical type, as well as the non-stationarity of consumer purchase behavior. Another important justification for this model choice, that will be later described, is the relative ease of estimating the model's parameters.

PURCHASE INCIDENCE BEHAVIOR

The incidence of consumer purchases is considered by means of two alternative models of behavior.

The Negative Binomial Distribution Model

Ehrenberg (1950), first proposed a Negative Binomial Distribution (NBD) model of aggregate purchase behavior based on individual purchases distributed according to the Poisson Distribution with the mean of the distribution being Chi-Square distributed over the population of consumers. The NBD, in addition to being easily fitted to empirical data, has appeared to be generally empirically viable (e.g., Chattfield and Goodhardt, 1973; Ehrenberg, 1965). Moreover, recent studies have given additional support to its general validity as it pertains to the modeling of product class purchase incidence behavior (Zufryden, 1975b, 1976, 1978). A similar model is proposed here to characterize the distribution of product class purchases.

Thus, consider a particular individual consumer (or family). Then, the probability that he (it) will make k product class purchases during (0,T) is given by the Poisson law:

$$
P_P(k|\mu,T) = (\mu T)^k \, e^{-\mu T}/k!, \quad k=0,1,2,\ldots
\tag{6}
$$

where μ = mean rate of product class purchases during $(0,T)$, $E(k) = \mu T$, and $Var(k) = \mu T$. It is well known that this law gives rise to exponentially distributed time t between purchases:

$$g(t|\mu) = \mu e^{-\mu t}, \ t \geqslant 0; \qquad (7)$$

with $E(t) = 1/\mu$ and $Var(t) = 1/\mu^2$. It is known that individual mean purchase rate varies over the population of consumers. If it is assumed that μ is distributed as Gamma over the population of consumers:

$$f(\mu|a,b) = b^a e^{-b\mu} \ \mu^{a-1}/\Gamma(a), \ \mu \geqslant 0, \qquad (8)$$

where a,b = constant parameters $(a,b > 0)$, $E(\mu) = a/b$ and $Var(\mu) = a/b^2$; then, the combination of the Poisson and Gamma distributions yields the expected (mean) probability that k product class purchases will occur during a time interval $(0,T)$ as the NBD:[3]

$$E[(P_P(k|\mu,T)] \equiv P_N\ (k|T) = \frac{\Gamma(k + a)}{\Gamma(a)\ k!} \ y^k (1 - y)^a, \ k=0,1,2,\ldots \qquad (9)$$

where

$$y = T/(T + b).$$

Hence, the NBD represents the proportion of individuals who make given numbers of product class purchase over a time interval (O,T).

The Condensed Negative Binomial Distribution Model

Rather than the Exponential Distribution of time between purchases, recent empirical work has indicated that it may be more appropriate to assume Erlang distributed interpurchase time t (see Chattfield and Goodhardt, 1973; Herniter, 1971; Zufryden, 1976, 1978). For example, the Exponential Distribution of individual consumer time between purchases upon which the NBD is based suggests that a consumer is most likely to repurchase the product class immediately following a purchase. This is because the Exponential Distribution has a zero mode. However, it would appear more reasonable that, as the time since the last product class purchase increases, the probability of repurchasing the product class should increase. In view of this fact, an Erlang Distribution model with parameter $c \geqslant 2$ which is dependent upon the time of last purchase would appear to provide a more realistic model on at least theoretical grounds. In particular, the Erlang distribution of order 2, which may be derived as a special case of the Gamma Distribution, has received both theoretical and empirical support as being superior to the Exponential model.[4] This model has the following form:

$$f(t|\mu,c) = \mu^c e^{-\mu t} t^{c-1}/\Gamma(c) \tag{10}$$

with t, $\mu > 0$ and c $= 2$.

It may be shown that the Erlang distribution of order 2 can be generated from a "condensed" Poisson Distribution in which every other product class purchase event is excluded (Chattfield and Goodhardt, 1973). That is, upon removing purchases 1, 3, 5, etc., generated from a Poisson process with parameter μ, the time between the remaining purchase events is Erlang with parameters c $= 2$ and mean $\mu/2$.

It has been shown that the Condensed Poisson process which relates to the Erlang Distribution may be stated as a function of the Poisson distribution (e.g., Chattfield and Goodhardt, 1973). Thus, the Condensed Poisson Distribution of individual product class purchases during (0,T), stated in terms of (6), is given by:

$$P_{CP}(k|\mu,T) = \begin{cases} P_P(0) + \frac{1}{2}P_P(1) & k = 0 \\ \frac{1}{2}P_P(2k-1) + P_P(2k) + \frac{1}{2}P_P(2k+1), & k=1,2,\ldots \end{cases} \tag{11}$$

Under the assumption that the individual consumer mean product class purchase rate is Gamma distributed over the population, as in (8), by combining the Gamma and Condensed Poisson distribution, it can be shown (see Chattfield and Goodhardt, 1973, or Zufryden, 1977) that the aggregate product class purchase distribution is a Condensed Negative Binomial Distribution Model (CNBD):

$$E[P_{CP}(k|\mu,T)] \equiv P_{CN}(k|T) = \begin{cases} P_N(0|T) + \frac{1}{2}P_N(1|T) & k = 0 \\ \frac{1}{2}P_N(2k-1|T) + P_N(2k|T) \\ \quad + \frac{1}{2}P_N(2k+1|T) & k = 1,2,\ldots \end{cases} \tag{12}$$

where

$$P_N(k|T) = \frac{\Gamma(k+a)}{\Gamma(a)\,k!} z^k(1-z)^a,$$

and $z = 2T/(2T + b)$. This model, as the NBD, represents the proportion of individuals who make given numbers of product class purchases over a time interval (0,T).

DEVELOPMENT OF COMBINED BRAND CHOICE-PURCHASE INCIDENCE MODELS

Now that the basic Logit-based Markovian model of brand choice and the purchase incidence models have been described, the paper proceeds towards the development of the overall integrated model structure. Recalling that two alternative model assumptions were made regarding individual product class purchase incidence behavior, *two* distinct model versions will be developed. The first, which combines a Logit-Markov and an NBD model, is given the achronym *LMN*. The second model, based on the alternative CNBD purchase incidence model, will be referred to as the *LMCN* model.

The Time Pattern of Market Share

A useful result, both in terms of further developments and model application, is the development of the time pattern of market share for brand A. To obtain this measure, first consider an individual consumer at a particular purchase occasion with respect to each of the two alternative brand choice states (A and O). If his initial state vector probabilities at n-1 are defined as $(P_{n-1}, 1 - P_{n-1})$, the probability $P_n(x)$ of purchasing brand A after purchase occasion n given the influence of a particular vector x is obtained by postmultiplying the initial state vector by the transition matrix T (5). Thus,

$$P_n(x) = P_{n-1} \frac{1}{1 + e^{-\psi_A(x)}} + (1 - P_{n-1}) \frac{1}{1 + e^{-\psi_O(x)}} \tag{13}$$

$$= P(A_n|O_{n-1},x) + [P(A_n|A_{n-1},x) - P(A_n|O_{n-1},x)]P_{n-1}.$$

Since it is assumed that the Markov process is stationary given a particular x, let

$$\alpha(x) = P(A_n|O_{n-1},x)$$
and $\beta(x) = P(A_n|A_{n-1},x) - P(A_n|O_{n-1},x).$
Therefore, $P_n(x)$ is of the form:

$$P_n(x) = \alpha(x) + \beta(x) P_{n-1} \tag{14}$$

Starting with an initial individual probability P_0 at the outset of the process and given a *fixed* x, it may be shown by recursive substitution that in general:[5]

$$P_n(x) = \alpha(x) \sum_{i=0}^{n-1} \beta^i(x) + \beta^n(x) P_0 \tag{15}$$

$$= P_\infty(x) + [P_0 - P_\infty(x)] \beta^n(x),$$

where

$$P_\infty(x) = \frac{\alpha(x)}{1 - \beta(x)} \tag{16}$$

is the individual steady state brand A choice probability given a specified vector x. Thus, given (15), the mean probability of purchase after the nth purchase occasion is:

$$E[P_n(x)] = m_n(x) = m_\infty(x) + [m_0 - m_\infty(x)]\beta^n(x), \qquad (17)$$

where $m_\infty(x)$, the mean steady state mean probability (or market share) for brand A, is identical to $P_\infty(x)$, and $m_0 = E[P_0]$ is the mean initial brand choice probability over the population of consumers.

In subsequent developments, it is assumed that brand choice is independent of product class purchase incidence. Thus, the market share $m_x(T)$, at any arbitrary time T, given a fixed x, is obtained by probability conditioning as:

$$m_x(T) = \sum_{n=0}^{\infty} m_n(x)\, P_\theta(n|T), \qquad (18)$$

where θ corresponds to either the NBD or CNBD distribution.

Specifically, for the LMN model, it can be shown[6] (see Appendix 1) that:

$$m_x(T) = m_\infty(x) + \frac{(1 - y)^a\,[m_0 - m_\infty(x)]}{[1 - \beta(x)y]^a} \qquad (19)$$

and since $y = T/(T + b)$,

$$m_x(T) = m_\infty(x) + \frac{b^a[m_0 - m_\infty(x)]}{[b - (\beta(x) - 1)T]^a}, \qquad (20)$$

Similarly, for the LMCN model, according to the developments of Zufryden (1977),

$$m_x(T) = m_\infty(x) + [m_0 - m_\infty(x)]\left\{ A\left[\frac{1 - z}{1 - Cz}\right]^a + (1 - A)\left[\frac{1 - z}{1 + Cz}\right]^a\right\}, \qquad (21)$$

where $z = \dfrac{2T}{2T + b}$, $C = \beta(x)^{1/2}$ and $A = \frac{1}{4}C + \frac{1}{2} + \frac{1}{4}C^{-1}$.

Mean Number of Brand Purchases Over Time

Given the time pattern of market share, it is possible to derive the mean of the aggregate *brand* purchase distribution over any specified time interval (0,T). First note that the average mean probability of purchase (i.e., market share) over (0,T) is given by:

$$M_x(0,T) = \frac{1}{T}\int_0^T m_x(t)dt. \qquad (22)$$

Following integration, in the LMN case,

$$M_x(0,T) = m_\infty(x) + [m_0 - m_\infty(x)] b^a \left\{ \frac{[b - (\beta(x) - 1) T]^{1-a} - b^{1-a}}{(\beta(x) - 1)(a-1)T} \right\}.$$

(23)

Alternatively, from the results of Zufryden (1977), the corresponding LMCN results become:

$$M_x(0,T) = m_\infty(x) + \frac{1}{2} \frac{[m_0 - m_\infty(x)]b^a}{(1 - a)T} \left\{ \left(\frac{A}{1 - C} \right) \right.$$

$$([b + 2(1 - C)T]^{1-a} - b^{1-a}) + \left(\frac{1 - A}{1 + C} \right) ([b + 2(1 + C)T]^{1-a} - b^{1-a}) \right\}.$$

(24)

In both cases, the mean number of brand purchases over $(0,T)$ is given by:[7]

$$MP_x(0,T) = M_x(0,T) \, aT/b.$$

(25)

Market Penetration

Provided that the proportion of individuals in the population who make no brand purchases over a specified period of time is known, market penetration estimates can easily be derived.

First consider the determination of the fraction of the population who make no purchases. Thus, consider a population of consumers. The proportion of individuals making $j = 0$ brand A purchases, given that N consecutive product class purchases have taken place, is given by:

$$(1 - m_0) \, P \, (O_N | O_{N-1}, x)^{N-1}, \text{ or}$$

(26)

$$P_x(j = 0|N) = (1 - m_0) \left[\frac{e^{-\psi} o^{(x)}}{1 + e^{-\psi} o^{(x)}} \right]^{N-1} \text{ for } N \geqslant 1.$$

(27)

For notational convenience, define $P_x(O|O)$ as $e^{-\psi} o^{(x)}/[1 + e^{-\psi} o^{(x)}]$. Hence, the marginal aggregate probability of 0 brand purchases over $(0,T)$ is obtained by conditioning (26) on product class purchase counts as:

$$P_x(j = 0|T) = P_\theta(0|T) + \sum_{N=1}^{\infty} (1 - m_0) \, P_x(O|O)^{N-1} \, P_\theta(N|T).$$

(28)

For the LMN case, this becomes (see Appendix 2):

$$P_x(j = 0|T) = (1 - y)^a + \frac{(1 - m_0)}{P_x(O|O)}(1 - y)^a \left\{ [1 - y P_x(O|O)]^{-a} - 1 \right\}.$$

$$(29)$$

For the LMCN-based case, according to (23) and the mathematical results of Zufryden (1977, p. 8):

$$P_x(j = 0|T) = (1 - z)^a \left(1 + \frac{za}{2} + \frac{(1 - m_0)}{P_x(O|O)} \right.$$

$$(30)$$

$$\left\{ (1 - z)^a \left[A(1 - \lambda)^{-a} + (1 - A)(1 + \lambda)^{-a} - \tfrac{1}{2}P_x(O|O)^{-1/2}a\lambda - 1 \right] \right\},$$

where $A = \tfrac{1}{4}P_x(O|O)^{1/2} + \tfrac{1}{2} + \tfrac{1}{4}P_x(O|O)^{-1/2}$
$\lambda = z\,P_x(O|O)^{1/2}$, and
$z = 2T/(2T + b)$.

From the above results, the cumulative brand penetration over $(0,T)$ is obtained as:[8]

$$P_x(j \geq 1|T) + 1 - P_x(j = 0|T). \tag{31}$$

Brand Purchase Distribution

Two methods are outlined to develop the aggregate marginal brand purchase distribution. This distribution provides useful information regarding the repeat purchase pattern in a population.

One method is to follow a combinatorial procedure similar to that developed by the author in a previous article (Zufryden, 1977). This approach is based on the development of likelihoods corresponding to possible strings of purchase sequences. Thus, define a particular individual's brand purchase sequence I_1, $I_2, \ldots I_N$, where

$$I_j = \begin{cases} 1 \text{ if jth purchase is brand A} \\ 0 \text{ if jth purchase is brand O.} \end{cases}$$

Also define the elements of the transition matrix (5):

$$P_x(I_j|I_{j-1}) = \begin{cases} P_x(A|A) & \text{if } I_j = 1, I_{j-1} = 1 \\ P_x(A|O) & \text{if } I_j = 1, I_{j-1} = 0 \\ P_x(O|A) & \text{if } I_j = 0, I_{j-1} = 1 \\ P_x(O|O) & \text{if } I_j = 0, I_{j-1} = 0, \quad j > 1. \end{cases} \tag{32}$$

Then the expected likelihood $L_x(I_1, \ldots, I_N)$ that a particular purchase string will occur can be computed from a knowledge of the corresponding sequence of binary numbers. Given that the initial individual brand choice probability is P_0, the general *expected* likelihood expression becomes:

$$L_x(I_1, \ldots, I_N) = [m_0 I_1 + (1 - m_0)(1 - I_1)] \prod^{N-1} \{P_x(A|A) I_j I_{j-1} +$$

$$P_x(A|O)I_j(1 - I_{j-1}) + P_x(O|A)(1 - I_j) I_{j-1} + P_x(O|O)(1 - I_j)(1 - I_{j-1})\}$$

$$(33)$$

From (33), the aggregate conditional brand purchase distribution given m product class purchases becomes

$$P_x(j|M) = \sum_{i \in J} L_x^{(i)} (I_1, \ldots, I_M), \qquad j = 0,1, \ldots, M; \qquad (34)$$

where the summation in (34) is taken over all likelihood values $L_x^{(i)} (I_1, \ldots, I_M)$ from sets i of J that include j brand A out of M product class purchases.

From (34), the marginal brand purchase distribution over an arbitrary time interval (0,T) becomes:

$$P_x(j|T) = \sum_{M=j}^{\infty} P_\theta(M|T)P_x(j|M), \qquad (35)$$

$$j = 0,1,2, \ldots, \text{etc.}$$
$$\theta = \text{NBD or CNBD.}$$

Computational experience has suggested that, even with the use of a computer, the approach to the development of $P_x(j|T)$ outlined above may often require tedious computations due to the combinatorial nature of (34) and the difficulty of obtaining (35) in closed form. Hence, an alternative approach is used which provides a good approximation of the $P_x(j|T)$ distribution while requiring little computational effort.

The approach is based on the assumption that $P_x(j|T)$ is approximately NBD. This appears a reasonable assumption in view of past empirical work (e.g., Chattfield and Goodhardt, 1973; Ehrenberg, 1950; Zufryden, 1976, 1978). Hence, $P_x(j|T)$ can be generated from a knowledge of only $P_x(j=0|T)$ and $MP_x(0,T)$, which are both obtainable in closed form (i.e., from (29) or (30) and (25) respectively). Hence, by a simple iterative estimation procedure (e.g., see Chattfield and Goodhardt, 1973, or Ehrenberg, 1950), one can easily obtain the time-varying parameters $a_T(x)$ and $b_T(x)$ for the corresponding NBD approximation (to either alternative model) and then generate values of $P_x(j|T)$, $j \geq 1$ given these parameters. According to this procedure, a different NBD approximation would thus be generated corresponding to any specified time interval *and* setting x of explanatory variables. Empirical evaluation has shown this to provide excellent approximation to actual marginal distributions $P_x(j|T)$.[9]

Brand Trial and Repeat Purchase

Several other results may be derived from the model which may provide useful information to marketing managers.

For example, the proportion of new triers of brand A during a particular period of length ΔT may be obtained. Thus, given two consecutive periods of lengths T and ΔT respectively, the proportion of new triers during ΔT is given by:

$$P_x(j \geq 1 \text{ in } \Delta T | j = 0 \text{ in } T) = P_x(j \geq 1 | T + \Delta T) - P(j \geq 1 | T). \quad (36)$$

Similarly, by applying conditional probabilities, the repeat purchase ratio may be computed. This measure is defined as the proportion of individuals who purchase brand A at least once during an interval ΔT, given that they have purchased this brand at least once during the previous period of length T. Mathematically, this is stated as:

$$P_x(j \geq 1 \text{ in } \Delta T | j \geq 1 \text{ in } T) = \quad (37)$$

$$\frac{P_x(j \geq 1 | T) + P_x(j \geq 1 | \Delta T) - P_x(j \geq 1 | T + \Delta T)}{P_x(j \geq 1 | T)}.$$

Both of the above measures are obtained directly from (31).

The results obtained thus far are conditional upon a particular setting of the explanatory variable vector x. However, the market will be composed of market segments that are each subject to a different vector of explanatory variables. Hence, if it is desired to derive model results that are unconditioned on x, it is necessary to multiply results by the probabilities P(x) of the occurrence of the alternative x values and sum over all possible x values. For example, in the case of all categorical explanatory variables, the repeat purchase ratio becomes

$$P(j \geq 1 \text{ in } \Delta T | j \geq \text{ in } T) = \sum_x P_x(j \geq 1 \text{ in } \Delta T | j \geq 1 \text{ in } T) \, P(x).$$

Unconditioned results may similarly be obtained for any of the other results that have been derived.

ESTIMATION OF MODEL PARAMETERS AND EMPIRICAL CONSIDERATIONS

Despite the mathematical complexity of the model in terms of the number of parameters involved, extremely simple methods exist to estimate model parameters. This fact is of considerable significance since much simpler stochastic models that have been previously developed (e.g., the Linear Learning model) in fact require much more complex estimation methodologies (see Massy, Montgomery, and Morrison, 1970).

The b_i coefficients of the Logit model may be obtained through the technique of weighted least squares (WLS) which can be applied to the linear model:[10]

$$\psi(x) = \ln\left[\frac{P(A|x)}{1 - P(A|x)}\right] = b_0 + \sum_{i=1}^{I} b_i x_i + \epsilon. \qquad (38)$$

The Logit model approach is superior to alternative approaches such as Automatic Interaction Detection (AID) or dummy-variable regression, given its many appealing statistical properties in the present context (e.g., see Green, Carmone, and Wachpress, 1977, pp. 32–54). The latter methods are not statistically appropriate to estimate functions involving a dependent variable which involves a probability that must naturally fall within the range (0,1). Moreover, given the ready availability of stepwise regression programs, the estimation procedure may conceptually be used to arrive at set of relevant explanatory variables that best explains brand choice behavior in a particular problem situation.

To illustrate the application of the Logit model, assume that x includes $I = 3$ explanatory variables:

x_1 = price differential of brand A relative to competition at time of purchase (i.e., brand price less the average price of competing brands per package)

x_2 = an indicator variable denoting the presence ($x_2 = 1$) or absence ($x_2 = 0$) of a deal for brand A at a particular purchase occasion:

x_3 = last brand purchased indicator (1 if A, 0 of O was purchased last time).

In the case of the continuous variable (price differential), assume that observations are made under two price levels (say 3¢ and 5¢ per package). Assume that data is available from which observations on x are known relative to each consumer's purchases. Then, each purchase occasion can be categorized in one of eight possible cells, as shown in the three dimensional matrix of Figure 2. For each of the cells, (i = 1,2, ... 8) the proportion of product class purchases which were made for brand A, $P_i(A|x)$, can be determined. In this particular example, there would be eight observations on x and the related $P_i(A|x)$ values to be converted to corresponding $\psi(x)$ as in (38). The WLS procedure may then be applied to obtain the coefficients b_0, b_1, b_2, and b_3 of the linearized model.

It is noted that the entries in each cell are purchase specific. That is, a particular consumer's purchases are entered in the particular cell corresponding to the explanatory variable observations at the time of purchase. The model, however, has the added flexibility of including consumer specific explanatory variables as well. For example, such segmentation variables as brand loyal, heavy buyer,

Figure 2. Illustration of Purchase Categorization for Logit Model

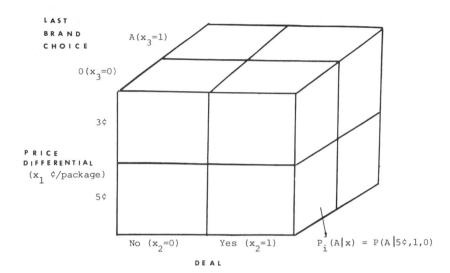

store loyal, deal prone, price sensitive, family size, or others can easily be incorporated within the general model structure.

The purchase incidence parameters (a and b) of the NBD and CNBD models are easily obtained by available statistical procedures. The most commonly used technique is an iterative approach which has been routinely applied in a number of previous studies (i.e., see Chattfield and Goodhardt, 1973, or Ehrenberg, 1950). This approach consists of setting the theoretical expression for the proportion of no purchases to the corresponding observed proportion. Given the additional knowledge of the mean number of purchases, it remains to determine one parameter through an iterative root search alogarithm.

When fitting the product class purchase incidence model, it may be necessary to fit different model parameters according to the cell classification. For instance, "loyals" may have different purchase incidence behavior than other consumers. In most cases, the empirical situation involved should dictate the need to perform such segmentations due to consumer heterogeneity or dependence of the brand choice and purchase incidence process.

MODEL APPLICATIONS

In order to illustrate the potential applications of the model, consumer panel data from the Market Research Corporation of America (MRCA) were used. The nature of these data has been described in several previous studies (e.g., Jones, 1970a, 1970b; Massy, Montgomery, and Morrison, 1970, Ch. 5; Zufryden,

1976, 1978). This data covered purchases of dentifrice (defined as the product class), including *Crest,* which was the particular brand of interest in this application. The period of study followed the date of endorsement of Crest as a decay preventive dentifrice by the American Dental Association (ADA) in August 1960). Empirical results, pertaining to product class purchase incidence behavior, from a previous study by the author were used in this application (Zufryden, 1976). Table 1 provides a summary of the parameter estimates of the NBD and CNBD product class purchase distributions as well as the observed and estimated probability values corresponding to the first 4 months following the ADA endorsement of Crest.[11]

First, a simplified version of the brand choice model was used, whereby an ordinary Markov process was estimated based on a unidimensional classification of consumers according to last brand purchased only. Thus, the following transition matrix was obtained from an analysis of consumer purchase sequences over the 4-month period following the ADA endorsement:

PURCHASE AT OCCASION n

$$
\begin{array}{cc}
 & \begin{array}{cc} A & \quad O \end{array} \\
\begin{array}{c} \text{PURCHASE} \\ \text{AT OCCASION} \\ n - 1 \end{array}
\begin{array}{c} A \\ \\ O \end{array}
& \begin{bmatrix} .72 & .28 \\ .10 & .90 \end{bmatrix}
\end{array}
$$

Table 1. Contrast of Fit of NDB and CNBD Alternative Aggregate Product Class Purchase Distributions[a]

No. of Purchases	Actual	NBD	CNBD
0	.265	.263	.256
1	.296	.277	.299
2	.207	.200	.194
3	.103	.122	.114
4	.060	.068	.063
5	.028	.036	.034
6	.012	.018	.018
7	.010	.009	.010
8	.007	.004	.005
9	.002	.002	.003
10	.002	.001	.001
11	.002	0	.001
12+	.006	0	.002
a		2.710	1.470
b		6.273	3.402
Mean	1.728	1.728	1.728
Variance	3.650	2.831	3.011

[a] Based on the 4-month period following the ADA endorsement.

The initial Crest share was estimated from the data as .20 at the outset of the ADA endorsement. From these transition probability estimates, the following Logit model parameters were derived:[12]

$$b_0 = -2.19722$$
$$\text{and}$$
$$b_1 = 3.14168$$

In the above base case situation, no explanatory variables other than the last brand purchase were used.

In subsequent model illustrations, arbitrary parameter values b_1 and b_2 (assumed as $-.48$ and $.90$ respectively) were defined as the coefficients of the variables x_1 (average price difference per package of Crest relative to other brands) and x_2 (deal versus no deal offered on Crest at time of purchase). The resulting Logit model was then used as the basis for a simulation of the alternative models under hypothetical explanatory variable settings to provide a contrast against the results of the base case.[13]

Evaluation of Models in the Base Situation

The following discussion examines the models in the context of the base case situation. As a test of the ability of the combined models to adequately describe the Crest data, one can compare the brand purchase distributions from each of the alternative models to the actual distribution. Table 2 provides such a comparison based on the first 4 months following the ADA endorsement. The theoretical distributions were generated by the NBD approximation method previously described based on the values of $P_x(0|T)$ and $MP_x(0,T)$. The corresponding parameters $a_T(x)$ and $b_T(x)$ of the approximate NBDs over cumulative time so determined for each of the alternative models are given in Table 3. Referring back to Table 2, it is noted that the results of the LMN and LMCN models are

Table 2. Contrast of Fit of Alternative Brand Purchase Distributions[a]

Units Purchased	Actual	LMN	LMCN
0	.806	.781	.781
1	.109	.134	.134
2	.044	.048	.048
3	.018	.020	.020
4	.009	.009	.009
5	.004	.004	.004
6	.005	.002	.002
7	.001	.001	.001
8+	.004	.001	.001
Mean	.383	.373	.374

[a] Based on 4–month period following ADA endorsement.

Table 3.   Parameter Estimates for NBD
Approximation to Brand Purchase Distributions

Period	LMN		LMCN	
	$a_T(x)$	$b_T(x)$	$a_T(x)$	$b_T(x)$
1	.291	3.219	.333	3.688
2	.319	3.422	.320	3.422
3	.350	3.656	.336	3.516
4	.381	3.906	.358	3.680
5	.412	4.156	.381	3.852
6	.442	4.402	.403	4.027
7	.471	4.641	.424	4.195
8	.500	4.875	.444	4.359

virtually identical. Both give a reasonably good representation of the actual purchase distribution data.

It is recalled that the parameters of the models were estimated on the basis of only the first four-month period following the ADA endorsement of Crest. Given these parameters, it is of interest to obtain various market projections utilizing the subsequent 12–month data as a holdout sample. Hence, *all* of the following analyses examine the pattern of behavior of various market measures from the time of the ADA endorsement, considered as t = 0, over eight consecutive 2–month periods (including the 4–month period following the ADA endorsement and the one-year period thereafter).

Table 4 examines the projections of average Crest market share over time. It is noted that aside from a reasonably close compatibility within the early periods, future projections tend to follow the direction, but somewhat underestimate the actual pattern. The LMN model appears to provide marginally closer estimates. A look at the steady state value (.263) suggests that market forces during periods 3 thru 7 increasingly favored the purchase of Crest. The increasing momentum of

Table 4.   Projection of Average Market Share
per Period

Period	Actual	LMN	LMCN
1	.221	.209	.209
2	.218	.223	.224
3	.251	.233	.233
4	.274	.240	.239
5	.271	.245	.243
6	.278	.248	.247
7	.293	.251	.249
8	.268	.253	.251
Steady State		.263	.263

Table 5. Contrast of Projections of Mean No. of Brand Purchases

	Mean Number of Brand Purchases Over Cumulative Time Periods			Mean Number of Brand Purchases Over Consecutive Time Periods		
Period	Actual	LMN	LMCN	Actual	LMN	LMCN
1	.209	.180	.180	.209	.181	.181
2	.383	.373	.374	.176	.193	.194
3	.600	.574	.574	.224	.201	.201
3	.838	.780	.780	.242	.207	.207
5	1.069	.991	.988	.232	.211	.210
6	1.305	1.205	1.200	.244	.214	.213
7	1.574	1.421	1.414	.269	.217	.215
8	1.793	1.639	1.630	.225	.219	.217

the Crest promotional campaign after a brief period of relative inertia following the ADA endorsement and the resulting increase in the number of switchers to Crest appear to explain the actual trend. However, the parameters of the model which are based on the first 2 periods, obviously do not measure the full impact of future market forces. Consideration of explanatory variables other than the last brand choice would likely strengthen the validity of future market share estimates in this instance.

The models also provide projections of both the mean number of brand purchases over cumulative and consecutive time periods. Table 5 shows these results for consecutive 2–month periods. It is noted that both the LMN and the LMCN projections track the actual data observations quite well. However, the estimates of the LMN model are slightly (but negligibly) closer to the actual data. Interestingly, the models both tend to slightly underestimate the actual number of brand purchases over cumulative time periods as well as the actual mean number of brand purchases per period.

The models yield several other projections that may provide useful information

Table 6. Contrast of Brand Penetration Projections

	Cumulative Penetration			Incremental Penetration		
Period	Actual	LMN	LMCN	Actual	LMN	LMCN
1	.141	.131	.135	.141	.131	.135
2	.194	.219	.219	.122	.139	.144
3	.249	.288	.285	.149	.145	.149
4	.291	.346	.339	.158	.149	.153
5	.322	.396	.386	.148	.152	.156
6	.347	.441	.427	.156	.154	.157
7	.383	.481	.463	.183	.155	.159
8	.403	.516	.496	.153	.157	.160

Table 7.   Contrast of Brand Trial Projections

Period	Actual	LMN	LMCN
1	.141	.131	.135
2	.053	.088	.085
3	.055	.069	.065
4	.042	.058	.054
5	.031	.050	.047
6	.025	.044	.041
7	.036	.040	.036
8	.020	.036	.033

to marketing managers about their product and market. Table 6 provides projections of both cumultive and incremental brand penetration. In this instance, the estimates of the LMCN model appear generally closer than those of the LMN model, although both provide reasonably good estimates. In the case of the projections of new triers (Table 7), again the LMCN provides results that are closer to the actual data. However, in both cases, the actual trial proportions are somewhat overestimated over time. Table 8 contrasts the predictions of repeat purchase ratios from both models. As in the previous measures, the LMCN models tracks the actual data better. Both sets of estimates, however, tend to underestimate the actual data observations.[14]

The empirical analysis does not point to a clear superiority of either the LMN or LMCN models in all cases. Both perform reasonably well. However, the LMCN predictions of penetration, trial, and repeat purchase clearly dominate those of the LMN model. Although the LMN model provides marginally better predictions of such measures as mean number of brand purchases and average market share, the differences between models on these measures are practically negligible. Consequently, on an overall basis, the LMCN model would appear to be the favored alternative.[15]

Table 8.   Contrast of Brand Repeat Purchase
Projections

Period	Actual	LMN	LMCN
2	.489	.393	.436
3	.590	.391	.433
4	.611	.391	.432
5	.513	.392	.434
6	.601	.392	.434
7	.599	.393	.435
8	.525	.394	.436

Illustrations of Model Applications

The model offers a number of important potential applications from a decision-making standpoint. Given that the appropriate explanatory variables have been identified and the relevant parameters have been estimated, the models can be used to assess the relative impact of changes in the setting of a company's marketing mix. Consider now the additional marketing variables (price differential and availability of a Crest deal at time of purchase) and the corresponding Logit parameters previously discussed. Suppose that a marketing manager desires to evaluate the following alternative strategies:

Base Situation: Keep price differential at 0¢ $(x_1 = 0¢)$
                              Do not provide a deal on Crest $(x_2 = 0)$

Mix 1: a) Keep price differential at 0¢ $(x_1 = 0¢)$
             b) Provide a given deal on Crest $(x_2 = 1)$

Mix 2: a) Increase Crest price by 10¢/pkg. $(x_1 = 10¢)$
             b) Do not provide a deal on Crest $(x_2 = 0)$

Mix 3: a) Increase price by 10¢/pkg. $(x_1' = 10¢)$
             b) Provide a given deal on Crest $(x_2 = 1)$

The models may be used to simulate the three alternative marketing mix settings whose impact might be subsequently contrasted to the results of the base situation previously discussed. For example, Table 9 examines the corresponding Markov brand choice mechanisms. It can be noted that, whereas the availability of a deal would substantially increase the loyalty of Crest (and decrease the switching from Crest to brand O), an increase of price differential of 10¢ would substantially decrease loyalty. By offering both a deal and increasing price, there tends to be an offsetting effect that causes a net increase in Crest loyalty. The alternative switching matrices thus provide a direct view of the impact of particu-

Table 9. Brand Switching Matrices under Alternative Marketing Mix Settings

Alternative Mix Setting:

Price Differential:	$X_1 = 0¢$	$X_1 = 0¢$	$X_1 = 10¢$	$X_1 = 10¢$
Deal Availability:	$X_2 = 0$	$X_2 = 1$	$X_2 = 0$	$X_2 = 1$

$$A \begin{bmatrix} .72 & .28 \\ .10 & .90 \end{bmatrix} \quad A \begin{bmatrix} .86 & .14 \\ .21 & .79 \end{bmatrix} \quad A \begin{bmatrix} .61 & .39 \\ .06 & .94 \end{bmatrix} \quad A \begin{bmatrix} .80 & .20 \\ .14 & .86 \end{bmatrix}$$

Table 10.   Average Brand Market Share Projections under Alternative Marketing Mix Settings

Price Differential:	$X_1 = 0¢$		$X_1 = 0¢$		$X_1 = 10¢$		$X_1 = 10¢$	
Deal Availability:	$X_2 = 0$		$X_2 = 1$		$X_2 = 0$		$X_2 = 1$	
Period	LCM	LMCN	LCM	LMCN	LCM	LMCN	LMN	LMCN
1	.209	.209	.255	.256	.190	.190	.228	.229
2	.223	.224	.344	.347	.176	.175	.275	.276
3	.233	.233	.405	.405	.167	.167	.307	.307
4	.240	.239	.449	.445	.161	.162	.330	.328
5	.245	.243	.480	.473	.157	.158	.346	.343
6	.248	.247	.504	.494	.154	.155	.359	.354
7	.251	.249	.523	.510	.152	.153	.369	.362
8	.253	.251	.537	.523	.150	.152	.376	.369
Steady State	.263		.611		.143		.415	

lar strategies upon the switching behavior process from brand A to O and vice versa.

The extent of the impact of the alternative mixes on the pattern of market share over future time periods is shown in Table 10. The steady state shares point to the long-run direction given each mix. It is noted that the deal decision would result in a tremendous increase in market share (about twice that of the base case by period 8). On the other hand, raising price by 10¢ would cause market share to fall approximately 5% from that at the outset of the ADA endorsement. A

Table 11.   Summary of Simulated Average Number of Brand Purchases per Period under Alternative Marketing Mix Settings

Alternative Mix Settings:

Price Differential:	$X_1 = 0¢$		$X_1 = 0¢$		$X_1 = 10¢$		$X_1 = 10¢$	
Deal Availability:	$X_2 = 0$		$X_2 = 1$		$X_2 = 0$		$X_2 = 1$	
Period	LMN	LMCN	LMN	LMCN	LMN	LMCN	LMN	LMCN
1	.181	.181	.220	.221	.165	.164	.197	.198
2	.193	.194	.297	.300	.152	.152	.238	.239
3	.201	.201	.350	.350	.144	.144	.265	.265
4	.207	.207	.388	.384	.139	.140	.285	.283
5	.211	.210	.415	.409	.136	.136	.299	.296
6	.214	.213	.436	.427	.133	.134	.310	.306
7	.217	.215	.452	.441	.131	.133	.319	.313
8	.219	.217	.464	.452	.130	.132	.325	.323

Table 12.   Cumulative Brand Penetration under Alternative Mix Settings

Alternative Mix Settings:

Price Differential:	$X_1 = 0¢$		$X_1 = 0¢$		$X_1 = 10¢$		$X_1 = 10¢$	
Deal Availability:	$X_2 = 0$		$X_2 = 1$		$X_2 = 0$		$X_2 = 1$	
Period	LMN	LMCN	LMN	LMCN	LMN	LMCN	LMN	LMCN
1	.131	.135	.157	.159	.122	.126	.142	.144
2	.219	.219	.285	.284	.195	.196	.247	.246
3	.288	.285	.389	.381	.249	.247	.331	.326
4	.346	.339	.473	.458	.294	.289	.402	.392
5	.396	.386	.543	.520	.333	.326	.462	.447
6	.441	.427	.600	.572	.368	.359	.514	.494
7	.481	.463	.648	.614	.400	.388	.559	.534
8	.516	.496	.689	.650	.429	.416	.599	.570

combination of the two decisions would, however, result in a net increase in market share.

Table 11, which shows the simulated average number of brands purchased per individual per period, follows the general patterns exhibited by the alternative market share trends of Table 10. Whereas the deal decision would cause a significant increase in brand purchases, a price increase of 10¢ would result in a loss of the Crest franchise to other brands as the number of brand purchases would decrease over consecutive time periods as shown. Again, the combined decisions (Mix 3) show a net gain due to the apparent overwhelming effectiveness of a deal policy.

Table 13.   Brand Trial under Alternative Marketing Mix Settings

Alternative Mix Settings:

Price Differential:	$X_1 = 0¢$		$X_1 = 0¢$		$X_1 = 10¢$		$X_1 = 10¢$	
Deal Availability:	$X_2 = 0$		$X_2 = 1$		$X_2 = 0$		$X_2 = 1$	
Period	LMN	LMCN	LMN	LMCN	LMN	LMCN	LMN	LMCN
1	.131	.135	.157	.159	.122	.126	.142	.144
2	.088	.085	.128	.125	.073	.070	.105	.102
3	.069	.065	.104	.097	.054	.051	.085	.080
4	.058	.054	.084	.077	.044	.042	.071	.066
5	.050	.047	.069	.062	.039	.037	.060	.055
6	.044	.041	.057	.051	.035	.033	.052	.047
7	.040	.036	.048	.043	.032	.030	.045	.041
8	.036	.033	.041	.036	.029	.027	.039	.035

Table 14.   Brand Repeat Purchase under Alternative Marketing Mix Settings

Alternative Mix Settings:

Price Differential:	$X_1 = 0¢$		$X_1 = 0¢$		$X_1 = 10¢$		$X_1 = 10¢$	
Deal Availability:	$X_2 = 0$		$X_2 = 1$		$X_2 = 0$		$X_2 = 1$	
Period	LMN	LMCN	LMN	LMCN	LMN	LMCN	LMN	LMCN
2	.393	.436	.490	.541	.332	.374	.442	.488
3	.391	.433	.484	.527	.335	.380	.438	.480
4	.391	.432	.485	.525	.336	.382	.438	.478
5	.392	.433	.487	.527	.335	.381	.440	.480
6	.392	.434	.490	.530	.334	.380	.441	.482
7	.393	.435	.492	.533	.333	.379	.443	.484
8	.394	.436	.495	.536	.332	.377	.445	.486

Tables 12 through 14 provide further supporting results. As may be seen in Table 12, a decision to increase price would substantially slow down the cumulative penetration of the market, whereas the decision to deal accelerates penetration significantly. For example, the cumulative penetration after 5 periods under a deal policy exceeds that which would be achieved in the base case situation after as many as 8 periods. Tables 13 and 14, which respectively provide projections of brand trial and repeat purchase behavior over time under the alternative settings, further point to the danger of raising price both in terms of the erosion of

Table 15.   Brand Purchase Distributions under Alternative Marketing Mix Settings

Alternative Mix Settings:

Price Differential:	$X_1 = 0¢$		$X_1 = 0¢$		$X_1 = 10¢$		$X_1 = 10¢$	
Deal Availability:	$X_2 = 0$		$X_2 = 1$		$X_2 = 0$		$X_2 = 1$	
Units Purchased	LMN	LMCN	LMN	LMCN	LMN	LMCN	LMN	LMCN
0	.781	.781	.714	.716	.805	.804	.753	.754
1	.134	.134	.166	.163	.125	.126	.147	.146
2	.048	.048	.065	.064	.042	.042	.055	.055
3	.020	.020	.029	.029	.016	.016	.024	.024
4	.009	.009	.013	.014	.007	.007	.011	.011
5	.004	.004	.007	.007	.003	.003	.005	.005
6	.002	.002	.003	.003	.001	.001	.003	.003
7	.001	.001	.002	.002	.001	.001	.001	.001
8+	.001	.001	.002	.002	—	—	.001	.001

new triers and repeat purchasers over time. More specifically, Table 15 provides a complete view of the expected brand purchase distribution under the alternative mix settings for the 4–month period following the ADA endorsement. The overwhelming positive impact of a deal decision with respect to repeat purchase of Crest is clearly noted as the probability of occurrence of larger strings of Crest purchases becomes more pronounced in this case. Conversely, the distribution becomes more peaked at the origin under the price increase decision since the tendency to repeat Crest purchases would then substantially diminish.

CONCLUSION AND FUTURE DIRECTIONS

This paper has developed a model framework including two alternative model versions. These models combine a first-order brand choice and purchase incidence models within a general framework that permits the consideration of *any* explanatory variables that may be relevant to a given market situation.[16] Estimation methods were also discussed to permit the identification of relevant explanatory model variables as well as the estimation of model parameters.

A simplified version of the model was evaluated on the basis of consumer panel data. The empirical results showed that both the proposed LMN and LMCN provided a reasonably good fit to the empirical data in descriptive and predictive evaluations. However, one of the models, the LMCN model, appeared somewhat superior to the other. Then, on the basis of several simulated illustrations, it was shown how the models could be used to provide potentially useful information to marketing managers, on the basis of which alternative marketing decisions could be evaluated as to their potential effectiveness, and thereby enhance the marketing decision-making process.

This research effort represents a significant step forward in the area of stochastic models of consumer purchase behavior given the previous ignorance of marketing mix factors in the past literature. However, it by no means provides a final solution to the problem of modeling consumer purchase behavior in terms of its components of influence. Indeed, the proposed model suggests a number of future refinements and extensions, some of which are currently under study by the author.

For example, although the model considers the non-stationarity of consumer purchase behavior through a first-order Markov process, extensions of the model could include higher order processes such as infinite-order linear learning model forms.

At present, the model is considered as a two-state (i.e., two brand) process. However, by splitting up the "all other" brand state, a multi-brand Markov process could similarly be developed. Such extensions are feasible if a multivariate Logit approach is used, although the mathematics involved would obviously become more complex.

Although account is given to the heterogeneity of consumer behavior with respect to purchase incidence and initial individual brand choice probability, the model assumes that brand switching is homogeneous. That is, the transition matrix, which depends upon the explanatory variable vector x, is assumed homogeneous, at least within specific segments of the population. Future model extensions should, ideally, focus on model specifications such as that of a heterogeneous Markov process which would permit the heterogeneity of switching behavior to be specifically considered within the total consumer population.

The Logit model incorporates such behavioral phenomena as diminishing returns and saturation effects explicitly by virtue of its structure. However, the proposed basic model does not explicitly incorporate time effects such as advertising carry-over and memory decay. However, given the inherently linear structure of the Logit model form, it appears feasible to incorporate such aspects through the use of lagged explanatory variables. These and other model extensions, including the development of related marketing mix optimization models, are currently being investigated.

In conclusion, it appears that the proposed model approach opens the door to unlimited future research opportunities which, hopefully, may shed new light on the various facets of consumer purchase behavior from both theoretical and practical perspectives.

APPENDIX 1

Derivation of Market Share Function for the LMN Model

Consider the relation (18):

$$m_x(T) = \sum_{n=0}^{\infty} m_n(x) \, P_\theta(n|T), \qquad \text{with } \theta = \text{NBD},$$

Substituting $m_n(x)$ from (17) and $P_N(k|T)$ from (9),

$$m_x(T) = \sum_{n=0}^{\infty} \{m_\infty(x) + [m_0 - m_\infty(x)] \, \beta^n(x)\} \frac{\Gamma(n+a)}{\Gamma(a)n!} y^n (1-y)^a. \tag{1.1}$$

(1.1) can be written as:

$$m_x(T) = m_\infty(x) + [m_0 - m_\infty(x)] (1-y)^a \sum_{n=0}^{\infty} \frac{\Gamma(n+a)}{\Gamma(a)n!} [\beta(x)y]^n. \tag{1.2}$$

Consider any variable w $(0 < w < 1)$, since NBD probabilities must sum to unity:

$$\sum_{n=0}^{\infty} \frac{\Gamma(n + a)}{\Gamma(a)n!}\, w^n = 1/(1 - w)^a. \qquad (1.3)$$

Let $w = \beta(x)y$. Since $0 < \beta(x)y < 1$, then using relation (1.3) in (1.2), $m_x(T)$ becomes identical to (19). That is,

$$m_x(T) = m_{\infty}(x) + [m_0 - m_{\infty}(x)](1 - y)^a/[1 - \beta(x)y]^a.$$

APPENDIX 2

Derivation of Proportion of Population Who Make No Brand Purchases for the LMN Model

From (28), using the NBD, we obtain:

$$P_x(j=0|T) = (1 - y)^a + (1 - m_0) \sum_{N=1}^{\infty} P_x(O|O)^{N-1} \frac{\Gamma(a + N)}{\Gamma(a)N!}\, y^N(1-y)^a. \qquad (2.1)$$

The latter expression may be rewritten as:

$$P(j = 0|T) = (1 - y)^a + \frac{(1 - m_0)}{P_x(O|O)} = (1 - y)^a \sum_{N=1}^{\infty} \qquad (2.2)$$

$$\frac{\Gamma(a + N)}{\Gamma(a)N!}\, [y\, P_x(O|O)]^N.$$

Since $0 < y\, P_x(O|O) < 1$, using a similar approach to that of Appendix 1, the summation portion of (2.2) equals

$$[1 - y\, P_x(O|O)]^{-a} - 1. \qquad (2.3)$$

Substituting (2.3) into (2.2) yields (29). Thus,

$$P_x(j = 0|T) = (1 - y)^a + \frac{(1 - m_0)}{P_x(O|O)} (1 - y)^a \{[1 - y\, P_x(O|O)]^{-a} - 1\}.$$

FOOTNOTES

*This study was supported by a research grant (Summer 1977) from the University of Southern California. The author also wishes to acknowledge Dr. I. Abrams of the Market Research Corporation of America for providing the empirical data used in this study.

1. For notational convenience, purchase occasion subscripts (n) have been omitted.

2. The Logit model can also be extended to include a multi-brand market situation instead of combining all competing brands within one state.

3. See Zufryden (1975b) for a derivation of the NBD.

4. See Chattfield and Goodhardt (1973) and Zufryden (1976).

5. The derivation follows the same procedure used in Zufryden (1973).

6. Replacing $\beta + \lambda$ of Zufryden (1975c) by $\beta(x)$ leads to an identical derivation. Note that this result and others which are subsequently developed can be stated in terms of incremental time as well as cumulative time.

7. Note that the means of the NBD and CNBD distributions both equal aT/b. See Chattfield and Goodhardt (1973) or Zufryden (1975c).

8. The above formulas can also be applied to obtain incremental brand penetration results.

9. Other approximating distributions (e.g., CNBD, etc.) could be used in a similar way.

10. For a detailed discussion of the estimation of the Logit model in the instance of categorical variables, the reader is referred to Green, Carmone, and Wachpress. A Logit model consisting of a mixture of categorical and continuous variables can similarly be treated.

11. See Zufryden (1976) for a detailed empirical discussion of these results.

12. Note that since this simple model has only two parameters and two cell classifications, the parameters are uniquely determined by simultaneous equation solution using (38).

13. Note that when $x_1 = 0$ and $x_2 = 0$, the Logit model of the base case situation is obtained.

14. The reader may be interested in contrasting the results of the LMN and LMCN models with that obtained from other models applied to the same data base. The author has reported such empirical results in relation to the NBL, CNBL, NBD and CNBD models (Zufryden, 1976).

15. These results are consistent with the author's previous research, which also point to the superiority of another CNBD-based model (see Zufryden, 1976).

16. The proposed model framework may be extended to include alternative brand choice models. For example, in current research by the author with Professor J. Morgan Jones of the University of California at Los Angeles, a heterogeneous Bernoulli version of the proposed model has been developed and is currently being tested. The development of an infinite order model version is also currently in progress.

REFERENCES

Bass, F. M., and Wright, G. P., "Some New Results in Purchase Timing and Brand Selection." Krannert Graduate School of Management, Purdue University, Working Paper No. 583, December 1976.

————, Jeuland, A., and Wright, G., "Equilibrium Stochastic Choice and Market Penetration Theories: Derivations and Comparisons." *Management Science,* Vol. 22, No. 10 (June 1976).

Blattberg, R. C., "Stochastic Brand Choice Models: Is There a Future." Paper presented at the Joint Meeting of ORSA/TIMS, Miami, November 1976.

————, and Sen, S., "Market Segments and Stochastic Brand Choice Model." *Journal of Marketing Research* 13 (February 1976): 34–45.

Carmen, J., "Brand Switching and Linear Learning Models." *Journal of Advertising Research,* Vol. 6, No. 2, (June 1966): 23–31.

Chattfield, C., and Goodhardt, G. J., "A Consumer Purchasing Model with Erlang Interpurchase Times." *Journal of the American Statistical Association,* Vol. 68, No. 344 (December 1973): 828–835.

Ehrenberg, A. S. C., "An Appraisal of Markov Brand-Switching Model." *Journal of Marketing Research* 2 (November 1965): 347–363.

————, "The Pattern of Consumer Purchases." *Applied Statistics* 8 (1950): 26–41.

Frank, R. E., "Brand Choice as a Probability Process." *Journal of Business* 35 (1962): 43–56.

Green, P. E., Carmone, F. J., and Wachpress, D. P., "On the Analysis of Qualitative Data in Market Research." *Journal of Marketing Research* 14 (February 1977): 52–59.

Harrary, F., and Lipstein, B., "The Dynamics of Brand Loyalty: A Markovian Approach." *Operations Research* 10 (1962): 19–40.

Herniter, J., "An Entropy Model of Brand Choice Behavior." *Journal of Marketing Research* 10 (November 1973): 361–75.

————, "A Probabilistic Market Model of Purchase Timing and Brand Selection." *Management Science*, Vol. 18, No. 4 (December 1971).

Jeuland, A. P., "Heterogeneity of the Population with Respect to Brand Choice as a Determinant of Brand Switching." Paper presented at the Joint Meeting of ORSA/TIMS, Miami, November 1976.

Jones, J. M., "A Comparison of Three Models of Brand Choice." *Journal of Marketing Research* 7 (November 1970a): 466–473.

————, "Distribution of Probability of Purchase in Models of Consumer Brand Choice Behavior." Paper presented at the 11th American Meeting of TIMS, Los Angeles, October 1970b.

Kalwani, M., and Morrison, D. G., "A Parsimonious Description of the Hendry System." *Management Science*, Vol. 23, No. 5 (January 1977): 467–477.

Kuehn, A., "Consumer Brand Choice—A Learning Process?" *Journal of Advertising Research* 2 (December 1962): 10–17.

Lilien, G. L., "An Application of a Modified Linear Learning Model of Buyer Behavior." *Journal of Marketing Research* 11 (August 1974): 279–85.

Massy, W. F., Montgomery, D. B., and Morrison, D. G., *Stochastic Models of Buying Behavior*. Cambridge, Mass.: MIT Press, 1970.

Prasad, V. K., "A Brand Choice Model with Store as an Intervening Variable." Paper presented at the ORSA/TIMS/AIEE Joint National Meeting, Atlantic City, November 1972.

Styan, G. P. H., and Smith, H., "Markov Chains Applied to Marketing." *Journal of Marketing Research* I (February 1964): 50–55.

Zufryden, F. S., "An Empirical Analysis of Alternative Composite Stochastic Models of Brand Choice and Purchase Timing Behavior." Working Paper, Graduate School of Business, University of Southern California, 1976.

————, "Examining the Pattern of Response in a Media Model." *Management Science*, Vol. 22, No. 1 (September 1975a).

————, "The Prediction of Market Penetration and Repeat Purchase Behavior: A Stochastic Dynamic Model Approach." Paper presented at the Joint ORSA/TIMS Conference, Las Vegas, November 1975b.

————, "A Composite Heterogeneous Model of Brand Choice and Purchase Timing Behavior." *Management Science*, Vol. 24, No. 2 (October, 1977).

————, "A Study of Heterogeneous Models of Dynamic Purchase Behavior." Working Paper, Graduate School of Business, University of Southern California, 1975c.

————, "Media Scheduling: A Stochastic Dynamic Model Approach." *Management Science*, Vol. 19, No. 12 (August 1973).

————, "An Empirical Evaluation of a Composite Heterogeneous Model of Brand Choice and Purchase Timing Behavior." *Management Science*, Vol. 24, No. 7 (March 1978).

Research in Marketing

A Research Annual

Series Editor: **Jagdish N. Sheth, Department of Business Administration, University of Illinois.**

Volume 1. Published 1978 Cloth   333 pages   Institutions: $ 28.50
ISBN 0-89232-041-9   Individuals: $ 14.50

CONTENTS: **Research in Productivity Measurement for Marketing Decisions,** Louis P. Bucklin, University of California - Berkeley. **Simulation of Risk Attitudes in Joint Decision Making by Marketing Firms in Competitive Markets,** Ralph L. Day, Indiana University and Jehoshua Eliashberg, University of Missouri. **Interpretative Versus Descriptive Research,** Ernest Dichter, Ernest Dichter Associates International, Ltd. **The Household as a Production Unit,** Michael Etgar, State University of New York - Buffalo. **Some New Types of Fractional Factorial Designs for Marketing Experiements,** Paul E. Green, University of Pennsylvania, J. Douglas Carroll, Bell Laboratories and Frank J. Carmone, Drexel University. **Optimizing Research Budgets: A Theoretical Approach,** Flemming Hansen, A.I.M., Copenhagen. **Choosing the Best Advertising Appropriation When Appropriations Interact Over Time,** Haim Levy, The Hebrew University and Julian L. Simon, University of Illinois, **Advertising and Socialization,** John G. Myers, University of California - Berkeley. **Multi-Product Growth Models,** Robert A. Peterson, University of Texas - Austin and Vijay Mahajan, Ohio State University. **Advocacy Advertising: Corporate External Communications and Public Policy,** S. Prakash Sethi, University of Texas - Dallas. **An Empirical-Simulation Approach to Competition,** Randall L. Schultz, Purdue University and Joe A. Dodson, Jr., Northwestern University. **Field Theory Applied to Consumer Behavior,** Arch G. Woodside, University of South Carolina and William O. Bearden, University of Alabama.

Volume 2.   October 1979   Cloth   440 pages   Institutions: $ 32.50
ISBN 0-89232-059-1   Individuals: $ 16.50

CONTENTS: **Canadian and American National Character as a Basis for Market Segmentation,** Stephen J. Arnould, Queen's University and James G. Barnes, Memorial University of Newfoundland. **The Products' Needs Matrix as a Methodology for Promoting Anti-Consuming,** Michael A. Blech, San Diego State University and Robert Perloff, University of Pittsburgh. **The Cereal Antitrust Case: An Analysis of Selected Issues,** Paul N. Bloom, University of Maryland. **Gift Giving Behavior,** Russell W. Belk, University of Illinois. **A Process Model of Interorganizational Relations in Marketing Channels,** Ernest R. Cadotte, University of Tennessee and Louis W. Stern, Northwestern University. **The Product Audit System as a Tool of Marketing Planning,** C. Merle Crawford, University of Michigan. **Rudiments of Numeracy,** A.S.C. Ehrenberg, London Business School. **Evaluating the Competitive Environment in Retailing Using Multilicative Competitive Interactive Model,** Arum K. Jain, State University of New York - Buffalo and Vijaya Mahajan, Ohio State University. **The Parametric Marginal Desirability Model,** John F. McElwee, Jr., General Dynamics and Leonard J. Parsons, Georgia Insititute of Technology. **Carry-Over Effects in Advertising Communication,** Alan Sawyer, Ohio State University and Scott Ward, Harvard University and Marketing Science Institute. **Redlining in Mortgage Markets: Research Perspectives in Marketing and Public Policy,** Thaddeus H. Spratlen, University of Washington. **Psychological Geography,** William D. Wells, Needham, Harper & Steers Advertising, Inc. and Fred D. Reynolds, University of Georgia.

JAI JAI PRESS INC., P.O. Box 1678, 165 West Putnam Avenue, Greenwich, Connecticut 06830.

Telephone: 203-661-7602   Cable Address: JAIPUBL

Research in Law and Economics

A Research Annual

Series Editor: **Richard O. Zerbe, Jr., SMT Program,
University of Washington.**

The contributions to be included in this series represent original research by scholars internationally known in their fields. A few articles generally based on outstanding dissertations by younger scholars will also be included. The contributions will include theoretical, empirical and legal studies considered to belong to the law-economics genre.

Volume 1.	April 1979	Cloth	285 pages	**Institutions: $ 27.50**
ISBN 0-89232-028-1				**Individuals: $ 14.00**

CONTENTS: State Occupational Licensing Provisions and Quality of Service: The Real Estate Business, Sidney L. Carroll and Robert J. Gaston, University of Tennessee, Knoxville. **Dynamic Elements of Regulation: The Case of Occupational Licensure,** William D. White, University of Illinois, Chicago Circle. **Airline Performance Under Regulation: Canada vs. the United States,** William A. Jordon, York University. **Airline Market Shares vs. Capacity Shares and the Possibility of Short-Run Loss Equilibria,** James C. Miller, III, American Enterprise Institute flr Public Policy Research. **The Political Rationality of Federal Transportation Policy,** Ann F. Friedlaender and Richard de Neufville, Massachusetts Institute of Technology. **A New Remedy for the Free Rider Problem? Flies in the Ointment,** Roger C. Kormendi, University of Chicago. **Toward a Theory of Government Advertising,** Kenneth W. Clarkson, University of Miami School of Law, and Robert Tollison, Virginia Polytechnic Institute and State University. **Protecting the Right to Be Served by Public Utilities,** Victor P. Goldberg, University of California, Davis. **The Role and Resolution of the Compensation Principle in Society: Part One - The Role,** Warren J. Samuels, Michigan State University, and Nicholas Mercuro, University of New Orleans. **The Dynamics of Traditional Rate Regulation,** Patrick C. Mann, Regional Research Institute, West Virginia University. **Price Discrimination and Peak-Load Pricing Subject to Rate of Return Constraint,** David L. McNichol, U.S. Treasury Department. **Index.**

Supplement 1 to Research in Law and Economics

Economics of Nonproprietary Organizations

Editor: **Kenneth W. Clarkson and Donald L. Martin, Law and
Economics Center, University of Miami.**

	September 1979 Cloth	Ca. 330 pages	**Institutions: $ 28.50**
ISBN 0-89232-132-6			**Individuals: $ 14.50**

CONTENTS: Series Editor's Preface. Editor's Introduction.

MANAGERIAL CONSTRAINTS. **Managerial Behavior in Nonproprietary Organizations,** Kenneth W. Clarkson, University of Miami. **The Economics of Seat Pricing: Rose Bowl vs. Hong Kong,** Steven Cheung, University of Washington. **Delivered Comments,** Ross D. Eckert, University of Southern California and H.E. Frech, University of California - Santa Barbara. **Discussion.** MUTUAL ORGANIZATIONS. **Health Insurance: Private, Mutuals or Government,** H.E. Frech, University of California - Santa Barbara. **The Union as a Nonpropreitary Firm,** Donald Martin, University of Miami. **Delivered Comments,** Louis DeAlessi, University of Miami and Walter Oi, University of Rochester. **Discussion.** CHARITABLE ORGANIZATIONS. **Charity and Nonpropreitary Organizations,** Earl Thompson, University of California - Los Angeles. **Private Goods, Collective Goods: The Role of the Non-Profit Sector,** Burton Weisbrod, University of Wisconsin. **Delivered Comments,** Mark Pauly, Northwestern University and Armen A. Alchian, University of California - Los Angeles. **Discussion.**

GOVERNMENTAL ORGANIZATIONS. **Is There a Theory of Public Organizations?**, *C. M. Lindsay*. **Producing Knowledge in Nonpropreitary Organizations**, *Roland McKean*. **Delivered Comments**, *Andrew Whinston and James Buchanan*. **Discussion. General Discussion. Index.**

Volume 2.   Spring 1980   Cloth   Ca. 250 pages   **Institutions: $ 27.50**
ISBN 0-89232-131-8   **Individuals: $ 14.00**

CONTENTS: **Economic Analysis of Federal Election Campaign Regulation.** *Burton A. Abrams and Russel F. Settle, University of Delaware.* **The Quality of Legal Services: Peer Review, Insurance and Disciplinary Evidence,** *Sidney L. Carrol and Robert J. Gaston, University of Tennessee.* **Price Discrimination in the Municipal Electric Industry,** *Daniel R. Hollas, University of Michigan and Thomas S. Friedland, University of Illinois.* **The Resolution of the Compensation Problem in Society,** *Warren J. Samuels and Nicholas Mercuro, Michigan State University.* **Monopoly Profits and Social Losses,** *Levis A. Kochin, University of Washington.* **The Evaluation of Rules for Making Collective Decisions: A Reply to Kormendi,** *T. Nicholas Tideman, Virginia Polytechnic Institute and State University.* **Tort Liability for Negligent Inspection by Insurers,** *Victor P. Goldberg, University of California - Davis.* **The Economics of Property Rights: A Review of the Evidence,** *Louis De Alessi, University of Miami.* **The Problem of Social Cost in Retrospect,** *Richard O. Zerbe, University of Washington.*

A 10 percent discount will be granted on all institutional standing orders placed directly with the publisher. Standing orders will be filled automatically upon publication and will continue until cancelled. Please indicate with which volume Standing Order is to begin.

 JAI PRESS INC., P.O. Box 1678, 165 West Putnam Avenue, Greenwich, Connecticut 06830.

Telephone: 203-661-7602   Cable Address: JAIPUBL